Also from the Julian Jaynes Society

Conversations on Consciousness and the Bicameral Mind:
Interviews with Leading Thinkers on Julian Jaynes's Theory

Gods, Voices, and the Bicameral Mind:
The Theories of Julian Jaynes

The Julian Jaynes Collection:
Biography, Articles, Lectures, Interviews, Discussion

Reflections on the Dawn of Consciousness:
Julian Jaynes's Bicameral Mind Theory Revisited

The Minds of the Bible:
Speculations on the Cultural Evolution of Human Consciousness

THE PSYCHOLOGY OF ANCIENT EGYPT

RECONSTRUCTING A LOST MENTALITY

Brian J. McVeigh

Julian Jaynes Society

First Julian Jaynes Society Softcover Edition 2023

Library of Congress Cataloging-in-Publication Data

McVeigh, Brian J.
The Psychology of Ancient Egypt: Reconstrucing A Lost Mentality

1. Ancient Egypt 2. Ancient Egypt—Psychology. 3. Consciousness.
ISBN: 978-1-7373055-4-5 (softcover)

Cover and interior design by Marcel Kuijsten.
Front and back cover images by Olga Chernyak.

Julian Jaynes Society
Henderson, NV
julianjaynes.org

Printed both in the United States of America and internationally.

JJSING031424

Preface

"As I live on Truth, so I consume Truth. I have done what people say and that on account of which the gods are pleased. I have contented the god with that which he loves."
— *Book of the Dead*

THIS BOOK RECONSTRUCTS THE MENTALITY of Egypt within the framework of Jaynesian psychology. Simply stated, Julian Jaynes argued that before approximately 1000 BCE individuals, when confronted with an important decision, experienced supernatural visitations (what we call hallucinations). Eventually, as societies grew in complexity, individuals had to learn a new, more efficient mentality that allowed people to consciously introspect upon their problems.

The task for a project like this is convincing two audiences of the value of investigating a lost mentality. The first audience is interested in ancient civilizations — history, language, literature, religion, etc. — while the second audience has an interest in adaptations of the psyche. The first group of researchers may have a difficult time accepting the argument that human mentality can radically change over the centuries. Those researchers concerned with modifications to the psyche premise their investigations on evolutionary changes that transpired over an unimaginable time-scale. The notion that salient alterations in psychology could have happened as recently as three millennia ago is a startling proposition. But I argue that once we confront the facts on the ground, discard preconceived assumptions about the psyche, and apply what we know about neurocultural plasticity, a major development in the history of psychology becomes more than plausible.

This book is not a review or summation of ancient Egyptian religion or history, on which many fine books have already been written. It is an argument concerning what we can learn about human psychology from studying history. It challenges fundamental assumptions that have guided Egyptology, the study of other ancient civilizations, and the nature of human cognition.

The Promise of a Jaynesian Paradigm Shift

I will refrain from explaining in detail the nuances of Jaynesian psychology as numerous articles and books have already summarized, explored, and applied this framework. But a few words are in order concerning some major treatments.[1]

The best introduction to Jaynes is his own *The Origin of Consciousness in the Breakdown of the Bicameral Mind.*[2] Four other books, edited by Marcel Kuijsten, have introduced articles inspired by Jaynesian psychology as well as collecting together some of Jaynes's own writings that answer critics and flesh out his original arguments: *Reflections on the Dawn of Consciousness: Julian Jaynes's Bicameral Mind Theory Revisited*;[3] *The Julian Jaynes Collection: Biography, Articles, Lectures, Interviews, Discussion*;[4] *Gods, Voices, and the Bicameral Mind: The Theories of Julian Jaynes*;[5] and *Conversations on Consciousness and the Bicameral Mind: Interviews with Leading Thinkers on Julian Jaynes's Theory.*[6] A number of my own works have contextualized and tested Jaynes's hypotheses: *Discussions with Julian Jaynes: The Nature of Consciousness and the Vagaries of Psychology*;[7] *The "Other" Psychology of Julian Jaynes: Ancient Languages, Sacred Visions, and Forgotten Mentalities*;[8] *How Religion Evolved: Explaining the Living Dead, Talking Idols, and Mesmerizing Monuments*;[9] and *The Psychology of the Bible: Explaining Divine Voices and Visions.*[10]

Jaynes is often regarded as a researcher who presented a controversial theory about the psychology of archaic humankind. This is a short-sighted view. In fact a well-considered appreciation of his work demonstrates that his ideas herald a paradigm shift in understanding the inherent malleability of the human condition. This turn has profound implications in art, history, philosophy, and politics, as treated in my *A Psychohistory of Metaphors: Envisioning, Time, Space, and Self through the Centuries*;[11] *The History of Japanese Psychology: Global Perspectives, 1875–1950*;[12] and *The Propertied Self: The Psychology of Economic History.*[13] Jaynes's novel approach to the human psyche also has practical therapeutic applications, as I explore in *The Self-healing Mind: Harnessing the Active Ingredients of Psychotherapy.*[14]

Methodology and Seeing the "Big Picture"

Research is the product of two approaches that ideally should reinforce each other. The first utilizes primary sources that researchers have gathered themselves. This "raw material" comes from archaeological digs, multi-year fieldwork, ethnographic participant observation, questionnaires, surveys, interviews, translating texts, and collecting archival and historical documents. It can be very detail-oriented, obsessive about proper methodology, and often esoteric to non-specialists. But without the discipline, commitment, and sacrifice of researchers who have toiled away on seemingly obscure topics, the second approach would be impossible. This approach, relying more on secondary sources (scholarly books and academic articles), adopts a bird's eye view and summarizes what others have already concluded about the raw material. Reviewing and recapping research is valuable as it allows investigators to discover patterns not readily discernible from close-to-the-ground, granular methods. In other words stepping back permits us to see the "big picture." But such projects can be risky since the Devil is in the details and key aspects of the relevant topic can be overlooked, especially by nonspecialists. In any case, the arguments in this work are informed by theoretical concepts that I hope demonstrate how, assuming the details have not been neglected, big-picture investigations can bear fruit.

While I was a graduate student the dream of early American anthropology still held some purchase. The idea was to train researchers in the "four-field approach" (archaeology, linguistics, ethnography, and evolution). An explosion of knowledge and specialization has rendered the four-field vision impractical and no longer tenable. Nevertheless, conceptualizing *Homo sapiens* within a comprehensive context inspires a connecting of the dots that more conventional disciplinary methods not infrequently discourage. Though in one sense overly ambitious, taking into account artifacts (monumental and minor), sophisticated communication systems (language), social environment (enculturation), and biological adaptation (genetics) bolsters a big-picture perspective. This book does not *sensu stricto* apply the four-field anthropological approach, but it does find general inspiration in a cross- or even transdisciplinary perspective. This is significant. Such a view forces a researcher to come to terms with what is possible, probable, and improbable in the grand scheme of the human adventure.

Notes to the Preface

1. The interested reader is also directed to the Julian Jaynes Society at www.julianjaynes.org where a wealth of research, resources, and relevant materials can be found.
2. Jaynes, 1976.
3. Kuijsten, 2006.
4. Kuijsten, 2012.
5. Kuijsten, 2016.
6. Kuijsten, 2022.
7. McVeigh, 2016a.
8. McVeigh, 2018.
9. McVeigh, 2016b.
10. McVeigh, 2020.
11. McVeigh, 2016c.
12. McVeigh, 2016d.
13. McVeigh, 2015.
14. McVeigh, 2022.

Acknowledgments

Martin Seligman, who attended a class taught by Julian Jaynes at Princeton University, invited me to give a talk about Julian Jaynes at the Positive Psychology Center, University of Pennsylvania on January 21, 2019. Prof. Seligman, who recognized the importance of what Jaynes had to say, had sent out preparatory reading materials about Jaynesian psychology to faculty and graduate students prior to my talk. For this presentation I decided to apply Jaynesian principles to a very old civilization: "Lessons from the Archaeopsychology of Ancient Egypt: What Can We Learn from Spiritual Doubles and Divine Manifestations?"

I am certain that the attendees wondered what strange ancient Egyptian beliefs about hallucinated ghostly beings and divine revelations had to do with the more practical problems of positive psychotherapy. In any case, my arguments did not seem to persuade too many audience members (and it was not apparent that they had done the assigned readings). Nevertheless, besides being a great opportunity to meet interesting researchers and share my ideas, my presentation was fortuitous. As it turned out, it was during the talk when, explaining a PowerPoint slide listing the "features of conscious interiority" (FOCI), I had a revelation of my own.

For some time I was haunted by the intuition that Jaynes's understanding of consciousness contained something that had practical, psychotherapeutic implications. But I did not know how to expound upon that suspicion. Looking at that slide, with the FOCI neatly numbered, gave me an idea that in hindsight is simple and obvious: in the same way FOCI developed in response to major civilizational stressors as an upgrade in human mentality about three millennia ago, in the modern world FOCI can be cultivated to function as psychologically restorative measures for the individual, especially those suffering from mental distress or disorders. My mission, then, was to conceptualize each FOCI as an aspect of cognition with psychotherapeutically recuperative and reparative effects. I then set about building my project of a Jaynesian therapeutics revolving around the different FOCI, elaborating upon each one as a potentially curative form of mentation. The result was my *The Self-healing Mind: Harnessing the Active Ingredients of Psychotherapy* (2022). I point out this linkage between a forgotten, startlingly odd spirituality and more pragmatic applications (therapy) as a testament to the wide-ranging profundity of Jaynes's understanding of the history of the psyche. In other words, Jaynes's brilliant insights can illuminate countless corners of human psychology, whether in the distant past or in the present with our current concerns.

A number of individuals have offered advice and commented on this project. Marcel Kuijsten, as always, provided useful insights and editorial help and was instrumental in getting this book published. Bill Rowe, Barbara Greene, and Rune Nyord provided many useful suggestions. And Boban Dedović, drawing on his own expertise in ancient cultures and languages, also offered helpful advice. A special thanks to Philip Ardery for his exceptional editorial suggestions. For their indispensable guidance I am appreciative. I would also like to express my gratitude to Martin Seligman for giving me the opportunity to discuss Jaynes. Finally, I am indebted to my family and my wife, Lana, for their unending encouragement and support.

Notes to the Reader

For translations, I mostly relied on Raymond O. Faulkner's *Concise Dictionary of Middle Egyptian*.[1] Simplified definitions from this source have been faithfully organized by Mark Vygus.[2] I provided the transliterations but not the hieroglyphs (I do provide Gardiner's list codes for the hieroglyphs but I do not always list all variants; in such cases I insert "etc."). I have also used Petty in some instances.[3] In a few cases hieroglyphs were created using JSesh.[4] For occasional grammatical references I relied on James Hoch's *Middle Egyptian Grammar*.[5]

In some of the Tables that list terms I insert "Possible Translation" rather just than "Translation." From the context it should be clear that such caution does not invalidate my core arguments. However, since our understanding of the Egyptian language is evolving, such prudence is warranted.

For my purposes "ancient" describes the period from approximately 3000 BCE to 500 CE. Generally, I use "archaic" to designate the period from approximately 3000–1000 BCE in order to alert the reader to a major rupture in mentality that, according to Julian Jaynes, occurred during the Late Bronze Age (approximately 1200 BCE).

Notes

1. Faulkner, 2017.
2. Vygus, 2015.
3. Petty, 2012, 2013a, 2013b, 2016.
4. Rosmordue, 2014.
5. Hoch, 1997.

Contents

Preface vii

Acknowledgments xi

Notes to Reader xiii

Introduction: Towards an Archaeopsychology of Egypt 1

1. The Origins of Visions and Conscious Interiority 4

2. A Defense of Cognitive Relativism 12

3. The Mentality of Archaic Egypt 32

4. A Historical Synopsis of Egyptian Super-religiosity 54

5. The Cosmopolitical Realm: Creation, Gods, and Divine Energies 75

6. Voices, Visions, and Visitations from the Gods 101

7. The Theocentric Social Order and Divine Kingship 129

8. Inspiring Awe and Radiating Authority: Monumental Architecture 156

9. The Realms of the Afterworld: Transfigurations and Multiple Existences 174

10. Spiritual Doubles, Divine Manifestations, and Communicative Life-forces 192

11. "Heart" in the Psycholexicon of Ancient Egypt 218

Epilogue: Lessons from Archaeopsychology 229

Appendix A: Expressions with "Heart" 235

Appendix B: Basic List of Ancient Egyptian Psycholexemes 241

Glossary 248

References 255

About the Author 265

Index 267

Introduction: Towards an Archaeopsychology of Egypt

"For Maat will endure unto eternity. And go down to the grave with him who performs it. He will be buried, and the earth will enfold him, but his name will never vanish upon the earth, for he will be remembered because of his goodness."
—*Tale of the Eloquent Peasant*

An Agenda for Rethinking Archaic History

WHAT GAVE BIRTH TO CIVILIZATION? Have we really considered all the possible variables and catalysts that, in the grand scheme of humankind's history, produced an explosive trajectory that can be traced to about ten millennia ago when the agricultural revolution began? Chapter 1 outlines how this arc makes more sense when we see how increasing population pressures configured the human psyche. Specifically, as social units expanded in size, a communication system had to develop in which individuals, for purposes of social control, "heard" or "saw" authoritative beings who were not present. Upon this communication system a form of super-religious social management was ideologically built and elaborated. It consisted of glorified ancestors and radiant deities who visited and communed with mortals, as well as awe-inspiring kings who reigned in the name of the gods. But success breeds its own failure and eventually by about 1000 BCE the communication system that helped humankind through the agricultural and urban revolutions became obsolete. Humans were forced to culturally learn, via linguo-socialization, a new mentality — conscious interiority — that granted them a more efficient type of cognition.

These aforementioned claims about cognitive relativism and archaeopsychology invite reservations, doubts, and questions. Chapter 2 addresses the predictable objections. This is a crucial chapter and the reader may want to periodically return to and consult it when reading other parts of this book.

Individuals with a preconscious mentality, not unexpectedly, processed information differently and thus had a distinctive viewpoint on how the world works. For reasons that are explained later, archaic Egypt, along with other preconscious civilizations, operated along "paralogic" lines. This claim is fleshed out in Chapter 3 with a discussion of symbolic thought and examples about spatiality, time, mind–body dualism, a prescientific (versus "ascientific") worldview, perspective versus aspective aesthetic representations, and the spiritually efficacious use of "words of the gods" (hieroglyphs).

Though I do pay attention as much as possible to the chronological development of ideas (as this is crucial to any reconstruction of mentalities), the topics of this book do not neatly follow a historical ordering. Chapter 4, however, is intended to afford a synopsis of ancient Egyptian history seen through a Jaynesian perspective.

Key facets of archaic Egyptian super-religiosity are explored in Chapter 5 (cosmogonies, deities, and divine energies). In archaic civilizations individual behavior, and by extension sociopolitical order, were governed by audio-visual hallucinations interpreted as divine guidance (supernatural visitations). These are the topics of Chapter 6. How a theocentric social order, capped by divine kingship, was maintained, is the focus of Chapter 7. Chapter 8 investigates how monumental edifices instilled a sense of the sacred and established lines of communication among deities, kings, and mortals, while Chapter 9 examines the nature of the Afterworld, spiritual transfiguration, and relevant funerary texts.

Ancient Egyptians regarded the individuals as having access to a multiplicity of forms in which they manifested themselves after death. These forms are not "parts" that constitute an individual, but rather "shifting modes" of personal existence.[1] If we are to reconstruct the archaeopsychology of ancient Egypt, we have to address the fundamental notions of Ka (spiritual double), Ba (human-headed bird body–soul), Shadow (*šwt*), as well as a number of other related concepts. The challenge then becomes explaining the purpose of these entities.[2] This is the goal of Chapter 10. I argue that the Ka, Ba, etc., were hallucinated beings. Their descendants are present-day doppelgängers; such autoscopic apparitions appear when vestigial neurostructures that once subserved archaic hallucinatory experiences are for some reason activated.

According to Jaynesian psychology, a preconscious mentality was reflected in Bronze Age languages that lacked robust psycholexicons. Chapter 11 explores this issue by focusing on the crucial linguo-concept of "heart" and what this might tell us about how language metaphorically evolved from a period when individuals lacked a clear-cut and precise psychological terminology.

Notes to the Introduction

1. Žabkar, 1968, p. 1.
2. Cf. Jaynes, 1976, p. 189.

Chapter 1

The Origins of Visions and Conscious Interiority

"Yet you are alone, rising in your manifestations as the Living Aten: appearing, glistening, being afar, coming close; you make millions of transformations of yourself."
— *Hymn to the Aten*

What Gave Birth to Civilization? A Missing Variable

WHAT LED TO THE BIRTH OF CIVILIZATION? Variables commonly used to explain historical change include: (1) demographic pressures (population increases, fluctuating mortality rates); (2) techno-economic advances (agricultural surplus, improved carrying capacity, better storage techniques, pottery-making, calendrics, irrigation, metallurgy, literacy, mathematics, wheeled transportation); (3) sociopolitical structural changes (hierarchical layering, multiple peaks of political control, stratification, extra-kinship networks, proto-state formation, role diversification); and (4) legitimating ideologies (religio-political beliefs that motivate and unify communities). Missing from analyses are changes in the human psyche, which is a "black box" for many researchers.

In order to address this lacuna I give attention to how alterations to the functioning of human mentality were key catalysts in historical developments. The aforementioned variables are interrelated and operate as complex feedback loops so it is difficult to pinpoint an ultimate cause, and society and psyche cannot ultimately be disentangled since they mutually configure each other. However, for the sake of argument, I submit that the expansion of demographic scale has important consequences for cognitive processes.

My arguments, at the most abstract level, are premised on two long-term historical and interrelated processes: socio-externalization and psycho-internalization. The former describes the political, technological, and economic forces impacting an individual from the "outside," while psycho-internalization accounts for consequential changes "inside" the person (how external factors modify cognition).

Hallucinations as Adaptive

We do not usually associate "hallucinations" with "adaptation." We link the former with loose brain wiring that causes malfunctioning and the latter with advancement and progress. However, hallucinations were — and in their updated incarnation as semi-hallucinatory mental imagery are — adaptive. In other words, conscious mental imagery is the neuro-cultural descendant of florid but useful hallucinations. Elsewhere I have discussed hallucinations as superceptions that subsume several types: (1) extraceptions (audiovisual hallucinations interpreted as theophanic voices and visitations in archaic times); (2) vestigial extraceptions (anomalous behaviors, e.g., hallucinations still experienced by schizophrenics; also seen more benignly in autoscopy, out-of-body experiences, heautoscopy); (3) introceptions (mental imagery and other inner quasi-perceptions under voluntary control); and (4) coceptions (coinciding perceptions and introceptions; such overlapping deludes us into assuming that interior experiences are sensory reflections of reality).[1]

My arguments are premised on the notion that until about 1000 BCE, when confronted with a particularly novel, stressful, or challenging situation that required cautious deliberation, individuals in the Bronze Age heard the guiding "voices" of gods, ancestors, or divine rulers. These "voice–vision–volitions" (VVVs; sometimes rendered as "dreams") originated in right-hemispheric linguistic areas (the commanding "god")[2] that would communicate with left-hemispheric linguistic areas (the obeying "person") via audiovisual hallucinations. This "bicameral" ("double chambered") neurological substratum of intra-speech resulted from the development of language during the Neolithic period. Upon death, it was believed that chieftains or kings became living gods and henceforth existed in a divine condition, continuing their reign and providing authorization for those dwelling in the earthly realm. This was the basis of pharaonic theopolitics.

I will skip over an in-depth, detailed recounting of Jaynesian archaeopsychology and bicamerality, as this has been done elsewhere (see the Preface for references). Here it suffices to note that bicameral mentality and its concomitant socio-organizational traits of god-governed, priest-administered, and temple economies evolved to meet the demands of the agricultural revolution and urbanization. But demographic expansion, due to the very success of agrarian innovations and close-quarter, concentrated settlements, increasingly eroded communicative efficacy between ruler and ruled, amid the masses, and most importantly, among the different components constituting the individual psyche. As civilizations became larger, increasing complexity outpaced the governing function of divine visitations and visions. Simply put, economic success overcame the limitations of sociopsychological processes subserved by bicameral neurocultural structures.

The idea that archaic Egypt was governed by VVVs which cascaded down a sociopolitical pyramid becomes more believable once its relatively small demographic scale is taken into account, i.e., smaller population scales are more controllable. In the Old Kingdom, Memphis had about 6,000 inhabitants. Large provincial towns had perhaps 1000–2000, while their smaller counterparts had as few as 250.[3] In the New Kingdom, Luxor had perhaps 85,000, Pi-Ramesses 100,000, and Tanis 31,000. The major provincial centers had perhaps 15,000–30,000 inhabitants. Egypt was predominantly rural, so the majority of individuals lived in small-scale groupings that were presumably easy to psychopolitically manage. Though "no more than an educated guess,"[4] by around 2500 BCE, Egypt's total population was 1.5 million; by 1250 BCE, 3 to 3.5 million. By the time of Cleopatra VII (51–30 BCE), there were five to seven million Egyptians. During periods of famine, political disruption, and economic dislocation, demographic retraction was on the order of 30% to 40%.[5]

Communications Systems Breakdown: The Collapse of Bicameral Civilizations

By around the twelfth century BCE (depending on location), bicameral theopolities, though they had been repeatedly renovated in the past, were no longer up to the challenge of keeping pace with ever-increasing political economic dislocation. The gods, always ready to promise security and order in exchange for sacrifices, prayers, and litanies, could no longer convince mortals of why they deserved unquestioned obeisance.

An example of how religious ideologies grew in intricacy is the increasing saliency all over the world of celestial bureaucracies that mirrored the theopolities of earth-bound god–kings, divine deputies, sons of heaven, and priestly classes. Increasingly, heavenly beings communed with mortals using intermediary message-bearing angels, admonishing demigods, vengeful ghosts, and terrifying demons. Attempts were made to trim the tangled theological weeds by consolidating and reducing the members of pantheons — i.e., attempts at monotheism (or something like it): Ahura Mazda among the Persians, Yahweh in Israel, Marduk in Babylon, and Aten in Egypt. In Egypt, the common response was syncretism or uniting gods into pairs or triads in an attempt to combine different lines of communication. However, the voices of deities and ancestors grew too quarrelsome, the chains of command too long, and the exchange of information cumbersome. As the noise of social chaos increased, it became less clear whose orders should be followed. The consequence was eroded super-religious authorization and eventually, a systemic breakdown of the social system as witnessed by the Late Bronze Age collapse. Bicameral mentality could not meet the challenges of a neurocultural system stretched beyond its capabilities.

The Birth of a New Mentality

By around 1000 BCE, hallucinations could not keep up with sociopolitical disturbance and economic dislocation that had outpaced the god–mortal communication complex. A new mentality was needed. Stabilization was achieved by upgrading cognition. It was the breakdown of bicamerality that gave birth to conscious interiority. However, this was accomplished *not* by neurological means but by cultural developments, i.e., people had to learn, over a matter of centuries, how to cognize more efficiently via subjective introspectable self-awareness. Consequently, by the Late Bronze Age people had learned a new type of mentality better suited for navigating denser networks, higher multi-layered hierarchies, occupational diversification, sociocultural differences, and abstract hypothetico-speculation demanded by long-term planning. Eventually, from around the eighth to second century BCE (there is some geographical variation), the Middle

East, Greece, India, and China witnessed an unprecedented flowering, a religious, philosophical, political, and artistic fluorescence described by the philosopher and psychiatrist Karl Jaspers as the "Axial Age." This explosion of creativity was driven by a new mentality reflected in a shining subjectivity whose luminaries (Hebrew prophets, Thales, Solon, Plato, Aristotle, Confucius, Mozi, Buddha, etc.) outshined the admonishments of the now stonily silent, reticent gods.

Features/Functions of Conscious Interiority

Conscious interiority is a package of interrelated capabilities — hence FOCI, an acronym for "features/functions of conscious interiority." Overall, FOCI gave the human psyche the ability to interconnect its neurological components in a more efficacious way, forming novel neurocultural pathways that sped up information flow. This constellation of cultural psychological adaptations offered humans a new repertoire of abilities. These features increased abstraction, theoretical approaches, and a conjectural mindset more conducive to problem solving.[6]

The first and most primitive feature is the *spatialization of psyche,* or the belief that, within the individual, an imaginary space or introcosmos exists in which an "I" introspects. Spatialization allows people to "see" problems and their solutions "in" their heads (a mind-space linguistically constructed by spatial metaphors). Mental space generates the second feature, which is *introception,* or the production of mental imagery grounded in an inner quasi-sensory introcosmos. This inner place is modeled after the real, perceptual physical world.[7]

The third feature is *excerption,* or editing the stream of subjective scenes and sights our psyche presents to us in our personal introcosmos. The "I" edits from the "collection of possible attentions to a thing which comprises our knowledge of it … Actually we are never conscious of things in their true nature, only of the excerpts we make of them."[8] Excerption, then, is the "instance of selection that picks and chooses among the many options" that the psyche provides.[9] The fourth feature is *consilience,* or making a "slightly ambiguous perceived object" conform to some previously learned schema. Consilience or assimilation is "doing in mind-space what narratization does in mind-time or spatialized time. It brings things together as conscious objects just as narratization brings things together as a story."[10]

Self-individuation, or highlighting personal traits and privileging uniqueness as opposed to subsuming the individual within a larger collectivity, is the fifth feature. Possessing a highly-individuated selfness helps select out what is special about an individual, thereby enhancing the group's repertoire of talents and strengths. The particular features of persons received little if any attention in archaic Egypt. This is not just a preference for standardized or idealized portrayals; the very notion of individuality is lacking. It is quite difficult to recognize a single Pharaoh as a distinct personality.[11] Imagery "consistently hid the individuality of the kings under generalities," so rulers "remain totally impersonal to us."[12] The realistic representation of the face of Senusret III (ca. 1838–1818 BCE) stands out as an exception, precisely because it exhibits personal and emotional expression.[13]

The sixth feature, *self-narratization*, postulates a linear temporality upon which one's own self as protagonist is able to move about. This evoked a sense of control over one's destiny and enabled people to mentally "see" themselves and plan, thereby enhancing abstractive-hypothetical speculation. Once detached from the limitations of physical reality, excerptions provide the "I," not just with a panorama of past and present events, but with imaginary "could be's" and future possibilities. All this led to more efficient decision-making processing, i.e., it permitted people to simulate possible outcomes of potentially risky choices without actually having to act them out in the real world.

Self-authorization, the seventh feature, describes believing how one's own person ("I"), rather than gods or ancestors, has immediate control over one's behavior ("me"). Self-authorization replaced the earlier divine authorization of theopolitical societies; it is, as modern people experience it, volition, which is really another way of describing how our neurocultural components "talk" to each other. In unicameral societies a self affords the individual authorization. Intentionality is attributed to the "I," rather than external divine powers. Volition, as postbicameral individuals conceive of it, is a consciously interiorized experience, the distinct but indescribable feeling of an executive-commanding "I" controlling a subordinate-commanded "me."

From self-authorization ("who" controls one) comes the eighth feature, *self-autonomy* ("what" one can control). Assigning responsibility to the "inner person" rather than social groupings, natural forces, or divine powers leads to a sense of control over one's fate. This interiorization of behavior positions agency within the individual. Any discussion of concepts of autonomy leads to the notion of fate. In Egyptian, *š3* is translated as fate,[14] ordain,[15] order, predestine, assign, settle, determine, decide, foretell.[16] Another term for fate (or destiny) is *š3w*.[17] But we need to be cautious of these glosses because "fate" always presupposes its counterpart, i.e., human volition, and it is doubtful whether preconscious individuals could conceptualize this notion as we think of it.

Generated from an "I" introspecting upon a "me" is *self-reflexivity*, that indefinable subjectively self-aware experience of an ineffable abyss separating us from others and the world. This ninth feature describes an infinitely regressive "mirror image" effect that leads to a keenly-felt existentialist perspective.

Spatialization affords a pretend place where our physical person can be introceived as two different types of selfhood. These are the two final features of conscious interiority, already alluded to: the *observing self* ("I") and the *observed self* ("me").[18] The former is self-as-subject or an interiorized representation of one's physical person. This active aspect of selfhood is imbued with a sense of control, agency, and action. The "I" can move about in the introcosmos and experience inner quasi-sensory experiences. The "I" may have a behavioral (imagining oneself carrying out an action) or a physiological mode (monitoring one's appetite, fatigue, or physical discomfort). The observing self allows us to imagine ourselves doing something in order to assess if our planned action is effective, thereby avoiding the risks and hazards of the actual behavior. Needless to say, the self-as-subject drastically increases planning capabilities. The counterpart of the "I" is the "me," i.e., self-as-object. This controlled, passive aspect of selfhood is acted upon and monitored by the "I." Different "me's" can be conceived as various scripts we perform for others as well as ourselves; such multi-perspectivism allows the proliferation of role-diversity, a crucial element for coping with socioeconomic complexity.

Notes to Chapter 1

1. McVeigh, 2013.
2. Currently partially vestigial.
3. Butzer, 1999, p. 296.
4. Butzer, 1999, p. 297.
5. Butzer, 1999, p. 297.
6. Note, however, that paralogic is in fact the default mode of cognition; it is still seen in trancing, bizarre dream content, and runaway symbolic associations; more negatively, it

can characterize idea entanglement, delusional thinking, and superstitions that contradict the tenets of objective science.

7. Basically meaning introspection. However, "introception" is intended to stress how perception of the external objective world is fundamentally distinct from what is imagined and "seeable" within our interior subjective introscape, that is, conscious interiority is not, and it cannot be, reduced to sensory perception.
8. Jaynes, 1976, pp. 61–62.
9. Nørretranders, 1998, p. 243.
10. Jaynes, 1976, pp. 64–65.
11. Frankfort, 2000, p. 124.
12. Frankfort, 2000, p. 46.
13. Müller, 2009.
14. M8-G1-Z7-Y1.
15. M8-G43-Y1.
16. M8-G1-Y1A.
17. M8-G1-G43-Y1A; M8-G1-M17-M17-I14; M8-G1-M17-M17-Aa2, etc.
18. Two other FOCI might be mentioned: (1) concentration or the inner analog of sensory perceptual attention; and (2) suppression or censoring distressing thoughts, based on the physical action of turning away from something unpleasant.

Chapter 2

A Defense of Cognitive Relativism

"There is no shortcut to an understanding of the ancients."
— Henri Frankfort

OBJECTION: CONSCIOUSNESS IS BIOLOGICALLY EVOLVED, NOT LEARNED

THIS OBJECTION — i.e., conscious interiority is an innate neurobiological feature that is not culturally acquired — is the most frequent counterargument to Jaynes's cornerstone claim. Understanding cognitive diversity demands a subtlety of thought often absent from debates about changes in human psychology.[1] The problem is one of terminology and definitions and how discussions are weighted down with semantic baggage. This dragging around of unquestioned assumptions, comfortable certainties, and unchallenged dogmas configures thinking habits, hypotheses, and theoretical perspectives unawares. So much luggage makes it difficult to set off for new intellectual destinations. In particular, the trap of dualism ensnares many analyses: either something is internal (in or of the mind) or external (bodily or coming from outside the mind via enculturation). And when viewed across the centuries, how should the various expressions such as "different ideas," "different mentalities," "different psychological processes," and "different minds" be distinguished (assuming they can be differentiated)?

Let us begin with a question: does a Jaynesian archaeopsychological interpretation imply "deep-rooted cognitive differences" between cultures, past and present? On the one hand yes, but on the other hand, no. It depends on one's definition of cognition, consciousness, mentality, etc. Let us begin with answering "no" to the aforementioned question.

Conscious Interiority Does Not Result in Deep-rooted Cognitive Differences — Consciousness Is Learned, Not Innate

Archaic Egyptian kings performed rituals that made the sun rise each day, ensuring the rebirth of the cosmos. This is not a bad metaphor for describing how individual consciousness must be relearned within each individual through linguistic enculturation. Consciousness only emerges when one is taught to be conscious. Jaynes never claims that neuroanatomical changes occurred three thousand years ago. Consciousness is learned, and this learning must re-occur each time a person is socialized from birth. This means that if an infant were born today, put in a time machine, and transported back to Egypt ca. 2000 BCE, he or she would not be socialized to be conscious. By the same token, if an archaic Egyptian infant were transported to the twenty-first century, he or she would be raised to be conscious. But because many instinctively link consciousness with something inherently basic about mentation, an assumption is made that some "deep-seated" neuroanatomical change must have transpired when people invented via language, over a matter of centuries, an interiorized psychology.

Conscious Interiority Does Result in Deep-rooted Cognitive Differences

On the other hand, a Jaynesian psychology does indeed imply deep-rooted cognitive differences. Jaynes argued that culture itself has the power to radically configure the mind. He recognized, in a way very few have, the tremendous world-altering power of culture as a psychological variable. The problem is how we instinctively conceive of "culture" and its relation to the human condition. The commonly accepted view is that culture is layered over relatively invariant neurological strata, like icing on a cake. Such a view permits researchers to celebrate, marvel at, and portray all the colorful differences among the world's societies without calling into question their commitment to human diversity. At the same time, since culture is just a coating, their belief in politically-correct "psychic unity" is maintained. Any uncomfortable politically-incorrect misunderstandings (and chances of hindering their climb up the academic ladder) are conveniently avoided.

Psychic unity was theorized in the early twentieth century as an intellectual weapon to combat social Darwinism and racism. As admirable as this project was and is, it should not prevent us from understanding humanity's psychic diversity or push challenging questions off the table of potentially informative research. We still need to ask, what precisely has changed over the centuries and millennia? Where is the line between cultural/learned material and cognitive/psychological processes? The premise behind this work is a stratigraphic psychology: the study of the sociopsychological layers, accreting through history, helps us understand adaptation and how human mentality has radically changed.

Elsewhere I have introduced the competing metaphors of mind-as-vase versus mind-as-putty.[2] The former view is conventionally accepted and politically correct. It postulates that the shape of the container, which we all share, configures whatever "cultural content" society pours into it while the basic shape of the vase remains the same; enculturation is a secondary process.[3] The mind-as-putty views psychic content as remarkably flexible and moldable into whatever shape social forces require. The putty material is the same regardless of place or period so that enculturation is not a secondary layering over deep cognitive structures. This trope allows us to acknowledge the power of culture to configure minds without stipulating fundamental differences in the human neuropsychological apparatus.

Consciousness, as something exopsychic and imposed via socialization from the outside, has more in common with definitions of the family, religious beliefs, democracy, and other intellectual endeavors than neurophysiological processes. Or we might say that as a cultural form, consciousness is more like a technology (invented, innovated, and utilized by humans). In the same way we use software to upgrade our computers, we have adopted new cultural codes over the centuries — reflected in language — that drove more efficient sociopolitical organizations. Table 2.1 summarizes some aspects of the aforementioned discussion.

An example of someone who falls into the trap of assuming that Jaynes argued that historical developments resulted in "massive structural brain changes" is Charles Fernyhough. He writes that "it is inconceivable that such a gross structural change could have happened in the human brain within the past three millennia."[4] But of course this is not what Jaynes is arguing at all, as a careful reading of his book demonstrates.

Also like other critics, Fernyhough seems to suggest that Jaynes inordinately relies on the *Iliad* for evidence, when in fact Jaynes only presents

Table 2.1. Theoretical Perspectives on Cognitive Change Compared.

Theoretical Perspective	Causes	Changes via	Deep Changes?	
			No	Yes
Conventional View	Long-term Evolutionary Adaptation	Genetics	N/A	Neuroanatomical Level
Misinterpreted Jaynesian View	Recent Social Complexity	Learning/ Culture	N/A	Neuroanatomical Level
Correct Jaynesian View	Recent Social Complexity	Learning/ Culture	Neuroanatomy Unchanged	Psychocultural Level

this text as one example from an overwhelming corpus of ancient works. Fernyhough writes that "If voice-hearing really is a pervasive aspect of human experiences, we should find testimonies of it appearing through the ages."[5] The truth is we can find many testimonies; we just have to become familiar with the archaeological and historical record. But like many psychology researchers, Fernyhough is unfamiliar with the substantial amount of evidence pointing to the salient role of auditory hallucinations, especially before the first millennium BCE.

OBJECTION: CHARACTERIZING ARCHAIC EGYPTIANS AS PRECONSCIOUS IS SOCIAL DARWINIST

While a graduate student I objected when another student, discussing Neolithic stone tools, described their "evolution"; I stated that her analysis came dangerously close to social Darwinism. Yes, she politely explained, she understood the risks of simplistic social evolutionist views. However, it is perfectly acceptable to discuss how isolated domains of a culture, such as certain implements, improve over time. In retrospect, I was guilty of overreacting to the mention of one word: "evolution." But things and ideas do "evolve," in the sense of develop or improve, all the time. Commenting on technological progress does not one make a closet social Darwinist. We need to acknowledge the differences between the narrow definition of "biological evolution" (transmitted via genetics) versus the broader and looser "cultural evolution" (extragenetic information that is learned and socially transmitted). This distinction is not complicated, but it deserves attention since many have misinterpreted Jaynes's key argument, assuming that he contended that conscious interiority was a bioevolutionary outcome.

Cognitive Relativism

We are comfortable with cultural relativism. But mention of cognitive relativism or psychic diversity raises eyebrows. The controversy surrounding the work of the French scholar Lucien Lévy-Bruhl's views (1857–1939) on "primitive mentality" is a good segue into the present discussion. Though some have seen value in the work of Lévy-Bruhl, many dismiss his ideas out of hand, illustrating how reactive researchers can be.[6] Lévy-Bruhl proposed two basic mentalities, "primitive" and "modern." While the latter uses logical reflection, the so-called primitive mind feels comfortable with contradictions and lacks an objective view of reality. Instead, it engages in "mystical participation" (*participation mystique*). This describes the tendency to overlook or merge boundaries among things and between the natural and the supernatural realms.

Levy-Bruhl's views resonate with earlier animistic notions developed by ethnographers. These inspired the "mythopoeic" stage of intellectual development proposed by the Dutch archaeologist and Egyptologist Henri Frankfort (1897–1954) and his wife Henriette Antonia Frankfort (1896–1982). Mythopoeic means "of or pertaining to myth-making." The argument is that archaic peoples avoided thinking in terms of generalizations as well as universal and impersonal laws. Events were always dictated by personal beings such as gods and spirits, and the spiritual and everyday spheres were inseparable.[7]

Towards the end of his life Lévy-Bruhl, becoming his own best critic, revised his views.[8] In his *Les carnets* (1949) he wrote:

> let us expressly rectify what I believed in 1910: there is not a primitive mentality distinguishable from the other by two characteristics which are peculiar to it (mystical and prelogical). There is a mystical mentality which is more marked and more easily observable among primitive peoples than in our societies, but it is present in every human mind.[9]

The charges against Lévy-Bruhl by his critics, still heard, are unfounded when one reads his more subtle, revised views. Lévy-Bruhl did not contend that "primitive thought" is antilogical or alogical; a mentality must be understood on its own terms. And despite the prefix "pre" he did not mean, at least in his later thinking, that prelogical thought is a kind of antecedent stage.[10] What is important is that prelogic is present in all places and periods and is not restricted to "primitive" societies. Lévy-Bruhl emerges as a thinker ahead of his time and, assuming it carries a positive denotation, was a proponent of cognitive relativism. This is the notion that the "logic we bring to bear in our description of the world is *not* universal, but rather a function of our immediate techno-environmental circumstances and our particular linguistic and ideological heritage, and that no one logic is necessarily superior to any other logic."[11] Incidentally, when it comes to psychological terminology, Middle Egyptian is not robust (while in other semantic domains Middle Egyptian is highly developed). This indicates, I submit, a low level of conscious interiority. Changes in vocabulary, obviously, reflect developments in society and the practical needs of a language's users, whether we look at technological, economic, political, or kinship-related lexical domains.

Reason, Objective Truth, and Social Truth

A common mistake is to equate consciousness with logical reasoning. But "reason" and "logic" are two very different, oft-confused things. The former concerns thinking (which may be rational, irrational, superstitious, or sublime). Reason is to logic as conduct is to morality or health is to medicine.[12] We need logic because most reasoning is not conscious.[13] The purpose of logic is to discover objective truth as dictated by external standards. But truth may also be socially-defined. Such "social truth" is shaped by political, economic, and spiritual motivations and considerations. It is not a matter of whether ideas reflect reality; what is important is if a package of culturally-defined ideas are organized in such a way that they facilitate the attainment of social goals (social utility), whether they be religious or scientific.

Which truth we use depends on the particular task or goal at hand. If objective truth is our goal, then we use logic, which demands impartial discernment, the rigorous application of scientific methods, and mathematical measurement. Social truth is much messier (but no less important or useful as objective truth), and thus accommodates paralogic more readily (see below). The everyday world, overflowing with political ideologies, white lies, egotistical agendas, self-deception, and the occasional delusion, is "very little concerned with objective truth."[14] To get through the day (and our lives) we typically utilize a mixture of both social and objective truth. These two types of truth intersect within the individual in what we may call personal or subjective truth.

Paralogic Cognition

An updated term that subsumes prelogic and mystical participation is paralogic cognition. This describes putting aside the rules of logic, here defined as an external standard of truth that our limited perceptual and conceptual processes may not discern.

In a sense there is nothing unusual or abnormal about paralogic cognition. It is most obvious in hypnosis, a vestige of bicameral mentality. When a "hypnotized subject walks around a chair he has been told is not there, rather than crashing into it (logical compliance), and finds nothing illogical in his actions."[15] Such behavior occurs due to the "paralogic compliance to verbally mediated reality." In other words, the hypnotized readily accepts assertions about the world from an authority figure that are not objectively true.[16] The human predilection to follow authoritative commands seems innate and explains how bicameral voices governed entire societies. Like preconscious people, hypnotized individuals do not recognize peculiarities and inconsistencies in their behavior. They cannot readily "see" contradictions because having their consciousness suspended facilitates verbally-mediated authorization.[17] Paralogic cognition also characterizes hypnoidal mental states, such as "being in the flow," daydreaming, visualization, guided imagery, deep relaxation, and autosuggestion.

While paralogic thinking is particularly pronounced in and centrally characteristic of hypnosis, it saliently characterized the bicameral period. "Paralogic identification" describes how representations and the things they imitate are both endowed with the same reality; images share the same essence as their real-life counterparts. The image is not a mere copy or stand-in since it possesses the same reality-ness as the original (see "identification symbols" in the next chapter). Many examples from archaic civilizations illustrate this and it is obvious in "treating unmoving idols as living and eating, or the same god as being in several places at one time, or in the multiples of jewel-eyed effigies of the same god-king found side-by-side in the pyramids."[18] A paralogic mindset views belief (intention and desire), behavior (ritual reenactment), verbalizations (spells and recitations), and objects (religious paraphernalia) as different manifestations of the same unifying reality.

Paralogic cognition explains why, to the modern observer, it often seems that no distinction existed between the factual and the mythic for the archaic Egyptians.[19] Shaw writes how "some degree of confusion between real happenings and purely ritual or magical acts" was maintained in regards to kingship, implying that this was a political ploy. Certainly politics was involved, but this ideological maneuver resulted from paralogic thinking rather than an explicit conscious decision.[20]

OBJECTION: IF JAYNESIAN ARCHAEOPSYCHOLOGY IS CORRECT, THEN ALL ARCHAIC CIVILIZATIONS WOULD HAVE TO EXHIBIT BICAMERAL MENTALITY

And they do. In order to test Jaynesian psychology, elsewhere I proposed and applied the Bicameral Civilization Inventory (BCI) Hypothesis (whose items are listed below).[21] It postulates that from around 3500 to 1000 BCE certain features characterized *all* civilizational cores without exception.[22] We have become accustomed to assuming that such features were somehow "natural" to early human development, thereby losing sight of how strangely remarkable such global commonalities are. The accentuations, inflections, and patterning of BCI traits display notable variation,[23] of course, but the inventory of items is found in all archaic cultures. The reader is requested to drop his or her assumptions and ask why these were universal. The scientific challenge is to find one demographically-large society that does *not* fit the pattern of bicamerality (or a culture that lacks bicameral vestiges) rather than one that does.

The most robust evidence for bicameral mentality appears in Mesopotamia from around 3500 BCE and in Egypt from around 3000 BCE with prototypical traits dating back to 10,000 BCE. Due to a later chronology, bicameral features emerged somewhat later in North, South, and Central America.

Items in the Bicameral Civilization Inventory

- *Right-Hemispheric Activation (RHA).* Hallucinated self-commanding "auto-speech" originating in the right hemisphere's linguistic regions (now vestigial).

- *Voice–Vision–Volition (VVV).* As groups grew in size, social control-at-a-distance was needed and hallucinated voice–volitions (RHA) developed. VVVs, attributed to absent clan leaders, provided social control and authorization. Eventually, social control-at-a-distance was effected through writing, large monumental architecture, and other techno-communicative advancements.

- *Centrality of Ancestor Worship (CAW).* Divinized rulers and ancestors became gods issuing VVVs. Household ancestor cults were typically nested within larger hierarchies of overarching royal ancestor-worship.

- *Theocentric Social Order (TSO).* Theopolitical governance developed with the emergence of divinely-deputized or semi-divine rulers (e.g., pharaohs). Carvings, sculptures, texts, etc., portray rulers' claim to "hear" and obey a deity's commands (RHA and VVVs).

- *Objects of Hallucinatory Focus (OHF).* Hallucinatory aids broadcasted instructions, commandments, and warnings. Idols, statues, and effigies were treated as if alive, fed, paraded, taken on journeys, and into battle. These emitted holy power and authorized decision-making — in some cases portable OHF were used, e.g., the Ark of the Covenant of the Israelites.

- *Induction Methods for Right-Hemisphere Activation (IMRHA).* Music, poetry, and song were used in induction procedures to activate linguistic regions of the right-hemisphere (e.g., large eyes on statues).

- *Authority-Radiating Ceremonial Complexes (ARCC).* The influence of gods and divine rulers emanated from sacred administrative centers (e.g., pyramids, ziggurats, temples, megaliths, aggrandized tombs). These structures formed focal points of deity–mortal interaction. Evolved from simpler funerary sites, monumental mortuary architecture housed divinized rulers and OHFs, e.g., images, ancestral tablets, or the glorified remains of leaders.

- *Human Settlements Dominated by ARCC.* Urban dwellings and agricultural hinterland typically encircled a "house of the god(s)" or other ARCC that exercised control (TSO) over local inhabitants.

- *Doubleworld Mortuary Practices (DWMP).*[24] This is the belief that the deceased continued to live in the Afterworld. In some cases graves themselves became OHFs (e.g., elaborate grave furnishings, retinues, slaves, figurines that assist in Afterworld, mummification).

- *Supernatural Visitations (SV).* Messages from the beyond maintain moral order as direct-god–mortal communication (VVVs) eroded.

- *Intermediary Beings (IB).* As deities retreated to the heavens, their VVVs ceased, so intercessionary beings ensured that communication between mortals and gods still transpired via angels, guardian deities, revenants, ghosts, demons, or vengeful spirits.

- *Indirect Divine Communication (IDC).* After the gods retired to the celestial realm, visitations ceased while exopsychic practices developed to communicate with supernatural entities, e.g., divination, oracles, prophets, visions, "visitation dreams," revelations by IB.

- *Secondary Burials (SB).* When VVVs of ancestors ceased, then the dead would be permanently interred (DWMP).

- *Multiple Souls (MS).* One soul is divinized while another stays behind to communicate with mortals (DWMP). In Egypt the Akh typically played the role of the former, while the Ka and Ba functioned as the latter.

- *Undeveloped Psychological Lexicon (UPL).* Sociopolitical systems were not complex enough to require sophisticated interiorized linguo-concepts until after ca. 1000 BCE.

- *Metaphoric Mind-Words (MMW).* In response to increased social complexity, psycholexeme-rich languages replaced UPL and followed a linguo-conceptual trajectory of scaffolding based on spatial and bodily metaphors.

- *No Philosophical Tradition before ca. 1000 BCE.* The existence of the gods was not doubted and skepticism of the divine order was culturally impossible. Sustained philosophical skepticism or suspicion regarding the supernatural did not develop until after 1000 BCE.

- *Postbicameral Civilization Inventory.* The development of postbicamerality indicated a major rupture in human history, roughly corresponding to the Late Bronze Age Collapse in the Mediterranean and Middle East. The Postbicameral Civilization Inventory (PBCI) concerns relics of bicameral societies. Examples of Vestigial Bicamerality (VB) include shamanism, spirit possession, glossolalia, autoscopic phenomena (doppelgängers, heautoscopy), and neo-IDC.[25] Folktales, myths, old ghost stories, and legends about "little people" are also remnants of an earlier mentality. Another example of vestigial bicamerality includes what happens when conscious interiority is suspended, i.e., hypnosis and hyper-suggestibility.

OBJECTION: WHAT ABOUT ARCHAIC EGYPT'S SOPHISTICATED ACHIEVEMENTS? WASN'T CONSCIOUSNESS REQUIRED?

Sky-scrapping pyramids, massive temples, a relatively developed mathematics, three millennia of accumulated artistic creations and literature — surely the archaic Egyptians had to be self-aware. But one can think, cognize, manipulate complex conceptualizations, perceive the world, and learn even if nonconscious. This has been shown in the laboratory. Obviously the archaic

Egyptians would have had to be endowed with these sophisticated mental capabilities. But would they have had to be conscious as defined by Jaynes?

Everyone is an expert in the commonsensical sureties of space and time until confronted with the weirdness of Einsteinian general relativity, quantum physics, and string theory. Similarly, when it comes to conscious experience everyone thinks they are an expert despite not really investigating it from a scientific point of view. This is probably because it is hard to imagine not being an expert on something so close at hand and personal. From discussions with colleagues about Jaynesian psychology, I learned that the problem was not that they were unacquainted with interesting differences among historical periods. The real problem was that they were not familiar with their own experiences of subjective introspectable self-awareness, which is confused with perception, thinking, rational thought, and a host of other related phenomena (and nothing upsets someone more than telling them that their beloved pet is not conscious). Trying to expand and mine Jaynesian archaeopsychology is admittedly an exercise in exploring terra incognita. But however one defines consciousness, the default, common-denominator presupposition is that consciousness is neurobiologically innate, essential, and fundamental to all forms of mentation. This assumption needs to be challenged.

OBJECTION: HOW COULD SO MANY INDIVIDUALS HEAR THE SAME VOICE?

It is quite a trick of sociopolitical engineering to ensure that everyone was always given the same orders and commands. Would not social confusion and chaos result if people experienced different VVVs? First, remember that in bicameral theopolities, the average individual likely only heard voices relevant to their daily lives. Indeed, at least in the case of archaic Egypt, evidence suggests that only the monarch directly interacted with the gods and experienced "apex VVVs" or a community's highest and most authoritative hallucinations. In other words, the average Egyptian probably experienced SVs and VVVs from ancestors, deceased relatives, Kas, and Bas. Second, there is little reason to suppose that frequently experiencing hallucinations was necessary before approximately 1000 BCE. Not every situation in a bicameral civilization required one to hear the voices of their rulers or supernatural entities. Most human behavior was habit-determined, prescribed, and routinized. After all, the strict hierarchical, role-prescribed nature of archaic Egyptian society ensured that everyone knew his or her expected behaviors. Nonconscious schemas, ritualized patterns of activity, and social scripts were adequate for most decisions — as is the case, incidentally, even for conscious humans. Third, in the same way that modern humans believe that others share enough of the basic worldview for mutual communication, archaic Egyptians implicitly assumed that everyone was on the same page, whether they heard the same hallucinations or not. No one today doubts (except perhaps for philosophers) that holding differing individualized scenes of mental imagery threatens the relatively smooth operation of sociopolitical and economic systems.

Finally, social disorder and upheaval in fact punctuate Egyptian history. Most likely such disruptions were worsened by the interruption and tangling of lines of divine messaging. By the Late Bronze Age, destabilizing social complexity and the lack of clear authorization hastened the final breakdown of bicameral mentality during the Third Intermediate Period (1069–664 BCE). An obsolete mentality had been shoved off from the stage of history. Replacing it was a new introcosmos of introspectable subjectivity.

Population Size, Cognitive Scale, and Hearing Voices

Imagine a society in which accountants have not been trained in math. Societies do not function well if the cognitive scale of individuals is not calibrated to demographic size and demands. More concretely, a person must be able to effectively respond to certain levels of sociopolitical organization, economic subsistence patterns, and technological advancements (e.g., writing).

What follows is admittedly speculative. I introduce a number of theoretical constructs. Let us begin with the most primitive and elemental type of bicamerality: auto-communicative looping in which one "speaks" to — and thereby manages — oneself via hallucinations of one's own voice (self-talk). But once social groupings reach a certain size and hierarchy, even if relatively flat, enters the equation of social relations, and then matters become complicated (especially if one's superiors are not nearby). In this situation auto-communicative looping evolves so that one's own verbalizations are reprocessed and interpreted to be the commanding voice of one's superior. Such an arrangement is adequate for small-scale groupings, but once they grow in size, direct control of each and every individual via VVVs becomes untenable. As social stability is threatened by demographic burdens two mutually reinforcing processes emerge. The first is the development of legitimizing super-religious ideologies in which rulers, either deputized by the gods or imbued with a semi-divine nature, sit on top of the sociopolitical pyramid (along with a priesthood). The second is the evolution of apex VVVs that are experienced by a society's supreme theopolitical leader, such as a pharaoh. Authorization, of course, is not necessarily the same as experiencing VVVs, and social management is possible as long as individuals accept the authorization of the ultimate ruler and believe everyone else does (Table 2.2).

OBJECTION: THE CHANGE FROM PRECONSCIOUSNESS TO CONSCIOUSNESS COULD NOT HAVE OCCURRED SO QUICKLY

Two responses are required here. First, assuming that conscious interiority is socially acquired and not an inborn neurophysiological feature, there is no reason to believe that a cultural facet of civilization could not change over a matter of centuries. Second, the transition from preconsciousness to consciousness, if speaking within the time span of several millennia, was gradual. We have to avoid simple categorizations of preconscious bicamerality versus conscious postbicamerality, and acknowledge the stages

Table 2.2. Demographic Scale and Cognitive Scale.

Demographic and Sociopolitical Organization	Direction of Authorization	Extent and Type of VVVs
Bands	Auto-communicative Looping	Generated by and "heard" by the individual
Tribes	Ruler → Small Group	Apex VVVs experienced by individuals; VVVs from ancestors, deceased relatives
Chiefdoms	Gods/Ancestors → Ruler → Shamans → Large Group	Apex VVVs not commonly experienced by individuals; VVVs from ancestors, deceased relatives
Kingdoms/Large Kingdoms	Gods/Ancestors → Ruler → Priesthood → Very Large Group	Apex VVVs rarely experienced by individuals; VVVs from ancestors, deceased relatives; SVs from various numina
Breakdown of Bicameral Mentality about 1000 BCE		
Super-dense and Very Large Polities	Gods/Ancestors → Ruler → Priesthood → Very Large Group	VVVs cease and conscious interiority emerges; vestigial VVVs

of weakening bicamerality, semi-bicamerality, and proto-conscious interiority. A time existed when people were completely nonconscious. But once the historical "civilizational period" was established from around 3500 BCE, a range of mentalities emerged, with individuals being "partly subjective and partly bicameral"[26] and a "primitive partial type of consciousizing"[27] struggling toward full-blown conscious interiority. Holdovers from the earlier bicameral mentality (spirit possession, hypnosis, glossolalia, imaginary friends of childhood, voices heard by the mentally ill as well as nonclinical populations) indicate how we still share basic psychic structures with our predecessors.

Though generally a common list of ingredients is to be found in all civilizations, the emphases, combinations, and permutations of the BCI traits vary by place and period. Variations in populations, regional ecologies, economic particulars, the organization of theopolitical structures, etc., would result in discernible differences in the "authority, frequency, ubiquity, and affect of hallucinatory control."[28] Also, static stability would be a mischaracterization of super-religious societies. Despite any uniformities among bicameral civilizations (e.g., "large central worshiping places, treatment of the dead as if they were still living, and the presence of idols"), these societies were "not unchanging over time."[29] Indeed, "over and beyond these grosser aspects of ancient civilizations" many subtleties are apparent. "For just as we know that cultures and civilizations can be strikingly different, so we must not assume that the bicameral mind resulted in precisely the same thing everywhere it occurred."[30]

OBJECTION: THE REMNANTS OF OFFICIALDOM DISTORTS OUR PICTURE OF EGYPTIAN SPIRITUALITY

The immovable obviousness of stone works has survived, erected by officialdom with its own self-important and pompous imperatives. So we must wonder what materials have been lost that might reveal non-elite perspectives, especially as they relate to the observances, practices, and beliefs of common people.[31] The aforementioned misgiving raises the sticky issue, then, of how the elite, who controlled the resources and set the ideological agenda, erected monuments to themselves that to this day overshadow any contributions or ideas held by the masses who, it needs to be emphasized, constituted the vast majority.

But nothing from the extant evidence indicates that the populace adhered to views that were in any way fundamentally at odds with what we moderns have pieced together about archaic Egyptian super-religiosity. Despite differences between officialdom's worldview and a more popular perspective and the uneven preservation of sites and monuments, the quest for spiritual meaning takes us "through common territory."[32]

OBJECTION: THE ARCHAIC EGYPTIANS OBSESSED OVER DEATH — THIS DISTORTS ANY INTERPRETATION ABOUT THEIR PSYCHOLOGY

In other words, their focus on matters funerary was unusual, thereby warping our interpretations of their thinking. However, a comparison with contemporaneous civilizations does not bear this out. Granted, it does seem that compared to other places, the Egyptians elaborated their mortuary culture more floridly — tomb-building (pyramids), rituals (mummification), writings (the *Book of the Dead* and other texts) — but this is a matter of degree, not kind.

Super-religiosity seemed especially centered on death. This makes sense given bicamerality, with the belief in the animate dead who communicated with the living (VVVs, DWMP). It is moderns who, in historical perspective, are unusual. "Few cultures in this world exclude death and the dead from their reality as radically as we do."[33] Moderns deny death (as this writer, growing up in a family employed in the funeral industry, can attest). From a comparative anthropological perspective, "it is we, not the ancient Egyptians, who are the exception."[34]

Also, the perceived Egyptian obsession with death needs to be put in context. In Egypt, "more than any other culture, we encounter death in many forms, in mummies, statues, reliefs, buildings, and texts; but these were not images of death, they were counterimages, articulations of its negation, not of its affirmation."[35] Egyptian funerary representations rarely depict gruesome images of the dead. "There are no skeletons or putrefying corpses."[36] There has "never been so this-worldly a next world, this-worldly not in the sense that the Egyptians envisioned Paradise, as Muslims do, after the fashion of an earthly pleasure house, but in the sense that in this world Egyptians were obliged to keep their hands full building it, conceptually colonizing it and ritually keeping it in motion."[37]

It is possible that the preponderance of information relating to the funerary practices of the Egyptians "merely reflects the imbalance in the preservation of evidence from burial and settlement sites."[38] In any case, the "fear of death and the unknown has always haunted mankind, but rarely finds expression in ancient Egyptian texts, and even then it is tempered by encouragement to enjoy life despite its brevity."[39] I suspect that this characterization applies to bicameral civilizations in general. This does not mean archaic peoples lacked any apprehension about death; it just means their orientation towards one's ultimate demise lacked the searing existential agony with which we moderns are more accustomed.

OBJECTION: HOW DO WE KNOW IF ARCHAIC ACCOUNTS WERE JUST MYTHIC STORYTELLING OR ACTUAL RECOUNTINGS OF EXPERIENCING DIVINE VISITATIONS?

Of course certain legends and tales from ancient times are fabrications. But there is no reason to doubt that many mytho-literary accounts and epics were inspired by hallucinatory encounters with the supernatural. I argue this point for three reasons. First, consider the overwhelming preponderance of evidence from all over the globe; surely this all means something of significance. Second, note that we have yet to find a civilization before about 1000 BCE with archaeohistorical evidence that was not super-religious. Third, we have to accept the prominent role of hallucinations (clinical and benign) still seen in modern times as well as semi-hallucinatory experiences (mental imagery); the ability to conjure up imagistic/imaginary/imagined scenery is a key facet of our psyche. Why have we evolved these capabilities? The simple answer is for social control.

Disentangling myth from fact can be challenging. But sometimes a new interpretative framework sheds light on historical realities. Consider the Narmer Macehead, an Egyptian decorative stone club from approximately five millennia ago. It depicts the king, gods, and goddesses interacting in a ceremony where captives and plunder are reviewed. Directly facing the seated king is a shrouded figure. Some have interpreted this mysterious person as a princess being offered for marriage or the king's child. Another view is that it represents a god attending the event.[40] I would go one step further and suggest that the figure is a visually hallucinated god.

The Problem of Translation

Related to all this is the issue of translation. Various challenges hinder the testing of Jaynes's proposition, such as misleading renderings of ancient texts. As if assuming that readers are allergic to strong religiosity, some translators impose modern sensibilities on earlier mentalities. A number of examples suggests a queasiness on the part of translators to let archaic Egyptians speak in their own voice (Table 2.3). For example, a footnoted exegesis on a portion of the enigmatic *The Man Who Was Weary of Life* explains that the "speaker is here not addressing his [Ba] as a separate entity. He is rather musing upon the joys and the peace which he will know in death. He addresses his [Ba] only as a symbol of addressing himself."[41] I contend that this interpretation, ignoring the historical context, distorts an earlier mentality as evidenced by this text whose alternative title might be *A Dispute Between a Man and His Ba.*

Table 2.3. Translations and Literal Renderings Compared.

Literal Translation	Common Reading	Source	Cited In
One whose Kas are harnessed	A man of standing	Stela of the Treasurer Iti of Imyotru	Lichtheim, 2006a, p. 89
An island of the Ka	Island of the Spirit	*Shipwrecked Sailor*	Simpson, 2003, p. 50
My heart began to follow my sleep	And I started / to drift off to sleep	*Teaching of King Amenemhet*	Simpson, 2003, p. 168
While his Ka will ...	While his mood will ...	*Maxims of Ptahhotep*	Simpson, 2003, p. 141
According as his Ka commands	Determined by his mood	*Maxims of Ptahhotep*	Simpson, 2003, p. 133
It is the Ka which stretches out his hands	It is his mood which prompts him to be generous	*Maxims of Ptahhotep*	Simpson, 2003, p. 133
This is an abomination of the Ka	This serves only to arouse the temper	*Maxims of Ptahhotep*	Simpson, 2003, p. 134
Do not separate your heart from him	Do not withhold your love from him	*Maxims of Ptahhotep*	Simpson, 2003, p. 135
He who pleases God	He who behaves in a decent manner	*Maxims of Ptahhotep*	Simpson, 2003, p. 135

SUMMING UP

At this point allow me to wrap up and summarize the key premises. The archaeohistorical record reveals elements of the BCI that formed worldwide commonalities. Such features have built upon each other through the centuries, forming global stratigraphic psychological patterns. The existence of such patterns, taken for granted, is a crucial datum itself. The evidence shows how human psychology has adapted over time. An exploration of these configurations demonstrates why the expansion of societal scale resulted in the reorganization of psychological processes (Table 2.4).

A Final Word on Probability and Evidence

I conclude this chapter with a comment about the likelihood that my claims in this project carry validity. The BCI Hypothesis allows us to view, within regions and across regions, a fact-pattern that follows a trajectory over a very long period. I contend that the evidence I offer falls well above "possible" but below "proven," occupying the "probable" (target) range, with variation depending on the particular hypothesis and evidence presented (i.e., likely, almost certain, highly likely) (Table 2.5).

Table 2.4. Suggested Chronology of Changes in Human Mentality.

Period	Bicameral Mentality	Conscious Interiority
?	Pre-bicameral Mentality	Preconscious
	Proto-bicameral Mentality	
Neolithic	Bicameral Mentality	
3000 BCE	Urban–literate Bicamerality	Incipient Conscious Interiority
	Weakening Bicameral Mentality	
	Semi-bicameral Mentality	Semi-conscious Interiority
1200 BCE	Breakdown of Bicameral Mentality	
1000 BCE	Vestigial Bicameral Mentality	Expanding Conscious Interiority
Future		

Table 2.5. Degrees of Probability.

Degree of Possibility	Level of Certainty	Percentage
Proven	Certain	100%
	Almost Certain, Highly Likely	93%
Probable	Likely Target Range	75%
Possible	Chances about Even	50%
	Unlikely, Probably Not	30%
Improbable	Almost Certainly Not, Highly Unlikely	7%
Impossible	Certainly Not	0%

Notes to Chapter 2

1. Some popular (mis)interpretations of Jaynes's arguments, based on less-than-cursory readings of his work, suggest that his views were archaeopsychiatric (e.g., archaic peoples were "schizophrenic"). But Jaynes never argued this.
2. McVeigh, 2016, pp. 11–13.
3. The "biological argument about human nature is linked to cultural history, with the biological framework merely a platform upon which cultural activity erected a superstructure in recent times." Warburton, 2009, p. 84.
4. Fernyhough, 2016, p. 137.
5. Fernyhough, 2016, p. 138.
6. E.g., the sociologist Stanislav Andreski wrote that in spite of its problems, Lévy-Bruhl's 1910 book (translated as *How Natives Think*) was a valuable contribution to anthropology.
7. Frankfort, et al., 1977.
8. Maleijt, 1974, p. 191.
9. Cited in Cazeneuve, 1972, p. 87.
10. Littleton, 1985, p. xx.
11. Littleton, 1985, p. vi, emphasis in original. Viewed against this background of his day, when the ranking of races and social Darwinism was widely accepted, Lévy-Bruhl's books "were the summit of moderation." Van der Veer, 2003, p. 180.
12. Jaynes, 1976, p. 41.
13. Jaynes, 1976, p. 41.
14. Jaynes, 1976, p. 41.
15. Jaynes, 1976, p. 390.
16. Jaynes, 1976, p. 390.
17. Jaynes, 1976, p. 391.

18. Jaynes, 1976, p. 391.
19. Shaw, 2000a, p. 16.
20. Shaw, 2000a, p. 4.
21. McVeigh, 2018.
22. Actually, if following a stricter standard of the scientific method, I should first propose the null hypothesis of the BCI Hypothesis: archaic civilizations existed that the list of items in the BCI does not apply to in any salient way, i.e., the task of the BCI Hypothesis is to find civilizations which the BCI does not describe. My hypothesis is that such attempts will be unsuccessful.
23. Jaynes is clear on this point. Jaynes, 1976, p. 194.
24. "Doubleworld" is borrowed from Bolshakov, 1997, 2001.
25. In some of these holdovers IMRHA is utilized to culturally activate vestigial language areas of the right hemisphere.
26. Jaynes, 1976, p. 300. This was the case elsewhere, e.g., the Inca Empire at the time of its conquest by Francisco Pizarro was perhaps a combination of bicameral and proto-subjective mentalities. Jaynes, 1976, p. 158.
27. Jaynes, 1976, p. 268.
28. Jaynes, 1976, p. 194.
29. Jaynes, 1976, p. 194.
30. Jaynes, 1976, p. 194.
31. We should note that the archaic Egyptians themselves had difficulty understanding their own texts, as is illustrated by, for example, the widely differing interpretations preserved in the glosses appended regularly to Chapter 17 of the *Book of the Dead.* Lesko, 1991, p. 88.
32. Shafer, 1991a, p. 3.
33. Assmann, 2005, p. 1.
34. Assmann, 2005, p. 1.
35. Assmann, 2005, p. 18.
36. Pinch, 2006, p. 147.
37. Assmann, 2005, p. 18.
38. David, 2003, p. 21.
39. Harrington, 2010, p. 122.
40. Millet, 1990.
41. Cited in Simpson, 2003, p. 181.

Chapter 3

The Mentality of Archaic Egypt

"A man should say that he may make his protection through magic, 'I am this pure Magic that is in the mouth and belly of Re. O gods, spirits, and the dead, keep away from me! I am Re, the radiant one."
— *Hymn to the Aten*

A MYTHOPOEIC WORLDVIEW

THE GREEK WRITER DIODORUS SICULUS who visited Egypt in the mid-first century BCE[1] described that country's religious behavior and beliefs as bizarre. But we must not forget that the "rational" Greeks themselves still held "irrational" (i.e., paralogic) beliefs as attested by Dodd's *The Greeks and the Irrational*.[2] Learned Greeks by the mid-first millennium BCE had adopted a logic grounded in conscious interiority. As did the well-educated Egyptians, no doubt. But the idea that many Egyptians still continued to embrace the dictates of a paralogic mindset (though not in all domains of their lives; they were after all conscious by the first millennium BCE) was strongly held. In any case, the views of Diodorus Siculus indicate not a difference between literal-minded Greek and hyper-mythologized Egyptian thought. Rather, the distinction concerns to which social circle an observer belonged (i.e., level of education) and to what degree bicameral vestiges were evident in that observer's society.

This chapter is intended to lay the groundwork of archaic Egyptian mentality. After treating how symbols operate and delineating the differences between "complexes" and "concepts," I discuss the meaning of a "prescientific" worldview; the complexes of space and time; how the new mentality of conscious subjective introspection "ruptured the cosmos"; and how the "words of the gods" (hieroglyphs) shaped reality.

SYMBOLS AND THE ANCIENT WORLD

Symbols are more than something that stands for something else by reason of conventional use or arbitrary association. We must drop the mistaken view that symbols are mere signs or reflections of a more "real" reality. Symbols motivate us, shape our behavior, and determine our interpretations of the world. They should be thought of as evocative devices for arousing, channeling, and domesticating powerful emotions such as hate, fear, affection, loyalty, and grief. A given society's values, institutions, and beliefs are organized into and around symbols, and often those in power use and manipulate symbols for their own ends (temples, pyramids, royal regalia, divine speech, ritual paraphernalia, etc.).

"Key symbols" are representations, signs, images, or iconic depictions that carry heavy significance. Also called dominant symbols or core symbols, these representations of weighty import may be a visual representation or a verbal expression, such as a single word. In fact, anything, including abstract concepts, can be a symbol. The important characteristics of key symbols include: (1) members of a certain society/community state that symbol X is important to them; (2) members of a certain society/community are positively or negatively aroused by symbol X (i.e., rather than being merely indifferent); (3) symbol X occurs in many different situations, such as in daily conversation or in other contexts, e.g., myths, rituals, artistic expressions, religious belief, etc.; (4) a certain amount of cultural elaboration surrounds symbol X, i.e., an extensive vocabulary may be used to describe details about symbol X, or the symbol may be put into various visual representations; (5) greater cultural restrictions surround symbol X, either in the sheer number of rules or severity of sanctions regarding its misuse.[3]

Key symbols operate in two ways, or we might say that they move in two opposite directions: summarizing and elaborating.[4] The former describes how symbols sum up or encapsulate many feelings and thoughts, bringing together complex ideas, so that one image or thing represents a system of meanings. Elaboration, on the other hand, sorts out complex, undifferentiated thoughts and emotions; this is an analyzing maneuver.

Important symbols can also be understood by examining their: (1) multivocality ("many voices"): this describes how one symbol can represent a spectrum of meanings; (2) condensation: one symbol can unify many diverse meanings and bring together different ideas. At the nonconscious level, these different ideas that make up one symbol may associate with and interrelate with other concepts; (3) ambiguity: because key symbols lack one single or precise meaning, and can accumulate additional meanings, allowing individuals to interpret, to a degree, the same symbol differently.[5]

REFLECTIVE SYMBOLS VERSUS IDENTIFICATION SYMBOLS

Homo sapiens are defined, vis-à-vis other animals, by their ability to symbolize the world around them. Indeed, human cognition is intrinsically symbolic. But we use two types of symbols. The first, reflective symbols, of which there are many examples, can be illustrated by the American flag. Its stripes represent the original thirteen colonies while the stars symbolize fifty states. Red stands for valor and hardiness, white, purity and innocence, and blue, vigilance, perseverance, and justice. Another example: the three colors of the French flag symbolize the motto of the revolution: blue = freedom; white = equality; and red = brotherhood. But we know that in the case of Old Glory, the number thirteen lacks an inherent causal connection to the founding colonies and that stars and states do not share a magical essence. We also know that the colors of the French flag have an arbitrary relation to revolutionary principles.

Identification symbols, however, are motivated by the belief that the relation between two things goes beyond mere reflective representation. In other words, two things share an ineffable essential identity. While reflective symbols signify, point to, indicate, mark, designate, direct to, or denote, identification symbols fuse, merge, and equate disparate things; they make causal connections, bring about relations, and elicit and provoke interactions that defy objective logic. These are paralogic operations. While reflective symbols are figurative, identification symbols carry a literalness of linkages. For example, portraying Egypt's enemies as small on temple walls was not figuratively symbolic (i.e., a mere artistic convention); rather, it was literally symbolic since a shrunken scale was a magical technique to rob power from one's foes. Another example: the murder of Osiris, being a cataclysmic event, was too dangerous to depict in temples.[6]

Reflective symbols and identification symbols coexist in ancient as well as modern societies, e.g., present-day Catholics believe in transubstantiation. However, I submit that, in preconscious civilizations, identification symbols were ubiquitous. In other words, it was possible that the ancient

Egyptians distinguished between the two types of symbols, but for them identification symbols played, by modern standards, a notably salient role.

EXAMPLES OF KEY IDENTIFICATION SYMBOLS

Consider some examples of key symbols. The sphinx *ḥw*[7] is undoubtedly second to the pyramids as the most recognized icon of ancient Egypt. Typically it had the body of a lion and the head of a king or queen (the latter were often depicted with wings) and guarded temples and tombs. They symbolized the unquestionable and awesome power of the ruler and their duty to defend Egypt and uphold Maat, the cosmic principles of balance and fairness. Some sphinxes had the heads of hawks or rams (*rhny*).[8] The double sphinx Aker (*ꜣkr*)[9] stood sentinel at the portals of the Afterworld. A type of sphinx with wings and a snake tail, Tutu, whose epithet at the Shenhur Temple was Who Comes to the One Calling Him,[10] was believed to be the offspring of the goddess Neit.

Another example of a key symbol was the Ankh (*ʿnḫ*),[11] the T-shaped cross with a loop handle. It was a very common element of design and was used as an amulet and often seen as a large scepter-like emblem carried by deities. It symbolized life-force, food, air, sexual fecundity, to live, be alive, and swearing an oath. It is unclear what it was supposed to replicate, though the same word for Ankh meant sandal or mirror; these may be clues to its original meaning which have been lost. Libation jars and vessels were made in the shape of the Ankh; water or wine would be poured through the loop of an Ankh as a form of blessing. Another key symbol is the Djed Pillar (*ḏd*).[12] It signified stability, endurance, and duration. Early on it may have meant a bundle of corn sheaves or reeds, but it came to mean the spine of Osiris and was also associated with Ptah. It may have stood for the axis mundi (world axis), uniting the earth and the sky.

Colors and Numbers as Key Identification Symbols

As in all cultures, colors possessed special symbolic powers and associations (Table 3.1). Certain numbers were inherently efficacious and appear repeatedly in rituals, spells, and invocations: two, three, four, and seven were meaning-laden numerals. Besides colors, numbers reflected cosmic principles and potencies (Table 3.2).

Table 3.1. Symbolic Associations of Colors.

Color	Symbolic Associations
Black	Night; death; Afterworld; resurrection; life; fertility (silt of the Nile); Anubis; Osiris; magical healing statues (interchangeable with green; interchangeable with blue for night sky)
Blue	Heavens; water; sky; life; rebirth; annual flooding of the Nile (recalling the primal flood of the Nile); fertility; Amun-Re; Ptah; Horus; Khnum; Re-Horakhty
Green	Growth; life; good deeds; resurrection; Osiris; Hathor; Afterworld
Red	Blood; fire; life; regeneration; sun's radiance; chaos; dangerous powers; Re; Seth; untamed vastness of the desert; dangerous lands and foreign places; red ink used to denote evil
White	Cleanliness; sacredness; ritual purity; garb of priests; used for sacred objects
Yellow	Gold; solar imagery; eternity; constancy; bones and flesh of deities

Source: Rankine, 2006, pp. 76–78.

Table 3.2. Symbolic Associations of Numbers.

Number	Symbolic Associations
One	The original unity from which creation emerges into plurality, gushing forth with emanations and manifestations
Two	Duality as the complementary aspect of unity, expressed in heaven and earth, light and dark, day and night, sun and moon, man and woman, young and old; Upper and Lower Crowns of Egypt, pairs of deities
Three	Plurality; trinities of deities to combine features or the family unit of deities (father, mother, child); three-season cycle (inundation, growing, harvest); three ten-day periods for the months; prayers typically offered three times; hieroglyphic convention of three images indicates plurality
Four	Totality; completion; four areas of cosmos (earth, sky, heavens, underworld); cardinal points addressed during rituals; north–south axis of the Nile and east-west axis of sun's journey; four legs of the cosmic cow; priests bathed four times per day
Seven	Perfection; sevenfold manifestations or aspects of deities; seven Bas of Re, Seven Hathors, Seven Arrows of Sekhmet, seven scorpions accompanying Isis on her trek to find the dismembered parts of Osiris
Eight	Intensification of the totality and completeness by doubling four; Ogdoad or eight primeval deities who precede creation; four gods and four goddesses in cosmogonies
Nine	Intensification of three by multiplying itself; Ennead if Heliopolis; all-encompassing group
Ten	Measurement of time and space; groups of ten occur in the months (three ten-day periods); a generation was thirty years (3 x 10)
Twelve	Measurement of time; twelve hours each of night and day; twelve months of the year

Source: Rankine, 2006, pp. 79–82.

Gods and Goddesses as Key Identification Symbols

The major gods and goddesses functioned as complexes with correspondences, correlations, and connections with amulets, animals, colors, concepts, plants, and symbols. For example, Sobek, a god of procreative and vegetative fertility, was a crocodile or crocodile-headed man who wore a sun disk with horns and plumes (Table 3.3). Sekhmet, a destroyer of demons and pestilence, was a lioness-headed woman who wore a wig, a solar disk, with the Uraeus serpent on her brow. Incidentally, the Uraeus, the spitting cobra, was donned by royalty in their crown. It denoted protection from enemies and symbolized the power of the Eye of Re. Sekhmet was known as the Mistress of Life. This fire-breathing deity was believed to accompany the pharaoh in battle and hot desert winds were called the "breath of Sekhmet" (Table 3.4).

COMPLEXES VERSUS CONCEPTS

We tend to forget that generalized, conceptual abstractions are the products of determined reasoning and mental labor; they do not arise naturally

Table 3.3. Symbolic Associations of Sobek.

Object	Symbolic Associations
Amulets	Figurines of Sobek indicating fertility and protection
Animals	Crocodile
Colors	Green
Concepts	Fertility; might; vegetation; water
Symbols	Sun disk with horns and plumes; water
Other	Carnelian; patron of fishermen; Nile comes from his sweat

Source: Rankine, 2006, p. 64.

Table 3.4. Symbolic Associations of Sekhmet.

Object	Symbolic Associations
Amulets	Figurines of Sekhmet
Animals	Lioness, cobra
Colors	Red
Concepts	Strength of the midday sun; divine retribution; fighting for the Evil Eye; fire; victory in battle; healing; misfortune (especially infectious diseases, setting bones)
Symbols	Charito; Leo (constellation and sign); rosettes, Sekhem; the Seven Arrows; sistrum; *w3ḏ* scepter;[13] Uraeus crown

Source: Rankine, 2006. p. 58.

or easily from the psyche. They require escaping from the powerful gravity of paralogic in order to enter the rarefied orbit of logic and impartial inquiry. On the other hand, a complexive idea possesses a functional concreteness, an over-abundance of associations, restricted abstraction, and limited logical coherence.[14] Though in archaic times individuals could conceptually construct higher-level categories and distinguish these from lower-level categories, quite often they saw little need to differentiate between superordinate and subordinate classification. There was a tendency to fuse the general with the particular.

MacDonald goes so far as to claim that archaic patterns of thought "do not differ from our 'modern' patterns in having different concepts, but in not having anything like concepts at all."[15] Instead archaic peoples relied on "complexes" (as opposed to logically thought-out concepts). A complex (1) "does not arise above its elements as does a concept; it merges with the concrete objects that compose it"; (2) its "abstracted traits are unstable and easily surrender their temporary dominance to other traits"; (3) the "basic level of complex formation may be the most inclusive level at which it is possible" to form a cognitive representation ("which is isomorphic to an average member of the class, and thus, the most abstract level at which it is possible to have a relatively concrete image"); and (4) it possesses an "over-abundance of properties, an over-production of connections, and weakness in abstraction."[16] According to one observer a "liberalism of interpretation, amounting at times to a chaotic indifference to consistency and meaning, is characteristic of [archaic] Egyptian thought."[17] However, nothing was random or arbitrary. For example, what we would call puns were for the ancient Egyptians a connection of meaning rather than mere coincidence. For example, men (*rmṯ*) literally came from the tears (*rmṯ*) of the gods. Much dream interpretation was based on punning, e.g., to dream of a harp (*bỉnt* or *bnt*) indicated evil (*bỉnt*), while to dream of a donkey (ʿꜣ) suggested one would be promoted (*s*ʿꜣ).[18]

"Magic" as a Complex Idea

Many key symbols operate as complexive ideas. As an illustration, consider the role of magic in the ancient world. Believers in magic make a distinction between "how" and "why" something happened. In other words, while they understood the immediate reason (the logical cause-and-effect) of an event, they seemed more concerned with an ultimate explanation of a happening (attribution of significance to an event). Such an assignment of import is illustrated by over-interpretation; patterns are seen to exist where, from a purely objective perspective, they do not in fact exist.

Anthropology, ethnography, and religious studies conventionally distinguish between magic (threatens the social order, unorthodox, unholy, personal use) and religion (sustains the social order, orthodox, holy, communal function). But this distinction, while possessing some validity, does not do justice to archaic Egyptian thought.[19] This is because in Egypt Heka (*ḥk3w*),[20] usually but misleadingly translated as "magic," was an enabling force used by all beings to succeed in their endeavors and obtain their desired ends.[21] Religion and magic were part of the same overarching cosmic order. Kings naturally possessed large doses of Heka, and in their official duties and rituals, utilized it for a variety of purposes. Heka allowed priests to act as intermediaries between this world and the supernatural realms. Magic was the binding force between the earth and other worlds, the link between mortals and the divine. Egyptians could not have imagined life without this cosmic power because it provided them with the opportunity to participate in the divine. Heka is best understood as a cosmic energy that was conjured up for a variety of reasons; it was not only utilized for untoward purposes outside the accepted and established system. Heka infused funerary, temple, and everyday domains.[22] Though anything out of the ordinary (e.g., dwarves) had high doses of Heka, it can be defined as the "divinely sanctioned force that initiated, permeated, and sustained nature itself."[23] It is tempting to view magic as a form of primitive science, but the former was not an experimental endeavor intended to understand the natural world in terms of impersonal forces. Indeed, magic was all about attributing personal agency, motives, and intentions to the surrounding world. [24]

COMPLEXES OF SPATIALITY

Nyord notes that the Egyptians did not "conceive of space in terms of sets of three dimensional coordinates."[25] They dwelled in a cosmogeography full of complexes and symbolic reference points. The known cosmos consisted of the sky or the divine realm, the earth (with Egypt in the center), and the Duat (commonly translated as the Underworld). They called their country Kemet (*kmt*), meaning Black Land. This referred to the earthy, rich, and black silt brought by the Nile's inundations; blackness was associated with regeneration, life, and rebirth. Beyond the civilized, cultivable regions hugging the Nile lay the desolate Deshret (hence "desert") or Red Land (*dšrt*). This was inhabited by marauding tribespeople and wild beasts. This arid region appeared red to the archaic Egyptians and this explains why redness became linked to danger and death. The south (Upper Egypt) is hot, dry, inward-looking, and the fertile soil was only a few miles wide on either side of the Nile. The north (Lower Egypt) is wider, flatter, cooler, and much more verdant. It was a region open to foreign influences as well as invasions. The two lands of Upper and Lower Egypt were symbolized by the White Crown (vulture, lily) and the Red Crown (cobra, papyrus), respectively.

Consider four types of spatial depiction. These all shared the same traits: more pictorial than planimetric; representing a nonperspective, bird's-eye view; not drawn at constant scale but instead precise measurements were "written where they are deemed important."[26] The first type were mythological and delineated features of the Afterworld. Funerary writings and images inscribed on mortuary objects (e.g., the floors of wooden coffins) overlapped in meaning with the second type, cosmological. These were formulaic portrayals of a cosmogeography studded with sacred landmarks and features. The third type were architectural plans for tombs and palaces. The final type were topographical that date to the late Predynastic Period (ca. 4000–3000 BCE). These depict the natural or cultural features of a portion of the earth's surface. Examples were narrative scenes inscribed on pottery, monumental walls, and stelae. However, these were not "maps" as we usually think of them (indeed, archaic Egyptian lacked a word for map). They were more like "pictures" but lacked any attempts at realistic verisimilitude. Another instance of topographical representations were cadastral maps (land surveys) for taxation purposes. The depiction that comes close to a map of a known geographical area in modern terms appeared late. It was probably prepared for Ramesses IV's quarrying expedition to the Wadi Hammamant in the eastern desert and was made around 1160 BCE.[27] The evidence seems to state that clear-cut maps were not used for economic or other practical purposes until the Ramesside period (1292–1069 BCE).[28]

COMPLEXES OF TEMPORALITY

In Salvador Dali's surrealistic painting, *The Persistence of Memory*, clocks melt in an eerie landscape, affording time both a strange concreteness and flexibility. This brings to mind how the archaic Egyptians "did not think of time as moving at the same rate for all classes of beings or in all parts of the cosmos."[29] A concrete–relative–cyclical view trumped an abstract–absolute–linear understanding of temporality. The earliest calendar was lunar and used for cultic purposes. But for the routines of an agricultural lifestyle, a solar system was developed with three "seasons": (1) Akhet (inundation); (2) Peret (growing); and (3) Shemu (lacking water). However, despite the emphasis on cyclical time, the *Coffin Texts* and the *Book of the Dead* (which due to its later date had a more clearly indicated sense of linear time) do state that the gods and the cosmos will eventually meet their ultimate demise.

Though the Egyptian language of the archaic era was chock full of concrete, specific words to describe the passage of events, it lacked an abstract, general term for time. The archaic Egyptians were certainly capable of conceptualizing temporality in linear terms for practical purposes and they used many expressions for time (e.g., *ꜣt*).[30] However, they lacked a notion of time as an absolute quantity; temporality had a particularized quality. Egyptians "attributed to substances and objects a 'right moment'"[31] so that "something occurs in its time" and certain events have their own time, i.e., the time provided for it or suited to things or people.[32]

Cosmic Time and Eternity

For the Egyptians, eternity was not a never-ending straight line trailing off beyond the horizon of the future but rather a continuation of an unchanging nowness. Indeed, it was a "flight from time's effects."[33] Translations for eternity are based on two terms. The first is *ḏt*,[34] meaning "unending sameness" or the changeless pattern of existence (eternal continuity). It occurs in a number of expressions. The rhythms of the cosmos move in a great cycle in which "everything had to change to survive and yet everything remained fundamentally the same."[35] Tombs were "houses of eternity," while temples were "mansions of eternity." In the Afterworld, time was absent in the sense that the passage of events, sickness, aging, or troubling incidents did not exist. In ritual reenactments, the "gods appear and speak once more the words they spoke 'the first time'" so that "change which has taken place is reduced to a reaffirmation of an unchanging truth."[36] The second term of eternity, *nḥḥ*,[37] designates "everlastingness" or continual renewal (eternal recurrence).[38]

The conceptualization of time by the archaic Egyptians fits in with their view of the universe, which was "essentially static."[39] Events transpired and movement occurred but change, "in so far as it was significant, was recurrent change, the life rhythm a universe which has gone forth, complete and unchanging, from the hands of its creator."[40] Single occurrences, odd events, and "historical circumstances were ephemeral, superficial disturbances of the regularity of being and for that reason unimportant."[41]

The gods lived in a continuous present accessed by ritual but they simultaneously also lived in the past, i.e., the time of the ancients (*rk*).[42] In the present, the "gods are powerful cosmic forces whose interactions are not governed by petty human concerns." In the past, "deities can appear as fallible beings with desires and emotions";[43] this was the beginning of time, the first primeval community of gods (*pꜣwt tpt*).[44] Osiris was the "Lord of Eternity" (*nb nḥḥ*) or "Ruler of Eternity" (*ḥkꜣ ḏt*). Other deities were linked to the different types of time, such as Re. The children of the creator god, Tefnut (moisture, e.g., morning dew) and Shu (dry, life-giving air) were linked to eternal continuity and eternal recurrence, respectively.

Many of the sources for Egypt's best known myths come from the first millennium BCE. Remarkably, some scholars have difficulty ascribing to Egypt a developed mythology before the Late Period.[45] Presumably this sentiment reflects how archaic Egyptians did not clearly distinguish between factual, impartially-written histories and supernatural accounts (i.e., mythology). Indeed, it was common in Egypt to use actual events as material for mythological accounts in order to highlight some cosmic truth. What mattered was not if something happened but rather what paralogic significance it held for society. This is a hallmark of mythopoeic thinking.

Time without History

Archaic Egypt "never had a genuine historian; this is a plain fact which must be accepted."[46] Like other archaic peoples, the Egyptians did not date important events along a line moving ahead into the future (i.e., with the "number of years that had elapsed since a single fixed point"). Rather, they measured, in a particularistic manner, time with the "years since the accession of each current king (regnal years)."[47] This was because the reign of each king was considered to have restarted the cosmopolitical clock anew. Events were commemorated but not narrated.[48] The absence of a continuous sense of time made exact dating and timing difficult.[49] Rulers were depicted "designed for eternity." Each figure "claimed eternal life by solidity and stolidity; by avoiding the appearance of flexibility, momentary action, or passing emotion; and by standing massive and motionless, sublimely freed from a single location in space or a single moment in time."[50]

Though a "future" in the modern sense of progress and radical social re-engineering demanded too much hypotheticality for preconscious people to conceptualize, the past was more readily accepted as having value. An unthinking acceptance of what had gone before, especially from the Middle Kingdom onward, granted the past an authorization that legitimated rulership and the entire cosmopolitical order. Being essentially recurrent, temporality was ahistorical, a process without results. The closest thing to historical records were annals, chronicles, and king lists. These "weighed down for more than thirty centuries the notations of historical facts in Egypt."[51] King lists were exclusively preoccupied with ancestor worship and ritual purposes, not with history. Examples of king lists include the Abydos Tablet from the mortuary temple of Seti I (1306–1290 BCE) which includes 76 rulers; the Karnak Tablet inscribed in the festival hall of Tuthmose III at Karnak; the Palermo Stone from Dynasty 5; the Saqqara Tablet (Ramesside period) that probably dated to the reign of Ramesses II (died 1213 BCE); the Turin Canon from the reign of Ramesses II, which begins with the dynasties of the gods and is probably the most reliable of the king lists; and the historian Manetho's list, consciously composed during the time of Ptolemy I Soter (ca. 367–282 BCE) and Ptolemy II Philadelphus (283–246 BCE).

Archaism, here meaning the conscious attempt to reproduce the art, dress, religions, and writings of an earlier time, emerged in Dynasty 26 (1938–1755 BCE), when an interest in archaeology and traditional customs became salient.[52] By then time had become more narrative and linear.

A PRESCIENTIFIC RATHER THAN ASCIENTIFIC WORLDVIEW

"In a world abounding with the presence and activity of gods and spirits, one did not study the processes of nature."[53] Divine agency accounted for everything, so that the cosmos was not open to human questioning. Consequently, the need to seek out impersonal causes, regular laws of nature, or to encourage an interest in the "movement of time" was unnecessary.[54] Science was "limited to measurement, building, and repair, with no interest in the future, no interest in chains of cause and effect, no interest in abstracted principles."[55] The archaic Egyptian "was no historian."[56] Things happened because the gods willed them to happen. And the "will of the gods needed no philosophical or logical analysis."[57] They "never tried to go back to the historical origin of a phenomenon and explain the series of events leading up to that phenomenon."[58] The FOCI of narratization was weakly developed.

Since mythopoeic thought personifies its surroundings and all observable phenomena, impersonal causation and philosophical abstraction were not front-and-center.[59] Egyptian philosophical inquiry, if it can be called that, is the "product of theology [or more accurately, theocentricity] and never becomes emancipated from it."[60] Indeed, we "need to always remember that the ancient Egyptian religion had no theology."[61] An "explicit and coherent explanation of Egyptian theology on the metalevel of theoretical discourse" was non-existent. A meta-framed perspective was also lacking in grammar, rhetoric, and historiography.[62] Knowledge was not a matter of speculating about abstract principles but, as seen in other parts of the preconscious archaic world, of presenting items of knowledge on a list. For instance, though certainly impressive, archaic Egyptian mathematics was limited to practical pursuits such as architectural engineering and measurement. Egyptian could be rich in detailed descriptions, but poor in grand abstractions. For instance, there were many words for earth, sky, and the heavens, but no term that abstractly expressed "world" or *cosmos mundus*. A "great number" meant millions of years.

The lack of a philosophical perspective meant that, for archaic Egyptians, the distinction between cause and effect was not always clear, or more accurately, did not matter. This is a consequence of a prescientific, paralogic worldview (not ascientific); it does not mean that they could not discern the difference between reason and consequence. Obviously, one cannot build and run a sophisticated civilization without at least sometimes discerning cause-and-effect relations. It just means that an advanced scientific perspective was not predominant in many circumstances. Several answers to one question were acceptable; a multiplicity of perspectives encouraged; categorizations were not mutually exclusive; and multifaceted aspects of the same situation were acknowledged. The cosmopolitical, pivoting around a powerful sense of duality and balance, was held together by the key symbol of Maat (truth, harmony, law, morality, justice), which governed daily actions and moral principles.

HOW CONSCIOUS INTERIORITY RUPTURED THE COSMOS

The emergence of conscious interiority fractured the world, splitting it into an internal psychoscape from which one can "look out" and observe the external physical terrain. This bifurcation of reality is usually associated with mind–body dualism, but actually it implicates a number of issues: (1) how differences between visual and auditory processing influence the way we perceive/conceive the world; (2) psyche versus physicality; (3) the perceptual aspects of perspective; (4) the spiritual and material realms; and (5) deceit.

(1) Voices and Visions: Two Types of Knowing

Let us begin with the differences between engaging with the world aurally or visually. Auditory experiences collapse the distance between the perceiver and the source of sound; one cannot easily escape from the words someone speaks to us. What we see, however, can be controlled by simply averting our gaze or turning our heads away. Moreover, vision accesses objects at a distance, therefore implying the existence of an external world that is distinct from — and "outside" of — the mind that perceives it.[63]

Assuming that Jaynes is correct about superceptive voices and visions (i.e., hallucinations), the distinction between hearing and seeing has important implications for historical changes in cognition. One cannot flee divine voices, but one can turn away from others who are speaking to us, as well as averting one's attention away from material representations of the divine and textual information. This grants the individual a measure of control; it also allows the cultivation of an interiorized visual landscape that can be viewed by an internal "I" that helps erode bicameral mentality. The emergence of conscious interiority, then, can "in a certain vague sense be construed as a shift from an auditory mind to a visual mind."[64] Visuality, then, seems to undergird mind–body dualism.[65] Moreover, visuality becomes part of the powerful metaphor of "knowing is seeing," a common trope in many languages.

(2) Evidence of Mind–Body Dualism?

Did the archaic Egyptians have a notion of mind–body dualism? If yes, this challenges Jaynesian claims about a lack of introspectable experiences in preconscious times.[66] Certainly no evidence of an explicit, theorized Cartesian mind–body split exists in bicameral civilizations, and it seems clear that archaic Egypt was a "culture that did not operate with a primary ontological mind–body distinction."[67] However, a type of weak proto-dualism can be detected (as evidence see the section on deceit below). In the *Pyramid Texts,* a sort of primitive dualism is present in how the Ba (human-headed bird soul) is opposed to the body (*ḏt* or *ẖ3t*).[68] This complicates but is not lethal to a Jaynesian approach.

If Jaynes's theories are correct, preconscious civilizations should lack certain things, such as a tradition of philosophizing that engages in speculative, hypothetical, abstract, and difficult-to-answer problems, as well as the difference between one's inner experiences and one's physicality. In other words, in ancient civilizations, speculative meditation on mind–body dualism was absent before approximately the mid-first millennium BCE.

New conceptions of spatiality also drive mind–body dualism (and vice versa). Dualism produces two types of space. The first is introspectable, i.e., an invisible, intangible private arena accessible only to an inner self. The second is visible in the conventional sense, i.e., an exterior, physical space publicly apparent to others. "If body and soul are ontologically different, it tends to follow that the 'inner' world of human experience is qualitatively different from the 'outer' world."[69] An important clue to what degree a culture has interiorized the first type of space is how — or if — they utilized perspective.

(3) Perspective and Aspective

Perspective introduces not only depth into depictions but also "distance into the mind." In other words, perspective highlights how a key feature of interiority, the spatialization of the psyche, turns it into an introcosmos. Perspective means placing the observer into the represented scene while positioning the mind's eye within the individual in such a way that it "looks out" from the person, thereby bolstering interiorization and establishing mind–body dualism. It provides the mind's eye with a more multidimensional and textured introscape to observe relative to the actual perception of the external world. Perspective highlights the difference between perception (what one's senses detect or "see") and introception (what one's mind's eye "sees").[70] Perspective is not just about measuring reality; it is also an attempt to grant the conscious interiorization of reality an inherent value.

Brunner-Traut uses the term "aspective" to describe the lack of perspective in Egyptian depictions and how objects are portrayed as aggregates of separate parts. She elaborates upon this notion, which is more of a conceptual than a perceptual issue, by extending it to how the Egyptians conceived the human body, state, social relations, spirituality, writing, and mathematics. Aspective means "purely additive stringing together or aggregating of elements without organizing, structuring principles that would make them appear to be parts of a subordinate whole."[71] With an aspective view, parts of an object are not visible but may be shown in a "false transparency."[72] For instance, in many scenes the body appears as a "marionette," an "aggregated multiplicity of individual limbs, not an organic whole controlled from the center outward."[73] Brunner-Traut attributes this way of thinking to the dominance of the brain's right hemisphere; aspective cognitive processing contrasts with the left-hemisphere dominance of the Greek tradition. This argument resonates with Jaynes's theory about bicamerality. Note, however, that Jaynes stressed how *cultural changes* configured hemispheric interactions, i.e., brain anatomy in and of itself does not determine cultural patterns.[74]

Related to the aspective approach is how Egyptian aesthetics depicted figures stereotypically with frontal eyes and shoulders and a profiled face. The aim was to visually unfold a concept, not reflect reality the way a photograph might. Egyptian iconography used relative size to indicate status differentials between victor and vanquished, king and subject, and the gods and king/priests.[75] Here we might note that, arguably, it was not until the beginning of the New Kingdom that art began to incorporate a degree of secularization.

(4) Another Dualism: No Distinction between the Spiritual and Material

I submit that if individuals lack an abstract concept of mind, it is difficult to conceive of the spiritual as a dimension clearly separate from the material world. This is because, arguably, mind–body dualism reflects the difference between the realms of the introspectable (invisible to others) and the visible (apparent to everyone). Being invisible to others, the mind became the enchanted and mysterious place to which the numinous entities retreated as individuals acquired consciousness. Mind–body dualism, then, is actually part of a larger cosmic split that includes a division between the spiritual and the material.

The Ka, Ba, and other aspects of Egyptian archaeopsychology cannot be understood as belonging to the spiritual realm in the modern sense since a purely immaterial, ethereal existence was foreign to the archaic Egyptians. The non-material — in the sense of something otherworldly and spiritual — appeared much later in Egyptian thinking; for most of pharaonic history, Egyptian thought is best characterized as monosubstantial. The "spiritual," in the sense of being energetically immanent in this world, rather than as a state of existence distant and transcendent, was how the archaic Egyptians viewed matters. They lacked what is understood by moderns as a psychological realm dwelling within the individual; instead of psychic content (at least in later periods), spiritual entities existed inside the person. This is evidenced in an inscription from the statue of Nebneteru, High Priest of Amun (thirteenth century BCE): "The heart is a god, / The stomach is its shrine, / It rejoices when the limbs are festive!"[76] And from the *Prayers of Paheri* we learn that "In the favor of the god who is in you, / I knew the god who dwells in man" (1506–1468 BCE).[77]

(5) Dualism and Deceit

Dualism can concern the distinction between what one really thinks and how one actually presents one's self — i.e., deceit. Jaynes wrote that long-term deceit or treachery (or more charitably, to be calculating) is impossible for animals or for bicameral individuals. Note Frankfort's view that among the archaic Egyptians a "separation between intention and execution" was absent.[78] "Long-term deceit requires the invention of an analog self that can 'do' or 'be' something quite different from what the person actually does or is, as seen by his associates."[79] Jaynes would later temper his claims about the lack of "treachery" in bicameral societies (i.e., long-term deceit) in conversations he had with this author, and certainly evidence exists that archaic Egyptians, cognizant of the risks of revealing one's thoughts or opinions, engaged in machinations: "Do not empty your belly to everyone, / And thus destroy respect of you; / Broadcast not your word to others, / Nor join with one who bares his heart. / Better is one whose speech is in his belly / Than he who tells it to cause harm" (*Instructions of Amenemope*, ca. 2300–2150 BCE).[80] In the *Instructions of Prince Hardjedef,* we are advised that "The trusted man who does not vent his belly's speech, / He will himself become a leader" (ca. 2450 to 2300 BCE).[81] But texts from the postbicameral period arguably contain more maxims premised on a clear distinction between "inside mind" and "outside body." For example, in the *Instructions of Papyrus Insinger* (compiled in the first century CE but perhaps dating from the late Ptolemaic era), we are told that "He who guards his heart and his tongue sleeps without an enemy" and "Do not reveal what is in your heart to your master when (he is) deliberating."[82]

HIEROGLYPHICS: HOW THE WORDS OF THE GODS SHAPED REALITY

Hieroglyphs can be traced back to the beginnings of pharaonic civilization. Though we often associate hieroglyphs with spiritual endeavors, the fact is early on they were developed for practical uses, such as tax payments, royal possessions, gifts made by the king to the gods, etc.[83] This was the case in other archaic civilizations, e.g., the motivations behind the invention of writing was for measuring, counting, calculating, and taxing.[84] However, we must remind ourselves that in the super-religious context, no real distinction existed between matters this-worldly and otherworldly, the mundane and the sacred, the material and spiritual. Whether for the warehouse or for the Afterworld, recordkeeping was part of the same cosmic machinery.[85] Noteworthy also is that it was not until centuries after the invention of writing that the contents of an individual's psychic life was recorded, indicating a lack of an interest in the interior life of protagonists.

Hieroglyphs (*mdw nṯr*) — or god's words[86] (divine words,[87] sacred writings,[88] or written characters, word of God, divine decree[89]) — are informed by the paralogic notion that the sign/representation is what is signified/represented. Hieroglyphs were intended to be read by the gods[90] and utilized by a theopolitical scribal elite who had a sacred relationship with those gods.[91] Very few Egyptians could read them. Rather than the spoken language, the guiding principles of the archaic Egyptian writing system originated in ideologized ceremonies.[92] Though the Mesopotamians eventually dropped their pictorial form and developed a more efficient writing system, the Egyptians maintained a dual system, reserving their pictorial script for special spiritual purposes.

The sacred effectiveness of hieroglyphs — which are complexive, identification symbols par excellence — were enhanced by their aesthetics. Craftsmen were able to "merge flawlessly a verbal message and a decorative or symbolic image in one harmonious composition."[93] Besides being inscribed in architecture, hieroglyphs were also used on furniture and other objects of the minor arts. In many tombs, the text and the accompanying scenes are closely related. Indeed, it is often "difficult to decide whether the scene acts as a determinative for the text, or whether the text is a literary complement for the scene."[94] Hieroglyphs, which were imbued with an animating power,[95] activated rituals.[96] Figures in a scene were accompanied by hieroglyphs that identified the person plus what he or she was saying. In a temple, the king "speaks" the offering ritual to the gods, and the gods "reply with the appropriate reward speech."[97] The scent and smoke of burning incense allowed the gods to inhale the spiritual essence of hieroglyphs.[98] Sacred writing enhanced the power of gestures, dancing, and the incantations of ceremonies.[99] Since the name of an object/person contained the essence of that object/person, removing a person's name could end their existence. Such redaction was used "against both human beings and gods as a political and religious act of denial of existence."[100] And since carved images on tomb walls would come to life, they might pose a threat. In the burial chambers of Tei and Pepy I, animal hieroglyphs were mutilated, e.g., animal signs lacked legs, birds had their heads cut off, and knives were inserted into snakes and crocodiles.[101]

Despite the inextricable nature of the divine and practical, an incipient secularization that marked the mundane from sacred purposes did emerge. While hieroglyphs continued to be used in monumental inscriptions throughout archaic Egyptian history, a parallel writing system developed in order to write more quickly. Called hieratic (from the Greek *hieratiká* for "sacred"), this was a simplified, cursive hieroglyphics written on papyrus in ink. It was used for administrative and literary purposes. By the seventh century BCE, an even more cursive system was being used called demotic.

Notes to Chapter 3

1. Cf. Pinch, 2002, pp. 40–41.
2. Dodds, 1951.
3. Ortner, 1973.
4. Ortner, 1973.

5. Turner, 1967.
6. Pinch, 2006, p. 18.
7. V28-G43-E23; V28-G43-E23-Z1. A related term was *m3i* (E22) meaning lion, lion shaped image (of king), sphinx.
8. D21-O4-G1-N35-X1-Z5.
9. G1-V31-D21; G1-V31-D21-N18.
10. Tutu means "image" (*twtw*); X1-G43-X1-G43-A53-A53-Y1-Z2.
11. S34; R11-Z1.
12. R11-Y1-R11-G7.
13. M13.
14. MacDonald, 2005, p. 226.
15. MacDonald, 2005, p. 223.
16. MacDonald, 2005, p. 227.
17. Kirk, 1970, pp. 208–209.
18. Pinch, 2006, p. 68.
19. Ritner, 2001a, pp. 321–326.
20. F22-R12; V28-D28-Y1-A40-Z3.
21. For the leading work on Egyptian magic, see Ritner, 2008.
22. Pinch, 2006, p. 9.
23. Ritner, 2001a, p. 321.
24. Pinch, 2006, p. 16.
25. Nyord, 2015, p. 163.
26. Harrell, 2010, p. 241.
27. Harrell, 2010, pp. 239–240.
28. Morenz, 1992, p. 9.
29. Pinch, 2002, p. 57.
30. F3-X1-N5, etc.
31. X1-D21-M17-M4-N5-Z1, etc.
32. Morenz, 1992, p. 76.
33. Kadish, 2001, p. 409.
34. F40X1-Y2-Y2-Y2-I10-X1-N17; I10-79; I10-X1-N16; I10-X1-N18; I10-X1-N35; N35-I10-X1-N17; I10-X1-Z1-I10-X1-N16.
35. Pinch, 2002, p. 65.
36. Frankfort, 2000, p. 136.
37. N35-F18; N35-V28-V28-N5; G21-V28-N5-V28; G21-V28-V28-N5.
38. Kadish, 2001, pp. 405–409.
39. Frankfort, 2000, p. 49.
40. Frankfort, 2000, p. 50.
41. Frankfort, 2000, p. 50.
42. D21-V31-G43; D21-V31-N5; D21-V31-N5-N23, etc.
43. Pinch, 2004, p. 75.
44. G40-X1-X6-D1-Q3-X1-A40-Z3
45. Pinch, 2002, pp. 31–32.
46. Sauneron, 1960, p. 141.
47. Shaw, 2000, p. 7.
48. Shaw, 2000, p. 4.

49. Sauneron, 1960, p. 141.
50. Wilson, 1965, p. 53.
51. Sauneron, 1960, p. 141.
52. David, 2003, p. 414.
53. Wilson, 1965, p. 313.
54. Wilson, 1965, p. 314.
55. Wilson, 1965, p. 313.
56. Wilson, 1965, p. 3.
57. Wilson, 1965, p. 314.
58. Wilson, 1965, p. 314.
59. Warburton, 2009, p. 85.
60. Morenz, 1992, p. 11.
61. Gee, 2009, p. 3.
62. Assmann, 2005, p. 9.
63. Fóti, 2003.
64. Jaynes, 1976, p. 269.
65. Nyord, 2015, p. 135.
66. The recognition of psychosomatic problems is evident in the post-bicameral in the *Instructions of Papyrus Insinger* (probably latter part of the Ptolemaic period, compiled in the second century CE): "If the heart worries about its owner it creates illness for him" and "When worry has arisen the heart seeks death itself." Cited in Lichtheim, 2006c, p. 200.
67. Nyord, 2015, p. 136. See Finnestad, 1986, "On Transposing Soul and Body into a Monistic Conception of Being: An Example from Ancient Egypt."
68. Gee, 2009, p. 14.
69. Nyord, 2015, p. 163.
70. McVeigh, 2016b, p. 64. Cf. Sörbom's hypothesis that the "Greek art revolution" of the fifth and fourth centuries BCE resulted in a concomitant development of body–soul dualism. Sörbom, 1994.
71. Assmann, 2005, p. 26.
72. However we must cautiously approach the claim that the archaic Egyptians "perceived only individual details and was incapable of seeing larger unities." Assmann, 2005, p. 26.
73. Assmann, 2005, p. 26.
74. Brunner-Traut, 1990, pp. 158–164; cited in Nyord, 2015, p. 141.
75. It is useful to distinguish between paratactic and hypotactic perspectives. The former means placing things side by side. In writing or speaking (or as a literary technique) it denotes preference for short, simple sentences sans conjunctions or the use of coordinating (rather than subordinating conjunctions). Hypotactic means connecting words in an explicit fashion (between clauses or sentences). The idea is to show a logical relationship. Unlike parataxis, which simply juxtaposes clauses or sentences, hypotaxis relies on the syntactic subordination of one clause to another. At the representational level, paratactic means "non-functional," "conceptual," or "ideoplastic" (symbolic art created by mentally modified natural artistic subjects). Cf. Waburton, 2009.
76. Cited in Lichtheim, 2006c, p. 22.
77. Cited in Lichtheim, 2006b, pp. 18–19.
78. Also, supposedly no separation existed between "capabilities and success." Frankfort, 1978, p. 68.

79. Jaynes, 1976, p. 219.
80. Chapter 21. Cited in Lichtheim, 2006b, p. 159.
81. Cited in Lichtheim, 2006a, p. 67.
82. Cited in Lichtheim, 2006c, pp. 202, 203.
83. Pinch, 2004, pp. 21–22.
84. Wilson, 2003, p. 216.
85. Wilson, 2003, p. 8.
86. R8-S43-Z1-G7-Z3A.
87. R8-S3-Z1-Z3.
88. R8-S43.
89. R8-S43-Y2; R8-S43-D46-G43-A2; R8-S43-D46-Y1-Z2; R8-S43-S43-S43; R8-S43-V12-Z1; S43-D46-G43-Y1-Z2-R8.
90. Wilson, 2003, p. 53.
91. Wilson, 2003, p. 38.
92. Wilson, 2003, p. 38.
93. Silverman, 1997, p. 243.
94. Silverman, 1997, pp. 242–243.
95. Wilson, 2003, p. 52.
96. Wilson, 2003, p. 59.
97. Wilson, 2003, p. 45.
98. Wilson, 2003, p. 452.
99. Wilson, 2003, p. 60.
100. Wilson, 2003, p. 59.
101. Wilson, 2003, p. 59.

Chapter 4

A Historical Synopsis of Egyptian Super-religiosity

"Be vigilant against the approach of eternity, cherish length of life, for, as is the saying, 'To do Maat is the breath of the nostrils.'"
— *Tale of the Eloquent Peasant*

A FULLY CONSCIOUS BELIEVER in religion assumes that a loving relationship with some supernatural entity is inherent to spirituality. But this is a modern presumption. For many centuries in archaic Egypt individuals could only approach the gods indirectly via the mediation of priests. However, this began to change as individuals sought out more personal relations with the deities. Such a connection was the cornerstone of piety, which is defined as the "personal, individual expression of faith in and devotion to a deity, as opposed to institutionalized religious practice, which was traditionally the preserve of the king."[1] This change became evident during the Middle Kingdom, and as argued below, signaled the interiorization of faith, one of the most significant transitions in human religiosity.

What follows is a thumbnail sketch of ancient Egyptian history. A note on dating. For dates before 664 BCE the margin of error ranges from ten to twenty years. Before the New Kingdom (or ca. 1300 BCE), it may range as much as fifty to a hundred years for the Early Dynastic Period (ca. 3000 BCE). From 664 BCE dates are precise. In the third century BCE, an Egyptian priest named Manetho composed a list of dynasties in his *Aegyptiaca* (now lost) for the "pharaonic period," roughly from 3000 to 332 BCE. His chronology provides a sense of continuity that the careful historian should question due to overlapping reigns and periods of political disunity. Some dynasties only ruled parts of Egypt. Dynasty 7 may not have even existed, Dynasty 14 was probably contemporary with Dynasty 13 or 15, and Dynasty 16 was contemporary with Dynasty 15. But as a general guide, Manetho's framework is useful. Modern Egyptologists traditionally distinguish between periods of relative political unity, prosperity, and stability (kingdoms) and three "intermediate periods," often characterized by political disunity, rivalries, and social disorder (Table 4.1).

Neolithic and Predynastic Periods

The earliest evidence of Egyptian spirituality is found in the Neolithic period (from around 7500 BCE). Human burials, megaliths, and stelae with possible astrological/astronomical significance have been found, as have

Table 4.1. Periodization of Ancient Egypt.[a]

Years–BCE	Period	Dynasty	Type of Mentality[b]
7500-5000	Neolithic	Dynasty "0"	Preconscious bicameral
5000–4000	Badarian		
4000–3650	Naqada I		Classic bicameral
3650–3300	Naqada II		
3300–2950	Naqada III = Protodynastic		
2950–2575	Early Dynastic	1 to 3	Weakening of bicameral mentality
2575–2125	Old Kingdom	4 to 8	Semi-bicameral/ Semi-conscious
2125–2010	First Intermediate	9 to early 11	Emerging, proto-conscious interiority
2010–1630	Middle Kingdom	12 to 13	Bicameral mentality's final breakdown[c]
1630–1539	Second Intermediate	14 to 17	
1539–1069	New Kingdom	18 to 20	Conscious interiority
1069–664	Third Intermediate	21 to 25	
664–332	Late Period	26 to 31	
332–30	Ptolemaic Period		
	Macedonian Dynasty (332–309)		
	Ptolemaic Dynasty (309–30)		
30 BCE–4th century CE	Roman Period		

[a] Dates are based on Wilkinson, 2010.
[b] The timings of types of mentality are approximate and somewhat speculative.
[c] Corresponds roughly to the Late Bronze Age Collapse.

sacrificed cattle buried in stone-roofed chambers in Nabta Playa (perhaps the first inklings of what would become the Hathor cult). The Badarian cultural phase, from about 5000 to 4000 BCE, was characterized by life in small villages and a rudimentary economy of farming, hunting, and fishing. The dead were buried in simple pit graves facing west. Grave goods, that appear to be personal items, have been found and the deceased were wrapped in reed matting or animal skins. Some of the dead were accompanied by carved-ivory female figurines. In the Naqada I phase (Amratian culture), from about 4000 to 3600 BCE, spirituality is evident in how each village had its own token animal deity. Amulets have been found, and the deceased were buried with food items, weapons, figurines, decorations, malachite, and sometimes canines.

From about 3650 to 3300 BCE, during the Naqada II phase (or Gerzeh culture), major changes occurred. Theocentric developments reflected changing sociopolitical conditions. Settlements coalesced to form bigger units that in turn became capitals overseeing an area. These would eventually develop into the administrative units called nomes. Each population center had its own chieftain and deity. Structures slightly larger than the typical house were constructed from wood, wickerwood, reed, and mud; these were probably shrines housing images of gods (early AARC). Local gods evolved to become deities who conquered or absorbed other areas. In a pattern seen in Mesopotamia, a victorious god would subordinate the vanquished deities, or perhaps the conquered deity would become a follower of the victor. A differentiation in burial customs between leaders and commoners became apparent, with leaders entombed in monumental brick bench-shaped superstructures (*mastaba*)[2] with recessed brick paneling on the façade, multiple chambers, and underground substructures for the body.[3] Metalwork, painted pottery, monumental brick architecture, advances in craftsmanship, and the first evidence of writing are evident.

Protodynastic Period: 3300–2950 BCE

Naqada II culture would gradually spread northward. What was to become the two kingdoms of Egypt were groupings of people scattered into communities and settlements. Farming, pottery, and copper smelting were developing. The Naqada III phase, from about 3300 to 2950 BCE, witnessed proto-state formation with kings heading emergent but powerful theopolities. This phase is known as the Protodynastic Period (Semainian culture), or Dynasty 0. The names of kings were inscribed in the form of *serekhs* (a type of heraldic crest) on tombs, pottery, and other materials. This cultural period saw small city-states and socially stratified cemeteries appear. It was at this time that the worship of stars and constellations emerged; this star cult predated the better known solar cult. The last phase of the Protodynastic Period[4] saw the first successful attempt to unify Egypt into a large territorial state. At around this time, centers of power had emerged in Naqada, Hierakonpolis, and Thinis. At Abydos evidence of writing is seen as well as the construction of necropolises.

Early Dynastic Period: 2950–2575 BCE

The Early Dynastic Period is called the Thinnite era, from Thinis (or This; near Abydos) which became a spiritual center. This era lasted about 300 years and includes the first two dynasties.[5] It saw the construction of monumental architecture using mud-bricks. Succeeding rulers of the first two dynasties established the germ of what would develop into a full-fledged political system. Eventually state structures consolidated control over the populace, rebels and invaders were subdued, Libya and Nubia were invaded, and trade networks with Syrio-Palestine expanded.

According to legend, gods, including Horus and Osiris, ruled Egypt before unification.[6] Then a series of semi-divine kings, demi-gods, and god-kings took over (the Horus Kings or Followers of Horus). Some of these semi-mythological rulers may have been actual leaders of Buto and Hierakonpolis.

The legendary warrior-king King Menes (or Men) united Upper and Lower kingdoms and fought north from Thebes (modern Luxor) to Memphis. Menes may in fact have been Narmer, the founder or forerunner of Dynasty 1. Or he may have been Hor-Aha (Aha), another contender for the first king of Dynasty 1.[7] In any case, Menes moved the capital north (near Abusir) to Inebu-hedj (the "white walls"), later known as Men-nefer (Enduring and Beautiful) or as is commonly known by its Greek name, Memphis.

The Old Kingdom: Establishing the Core Elements of Egyptian Super-religiosity

By the Old Kingdom (2575–2125 BCE), Egypt had become a highly centralized and organized theopolitical system. Most of the main beliefs that characterized Egyptian theocentricity were already established by the Old Kingdom, such as the solar cult and pharaohs who were believed to be "sons of Re." The theopolitical bicameral order was probably the most stable it would ever be: "Internal dissent was minimal, and support for the system was genuine and prevalent. Coercive state mechanisms, such as police, were conspicuous by their absence."[8] Pharaonic monocracy reached its zenith. Eventually, local militias were organized into a more permanent standing military to deal with Egypt's enemies.

But the seeds of royal decline were being sown. Though the king theoretically owned all the land, wealth, and people, the royal estates gradually passed into an ever-widening circle of inheritance and were increasingly divided into smaller units. Royal lands were given to nobility and officials. From Dynasty 4 onwards, royal decrees exempted the personnel and possessions belonging to the pyramid temples and pyramid cities from taxation and drafts of enforced labor. In the long-run this decreased the king's resources. While pharaonic monarchy's position diminished and the kingship became more humanized, the sway of the nobles and priests increased. Also in Dynasty 4, the highest offices became closed to royal relatives and were taken over by lower-born individuals who were given the honorific title "king's son."[9] Meanwhile, by Dynasty 5, new nomarchs (provincial governors) became hereditary, more assertive, and independent. Decentralization and the fragmentation of unified state power were in the offing. During Pepy II's (2260–2175 BCE) reign, the collapse of the Old Kingdom saw power shift to the nomarchs. The latter adopted some of the royal rituals associated with the king and had the *Pyramid Texts* included in their burials, so that they too had access to the Afterworld. Nomarchs started to reside permanently in the nomes they administered, allowing a provincial elite to coalesce.

The First Intermediate Period: The First Collapse

At the close of Dynasty 6, insurrection weakened the power structures, while foreign incursions by Bedouin peoples threatened the center of power in Memphis. All this led to chaos. During the fifty years of Dynasties 7 to 8, 25 kings ruled. A number of challenges, rooted in the Old Kingdom, led to the problems of the First Intermediate Period (2125–2010 BCE), during which centralized government went into steep decline. Civil war, famine, poverty, and disease stalked the land. Graves and monuments were ravaged and a "pessimistic literature" developed. The nomarch of Herakleopolis in the north claimed royal power as Akhtoy I (2160–2025 BCE). His descendants were eventually challenged by the rise of Dynasty 11, based in Thebes. It became a battle over who controlled Middle Egypt, as two independent dynasties competed for complete dominance. Nebhepetre Mentuhotep II (ca. 2051–2030) from Thebes, relying on the resources of Nubia, eventually reunified the country and restored political centralization and social order.

Middle Kingdom: The Discovery of the Individual

During the Middle Kingdom (2010–1630 BCE), the reciprocal processes of socio-externalization and psycho-internalization were evident in how, as individual interiority became salient, the authorities reacted to growing autonomy among the masses by exerting more control. As interiority increased, kings became more absolute in order to control individuals who were now acquiring a proto-form of self-autonomy and self-authorization. A more intense intrusion into private life became evident, as control over individuals increased as did the obligation that everyone owed the monarchy unquestioned loyalty. During this period a "more human scale" developed and individual human beings became "more significant in cosmic terms."[10] The gods lowered themselves in this "age of greater humanity."[11] A "direct personal access to deities rather than via the king or priests" was part and parcel of the attention given to what we would label personal piety.[12] These developments were seen in the growth of a confident middle class, a richer literature (cf. the *Story of Sinuhe*, the *Shipwrecked Sailor*, *Hymn to Hapi*, *Satire of the Trades*), and more provisions for burial.

By Dynasty 12 (1938–1755 BCE), the authorities began to realize the usefulness of instilling fear in order to stabilize governance. This change in mentality suggests an increased emotionalization, a feature of interiority. "In their determination to establish rock-solid internal security, they outdid all their predecessors, deploying sophisticated propaganda alongside brute force, subtle persuasion backed up by terror tactics."[13] Meanwhile the influence of the central state became more pervasive in regional areas, as it attempted to minimize the power of the uppity nomarchs.[14]

The "Democratization" of the Afterworld and Spiritual Practices

Developments toward the end of Old Kingdom undermined the stone-solid sureties of monarchical prerogatives (as evident in the *Instructions for Merikare*). Kingship underwent major changes, and individual and personal qualities of rulers (self-individuation) became more apparent. In the Old Kingdom, only the pharaoh was granted mummification and thus a chance at an eternal and fulfilling existence in the Afterworld. But by the Middle Kingdom, all dead were afforded the opportunity so that immortality was achievable by anyone.

While wealth and social status are easily observed, and in a sense behaviorally measureable (relatively speaking), the interiorized dimensions of a person's life — living virtuously, performing funeral rites correctly, worshipping the gods in a devoted fashion — could now open the doors to the Afterworld. The expanding psychologicality of average people is also seen in how wooden models, statuettes of the tomb-owner (as well as of other members of the family, servants, soldiers, musicians, concubines, and animals) were placed in private tombs.[15]

Throughout the Middle Kingdom, the use of the *Coffin Texts* became more widespread. These were written inside coffins and used pictorial vignettes painted on coffins used by the less wealthy (e.g., shields, a quiver, and a bow and arrow).[16] Also painted on coffin exteriors was the Eye of Horus (Wedjat), a symbol of protection, royal power, and good health. These allowed the deceased to look out on the world. But by the end of the Middle Kingdom, the *Coffin Texts* were no longer in common use. Though inspired by earlier precedents, a new guide, the *Book of the Dead*, became popular. The adoption of funerary texts was part of a larger trend in which the power of the nomarchs increased; they adopted some of the royal rituals associated with the king so they too had access to the Afterworld.

Interiorization and the Emergence of Piety

As the hierarchies of the pharaonic theopolitical order became flattened, the emergence of closer, individualized relations between gods and mortals allowed a more demotic and interiorized pious religiosity to flourish. Two mutually interrelated processes were at work. First, demographic expansion meant that the streamlined communicative hierarchy of god → king → priesthood → populace became strained. Individuals needed their own lines of divine messaging. This led to the second process:

a personalized connection to the gods entailed the expansion of a more interiorized psychologicality which increased the emotionalizing of relations. These changes are indicated in the archaeohistorical and textual record. For instance in the Amarna Period, during the reign of Aya (ca. 1320 BCE), songs expressive of pain and sadness emerged.[17]

In general, evidence of personally devout sentiments prior to the New Kingdom is limited, which fits in with the bicameral-to-conscious trajectory. A number of trends indicate a more interiorized and pious spirituality. First, by the close of the Middle Kingdom, the first representations of nonroyal persons worshiping a deity appeared on nonroyal stelae. And by the early New Kingdom, images of deities regularly began to appear on nonroyal monuments."[18] Second, while family and themes of daily life were prominent in the Middle Kingdom, during the New Kingdom mortuary decoration "shifted towards the relationship between the deceased and the gods."[19] By Dynasty 19, the introduction of deities in private tombs suggested heightened devotion at the commoner level. Third, the shift away from the ancestors and toward gods reflected a more self-individuated spirituality that was escaping the orbit of a communal, lineage-based worldview. Fourth, a number of elements are found in prayers, hymns, and votive offerings expressing reverence.[20] The first words concern listening on the part of the deity: "one who heard petitions"; "who comes at the voice of the poor in need"; and "who comes at the voice of him who calls to him." Then petitioners described themselves as poor and humble and made apologies for any transgressions. Next they accepted the god's punishment and use the formulaic expression "seeing darkness by day" to articulate the pain of being separated from their god. Finally, a promise is made to proclaim the might of the god to all the world and an account is given about the god's answer to the prayer. Related to the rise of personal piety was the increase in penitential texts and the belief that the gods could forgive human sins, suggesting a new-found sense of interiorized guilt. We should also note that piousness was reflected in theophoric names, which became especially common in the Late Period, an era when individualized feelings were at their height.

Though it is untrue that "the theme of Gods' wrath is practically unknown in Egyptian literature,"[21] nevertheless in archaic Egypt no sense existed of humankind in rebellion against the divine order. Sometimes the human–god relationship was conceptualized as one between servant (*bꜣk*) and master (*nb*). Many words denote evil acts, "but I doubt whether any should be rendered by 'sin,' if one grants that word its proper theological connotation."[22] An ethical misstep was more like an aberration. But this changed by the Ramesside Period, when expressions of an intimate relationship with a specific deity were not uncommon. Resonating with this age of personal piety was a more existential perspective and a feeling of personal inadequacy, accompanied by a stronger sense of sin.[23] Previously one's fate depended on one's behavior in accordance with Maat, but now individuals came to be seen as directly responsible to a god who "personally intervened in the individual's life and punished wrongdoing."[24]

Spiritual Self-individuation: The Osirian Cult

The rise of Osiris, whose beginnings are obscure, illustrates well the democratization of the Afterworld.[25] This god "eclipsed a host of other, more ancient funerary deities."[26] For example, the townspeople of Djedu had worshiped a local god called Andjety, who was believed to have been an earthly ruler who had been resurrected after death. Eventually Djedu became the main center of Osiris worship in Lower Egypt, absorbing the features of Andjety. The leveling of the funerary cult of the kings and that of the commoners began in the First Intermediate Period. By end of the Middle Kingdom, everyone hoped that they could partake of the potency of Osiris. This god of the people was linked to the underground spiritual world, the Fields of Reeds, "eternal springtime, unfailing harvests, and no pain or suffering."[27]

Changes in Mentality as Reflected in Literature

Classifying Egyptian literature is highly problematic since the boundaries between what we would call genres do not fit modern definitions. But what is noteworthy for our purposes is how the vast majority of archaic Egyptian texts possess an authoritative sensibility animated by a super-religiosity (Table 4.2). What has been referred to as "wisdom literature" actually subsumes various types of texts that differed in purpose. Foster suggests "didactic literature," meaning writings intended to convey information, teach, or persuade.[28] It includes maxims and teachings (*Instructions of Ptahhotep*); complaints (*Eloquent Peasant*); lamentations (*Admonishments of Ipuwer*); "prophecy" (*Prophecy of Neferti*); and the passing on of important information (*Instructions of Amenemhet*). Significantly, most of these writings, like

Table 4.2. List of Some Important Writings from Archaic Egypt.

No.	Text	Dynasty
1.	*Instructions of Kagemni*	4–6
2.	*Maxims of Hordjedef (Djedefhor)*	5
3.	*Instructions of Ptahhotep (Precepts of the Prefect, the Lord Ptah-hotep)*	5–6
4.	*Instructions for Merikare*	9–10
5.	*Instructions of a Man for His Son*	12
6.	*Loyalist Instructions*	12
7.	*Admonitions of Ipuwer (The Admonitions of a Prophet)*	12–13
8.	*Eloquent Peasant*	12
9.	*Words of Khakheperresonb*	12
10.	*Dispute between a Man Who Was Weary of Life and His Soul*	12
11.	*Prophecy of Neferti*	12
12.	*Loyalist Instructions from the Sehetepibre Stela*	12
13.	*Fowler's Speech*	12
14.	*Satire of the Trades (Instructions of Khety)*	12
15.	*Instructions of Amenemhet (Teaching of Amenemhet I to His Son Senusret)*	12
16.	*Instructions of Anii*	18
17.	*Regulation Laid upon the Vizier, Rekhmire*	18
18.	*An Ideal Autobiography*	18
19.	*Equipment of a Syrian Expedition (Koller Papyrus–Model Letter)*	18
20.	*Warnings to the Idle Scribe (Koller Papyrus)*	18
21.	*Papyrus Anastasi I: A Satirical Letter*	19
22.	*Instructions of Amenemope*	19–20
23.	*Teachings of Amennakht*	20
24.	*Instructions in Letter-Writing by Nebmare-nakht (Lansing Papyrus)*	20
25.	*Demotic Papyrus of Moral Precepts*	32

archaic Egyptian belles letters (whether lyric or narratives) were grouped in two-line units or couplets (IMRHA).[29]

The implosion of state authority at the close of the Old Kingdom resulted in almost 130 years — the First Intermediate Period — of socioeconomic dislocation, rebellions, and the local usurpation of power. After the central authorities re-established control, the elite literate class generated what has been called pessimistic literature.[30] These meditations on sociocosmic chaos were all composed during the Middle Kingdom.

This was an era when literature flourished and is conventionally regarded as the "classical" or "golden age" of Egyptian writing. A more reflective, distanced attitude to society is apparent, as well as the sense that one's present life is to be enjoyed and thoughts of death kept at bay. This is not full-blown existentialism, and was probably restricted to very small literate, elite circles, but changes in mentality are clear. Pessimistic literature displayed an apprehension of how tradition had been lost as well as the isolated individual detached from the sureties of an ordered society, driving a measure of self-individuation. Three themes unite these writings (that categorically overlap with "wisdom literature").

The first theme is how the gods have shirked their responsibilities. The deities are accused of allowing disorder to reign during the end of the Old Kingdom. In *The Admonitions of Ipuwer*, it is proposed that the god Atum, withdrawing from the world, should be held accountable for allowing people to develop into evil beings. Atum has betrayed humankind. In *The Prophecy of Neferti*, it is proposed that Re needs to go back to square one and "begin creation anew." Such writings, though significantly they never questioned the existence of supernatural entities, were nevertheless an important step toward philosophizing about human morality — were people innately bad or were the gods themselves somehow responsible for the blight of evil?

The second theme concerns life in an unstable, insecure world. Corrupt royal advisors, the disintegration of trade networks, and civil war ripped apart the sociopolitical fabric. Fields were abandoned and granaries left unfilled. Hunger and greed stalked the land, as did robbers and thieves. Inadequately supplied temples, desecrated tombs, and the eviction of priests lead to deep feelings of hopelessness and lamentation. Skepticism was mounting. In the *Song of Intef*, a pessimistic hymn, the rewards of the Afterworld are uncertain and funerary preparations are useless. However, Fox claims that the Song of Intef does not deny the Afterworld. Rather, it simply emphasizes how the living do not have the ability to know about life after death. Also, it has been suggested that the *Song of Intef*, usually attributed to the First Intermediate Period, may in fact be from the Amarna Period, when existence after death was thought to be less cheerful and darker.[31] The very reality of the Afterworld seems to be questioned and in some cases death is welcomed.

In a testament to the still-steady influence of divine rulership and theocentric ideals, none of the writings hold the king directly responsible.

However, monarchical accountability for disorder is certainly implied. Such hinting at the fallibility of the pharaoh is another step toward a less theocentric and a more human-centric psychology.

The third theme of pessimistic literature is noteworthy for how it advocates standards of justice toward which Egyptians were expected to aspire. The king will reign magnanimously, civil unrest will cease, and foreign enemies will be defeated. Proper religious observances, the maintenance of funerary cults, and a well-oiled and equitable economy will be the order of the day. These writings did not propose "progress" in the modern sense, since they looked back nostalgically to a golden past, not a future born of revolution. Their hope was to restore a lost justice, not radically re-engineer society. *The Prophecy of Neferti* contrasts the disordered world of the First Intermediate Period with that of Middle Kingdom. Set in Dynasty 4, but most likely written in Dynasty 12, in this account the sage Neferti is summoned to King Sneferu's court (2575–2545 BCE). He predicts terrible events that will befall Egypt but states that matters will be rectified by "Ameny." Presumably Ameny was Amenemhat I (1938–1908 BCE), making this "prophecy" retrospective, not prophetical; it was an attempt to legitimate strong centralized authority. Similarly in the *Admonitions of Ipuwer*, a sage warns a sickly king (possibly Pepy II) that unless traditions are restored, state structures will implode, famine spread, and criminals will run wild.

The *Dialogue of a Man with his Ba* envisions the next world as an idealized existence with the punishment of malefactors and well-provisioned temples. The *Instructions for Merikare* examines how the king should behave to ensure social justice by respecting traditions, performing rites, and maintaining the mortuary cult. The *Eloquent Peasant* portrays a just society that mercifully cares for the down-trodden and swiftly disciplines wrongdoers.

Second Intermediate Period: Another Round of Chaos

Though it is difficult to judge the scale of destabilization, by the end of the Middle Kingdom social disorder returned, perhaps evidenced by how Dynasty 13 witnessed an abrupt decline in the scale of royal tombs.[32] The unremarkable but troubled Dynasty 13 (it had at least fifty kings and lasted over 125 years) and a weakened Dynasty 14 set the stage for the Second Intermediate Period (1630–1539 BCE). Dynasty 14 was one of political fragmentation that saw several kings come and go without stabilizing the political landscape. Egypt was squeezed between the Kingdom of Kush in the south and immigrant populations in the north. Semitic newcomers, the Hyksos, came in from the east. The six Hyksos kings of Dynasty 15 (1630–1520 BCE) competed with the native rulers in Thebes. The Hyksos made an alliance with the Kushites, putting further strain on what was left of Egyptian power. Kamose (1541–1539 BCE), and then his brother Ahmose (1539–1514 BCE), fought against and finally defeated and expelled the Hyksos. The latter founded Dynasty 18 (1539–1292 BCE).

New Kingdom: Resurgence and Imperialist Expansion

The New Kingdom (1550–1069 BCE) was an era of recovery and growth. Nubia was targeted in several military campaigns and Egypt occupied areas as far south as the Nile's Fourth Cataract. Parts of the Near East also fell to Egyptian dominance and vassal states were established. The new Egyptian empire competed vigorously with the Hittites until they reached an agreement under Ramesses II. Memphis continued as the capital while Thebes became the spiritual center of a rejuvenated and prosperous theopolity. Expanded trade brought in considerable wealth that polished Egypt's cosmopolitanism and flourishing artistic traditions. The pharaohs, especially Amenhotep III (1390–1352 BCE) and Ramesses II (the Great), built sumptuous monuments to display their confidence and glory. Meanwhile, the "overall pattern of worship suggests a trend towards localism, as well as a certain level of exclusivity regarding state gods and the relationship with the king."[33] The New Kingdom ended with Rameses XI's death (1099–1069 BCE).

Interiorization Accelerates: The Enigma of Akhenaten

Of all the pharaohs, Akhenaten (Amenhotep IV; ca. 1353–1336 BCE) is the most "controversial and enigmatic."[34] His seventeen-year reign was "entirely unprecedented and radically at odds with the previous seventeen centuries of ancient Egyptian religions tradition."[35] He is known for elevating the Aten or Sun Disc from supreme god to sole god and not tolerating other deities.[36] This pharaoh has fascinated scholars since he seems to have been the world's first monotheist, or perhaps more likely, he set in motion the theological currents of what would become monotheism, perhaps influencing Judaism's turn from henotheism to the Yahweh-only cult in the sixth or fifth century BCE.[37] Akhenaten's so-called reforms must be seen in the context of the rise of interiorized spirituality. A key objective of his was to reverse the individuation of religion and restore the monarch to a secure theocentric role as the only intermediary between the people and one god.[38]

Akhenaten did not "instigate a spiritual shift de novo" or invent a new style; his changes were not a "revolution."[39] However, he did speed up the spread of the deeply rooted solar-based theology of his father and grandfather. In this sense, he was a traditionalist who wished to return to an older spirituality. Solar worship grew in popularity during the reign of Amenhotep II (Amen Is Content) (1427–1400 BCE). The latter's son, Amenhotep III, was influenced by his wife Tiy (ca. 1410–1340 BCE), who popularized the Aten (*i͗tn*), originally depicted as a sun disc with rays of outstretched arms, as a major deity. Amenhotep IV, the son of Amenhotep III, motivated by a combination of personal belief and the wish to break the power of the Amun priesthood, vigorously promoted the Aten as the supreme god of Egypt.

Amenhotep IV changed his name to Akhenaten (Effective for the Aten) and founded a new capital, Akhetaten, the Place Where the Aten Becomes Effective (or Horizon of the Sun Disc). Hoffmeier believes Akhenaten experienced "some sort of theophany" that led to the founding of Akhetaten and Atenism.[40] Such revelations became rarer as the Late Bronze Age came to a close, e.g., Moses's encounter with Yahweh in the form of a burning bush. But in archaic Egypt, such divine appearances were not unusual, at least among those closest to the gods (i.e., the pharaohs). Akhenaten's thinking had been "foreshadowed by his father's apotheosis."[41] Under Amenhotep III, the king had become the solar orb, while under Amenhotep IV, the solar orb had become the king.[42] Amenhotep IV was declared "nothing less than a co-regency, with himself and the sun god as joint sovereigns."[43] The Sun Disc proclaimed a celestial pharaoh, with Akhenaten as the Aten's earthly representative. Other gods were banned in representations and Akhenaten became the sole mediator between divinity and mortals; he became the center of devotion, through which all people had to go to encounter the divine. A state-sanctioned and heavily enforced iconoclasm ensured that only the Aten would be recognized. "To much of the population, the orgy of vandalism must have felt like the ritual murder of their most cherished hopes and beliefs."[44] Not surprisingly, a preoccupation with the king's personal safety led to an "atmosphere of paranoia."[45]

Under Akhenaten, the myths associated with the traditional funerary deities were discarded. The Aten was to rule over not only the living but also the deceased. Osiris was banished and the promise of the traditional Afterworld was denied. Aten became the only gateway for the deceased to the other world. But the new theology "offered a poor substitute." After death, "devotees of the Aten would haunt the altar of the sun temple by day,"[46] warmed by the Aten's rays and partake of the offerings from the temple.[47] In the evening they would "sleep the sleep of the dead in their tombs."[48] Only the "royal family would escape to enjoy an eternal life with their god."[49]

Also under Akhenaten architecture was transformed. The traditional design of courtyards leading to dark sanctuaries was done away with. Instead, temples were constructed to be more accessible (but not to commoners), with roofs open to the sky, allowing the Aten's rays, sometimes depicted with hands clasping the Ankh (sign of life), to directly reach the sacrificial altars. On monuments, intimate scenes of lifelike quality from the daily life of Akhenaten and his wife playing with their daughters graced the walls. The codified symbolism of traditional convention was abandoned, suggesting more attention to an interiorized, self-individuated outlook. In its stead was realism, naturalism, and spontaneity. Space was depicted as whole rather than a juxtaposition of scenes, left/right hands and feet were distinguished, and movement was represented as was depth. The introduction of perspective went against the conventional aspective approach to aesthetics. As for the king himself, every aspect of his "face and body was deliberately distorted"; the effect was "both frightening and surreal."[50] Explanations for such bizarre depictions vary (e.g., he was deformed by disease), but perhaps such representations carried a particular meaning known only to Akhenaten.

Several developments related to Akhenaten's attempt at theopolitical reorganization indicate a major shift in the psychology of spiritual history. The first concerns an aniconism aimed at Egyptians' traditional deities. This signaled the stirrings of a formalized creed or religious faith different from a super-religious mindset that never questioned the gods. "A god being proclaimed false and his cult being decreed to destruction was an unheard-of-action in the history of not only Egypt but probably of the whole of humanity."[51] The second development concerns how centering Atenism around the person of the sovereign and the mythologized personality cult was in fact a case of brazen self-individuation.[52] Finally, the persecution of dissenters and the existence of a repressive apparatus to enforce what seems to be faith in the modern sense suggest the emergence of consciously-interiorized fear, an emotion used by rulers to ensure their power.[53] Indeed, Akhenaten's experiment was one of the earliest, if not the first, "known attempts in human history at establishing an early totalitarian state."[54]

Akhenaten's rupture with traditional Egyptian spirituality was short-lived. After his death the priesthood that he had dismantled was re-established, traditional temples and shrines renovated, and new statues installed. This almost immediate return to tradition is a testament to the solidity of Egypt's theocentric worldview and its permeation of all facets of life. But Akhenaten's theopolitical impulses, while difficult to understand and dictatorial by today's standards, strongly evidence a more self-reflexive psychology that took hold at least in the mind of one individual.

Third Intermediate Period: The Final Break from an Obsolete Mentality

Around the time of the Late Bronze Age collapse, Egypt held together as a political unit, fighting off the Libyans under King Merenptah (1213–1204 BCE) and the Sea Peoples under Ramesses III (1126–1108 BCE). However, Egypt did lose control of its territories in Asia and saw a reduction in contacts with areas beyond its borders. More significantly, it suffered internal disorder and social upheaval and by Third Intermediate Period would experience political fragmentation. Egypt's three Intermediate Periods (which might be considered "dark ages," though this characterization needs serious qualification) suggest sociopolitical disorder and chaos. But the last Intermediate Period (1069–664 BCE) overlapped with one of humankind's bleakest times. Indeed, The First and Second Intermediate Periods were 115 and 91 years long respectively, while the final and Third Intermediate Period, lasting 405 years, was considerably longer.

The Late Bronze Age Collapse and the Birth of a New Mentality

During the sixteenth century BCE, no state was strong enough to dominate the Near East. But by around 1350 BCE, consolidation led toward eight powers: Mycenae, Arzawa, Hatti (Hittites), Mittani, Assyria, Babylonia, Elam, and Egypt. By around 1220 BCE, this number was reduced to six: Mycenae, Hatti, Assyria, Babylonia, Elam, and Egypt. What had developed was an impressive archaic version of an international order, stitched together by cultural exchanges, trade, diplomacy, and economic integration. Then it all fell apart.

The catastrophic collapse was a rolling event between 1225 and 1175 BCE (in some places, a bit later).[55] The "far-reaching civilizations that were still flourishing in the Aegean and the ancient Near East in 1225 BCE had begun to vanish by 1177 BCE and were almost completely gone by 1130 BCE."[56] An "almost complete restructuring of society took place over most of the Near East."[57] The sociopolitical landscape of whole swathes of the world was completely different by 1000 BCE. Empires either collapsed completely or were drastically reduced in size and influence. Large centralized polities were replaced by smaller city-states. Urban residents became pastoralists while semi-nomadic peoples acquired power by moving into cities. It took decades, and in some places centuries, to rebuild. The result was the "total disappearance of the system that had characterized the Near East in the preceding centuries."[58] The effects were strongest in the eastern Mediterranean (Aegean and Anatolia); civilizational collapse extended eastward with less force into the inland areas.

For some the Late Bronze Age collapse is a controversial topic. Others deal with the mystery of this great calamity by simply arguing that in fact there was no "collapse." In any case, a long list of reasons has been given for the Late Bronze Age implosion: invasions, rebellions, and an assortment of ecological stresses such as earthquakes, famines, floods, and droughts. But the mystery is that no one variable can account for the cascading rapidity and widespread destruction. Why was it so systematic and extensive? Why was the breakdown comprehensive, as if a multiplier effect in which the repercussions of each variable were magnified, resulting in a "perfect storm"? And why did it take so long to recover from this collapse? After all, as noted by the historian Eric Cline, "none of the individual factors would have been cataclysmic enough on their own to bring down even one of these civilizations, let alone all of them."[59]

Renfrew lists key processes of general civilizational collapses: (1) the breakdown of the central administrative organization; (2) the disappearance of the traditional elite class; (3) an imploding of the centralized economy; and (4) settlement shift and population decline. It may have taken a century for all processes of the collapse to be completed.[60] The Late Bronze Age breakdown seems similar to what may have occurred in different periods in the Indus Valley, among the Maya, and Old Kingdom Egypt.[61]

A type of tautology surrounds discussions about the Late Bronze Age collapse. Working from the complexity theory perspective, Dark introduces "hyper-coherence" into the debate: "when each part of a system becomes so dependent upon each other that change in any part produces instability in the system as a whole."[62] As systems become more complex and the "degree of interdependence between their various constituent parts grows, maintaining the stability of the overall system becomes difficult.[63] But as Cline notes, does hyper-coherence really advance our understanding? "Is it more than just a fancy way to state a fairly obvious fact, namely, that complicated things can break down in a variety of ways?"[64] To posit as an explanation that the "more complex a system becomes, the more likely it will collapse" is not very explanatory.

The Breakdown of Bicameral Mentality as a Multiplier Effect

Rowe reviewed recent attempts at explicating the Late Bronze Age collapse.[65] He concludes that a new model is called for, one that "identifies a core weakness that is independent of local geography, weather, and other regional variations."[66] We need a common denominator, whether the systems in question are viewed externally or internally. I contend, along with Rowe, that the missing variable is the individual psyche. Rowe writes that a Jaynesian interpretation fits the bill as an explanation, and here I submit that, while foreign invasions, civil wars, and environmental pressures certainly played a part, the inadequacies of bicameral mentality acted as a multiplier effect that spread the chaos. What is remarkable about the Late Bronze Age is how quickly the entire proto-international system unraveled; this means it could not have been "accidental that all societies experienced drastic change at this time."[67] What is notable is that internal causes as well as external shocks to sociopolitical systems are evident.

Previously the inherent instability of urban–literate bicameral theopolitical systems played a role in the cycle of civilizational fall and rise witnessed not just in Egypt but in other parts of the archaic Near East. But by the thirteenth century BCE, things were different. Being interconnected in new and profound ways facilitated the cascading of confusion through the world's political economic systems. The weaknesses of bicameral mentality acted as a multiplier force, magnifying the instability of god-governed systems and exposing the overstretched and overtaxed lines of theopolitical communications. The consequence, evident after 1000 BCE, was a massive upgrade in sociocognition, i.e., conscious interiority. The worldview that dominated archaic thinking — "as above, so below" — became "as above, so below, and so within" (i.e., macrocosmos, microcosmos, and introcosmos).

During the Third Intermediate Period, Egypt saw decentralization, control by hereditary priesthoods, mass migrations, foreign rulers, and large populations of Libyans settle in Egypt. But depending on the exact dates it was also a "period of relative peace and prosperity";[68] witness the glorious achievements of the Ramesside Period (e.g., mummification was perfected) (Dynasties 19 and 20; 1295–1069 BCE). By Dynasty 21 (1069–945 BCE), Egypt was formally divided. Until Dynasty 24, kings from the Delta region ruled the north, while high priests of Amun in Thebes and local rules governed the south. A number of kinglets and principalities co-existed.

Foreign Influences and the Late Period

Beginning in Dynasty 23, Libyan kinglets took over parts of Upper Egypt (838–720 BCE) or ruled more extensively as pharaohs until Dynasty 24 (740–715 BCE) when native control was re-established. Dynasty 25 (728–657 BCE) again saw foreign rule (Nubian/Kushite). In 664 BCE the Assyrians pillaged and plundered Thebes and Memphis. Dynasty 26 (664–525 BCE), or the Saite Period (from the capital of Sais), saw the last native rulers to govern Egypt before the Persian invasion and marked the beginning of the Late Period (664–332 BCE). Dynasty 27 (First Persian Period; 525–404 BCE) and Dynasty 31 (Second Persian Period; 343–332 BCE) saw foreigners govern Egypt. The Persians wisely left the bureaucratic system largely intact under a layer of Persian administrators, and for the most part allowed Egyptians to manage their own affairs. They adopted ideas of pharaonic rulership by utilizing cartouches, maintained temples, and respected local customs.[69] Though some limited strife was not unexpected, life more or less continued as before. This was a testament to the centuries-honed solidity of traditional Egyptian sociopolitical structures.

The Macedonian Greek conquest of Egypt ushered in the Hellenistic era. This "east-meets-west" encounter was one of conflict, co-operation, and a rich confluence of traditions. The Ptolemaic Period (332–30 BCE) can be divided into the Macedonian (332–309 BCE) and the Ptolemaic Dynasties (309–30 BCE). Egypt became a Roman province in 30 BCE.

Notes to Chapter 4

1. Ockinga, 2010, p. 44.
2. Arabic for "bench."
3. David, 2003, pp. 42–42.
4. Some refer to the Predynastic Period as "dynasty zero."
5. Dynasties 1 and 2 (2950–2650 BCE) are also referred to as the Archaic Period.
6. No archaeological evidence of a war of unification has to date been found.
7. Three royal names are associated with Dynasty 0: the Kings Iri-Hor, Ka, and Narmer. The latter is well attested.
8. Malek, 2000, pp. 100–101.
9. Silverman, 1997, p. 24.
10. Callender, 2000, p. 183.
11. Callender, 2000, p. 183.
12. Callender, 2000, p. 181.
13. Wilkinson, 2010, p. 141.
14. Callender, 2000, p. 174.
15. David, 2003, p. 21.
16. Not found in the *Pyramid Texts*.
17. Assmann, 2005, p. 114.
18. Ockinga, 2010, p. 44.
19. Harrington, 2010, pp. 48–49.
20. Ockinga, 2010, p. 45.
21. Frankfort, 2000, p. 77.
22. Frankfort, 2000, p. 73.
23. Wilson, 1965, p. 299.
24. Ockinga, 2010, p. 45.
25. Callender, 2000, p. 180.
26. Wilkinson, 2010, p. 131.
27. David 2003, p. 160.
28. Foster, 2001, p. 503. Per Foster, what is called "instructions" or "teachings" (*sbȝyt*) does not cover all the types of writings that fit under the rubric of didactic writing. Foster, 2001, p. 503.
29. Foster, 2001, p. 507.
30. Key examples include: *Admonitions of Ipuwer*; *Complaints of Khakheperresonb*; *Dialogue of a Man with his Ba*; *Eloquent Peasant*; *Instructions for Merikare*; *Prophecy of Neferti*; *Teachings of Amenemhet*.
31. Fox, 1977.
32. Tyldesley, 2019, p. 82.
33. Harrington 2010. p. 102.
34. Wilkinson, 2010, p. 257.
35. Wilkinson, 2010, p. 265.
36. Wilkinson, 2010, p. 269.

37. Hoffmeier, 2015.
38. Ockinga, 2010, p. 44.
39. Tyldesley, 2019, p. 133.
40. Hoffmeier, 2015, p. 143.
41. Wilkinson, 2010, p. 265.
42. Wilkinson, 2010, p. 259.
43. Wilkinson, 2010, p. 259.
44. Wilkinson, 2010, p. 270.
45. Wilkinson, 2010, pp. 273, 274.
46. Tyldesley, 2019, p. 130.
47. Wilkinson, 2010, p. 272.
48. Tyldesley, 2019, p. 130.
49. Tyldesley, 2019, p. 130.
50. Wilkinson, 2010, p. 259.
51. Kulmar, 2018, p. 119.
52. Kulmar, 2018, pp. 122, 125.
53. Kulmar, 2018, p. 124.
54. Kulmar, 2018, p. 119.
55. Cline, 2014, p. 172.
56. Cline, 2014, pp. 173–172.
57. Van De Mieroop, 2016, p. 217.
58. Van De Mieroop, 2016, p. 203.
59. Cline, 2014, p. 162.
60. Renfrew, 1979.
61. Cline, 2014, pp. 161–162.
62. Dark, 1998.
63. Dark, 1998.
64. Cline, 2016, p. 168.
65. See Rowe's review of Cline, 2014 and Drews, 1995. In Rowe, 2016.
66. Rowe, 2016, p. 94.
67. Van De Mieroop, 2016, p. 210.
68. Tyldesley, 2019, p. 174.
69. Tyldesley, 2019, p. 192.

Chapter 5

The Cosmopolitical Realm: Creation, Gods, and Divine Energies

"Hail Atum, who makes the sky, who created that which exists ... Lord of all that is, who gave birth to the gods!"
— *Hymn to the Aten*

EGYPTIAN DEITIES: THE BASICS

Egyptian gods and goddesses "have been worshipped for fully three-fifths of recorded human history."[1] The actual number of deities is unknown, but it may have ranged from 1,500 to 2,000. Of these about 1,500 are known by name.[2] A much smaller number, perhaps thirty, might be considered major;[3] these often represented cosmic forces. Such a storied, rich, and enduring legacy deserves attention for what it may tell us about human spirituality and its relation to archaeopsychology.

Ancient Egyptian is replete with terms for "god" and related notions as well as divine epithets. For example, Osiris was known as the Weary One, the Dismembered One, the Inert One, and Lord of the Duat. The most common term translated as god is *nṯr*.[4] It appears in numerous expressions, such as "every god" (*nṯr nb*) (Table 5.1).[5] But *nṯr* is often better understood as a vague sense of sacredness (*nṯry*, *nṯrỉ*) that could infuse animals, objects, and people.[6] It was used to describe personified concepts, pharaohs, strange beings, and lesser numina. Other terms translated as god include *wntỉ*;[7] *ỉsds*;[8] *ỉtnw* / *ỉṯnw*;[9] and *ỉḥty*.[10]

In many ways the gods were anthropomorphic. They shared with people virtues and vices, strengths and frailties. Being created entities, the gods could be subject to death. Like humans, they had physical needs and this explains

Table 5.1. Examples of Expressions with *nṯr*.

No.	Terms	Possible Translation
1.	*iry nṯr*[11]	One who belongs to god
2.	*ẖ nṯr*[12]	Holy enclosure, sanctuary (?)
3.	*fdt nṯr*[13]	God's sweat (ritual fragrance)
4.	*i͗t nṯr*[14]	Father of the gods (Osiris)
5.	*mwt nṯ*[15]	God's mother (Isis)
6.	*tꜣ n hiney nṯr*[16]	God's acre, cemetery, necropoli
7.	*ḥtp nṯr*[17]	Oblations, divine offerings
8.	*it nṯr*[18]	God's father (priest)
9.	*nṯr / nṯri͗*[19]	Divine, sacred
10.	*ḏrt nṯr*[20]	Hand of God (priestess title)
11.	*šwyt nṯr*[21]	Sacred figure, image (of god)
12.	*ẖrt nṯr*[22]	Necropolis
13.	*ḥm nṯr*[23]	Prophet, god's servant, priest
14.	*ḫt nṯr*[24]	Divine matters
15.	*ḫm nṯr*[25]	Incense
16.	*mḏꜣt nṯr*[26]	God's book, divine record
17.	*nṯr mnw / mnw nṯr*[27]	Sanctuary
18.	*ḥbs nṯr*[28]	Apron (god's clothing)
19.	*sṯꜣ nṯr*[29]	Corridor (in a tomb)
20.	*ḥmr nṯr*[30]	Prophet

why priests tended to god-statues on a daily basis, cleansing, feeding, dressing, and taking them on outings. Gods had homes in their temples and cult centers, made appearances at festivals, and were known for their roles and associations with natural phenomena. The gender of deities was almost always indicated while "hermaphroditic or androgynous images were rare."[31]

Egyptian gods could "extend their being endlessly, achieving this through a range of different names, manifestations, and actions, or through combining with other gods."[32] They were "always in the process of construction, undergoing change" and adopting new aspects; they were never a "finished entity."[33] For instance, Horus had two main forms that sometimes were regarded as different aspects of the same deity, or perhaps even separate deities: Horus the Great or Horus the Elder and Horus the Younger (the son of Osiris and Isis) (Table 5.2).[34] Each god usually had several

Table 5.2. Symbolic Associations of Horus.

Object	Associations
Amulets	Cippi (magical stelae for healing); amulets for protection from snakes and scorpions
Animals	Falcon; falcon-headed crocodile; hawk
Colors	Gold; blue
Concepts	Sun; clear vision; kingship; planets (Venus, Mars, Jupiter, Saturn); protection; victory
Plants	Acacia; myrrh
Symbols	Winged solar disk; Eye of Horus

Source: Rankine, 2006. p. 41.

spheres of interest and specialization that typically overlapped with those of other gods.[35]

Besides divinities, in principle any person, as well as any animal, could be the focus of a complex of beliefs and ritual behaviors usually linked to a locale (i.e., a cult). Royal cults of deified kings, and the king's ancestors, of course, are well known. Royal cults also existed at the popular level and in temples of gods. Many were dedicated to funerary concerns. Though relatively rare, cults for the living king were not unknown. Cults for deified individuals were unusual but well-attested; these were for those who had achieved stature and recognition in their profession. Some cults were private and for personal, familial, and ancestor-focused religious practices.[36]

Hieroglyphs provide four ways of writing "god." The first was of a seated deity.[37] The second was a falcon (often on a standard; evidence exists that divinities in the form of animal figures perched on a staff were venerated).[38] The third was a staff wrapped in cloth[39] or a stick draped by bands or ribbons representing some divine power. The last was a five-pointed star.[40] The determinative sign for god suffixed the name of any unusual or exotic creature and even the hieroglyphs themselves might be regarded as gods.[41]

The Physical Forms of Gods

The physical form of the deities merely afforded them a visible, recognizable appearance. However, their perceptual manifestations were limited and could not contain their many roles, characteristics, and functions. And whatever their appearances, these did not necessarily indicate their true or hidden form, as the gods and goddesses were "unknown" and "mysterious." Their secretive and mystifying nature no doubt amplified their authoritative sway over devotees. In terms of appearance, four types of deities can be postulated. The first were anthropomorphic. These were often the "cosmic" gods and goddesses, or those representing geographic areas (rivers, mountains, cities, and estates). The second type were zoomorphic, which can be subdivided into male (e.g., bull, ram, falcon, lion) or female (e.g., cow, vulture, cobra, lioness). Also, portrayals of a deity in purely animal form might have a solar disk, a special collar, or other jewelry to denote divine status. The third type were bimorphic or hybrid (half-human, half-animal). These came in two forms: either human-headed with animal body or animal-headed with human body. The latter form was more common. The head is the essential element of bimorphic deities. The final type are composite deities which combine "different deities or characteristics rather than representing an individual god in a particular guise."[42] Fantastic images — sphinxes, griffins — were unusual though they were represented.[43] Composite god forms typically donned a wig or wig-cover, to both "aid the transition between the human body and the animal head and to stress the divinity of the figure."[44]

Groupings of deities were quite common. The use of pairs and trinities (and other groupings) was a way to manifest different modalities or aspects of gods. Dyads, rather than concentrating on the differences between coupled gods, usually stressed their complementary nature, as a way of expressing the essential duality of existence.[45] Triads typically stood for a divine family unit of father, mother, and child. Tetrads symbolized the four cardinal directions or a kind of spatial or geographic totality. Next came pentads, hebdomads, ogdoads, enneads, and then dodecads. In general, the higher the number, the more abstract the reason for bringing gods and goddesses into a unit.[46]

Monarchical Gods

Kings and the gods were inextricable. Kingship on earth was paralleled by how the gods ruled as monarchs in their own divine realm. Gods-as-kings and kings-as-gods both were key elements of the cosmopolitical order and were different sides of the same coin. Hymns to gods often referred to them as kings and they were depicted wearing crowns. The "image of the enthroned god or goddess is probably more commonly found in Egyptian art than examples of enthroned human kings — showing the motif's importance for the portrayal of deities."[47] The gods, after all, had ruled on earth in the mythical past. In different periods, one god was elevated to the role of a monarch over other deities, e.g., Horus, Re, or Amun. The distinction between god and king was almost completely blurred when the Aten celebrated his own royal jubilee.[48]

TYPES OF GODS AND OTHER SUPERNATURAL BEINGS

Below I organize the multitude of Egyptian deities and demi-gods into six groups. This categorization is rather arbitrary and by no means represents an indigenous theological attempt at classification.

(1) Natural Phenomena, Cosmic Functions, and Abstractions

Many gods were close at hand and personal (local or tribal). However, others were distant, remote, and impersonal. These personified the forces of nature (sun, moon, stars, etc.) or abstract, universal concepts (Maat).[49] An example of personification is Hu, which is the deification of authoritative or divine utterances (these were arguably related to VVVs). This Egyptian deity, associated with the sensation of taste and nourishment, was mentioned in a document in a Temple of Heliopolis from the reign of Senusret I (1918–1875 BCE). Some gods could be universal, while still retaining links to a geographical area (though not all gods developed their role beyond a local significance). Also, local manifestations of great gods "existed to emphasize a special aspect of that deity's nature."[50] Some deities, such as Re, Osiris, Ptah, and Amun always possessed universal aspects and were never limited to a certain geographical region.[51] Other examples of the deification of a facet of the cosmos are the god Heka (magic), a "force that animated, compelled, and protected the gods and subsequent creation,"[52] and Sia, who personified knowledge and understanding. Sedjem personified hearing. Hapy personified aspects of the Nile's inundation (interestingly, there was no deity of the Nile itself). Shai, who might take the form of a snake and could be identified with any of the creator deities, personified destiny. Seth personified evil, as did Apophis, the Great Serpent, enemy of the sun god Re.

Animals were regarded as incarnations of specific gods (or at least manifesting some key facet of a deity). Thus we find creatures associated with a temple's god venerated while alive and mummified at death. At the Temple of Kom Ombo (twenty-five miles north of Aswan), the southern precinct is dedicated to the crocodile god Sobek. In a pool in the sanctuary dwelled a crocodile, an avatar of the god, which was venerated and mummified at death. At Serapeum at Saqqara (near Memphis), a cemetery is filled with the mummified remains of Apis bulls.

Pets were also mummified and offerings proffered to sustain them in the next world. They were often like Osiris, in mummiform. In later periods, animals were sometimes sacrificed in gratitude when a deity answered a prayer or perhaps to carry a message to a god. Mummified hawks, dogs, baboons, cats, rams, crocodiles, and cattle have been found in the hundreds of thousands. Such zoolatry on the industrial scale led to the extinction of a number of animal species. Four million ibises were found at one animal necropolis devoted to Thoth at Saquarra.

(2) Local and State Deities

In the archaic world, political realities and theological aspirations were intertwined. Local gods might evolve to become deities of larger areas, or they might be conquered or absorbed by a victorious god who would subordinate the vanquished deities, making the conquered deity a follower of the victor. State-level gods were changed out, e.g., in Dynasty 11 a Theban deity, Amun, replaced Montu (the falcon-headed god of war) as the supreme state god (Table 5.3). A local god "could be incorporated into a higher one, and lose his separate identity, or he could assert himself and be allotted a place with other deities in a hierarchically structured pantheon."[53] Lesser deities presided over a shrine, and every settlement had its shrine dedicated to a god or goddess. Each city or town also had its own god (*nṯr nwty*). Higher up the theopolitical hierarchy, each of the 42 nomes (administrative districts) had its official deity or group of gods.[54] The nomarch functioned as the high priest of the local deity. Despite any theopolitical vicissitudes, the Egyptians never abandoned their local gods.

(3) Funerary Deities

Osiris was originally associated with the Delta, the fertile earth, vegetation, and the Afterworld. He became master of the underworld, linked to the colors white (mummy bandages), black (fertile Nile soil), and green

Table 5.3. Symbolic Associations of Amun.

Object	Associations
Amulets	For eye ailments
Animals	Serpent; bull; ram (with curved horns); Nile goose; lion; bee
Colors	Blue, red
Concepts	Protector of the common man; protection from crocodiles, scorpions and other dangerous animals; fertility; invisibility; oracle, strength; wind
Symbols	Twin feather plumed crown; ammonite

Source: Rankine, 2006. p. 31.

(vegetation). He was represented in mummiform (body wrapped like a mummy with arms crossed). Osiris would become associated with the deceased king (while the ruler-to-be was identified with Horus). Another important funerary deity was the jackal or jackal-headed Anubis. He performed embalming, was associated with cemeteries, and ruled the underworld. Thoth (Djehuty), depicted as either a baboon or ibis (or ibis-headed) and associated with the moon, knowledge, and scribes, recorded the proceedings of the weighing of the heart. A tribunal of forty-two deities, in texts listed by their names and either a geographical area or some other characteristic, observed the ceremony. These gods had attention-grabbing names, such as Swallower of Shades; Bone Breaker; Doubly Evil; Demolisher; Owner of Faces; You Who Acted Willfully; You of the Altar; Blood Eater; Eater of Entrails; See Whom You Bring; Green of Flame.[55] Ammit, the "gobbler," who had the head of a crocodile, the front part of a panther or lion and the rear of a hippopotamus, would devour the deceased's heart if the judgment was not favorable.

The Afterworld had many gates, portals, and pylons that the sun god passed through on his evening journey. The transfigured king, as part of the sun god's barque-riding entourage, as well as the deceased, also needed to trek to their new existence. Special deities guarded these liminal areas. Minor gods demanded from the deceased their secret names in order to pass. What can be called "cavern deities," listed in the *Book of the Dead*, were involved in the punishment of the dead (often by beheading). These deities, however, also aided the "justified dead."[56] There were also deities for the hours of the day and night that corresponded to geographical locations in the Afterworld.[57]

(4) Household and Personal Gods

While high-ranking gods could hear the prayers of commoners, they usually could only be approached during festivals. But the Egyptians had more immediate access to the divine in the form of household gods. In later periods commoners desired closer relationship with the gods and this is apparent in a more intimate devotion to personal deities (the latter are not strictly speaking household gods). Here we should note the difference between "domestic religion" and "family religion." The former centers on a household, while the latter concerns a kinship unit that presumably can practice religion in various locales besides the house.[58] Also, to be clear, household gods (e.g., protective deities) are not necessarily "family gods" or ancestors, who also received devotion.

Two examples of household deities, associated with family life, especially women and children, were Bes and Taweret. The former was a musical-instrument playing bandy-legged dwarf with lion's ears, main, and a tail. More like a spirit or benevolent demon, Bes donned a feathered headdress and an animal pelt and carried an amulet (*sꜣ*) for protection. The goddess Taweret, associated with pregnant women and childbirth, was depicted as an upright hippopotamus with pendulous breast and a protruding stomach, crocodile tail, and a leonine muzzle. She wore a modius (a cylindrical headdress) surmounted by two plumes, sometimes with horns and a disc. The modius symbolized powers over fecundity. Taweret was sometimes shown clutching an Ankh and *sꜣ* (protective) and *tiit* (protection of women and childbirth) amulets.

(5) Demons: Wanderers and Guardians

What are translated as "demons" were really minor divinities (Middle Egyptian lacks a word for "demon"). Though sometimes called *nṯr*, demons were not in the same category as gods and were not as hostile to humans as the English word "demon" suggests. Their status is defined by being clearly subordinate to the major deities and performing specific functions and tasks. Unlike deities, demons lacked cults (at least until the New Kingdom) and were not mentioned in creation accounts.[59] The category of demon was never well-defined. For example, the Slaughterers or Butchers (gods aiding Re in fighting or *ḫꜣtyw*[60]) were also known as messenger demons; but they could also bring disease.[61] A demon might be promoted to a higher level of divine status, becoming in effect a god.[62]

During the Ptolemaic and Roman periods, demons had evolved to become deities in their own right and saw cults dedicated to them.[63]

In order to highlight their fearful nature and "otherness," demonic beings possessed hybrid human–animal appearance and theriomorphic features. This was in contrast to certain deities who were anthropomorphic; such beings presumably symbolized humanization and membership in the civilized sphere. As with many gods and goddesses, reptiles (especially snakes), aspects of felines, canids, donkeys, baboons, hippos, goats, bulls, insects, scorpions, falcons, or vultures might be components of a demonic or divine body.[64]

Demons typically lacked names but had epithets: Swallower of Shadows; Big and Fiery; Bellower; The Rapacious One; He Whose Face Is Hot. One demon's name, impressively longwinded, deserves special mention: God Who Lives on Meat-sacrifice Dog-faced, Human-skinned, Keeper of the Bend of the Waterway of Fire, Who Swallows Shadows, Who Snatches Hearts, Throws the Lasso and Yet Is Not Seen.[65]

Lucarelli divides demons into two main classes. The first were "wandering demons" who moved between this world and the next. They often operated as "agents of punishment" or "messengers" under the command of a god or goddess. However, though they typically worked as divine emissaries, they occasionally also acted "independently from the divine will."[66] Wandering demons were usually regarded as malevolent, visiting upon the unfortunate diseases, misfortunes, and nightly terrors. They were also known to haunt houses.[67] The second class were "guardian demons." These creatures were tasked with protecting sacred places from intrusion or pollution, as well as safeguarding pits, caves, and tombs which were believed to be portals to the Afterworld.[68] Some demons might even be considered "benevolent genii"[69] who protected gods, the king, or the deceased. Whereas wandering demons invaded spaces (such as dwellings and bodies), guardian demons, who were basically benevolent, stood as sentinels at liminal, transitional places, such as gateways and entrances.

(6) Foreign Gods

A number of gods of foreign origin from Nubia, Ugarit, and Canaan found their way onto the Egyptian spiritual landscape, e.g., Astarte (a western Semitic war-goddess, identified with Sekhmet), Baal (a Semitic god introduced by the Hyksos, identified with Seth), and Reseph, Hauron, Anat, and Qedeshet. They were often identified with indigenous Egyptian deities but as they had their primary cults outside the boundaries of Egypt and a historical presence in a foreign land, they continued to maintain their non-Egyptian identities and retain non-Egyptian names.[70] During the latter part of the first millennium BCE, Greek influence introduced even more gods and goddesses into the already overcrowded Egyptian pantheon, e.g., Apollo (identified as Horus by the Greeks), Demeter (Greek goddess of the earth, identified with Isis), and Harpocrates (Greek version of Horus-the-Child). The incorporation of these deities demonstrates the absorptive, flexible, and ever-changing nature of Egyptian spirituality.

THE ONE AND THE MANY

With all the references to cosmic forces, animating powers, and deities regularly teaming up to form dyads, trinities, and other groupings, one can be forgiven for wondering if, behind all the diversity, a belief in a fundamental, underlying oneness existed. Morenz saw a classification of deities into (1) "families of kindred deities" and (2) the "specialized functions which particular gods performed." But behind differences and the plurality of gods, a basic unity can be discerned.[71] Hornung contended that the Egyptians took a dualistic, complementary perspective of "One and Many" toward matters spiritual (not as either/or but both/and); "god is a unity in worship and revelation, and multiple in nature and manifestation."[72] The Egyptians "sought to effect an intellectual compromise between unity and plurality and to reconcile them to one another."[73] The One is ubiquitous, impersonal, universal, total, and complete, while the Many is local, personal, particular, limited, and partial.

Assmann attempted to account for the paradox of the "One and the Many" by proposing "generation" and "emanation."[74] In the former, the One produces the Many; this is apparent in the various cosmogonies. Emanations meant that the One is present in the Many; this is illustrated by syncretism. In the Atenism of Akhenaten, the idea of emanation is absent. Only through generation does Aten create the cosmos. Though immanent in the visible world, Aten also transcended his creation.[75]

The sun exemplifies the One–Many dynamic in how the divine, natural phenomena, and the cosmopolitical order are essentially and paralogically enmeshed. Arguably the solar orb was Egypt's pre-eminent deity, and numerous names and epithets indicate the sun as god. Horus (The

Distant One), was manifested as a falcon or falcon-headed man and could represent the sun as creation. Re, the ram or a falcon-headed man wearing a sun disc and a cobra headdress, was the solar aspect of creation. Khepri (The Evolving One) was the sun at dawn and was represented with the hieroglyph of a scarab or a scarab-headed man. Atum represented the sun as the culmination of creation and was depicted as a man and was associated with the setting sun. Amun-Re, a man crowned with two tall plumes, was the sun as the manifestation of Amun during the New Kingdom. The Aten, the visible disc of the sun, was a medium through which the sun's rays came into the world and became the key theocentric symbol of Akhenaten. Table 5.4 lists other solar gods.

Related to the One–Many dynamic was a god's relation to his or her multiple expressions. The Egyptians distinguished between a divinity's image and its "true form." The latter was inaccessible and infrequently revealed, if ever. However, here "image" was not conceptualized as a mere reflection or representation of a divinity. A god's manifestation (e.g., in statuary form) was as real as its hidden aspects. Thus Amun, the king of gods, took his *ȝbwt* (appearance)[76] in each god, while his *ḫprw* (form)[77] was in the Nile flood.[78] How a divinity relates to its image is described with the verb *sḫn*. This can mean bind together; meet; visit; occupy; embrace; repose; rest at; alight; dwell (nominal form: resting place).[79] The other relevant term is *ḫni*, meaning to alight; descend; rest on; to be confined. This merging of god and image is also described as joining (*snsn*; or in the Memphite tradition, entering — *ʿḳ*).[80]

Table 5.4. Solar Gods.

God's Name	Description
Mnevis	The bull of the sun god
Benu	Associated with rebirth
Herishef	Depicted as a long-horn ram with Atef-crown and sun disc headdress
Mandulis	A man with a headdress of ram horns, plumes, sun disc, and cobra
Ra-Horakhty or "Horus in the Horizon"	The god of the morning sun
Harpocrates or "Horus the Child"	Represented the rising sun and protected one from snake bites and scorpion stings
Horemakhert or "Horus in the Horizon"	The god of the east and the new born sun

A Cosmic Fundament?

The notion of an animating fundament of the universe finds expression in *sḫm*, which can mean a power personified as a deity;[81] mighty one or cult-like figure (of a god on earth);[82] shrine or place of worship;[83] or book of spells (magical book).[84] As an adjective it denoted powerful and mighty[85] (it could mean potentate[86]). And note the expression "powerful in body" (*sḫm ẖt*). A cognate pointing to the intersection of cosmic energy, religious objects, and divine beings is *sḫmw*, which had associations with the dead and gods.[87] It could mean cult statues, shrines, place of worship[88] or the mighty ones (powers).[89] "Power" may be better conceptualized as "efficacy," which may "serve as a common denominator for the immense variety of cult objects."[90] Related to all this is the long list of expressions with Ankh (*'nḫ*)[91] — e.g., force of life (*nḫt 'nḫ*)[92] — indicating vitality, living, and sustenance.

One may speculate that the One, in its primordial unmanifested form, was the original cosmic stuff that existed before the gods. This primeval power is immanent in natural phenomena, animals, storms, floods, plagues, and in higher concentrations takes personalized form in gods, kings, and special individuals. It is a force that underlies all beings, a sort of unified polytheism with pantheistic undertones. But we need to proceed with caution when proposing that the pre-Late Period Egyptians conceived the various facets of reality as manifestations of a single Godhead, even if an impersonal one, as this suggests a level of theological abstraction that I doubt existed. Polytheism, pantheism, monotheism, etc., are modern concepts applied to past societies that did not see the need to theorize such concepts. The principle of the "gods are many but the Godhead is one" may sound appropriate, but it does not necessarily resonate with the archaic Egyptian view.

Sometimes the archaic Egyptians would mention "the god" which has led some to suggest that monotheism was part of the Egyptian spiritual tradition. But probably such references were to a specific deity. In any case, "monotheism" can mean different things. For the sake of argument, it needs to be distinguished from henotheism, which acknowledges the existence of other gods but focuses worship on one deity (this describes the early Israelites). There is also summodeism, which describes a supreme god sitting atop a polytheistic pantheon, "whose multitude of deities exists as hypostases of the high god by virtue of his transforming himself into the many."[93] In such a system multiple gods exist only because a singular god is able to transform him- or herself into many different deities. The argument might be made that summodeism characterizes the New Kingdom, particularly the Ramesside period, when hymns were composed for a deity that was a "kind of universal super-transcendent god" with other deities as secondary emanations.[94]

SYNCRETISM: HOW BLENDING AND BLURRING OF THE DIVINE FACILITATES COMMUNICATION

The very nature of the deities shouts paralogic. Gods and goddesses could be in more than one place simultaneously. The form, name, and epithets of deities seem to have been "variable almost at will, and are often interchangeable with those of other deities."[95] A deity could be the Ba (soul-manifestation) of another god; this allowed a supernatural entity to take on additional names and attributes. A deity could split into a pair or merge with another divinity. The "union is not a static or lasting one, but rather a dynamic inhabitation ('indwelling') by one of the other, which does not limit the independence or mobility of either partner."[96] Such unions were neither permanent nor exclusive and gods would retain their own identity.

Syncretic shifting and combining of sacred identities had practical and self-serving political motivations (among the priesthood), but arguably they were attempts to accommodate multiple lines of communication. Rather than wasting efforts on disentangling communication lines or having supernatural entities compete for the attention of devotees, it was more expedient to accept and acknowledge multi-VVVs that could be centered in one supernatural entity.

Syncretism transpired in two ways: by the assimilation of a less important god by a greater one or, more rarely, a minor god absorbing some characteristic of a greater deity.[97] These unions were symbolized by combining names, e.g., Atum-Khepri, Re-Horakhty, Amun-Re. Sometimes three or more deities were linked.[98] The two ways to view syncretism may not have been mutually exclusive in the paralogic mindset of the archaic Egyptians. From one perspective, syncretism effectively creates a third god where there were originally only two.[99] From another perspective, a god did not subsume the identity of another; rather each deity maintained his or her individuality.[100] According to Morenz, the Egyptian gods possessed personality but not individuality. In other words, each god had a "sharply delineated character peculiar to him [or her] alone," since unstable liaisons and the "transposing of qualities from one to the other" were common.[101] This point about missing individuality resonates with the absence of self-individuation, a key feature of the consciously interiorized person: "The indeterminateness of Egyptian gods corresponds, mutatis, mutandis, to the relative lack of individuality in Egyptian art and literature."[102]

Syncretism seems to be an expression of the unity–plurality principle. The Egyptian pantheon abounds with syncretism. Though individual gods still remained as "separate hypostatic deities," their syncretism expressed the unity of divine power.[103] A good example is Amun–Re. The Amun facet of this divine amalgamation was secret, hidden, and mysterious, but the Re facet was visible and revealed.[104] Later, Amun-Re would become the champion of the poor and a beacon for personal piety.

THE QUESTION OF EGYPTIAN MONOTHEISM

Another issue in discussions of monotheism, informed by Judeo-Christian thought, is the transcendent nature of the Godhead. So it needs to be asked if transcendence characterized Egyptian gods. In other words, were any of the Egyptian gods conceived to have the capability to exist in the realm of the absolute and limitless?

Some debates (e.g., whether monotheism had a place in pharaonic Egypt or whether some pharaohs thought of themselves as gods) view things from a Judeo-Christian theological perspective that insists on drawing a sharp line between divinity and mortals. This would have been foreign to the Egyptian worldview. The archaic Egyptians were comfortable with a paralogical view of divine kingship: "On the one hand the god–king is to ride alongside Re in the celestial boat of the sun god and to act as a judge in the realm of Re, while on the other hand he is clearly said to be one with the solar god."[105]

An interesting conceit of the modern world is that an absolutely transcendent Godhead that lacks physical form is somehow more advanced than traditions with zoomorphic or hybrid forms of divinity. Egyptian gods and goddesses not only possessed mortal-like features but might have human bodies topped by animal heads (the reverse was rare). A candidate that comes closest to the transcendent criteria is the god Amun (*imn*). With the possible exception of Osiris, Amun is the best documented of all the Egyptian deities.[106] A primeval deity and associated with creative energies of the cosmos, Amun was conceived as an invisible, unknowable force dwelling far beyond the boundaries of the cosmos. His creative role was stressed in the Middle Kingdom, but even as early as the *Pyramid Texts* there are indications of his important role. By the New Kingdom he "became the greatest expression of a transcendent creator ever known" in ancient Egypt.[107] Amun "remained apart from his creation, totally different from it, and fully independent of it."[108] His "imperceptibility" granted him an absolute otherness and unqualified holiness.[109]

Another candidate for archaic Egyptian monotheism was Akhenaten's worship of the Aten, the sun disk. This was probably the closest the Egyptians came to monotheism. However, Akhenaten's sharing of divinity with Aten (was the king himself a god?) disqualifies this unusual, short-lived tradition as pure monotheism. Moreover, the king and queen worshiped the Aten directly, while their subjects could in principle only approach the Aten indirectly through the mediation of Akhenaten. And note that his queen, Nefertiti, also possessed divine attributes.

HEKA: THE COSMIC ENERGIES THAT ENABLED EFFECTIVENESS AND SUCCESS

The saliency of other terms for what we would call magic indicates how salient this idea was in the ancient Egyptian world: *ḥkꜣwt* (sorcery, magic);[110] *nht* (magical protection);[111] *ḏꜣw* (protective magic);[112] and *ḥkꜣ* (bewitch, be bewitched or magic, magic spell, magical influence).[113] Other associated concepts were *štꜣ*[114] and *štꜣw*[115] (secret, unknown, transfigured beings, necropolises, the hidden forms of gods).

Re reportedly created Heka. This allowed humans to call upon the supernatural entities and to have some control over their own destinies as mortals. Such power was elevated to a divine status when used by the deities and was considered a simple form in the hands of humans. Heka was not necessarily subversive and was utilized for purposes of the state. Magic, then, was a divine gift used for the benefit of all beings. An epithet of gods was Great in Magic (*wr ḥkꜣw*).[116] Crowns also shared this epithet (*wrt ḥkꜣw*).[117] This primary cosmic force was personified by the god Heka who was the eldest son of the universal creator.[118] This deity was the cosmic energy that made creation possible and guarded the world from chaos. He was described as the Ba of the solar god.[119]

The line between magicians and priests was blurry, since the latter were regarded as paid specialists. Heka involved a spell, ritual, and a magician.

The latter (*ḥk3y / ḥk3w*)[120] played various roles, such as a *šnw* (conjurer, exorcist)[121] or *rḫt* (wise woman, female healer, skilled woman).[122] It is unclear what a *s3w* (magician, amulet maker)[123] did exactly, but perhaps he made amulets or ritually infused amulets with Heka (e.g., for wet nurses, midwives). Terms for charm included *3ḫw,*[124] *ḥk3,*[125] and *ḥk3w.*[126]

The many expressions denoting "magic words" and spells indicate how potent language itself was considered (Table 5.5).

In the context of magical forces *swnw* should be mentioned. This meant a "doctor," but one who applied magico-medical arts, making no distinction between what we might call "superstition" and "science." The inseparability of magic and medicine is apparent in the *Ebers Papyrus,* which dates to around 1550 BCE. With its 700 magical formulas, incantations, and folk remedies, it is the oldest text of its kind and treats demon-caused and bodily-based illnesses. Significantly, it did not bifurcate the physical and what we would term psychological disorders (i.e., no mind–body dualism). Akhu (*3ḫw*) also meant magical power. It was associated with the stars, deities, and the blessed dead (*3ḫ*) (Table 5.6).

Table 5.5. Magic Words and Related Expressions.

No.	Term	Possible Translation
1.	*p'p'*[127]	Magic word
2.	*phti*[128]	
3.	*pṯti*[129]	
4.	*s3ti*[130]	
5.	*ṯwbs*[131]	
6.	*ṯnnwy*[132]	
7.	*ṯthnw*[133]	
8.	*rk*[134]	
9.	*rr*[135]	
10.	*mwy*[136]	
11.	*miw*[137]	
12.	*mtwti / m tiwti*[138]	
13.	*fnnwy*[139]	
14.	*hm*[140]	
15.	*šnt*[141]	Spell, conjuration, curse
16.	*ḥmwt r*[142]	Magic spell
17.	*šmw*[143]	Class of incantations, magic spell, omens
18.	*r ḏdw*[144]	Spells

Table 5.6. Meanings of Akhu.

No.	Possible Translation	Term
1.	Sunlight, sunshine, light[146]	*ꜣḫw*
2.	Sunlight, sunshine, radiance (of a god)[147]	
3.	Power (of god), mastery (over work)[148]	
4.	Akhs, spirits (of the dead)[149]	
5.	Glorified[150]	
6.	Benefactions, good excellent things, glorifications, ability[151]	
7.	Power (of god), magic, magical words, useful knowledge, mastery[152]	
8.	Power (of god), mastery (over work), skills, expertise, craft[153]	
9.	Spirits, personalities[154]	
10.	Magical charms[155]	
11.	Good things, kindness, (what is) useful, beneficial[156]	

CREATION MYTHS AND THE MOVE TOWARDS TRANSCENDENCE

No single account of creation became dominant in ancient Egypt. In fact, any god or goddess of any temple might be considered as a creator deity, though the most important creator gods were Atum, Amun, Ptah, Khnum, and Aten.[157] But differing accounts seem to be variants on a single theme: all existence was derived from an original source that transformed the oneness of the creator god into multiple life forms. To some degree, all the various accounts "appear as kaleidoscopic variations of core mythic elements."[158] Also, creation did not result from impersonal forces but was a manifestation of the personal wishes and desires of supernatural entities.[159]

The archaic Egyptians saw no contradiction between the co-existence of stasis (from the start, creation is perfect and complete) and change (life is dynamic).[160] Stasis can be characterized as "eternal sameness" (a state of existing) while "eternal recurrence" indicated cycles and repeated development.[161] Though there was a "first time," creation occurs daily. In this sense existence was timeless. A good analogy is how, in a play, the characters and script can remain invariable, but the actors and settings change as the performance is restaged each day.[162] Concrete events and creation were being continually re-enacted in nature and history.[163] An alpha and omega perspective was absent (as this linear conception of cosmic time that came on the world scene sometime in the first millennium BCE). Unlike people, the gods had left earth for divine realms far above or below the terrestrial realm and dwelled in a mythological past that was, from the modern perspective, odd, since this pastness was paralogically present and exerted an influence all around the living.

Creation was "thought of as occurring both in the past and the present, since new lives continued to come into existence."[164] It had "been fully good from the Beginning and needed only to be reaffirmed in its unchanging rightness."[165] Creation itself was a "complete revelation";[166] this precluded the need for extraordinary, episodic revelations or one-and-done incarnations (e.g., Jesus). The universe had been static from the beginning. This is why few texts deal with the end of time or the destruction of humankind.

The most important cosmogonies, which evidence gradual steps towards a more philosophical and less super-religious worldview, are: (1) Elephantine; (2) Hermopolitan; (3) Heliopolitan (arguably the most important); (4) Theban; and (5) Memphite. The latter two, originating during the latter part of the New Kingdom, not surprisingly exhibited more abstract thought, as well as signs of increased interiorization.

The Elephantine Tradition: Creating from Clay

Khnum (or Khnemu) was a god of fertility, associated with procreation and water. He was represented as a ram with horizontal twisting horns or as a ram-headed man. This deity crafted the gods, animals, and humankind from clay on a potter's wheel. While modelling people, he paid particular attention to how the human body was made and the installation of organs. Khnum was the god of the island of Elephantine and became known as the lord of the Nile's First Cataract. He became a member of a triad with the goddesses Satis and Anukis.

The Hermopolitan Tradition: Creation from the Natural Elements

Elements of the Hermopolitan tradition are evident in the *Pyramid Texts* of the Old Kingdom and the earliest version is from the Middle Kingdom. However, no coherent version has survived, but it can be pieced together from references from the New Kingdom. This tradition was centered in Hermopolis Magna (renamed in the Graeco-Roman period), originally the cult-center of Khmun (hence "group of eight"), the chief city of the god Thoth. The story begins with a vast, featureless ocean covered in darkness, symbolizing chaos and the unformed. Four male–female pairs of personifications of the natural world set creation in motion: (1) Nun and Naunet (primordial waters); (2) Amun and Amaunet (air or hidden power); (3) Kuk and Kauket (darkness); and (4) Huh and Hauhet (formlessness or infinity; associated with the force of flooding).

The "group of eight" gods constitutes the primal forces driving forward the creation of the universe. The male gods were frog-headed, while the goddesses were snake-headed. These eight elements collided, producing the cosmos. Two versions of the following events are provided. In one, a primeval mound emerged (Isle of Flames) from where life emerged. The god Thoth placed a cosmic egg on the mound. When the egg hatched, the sun ascended to the sky. In another version the petals of a lotus flower (personified as Nefertem) floating on the primordial ocean opened, out of which arose the sun (identified as Horus). Associated with the Hermopolitan Tradition is Amun Kematef (He Who Has Completed His Moment).

The Heliopolitan Tradition: From a Primordial Unity to an Assortment of Forms

Before creation — or the "time before two things evolved in this world" — there was only wateriness (*nwj*), inertia (*nnw*), infinity (*ḥḥw*), darkness (*kkw*), uncertainty (*tnmw*; literally "lostness"), and hiddenness (*imnw*). These terms first appeared in the *Coffin Texts* (ca. 2000 BCE). This precosmic state was personified as the god Nun or the Watery One; though associated with inertness Nun also symbolized rejuvenation and rebirth (the masculine form of Nut). The negative potentiality of the precreation cosmos was contrasted with the positive reality of the created world which was dry, active, bounded, full of light, and tangible.[167] The solar creator deity Atum (Lord of Totality, the Completed One, the All, Lord of the Limit) was inert and floated with Nun.[168] Atum then evolved from a primordial singularity into a multiplicity of forms, an evolution of evolutions.[169] By masturbating (or in one version sneezing), the self-evolving deity Atum produced the deities Tefnut and Shu, personifying moisture and air, respectively. This male–female pair produced Geb (the earth) and Nut (the sky). The "group of nine" in Heliopolis (the City of the Sun was composed of the gods Re, Atum (the Bull of the Ennead), Tefnut,

Geb, and Nut, along with the offspring of the latter two gods, Osiris, Isis, Seth, and Nephthys.

The word used to describe Atum's image could also refer to reliefs, paintings, sculptures, and "divine speech" (hieroglyphs); all these are imagistic representations of an idea, whether pictorial or verbal, i.e., creation itself is an "image" of the creator's concept.[170] Eventually Re took over the relevant attributes and became the self-originating Re–Atum.

The Theban Tradition: A Step toward Transcendence

This tradition, bolstered by the growing power of the Theban priesthood during the Middle Kingdom, regarded what was originally a local deity called Amun as the true creator of the cosmos, the source of power for all gods. Amun, or the Unknowable or the Hidden, is attested to at least from ca. 2350 BCE in the *Pyramid Texts*, but his "self-concealing" transcendent nature is a later development apparent by the New Kingdom (ca. 1539 BCE).[171] Though he is self-engendered and pantheistically immanent, he was conceived to exist before his creation and was independent of his cosmic handiwork. During the reign of Ramesses II (ca. 1279–1213 BCE) Theban priests conceptualized a sort of monotheism. Indeed, a theology developed that is centered on a trinity: (1) Amun (hidden identity); (2) the sun (face); and (3) Ptah (body).

The Memphite Tradition: A Philosophical Tradition

The Memphite Tradition, originating in the city of the Ptah (Memphis; from Men-nefer), is notable because, compared to earlier cosmogonies, it presents universe-making as an abstract process. Ptah, who was an older creator deity from the Old Kingdom, took on the trappings of transcendence, since his creative activities did not directly require precosmic raw stuff. Rather than an immanent deity ensnared in the very processes it generated, Ptah was a self-created primordial god. He was a "creative and controlling intelligence";[172] existence came about through his words.

The Memphite myth, carved on the eight-century BCE black granite Shabaka Stone, "conveys some advanced philosophical concepts which are not usually encountered in Egyptian mythology because the language was not rich and profound enough to express such ideas."[173] I submit that these "advanced philosophical concepts" could not have existed prior to the Ramesside Period (1100 BCE), and indeed, this is when the Memphite Tradition was most likely composed (or possibly even later). This collection of ideas indicated conscious interiorization that centers on the activity of the heart, the organ of thought (not the brain, which was discarded as a waste product during embalming).

According to the Memphite Tradition, first came the gods, the towns and shrines to house them, people, and then animals. The various gods were mere variations of Ptah's "tongue" (or voice?).[174] Three elements are involved. First Ptah conceives of something in his heart; this is called Sia (*sia*) or divine knowledge.[175] Next, Ptah brings it into being through creative speech or Hu (*ḥw*); this is a command, an authoritative utterance. Such divine naming makes thoughts real in the same manner hieroglyphs do. In other words, the very act of naming things calls them into existence paralogically; there is no difference between word and object.[176] The final element is Heka, or the magical divine energy that animates existence. The close link between magical energy and words (both spoken and written) is evident in Spell 261 (*To Become the God Heka*) of the *Coffin Texts*. This recitation describes how the mystical vitality of the god Heka, even prior to cosmic duality and the creative utterance (Hu), animated all creation, including other gods. Heka is He Who Consecrates Imagery and Lord of the Ka-spirits. This linkage between magical efficacy and language reoccurs in Spell 648, in which millions of Ka-spirits "within his mouth" operated as powers that infused creation with a life-force.[177]

The heart and tongue of Ptah play a prominent role in the Memphite cosmogony; the heart thinks (*kꜣi*), while the tongue commands (*wḏ*). Though we must be wary of translating Sia as an "objectified conception" of mind, since this amounts to imposing "modern categories upon the texts," it is a fairly abstract notion containing a degree of psychologicality. "It is generally agreed that the ancient Egyptian language, like the Sumerian, was concrete from first to last. To maintain that it is expressing abstract thoughts would seem to me an intrusion of the modern idea that men have always been the same."[178] Jaynes even goes so far as to write that the very word "created" may "also be a modern imposition, and the more proper translation might be *commanded*."[179] The Memphite tradition is "essentially a myth about language, and what Ptah is really commanding is indeed the bicameral voices [VVVs] which began, controlled, and directed Egyptian civilization."[180] Morenz, incidentally, notes the parallels with the creator's divine utterance (calling reality into existence) and how "in a sacrosanct monarchy people automatically carried into effect the commands given to them — and it was a command (*wḏ*) that "issued forth from the god's tongue."[181]

Notes to Chapter 5

1. Wilkinson, 2003, p. 7.
2. Wilkinson, 2003, p. 7.
3. David, 2002, lists 104; Morenz, 1992, 90; and Oakes and Gahlin, 2006, about one hundred.
4. R8; R8-A40; Z1-R8.
5. R8-N35-V30-G7-G7-Z1.
6. See R8-X1-D21.
7. E34-N35-U33-A40.
8. M17-S29-D46-O34-W24-A40.
9. M17-V13-N35-W24-G43-D19.
10. M17-V28-X1-Z4-F28.
11. D21-R8.
12. F32-X1-R8-01.
13. I9-D46-X1-N35A-R8-A40.
14. M17-X1-R8.
15. G14-X1-R8.
16. N16-Z1-N23-N35-R8-T28-D21-Z4-Y1.
17. R4-X1-Q3-R8-X2-W22-Z8.
18. R7-R8-M17.
19. R8.
20. R8-D46-X1-Z1.
21. R8-S36.
22. R8-T28.
23. R8-U36.
24. R8-Aa1-X1-Y1-Z2.
25. R8-Z5-Z5-Z5.
26. R8-Y1A.
27. R8-X-D21-Y5-W24-W24-W24.
28. R8-V28-D58-S29.
29. R8-V2-D54-O1.
30. R8-U36-Z1-Z7-A1-Z2.
31. Silverman, 1991, p. 21.
32. David, 2001, p. 56.
33. David, 2001, p. 56.
34. Pinch, 2002, p. 128.
35. Pinch 2004, p. 40.
36. Lesko, 2010; Ray, 2010; Teeter, 2001a; Thompson, 2001; Wegner, 2010.
37. A40.
38. G7.

39. R8.
40. N14.
41. R8.
42. Wilkinson, 2003, pp. 26–27.
43. Silverman 1991, p. 20. Interestingly in the Predynastic Period virtually no images of either human or animal forms have been found. Silverman, 1991, p. 13.
44. Goelet et al., 2015, p. 155.
45. Wilkinson, 2003, p. 74.
46. Wilkinson, 2003, pp. 76–79.
47. Wilkinson, 2003, p. 65.
48. Wilkinson, 2003, p. 66.
49. Silverman, 1991, pp. 33–34.
50. David, 2003, p. 57.
51. David, 2002, p. 57.
52. Ritner, 2001a, p. 321.
53. Morenz, 1992, p. 139.
54. Pinch, 2004, p. 63.
55. Wilkinson, 2003, p. 84.
56. Wilkinson, 2003, p. 80.
57. Wilkinson, 2003, p. 80.
58. Van Der Toorn, 2012, pp. 20–21.
59. Lucarelli, 2010, p. 2.
60. Aa1-M12-G1-G4-G43-T31-N33A.
61. M12-G1-G4-T30-G7-Z3.
62. Wilkinson, 2003, p. 81.
63. Lucarelli, 2010, p. 7.
64. Lucarelli, 2010, p. 5.
65. Szpakowska, 2009, pp. 802–803.
66. Lucarelli, 2010, p. 3.
67. Lucarelli, 2010, p. 4.
68. Lucarelli, 2010, p. 2.
69. Szpakowska, 2009.
70. Silverman, 1991, pp. 57–58.
71. Morenz, 1992, p. 142.
72. Hornung, 1996, p. 242.
73. Morenz, 1992, p. 29.
74. Assmann, 1997.
75. Assmann, 1997.
76. Appearance, aspect, outward form.
77. Appearance, shape, form, mode of being, transformation, development, stages of growth, (what) should happen, will happen, has happened, occurrence, become.
78. Morenz, 1992, p. 151.
79. Morenz translates *sḫn* as "coalesce." He also uses *ḫnm* but the semantic connection is unclear. Morenz, 1992, p. 151.
80. It is not clear if such habitation took place once or repeatedly, though it was probably the latter.

81. S29-Aa1-G17-S42-A40.
82. S42-A40.
83. O34-Aa1-G17-D35-O1.
84. S42-Z7-V12-Z1.
85. Y8-G17-Z7-Y1-A24.
86. Y8-G17-A24-D4-I9-A44.
87. Morenz, 1992, p. 17-18.
88. O34-Aa1-G17-Z2B.
89. S29-S42-G17-Aa1-G43-D40-Z2.
90. Morenz, 1992, p. 18.
91. S34.
92. N35-M3-Aa1-X1S34-N3-Aa1.
93. Ritner, 2001b, pp. 410–411.
94. Ritner, 2001b, pp. 410–411.
95. Wilkinson, 2003, p. 33.
96. Morenz, 1992, p. 140.
97. Wilkinson, 2003, p. 31.
98. Wilkinson, 2003, pp. 33–34.
99. Wilkinson, 2003, p. 35.
100. Wilkinson, 2003, p. 35.
101. Morenz, 1992, p. 141.
102. Morenz, 1992, p. 142.
103. Tobin, 2001, p. 83. Other permutations include Amun-Re-Amun, Amun-Re-Montu, Amun-Re-Horakhty, and Min-Amun.
104. Tobin, 2001, p. 84.
105. Wilkinson, 2003. p. 63.
106. Tobin, 2001, p. 84.
107. Tobin, 2001, p. 84.
108. Tobin, 2001, p. 84.
109. Tobin, 2001, p. 84.
110. V28-D28-G1-G43-X1-A1-Z2.
111. N35-O4-X1-Y1-Z2.
112. U28-G1-G43-V1-Z2.
113. V28-D28-G1-A2.
114. G5-N37-X1-U30-N16-N16; N37-X1-Z1-G1-Y1; N37-N16; N37-N16-U30-G1-9-Y1, etc.
115. G39-Z8-Z2; N37-X1-U30-G1-G43-M3-Z2; N37-X1-U30-G1-G43-Y1-Z2; N37-X1-U30-G1-Y1-Z2; N37-X1-U30-C1-Y1A, etc.
116. G36-D21-V28-D28-Z2; G36-D21-V28-D28-Z2-A40.
117. G36-D21-X1-V28-D28-Z2-S2; G36-D21-X1-V28-D28-Z2-S2-S4.
118. Ritner, 2001a, pp. 321–326.
119. Pinch, 2006, p. 10.
120. V28-D28-M17-M17-Y1-A40; V28-D28-G1-G43-A2, etc.
121. V7-N35-W24-Z7-A2-A1.
122. D21-Aa1-Y1-B1.
123. V17-G43-A1; V17-Z7-A1.

124. G25-Aa1-Z7-A2-Z2. Which also meant power of a god, magic, magical words, useful knowledge, mastery (G25-Aa1-G43-Z3).
125. F18-D28-A2-Z2.
126. V28-D28-G1-A2-Z3; V28-D28-G1-Z7-A2-Z3; V28-D28-G1-Z7-Y1-Z2, etc. Also means magic, magic spells, incantations.
127. Q3-D36-Q3-D36-F18-A2.
128. Q3-O4-U33-M17.
129. Q3-V13-U33-M17.
130. S29-Aa18-G1-U33-M7-D54.
131. V13-G43-D58-S29.
132. V13-M22-M22-G43-M17-M17.
133. V13-O4-W24-G43-N33A.
134. D21-Z1-V31-G1-A2.
135. E23-Z1-D21-Z1-A2.
136. G17-G43-M17-M17.
137. G17-M17-G43.
138. G17-U33-G43-U33.
139. I9-M22-M22-G43-M17-M17.
140. O4-G1-G17-G1-T14-Z5; O4-G1-G17-Z7-T14-Z5.
141. V7-N35-X1-V1-A2; V7-N35-X1-Y1-A2; V7-N35-X1-Y1-V1.
142. U24-X1-D21.
143. N40-G17-Z7-A2.
144. D21-Z1-I10-D46-Y1-Z2.
145. S29-E34-N35-W24-Z7-Y1-A24; T11-W24-G43-A1- T11-W24-Z1-A1, etc. Also *ḥry ḥkꜣ* (D2-D21-Z3-V28-D28-Z3).
146. G1-Aa1-G43-N8; G25-Aa1-N8; N8-G7.
147. N8-G43-A40.
148. G25-Ya-Z2; G25-Aa1-Y1-Z2; G25-Aa1-Z2-G43.
149. G25-Z2.
150. G25-Z7.
151. G25-Z7-Y1-Z2; G25-Aa1-Z7-Y1-Z2; X1-G25-Aa1-Z2.
152. G25-Aa1-G43-Y1.
153. G25-Aa1-G43-Y1-Z2; G25-Aa1-G43-Z3.
154. G25-Aa1-Y1-M17-M17-A51-Z3; Ga-Aa1-G43-G25-G25-G25.
155. G25-Aa1-Z7-A2-Z2.
156. M17-Aa1-Z2; N8-N8-N8.
157. David, 2002, p. 83. See Lesko, 1991, for a discussion on cosmogonies and cosmology.
158. Wilkinson, 2003, p. 19.
159. David, 2002, p. 83.
160. David, 2002, p. 83.
161. David, 2002, p. 83.
162. David, 2002, p. 83.
163. Morenz, 1992, p. 167.
164. Pinch, 2004, p. 75.
165. Wilson, 1965, p. 49.
166. Wilson, 1965, p. 3.

167. Silverman, 1997, 121.
168. From the root *tm*, meaning complete, finish.
169. Silverman, 1997, p. 123.
170. Silverman, 1997, p. 125.
171. Silverman, 1997, pp. 126–127.
172. Wilson, 1965, p. 60.
173. David, 2002, p. 87.
174. Jaynes, 1976, p. 186.
175. Personified as Sia, the god of knowledge, insight, and reason.
176. Similar to Ptah in the Memphite Tradition, the goddess Neith also used divine speech for purposes of creation.
177. Ritner, 2001a, pp. 321–326.
178. Jaynes, 1976, p. 186.
179. Jaynes, 1976, p. 186.
180. Jaynes, 1976, p. 186.
181. Morenz, 1992, p. 165.

Chapter 6

Voices and Visions from the Gods

"He who God loves, hears,
but he who God hates hears not."
— *Instructions of Ptahhotep*

THEOPHANIC AND REVELATORY EXPERIENCES

THERE ARE MANY EXAMPLES of the recorded words of gods. Merneptah (1213–1204 BCE), vexed by Egypt's enemies, dreamt that a huge statue of Ptah stood before him and extended a scimitar and said: "Take thou this. Banish thou the faint heart from thee."[1] Other examples are the Poetical Stela of Thutmose III (Tuthmosis III; 1479–1425 BCE), in which the god Amun-Re gives a speech,[2] and the Stela of Amenhotep III (1390–1353 BCE).[3] From an inscription about his coronation, we learn how Thutmose III was chosen by the oracle of Amun-Re for his kingly duty:

> [the statue] began wandering through the colonnade ...And the men leading it did not understand that it was looking everywhere for my majesty. When it reached me, it stopped ... I threw myself on my belly before him, I groveled in the dust, I bowed down in front of him ... he opened the gates of heaven for me, he unlocked the doors of the horizon and I flew up to heaven like a divine falcon ...[4]

Accounts of the appearance of a god (VVV) were "abundantly authenticated in Egypt," according to Morenz.[5] These reports refer to the continuous recurrence of what has long existed and is well known — like "stars in the evening."[6] Of course, not all recountings of divine appearances were hallucinatory, but references to theophanies arguably point to earlier periods when visitations by deities were not considered unusual.

Before proceeding, some background theorizing that links population growth, social control, neurolinguistics, and hallucinations will contextualize the issues surrounding VVVs.

POPULATION SIZE AND HALLUCINATIONS

Demographic scale configures linguistic change. In other words, as social units expand in size and become more complex (role diversification, social relations, technoeconomics, etc.), languages must keep up. Such changes have both neurological and cultural implications. The origin of voice-emitting supernatural beings can probably be traced back to pre-Neolithic times, sometime before or around the agricultural revolution. The idea is that right hemisphere's linguistic regions (RHA) developed hallucinatory "self-talk," i.e., a person would "hear" his or her own voice (or possibly that of an absent clan leader). Such auto-speech was a side effect of language comprehension, selected by socioevolution as a method of behavioral control. Such social management became necessary because early *Homo sapiens* lacked the ability to stay on task for time-consuming undertakings (stalking or chasing down prey, chipping away at stone tools to make them sharper, etc.).

> Let us consider a man commanded by himself or his chief to set up a fish weir far upstream from a campsite. If he is not conscious, and cannot therefore narratize the situation and so hold his analog 'I' in a spatialized time with its consequences fully imagined, how does he do it? It is only language ... that can keep him at this time-consuming all-afternoon work. A Middle Pleistocene man would forget what he was doing.[7]

Language provided humans with the capability to remind themselves by means of repeated hallucinated auto-speech how to complete enduring tasks. Articulate speech had become unilateralized in the left hemisphere, thereby freeing up the brain's right side for hallucinated voices that could maintain prolonged activities. This looping auto-command reminded an individual to stay on task when carrying out repetitive chores, ensuring social order, and economic productivity. Auto-speech was adequate for small-scale, close-knit, hunter–gatherer or early agrarian economics. But from approximately 10,000 BCE, the agricultural revolution brought about pressures whose social intricacy — increased demographic scale, economic specialization, more explicit, stable social roles — radically reconfigured auto-communication.

As group size increased, more and more social control-at-a-distance became necessary. In other words, divine voices and visions, generated by the right hemisphere (the commanding supernatural entity), communicated with the left hemisphere (the obeying "mortal"). The result was a neurocultural adaptation in which controlling voices were attributed to those further up a widening and towering social pyramid — i.e., divinized ancestors, departed rulers, god–kings, or the gods themselves. Bronze Age sociopolitical hierarchies, mediated through divine voices and visions, were reflected architecturally by sky-scraping ziggurats and awe-inspiring temples. Decision-making resulted from a dialogue between a dominant supernatural entity that "spoke" to a "person." "Revelations" were interpreted as the directives of absent clan leaders, ancestors, deceased/divinized rulers, or gods (similar to the command hallucinations experienced by people who hear voices today). As populations expanded and urbanization took root, then, verbal hallucinations provided social control and authorization became deeply entangled in theopolitical hierarchies.

DIVINE VOICES AND VISIONS IN ARCHAIC EGYPT

What is the situation in archaic Egypt? Before proceeding, two caveats are in order. First, interpreting the evidence is difficult. For instance, an image portrays a painter named Neb-Re in the Temple of Karnak thanking Amun for curing his son. We moderns are unsure as to how to interpret this. Is Neb-Re really kneeling before a statue of the god in the forecourt? Or is he experiencing a hallucinatory theophany of the god, who emerges "from the pylon of his sanctuary and manifesting himself to Neb-Re?"[8] Religious imagery since the beginning of the first millennium BCE was created by conscious individuals, though they harked back to preconscious times for inspiration. For example, in the barque chapel in the Temple of Luxor, a relief depicts Alexander worshiping his "god–father" Amun–Min, and at the Temple of Amun at the Siwa Oasis he is seen paying homage to his "father" Amun–Re. In another example a stela from the second century BCE in the Temple of Dendera shows the pharaoh Ptomley VIII Euergetes II (followed by his sister Cleopatra II and his wife Cleopatra III) making offerings to the triad of Amun–Re, Mut, and Khonsu. It is highly unlikely these representations were of actual extraceptive encounters, since they were made centuries after the breakdown of bicameral mentality. In other instances, the *Instructions of Papyrus Insinger* (probably from the latter part of the Ptolemaic period) tells us that it is the "god who gives calm and unrest through his commands"[9] and the "patience of a wise man is to consult with the god."[10] These examples, despite referring to speaking gods, come from an age when the deities had stopped visiting pharaohs, at least on a regular basis.

As for the second caveat, it is likely that only kings for most of the pharaonic period experienced directive hallucinations from the great gods; such experiences did occur among ordinary subjects, but perhaps were attributed to local deities, personal gods, ancestors, or other numina. Undoubtedly, not all representations of ruler–deity interactions were inspired by hallucinatory theophanic experiences. It of course depends on the period.

Divine Appearances

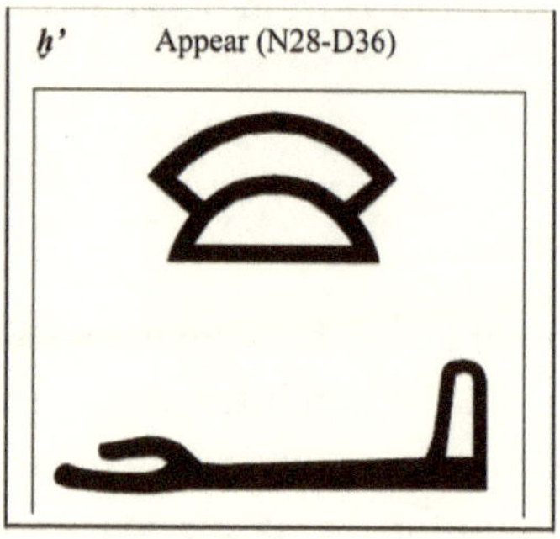

The term *ḫprw* has a host of meanings, such as appearance;[11] become;[12] form; shape; modes of being; change;[13] transformation;[14] evolution; development.[15] It appears in expressions such as "assume a shape" (*ir ḫprw*).[16] It can also mean "those living now" (Table 6.1).[17] Revelation might come through nature. For instance, at the end of Dynasty 11, the Vizier Amenemhet, while on an expedition, witnessed the god Min manifest himself via a pregnant gazelle that approached the Vizier's quarrying crew and then gave birth.[18]

Divine Emanations and Manifestations

In the same way deities could join and combine with others, they could also divide themselves into various emanations or Bau (*bꜣw*). This term actually had other similar meanings, such as a divine manifestation of an individual (Table 6.2).[43] Such manifestations could act as divine messengers (IB, SV) and were often ranked with "demons and ghosts as enemies of humanity."[44] Such emissaries were greatly feared.[45] Examples include

Table 6.1. Some Hieroglyphic Variants of "Appear."

No.	Term	Possible Translation
1.	*ḫꜥ / ḫꜥꞽ*[19]	Appear
2.	*ḫꜥ*[20]	(1) festival of appearance; (2) appear
3.	*ḫꜥ*[21]	Arise in glory
4.	*ḫꜥ*[22]	The appearing one (Re)
5.	*ḫꜥꞽ*[23]	Rise (of sun), appear in glory (of god or king), be shining (of kings)
6.	*ḫꜥ*[24]	Appear
7.	*ḫꜥt*[25]	Appearance
8.	*ḫꜥw*[26]	(1) crown; (2) rising (of sun, moon, stars), rise, appear in glory
9.	*ḫꜥw*[27]	Appearance in glory
10.	*ḫꜥw*[28]	Processional appearance
11.	*ḫꜥw*[29]	Manifestations
12.	*kꜣ*[30]	Appear
13.	*prꞽ*[31]	(1) go, come out, escape, be renowned, report; (2) display, show, be visible, be apparent (and other meanings)
14.	*prꞽ*[32]	Go forth, emerge, escape, issue, leave, proceed
15.	*pr*[33]	(1) be issued (supplies), delivered; (2) display, show, visible, apparent
16.	*prꞽ*[34]	Come forth
17.	*prꞽ ḫrw*[35]	Offer up (a sacrifice)
18.	*šfyt*[36]	Awfulness, respect, fear, majesty, majestic, appearance
19.	*sḫꜥ*[37]	Cause to appear (of a god or king), display (object), to arise
20.	*sḫꜥy*[38]	Cause to appear (of a god or king), display (object)
21.	*wbn*[39]	Rise, shine (of sun)
22.	*wbn*[40]	(1) rising; (2) rise, shine, glitter, appear, overflow, be excessive, run out of (fluid from body); (3) sprout, open up (of plants)
23.	*wbn*[41]	Rise, shine, to dawn
24.	*wbn*[42]	Shine

the Scorpion Goddess Serqet, who manifested as a woman with a scorpion on her head (She Who Causes [One] to Breathe) (note, however, in some contexts Serqet could be helpful). Significantly, most of the written evidence of hostile deities and messenger demons dates from the twelfth century BCE, when the need for IB and SV became salient, since the major gods had by now retired and grown reticent.[46]

Table 6.2. Meanings of Bau.

No.	Possible Translation	Term
1.	Souls, spirits[47]	*b3w*
2.	Souls, Bas[48]	
3.	Souls (of dead), manifestations[49]	
4.	Souls (of dead); glory, respect, authority, power, strength, fate[50]	
5.	Power[51]	
6.	Glory, respect, authority, power, strength, fate; might; impressiveness; souls; Bas[52]	
7.	Power, might, strength, will, glory, prowess, fame, wrath[53]	
8.	Souls (of dead), power, deed of power[54]	

Commands, Guidance, and Inspiration

Frankfort wrote that the "actions of the community were guided by the divine king with whom alone the other gods communicated."[55] I am not sure what Frankfort had in mind with the word "communicated," but I submit that hallucinatory, extraceptive experiences characterized such communication. Frankfort continued by writing that the "actions of individuals lacked divine guidance altogether."[56] Again I am not sure what he meant by "divine guidance," but I contend that the archaic Egyptians did receive divine communications (SV).

When direct god-to-mortal communication (VVVs) began to erode, the appearance of messengers from other realms increased to maintain the moral order (e.g., revenants, ghosts, demons, vengeful spirits). Frankfort also claims that we "do not even find that a rule of conduct or a set of 'teachings' is recommended as inspired or approved by a god."[57] This I think is debatable. In any case, perhaps the permeation of godly authorization into the sociopolitical fabric precluded such an explicitly stated need (in the same way many conscious individuals do not inquire about their ability to mentally introceive images).

Morenz describes the interactions between the divine and mortal worlds by classifying communication types into: (1) divine commandments; (2) divine guidance; and (3) divine inspiration.[58] These indicate increasing levels of conscious interiority. Divine commandments (VVVs) are common in myths, as when the gods order kings about. This category includes "commands of the king" (*wḏ nsw*) (or a royal decree, royal writ).[59] Next, with divine guidance, we discern the inklings of interiorization and self-autonomy. The heart (*ib*) is regarded as the gateway for divine guidance. From sometime during the 1500s BCE, a scribe writes that the "heart of a man [is] his God himself." We can see here the "organ through which God guides a man lacking in willpower, or at least unable to make up his mind."[60] Finally, with divine inspiration, the "heart which brings up its lord as one who hears [or] as one who does not hear." In other words, this organ itself is the focus of decision-making or it is utilized by divinity to elicit action. Thus the gods "caused that [thought] should be in their hearts"; "God puts [thought] into [a person's] heart to do it"; and "God put [all] this into my heart so as to make my lifetime on earth long."[61]

THE SELF-DEIFICATION OF KINGS

Though perhaps odd to the modern mind, kings could be depicted "in their normal guise offering to their divine alter egos."[62] In the New Kingdom, a king might be portrayed in his priestly capacity, "confronting his own divine image."[63] Amenhotep III makes an offering to his deified self in his temple at Soleb in Upper Nubia.[64] A relief of Sety I (1290–1279 BCE) from his temple at Abydos depicts him offering incense to his deified self. In the Great Temple of Abu Simbel, Ramesses II (1279–1213 BCE) of Dynasty 19 makes an offering to himself. In these depictions, noted one observer, the king is "worshipping not himself." Rather, the focus of worship is the "concept of deified kingship as represented in the royal *kꜣ* [inherited life force], which he embodies."[65] This may be a valid explanation, but arguably these depictions point to autoscopic hallucinations.

Just as the gods had a divine and worldly existence (in the form of images), the "living king was himself a manifestation of the earthly Horus, as opposed to the god Horus in the heavens. Thus, a king deified in his own lifetime — within the physical sphere — could sacrifice to his own self as a deity in the spiritual sphere" (Chart 6.1).[66]

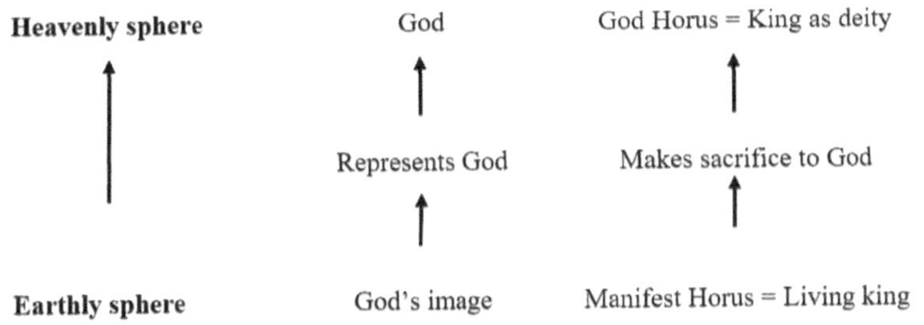

Chart 6.1. Correspondence between Heavenly and Earthly Spheres.

THE AUTHORITATIVE POWERS OF SPEECH

The very connective tissue of sociopolitical human communications is speech. In Egyptian cosmology, the voice carried a special meaning, conveying messages between gods, kings, and mortals. The term *ḥw*[67] — meaning (royal) ordinance, authoritative utterance, dictum, or command — most likely indicated auditory hallucinations. However, this divine speech operated at a grander, cosmic level, since as Hu it signified the creative commands that brought the world into existence. It was Hu, the words of the self-created primordial god Ptah of the Memphite tradition, that materialized his thoughts.[68] Authoritative verbalizations were personified as the god Hu. Speech, then, was at the intersection of cosmic creation, hallucinated verbalizations, and pharaonic control.

Voices from the Living Dead

To test Jaynesian psychology, an important line of research would be to investigate the role of "voice" and "hearing" in archaic Egyptian. Consider the epithet appended to the name of the deceased: "True of voice" (*mꜣʿ ḫrw)*[69] (also glossed as triumphant, deceased, be justified, vindicated). Originally this was applied to Osiris and Horus, with reference to their victories over their enemies, and was implicated in the judgment of the dead. But the expression "true of voice," rather than meaning the "acclaim that is given to an individual is true," supports Jaynes's contention[70] that the living were still hearing the voices of the deceased. From the point of view of the hallucinator, such voices could be trusted. A related term is *smꜣʿ ḫrw*,[71] meaning to justify (the dead, the living) and triumph. Also, note that the "invocation of offerings" (*prt ḫrw*) describes what was said to the dead when presenting them offerings. It literally means "the coming out to the voice."[72] And note the related expression *pri ḫrw*[73] that means to offer up (a sacrifice).

Hearing and Obeying

The counterpart of speaking is listening, and the term *sḏm*, besides meaning hearing, also meant to obey as well as solving a problem, suggesting the semantic overlap of listen–cogitate–submit, i.e., hearing a voice was tantamount to following a command (Table 6.3).

Table 6.3. Some Hieroglyphic Variants of "Hear."

No.	Possible Translation	Term
1.	(1) obey, understand, judge, satisfy (conditions); (2) hear (voice, etc.), hear of (something), listen (to)[74]	*sḏm*
2.	(1) solution (to a mathematical example), interrogation, examination; (2) attendant, servant; (3) listen, obey, understand, judge, satisfy (conditions); (4) hear (voice, etc.), hear of (something), listen (to)[75]	
3.	(1) solution (to a mathematical example); (2) obey, understand, judge, satisfy (conditions); (3) hear (voice, etc.), hear of (something), listen (to)[76]	

OBJECTS OF HALLUCINATORY FOCUS

Instances of paralogic identification were abundant in archaic Egypt. We are used to distinguishing a thing itself from its reproductions, replicas, and duplicates. But in archaic cultures, a cultic object was more than just a substitute; it was a living double imbued with efficacy and potency. Statues, after all, possessed a corporeality, and they required food, drink, and sex. Note that in Dynasties 5 and 6, statues of foreign captives were "executed"; the modern mind may see this practice as mere "ritual," but it is doubtful if the contemporary observers would always see much of a difference between reflective and identification symbols.

Images as Living Persons and "Distributed Personhood"

Archaic Egyptian was replete with terms for statues, effigies, and images, illustrating the centrality of super-religious anthropomorphic OHFs (Table 6.4). One term that meant statue — *twt*[77] — indicated resemblance, likeness, be in accord with, image, figure.[78] However, it also had the meanings of gather, be assembled, collected together,[79] complete,[80] full, entire,[81] perhaps suggesting that this cultic object acted to draw together, unite, and mobilize the various aspects of personhood.

A sense of the paralogic blurring of personages and their representations is apparent in how spiritual entities relied on statuary and other imagery to "presentify" their numinous power and effectiveness. The presentification of cultic objects of ancestors or gods makes what they stand for intensely manifest, thereby enhancing their very existence.[90] Statues permitted paralogic "physical self-multiplication."[91] A replica of a king or god, *snty*,[92] asserted its presence in statuary form. In the Old Kingdom,

Table 6.4. Terms for Statues, Effigies, and Images.

No.	Term	Possible Translation
1.	*ẖnty*[82]	Statue, effigy
2.	*ẖnty 'nḫ*[83]	Living semblance
3.	*pꜣ rḫ*[84]	Cult statue, divine image
4.	*šsp*[85]	Statue, image
5.	*sšmw*[86]	Statue, portrait, image, counterpart
6.	*sšm*[87]	Image
7.	*tỉt*[88]	Image, form, shape, figure, design, (written) sign
8.	*tỉt*[89]	Amulet

double or triple groups of statues "depicted the deceased in the company of himself."[93] During the Old Kingdom, the statue began to leave the personal sphere of the *serdab*, or statue chamber (*pr twt*),[94] and was set up in the cult chamber where it was visible.[95] Divinity was conceived as simultaneously dwelling in several places. For instance, Amun's Ba was believed to live in heaven, his body (*ḏt*) in the west, and his statue (*ẖty*) in Hermonthis, located south of Thebes on the west bank of the Nile.

Kjølby discusses the role private statues played during the New Kingdom in "distributed personhood" and "extended presence of the individual."[96] Making offerings to what might seem to us stony hard and silent statues was thought of as efficacious activities. A physical likeness referred to its powerful nature, how it functioned as an actual double for a personage. A word for statue or image[97] (*šsp*) could also mean to receive;[98] take; accept; or assume;[99] and note also the expression "receive offerings" — *šsp snw*.[100] Presumably such language indicated that statues were key components of a cycle of exchange between mortals and deities.

The idea that a statue was more than just a representation is evident in how some kings presented sacrifices to deified statues of themselves. In the later New Kingdom period, some statues were regarded as divine entities in and of themselves. They were given names, owned land, had their own attending priests, and were venerated as gods in their own right. Evidence for this is seen in a collection of artifacts known as the Horbeit Stelae. In one of these representations, the Seti-er-nedeh Stela, a deified Ramesses II (1279–1213 BCE) is depicted in western Thebes among Amun and Ptah in such a way that it is clear his statue possesses stand-alone divinity. In another stela, a colossal statue of Ramesses stands next to a smaller figure of the king who is apparently a divine manifestation of the statue.[101]

Merging Person and Representation

While it was believed that the Ba "entered" a statue, this was not exactly a spatially dualistic event (an entity from the outside entering the inside of a container). Such an interpretation is a later intellectual development. The external-versus-internal perspective, while descriptively accurate to a degree, fails to capture the more nuanced archaic Egyptian view. Rather than two separable entities coming together (indwelling, installation), the process was one of merging.[102] The modern clear-cut dualistic distinction between subject and object was absent.

The word *ḏt*[103] could mean one's actual body; an image; bodily form (of god, statues); self; or person. The distinction among these was not necessarily clear. Another relevant term is *'ẖm*,[104] meaning the sacred image of a god (*'ẖmw* / *'ẖm* can also mean voracious spirits or a crocodile as a demonic animal).[105] The "statue was a materialization of its owner, his mind, person, and identity."[106] It functioned simultaneously as agent (something imbued with power) and patient (something created and ritually acted upon) in relation to other participants.[107] The image was perceived as a "life-extender, a physical manifestation of a living being, hosting or giving form."[108] Manifesting in a statue was a mode of being (*ḫprw*). The statue of a god is not the "image" of that god but its body; it does not "represent" the deity's form but rather gives it form. In the same way a god manifested him or herself in a sacred animal or natural phenomena, a god is self-expressed via an image.[109]

This archaic way of thinking can be perhaps appreciated from the word used for "making" (*msi*)[110] a statue; it means to bear; give birth; to form; or fashion. The sculptor was known as *s'nḫ*;[111] this same term could mean to bestow life; perpetuate;[112] make live; preserve; revive (the dead); nourish; feed; perpetuate (name); sculpture.[113]

Eyes, Ears, and Audiovisual Hallucinations

The role of sensory stimulation in the effecting of communication cannot be neglected. For example, the radiance (of a god) (*i3ḫw*) is often encountered[114] or the radiant one (an epithet of the sun god) (*wbnni*).[115]

Especially popular in the New Kingdom was the prominent display of the "ear motif," seen in shrines placed on the outer walls of many temples.[116] Ears, presumably to persuade the deity to harken to the petitioner's pleas,[117] were carved on amulets, stelae, and votive statuettes to signify the listening of gods (or perhaps worshipers "hearing" the gods speak?).[118] Objects in the shape of the human ear have also been found.[119] Sometimes just one huge pair of ears was depicted, so as to drive home the point that a petitioner wanted to be heard. Examples include the "Ear Stela of Bai," representing the divine hearing of a worshiper's pleas. Another example is the Stela of Penbuy, dedicated to Ptah (from Dynasty 19).

Not surprisingly, eyes played an important role in representations; they could have a striking visual impact. Though speculative, it is possible that statuary with jewel-like glaring eyes locked in an observer's gaze, so that hallucinatory messages were more readily transmitted. Jaynes devoted attention to the salient role of eyes in ancient statuary. He notes that among many mammals, in particular primates, eye-to-eye contact can be used to establish authoritative relations. Eye-to-eye contact is extremely important as it implicates hierarchy and submission. In humans, however, its social significance is much more subtle and complicated. Jaynes argued that ocular iconography in past civilizations enhanced authority relationships and hallucinatory experiences.[120] In Egypt, eyes on stelae are quite common (usually in the Middle Kingdom). The "reciprocal act of seeing and being seen plays a fundamental role in Egyptian ideas about the manifestation of the dead."[121] Eyes signify the "presence of the deceased for the object of the mortuary rituals by positing a gaze which can be met by the 'audience' of the stela."[122] Note also how the god Sia was described as being in the eye of Re, so that the sun god could see and understand all events in the world.

The Wadjet (*wḏꜣt*),[123] an amulet of protection, exemplifies the power of the gaze. Known as the Eye of Horus (*wḏꜣ*)[124] or the Whole One, this symbol was associated with Hathor, Isis, and Sekmet, the cobra goddess (*wꜣḏt / wꜣdineyt*),[125] as well as being personified as the goddess Wadjet. It was a key element in the mythology of the Nile River. Symbolizing the sun and moon, it functioned as a separate spiritual entity. The Wadjet, typically made from blue or green faience, sometimes with semiprecious stones set in gold, was worn both by the living and by the deceased (in mummy wrappings). This protective insignia has a storied and complex mythology behind it: Horus lost his eye in battle with Seth while trying to avenge his father, Osiris. Horus's eye was broken into six pieces. Each fragment was linked to one of the six senses, as well as a specific fraction. Isis restored what came to be known as "the healthy eye."

Similar in meaning to the Eye of Horus, the Eye of Re (*ỉrt rʿ*),[126] was considered Re's daughter and protector, associated with fire and water; her fierce glance could destroy enemies while her tears created life. The Eyes of Re–Atum also could create new life, and other goddesses, such as Bastet, Hathor, and Mut were called the Eye of Atum and the Eye of Re. The eye of the creator god was thought of as different celestial bodies, such as the sun disk, the full moon, or the morning star.[127]

There is no reason to assume that hallucinatory experiences were limited to auditory or visual modes. Robyn Price applies a sensory analysis which goes beyond the vision-centered mode by examining tomb depictions of banquets and relevant mortuary texts from the New Kingdom (from around 1550 BCE).[128] She argues that the archaic Egyptians "recognized a certain scent as representative of divinity and that this fragrance could be used to identify divine presence."[129] For the Egyptians, the gods carried a particular smell. Such recognition would have been an extraceptive olfactory experience. Though speculative, the identifiable scent exuded by the gods was possibly a hallucination that evoked their invisible but divine presence.

The Use of Stelae

Stelae, pillar or vertical tablets made of stone or wood, used inscriptions, reliefs, or paintings to impart information. They came in numerous shapes and styles, and functioned as tombstones (usually placed outside tombs to name the tomb owner), boundary markers, and votive and commemorative monuments (to mark special events or to convey biographical information). The most common terms were *wḏ*,[130] *ʿḥʿ*,[131] and *ʿḥʿw* (also meaning monument, grave stone).[132]

Ancestor stelae "provided an interface for two-way communication between the living and the dead."[133] In Deir el-Medina, within the artisan district near the Valley of the Kings at Thebes, about 55 stelae have been recovered. The function of what have been called ancestor busts is not clear. They have mostly been discovered in houses and may have been intended to protect the family, as was apparently the case with anthropoid bust amulets.[134] They mostly date from the New Kingdom and have been found mainly in Deir el-Medina. Whatever their exact purpose (possibly OHF), they evidence ancestor cult practices.

THE WRITTEN WORD AND DIVINE COMMUNICATION

The main purpose of hieroglyphs was to allow the king to communicate with the gods and ancestors for the sake of humanity.[135] They were believed to possess an active potency that could shape reality and may have operated as a type of OHF in certain contexts. Since iconography was not merely representational but functional, one could share this potency by touching images and inscriptions. Besides rulers, ritual objects, monumental architecture, and other OHFs, the written word may have elicited extraceptive experiences. Hieroglyphs (*mdw nṯr*) — sacred writings,[136] word of god, divine decree[137] — may have been "heard" (hallucinated) by those who could read or had access to them. And note that some of these sacred writings were not merely ornamental, since they were often inscribed in areas or on funerary goods where "they would not be visible once the burial was sealed."[138] This was also true of sculptural works, which were "immured in a dark chamber, far removed from the gaze of potential viewers."[139] The written word and images were integrated in representations. This is seen in the use of *twt*[140] (cult statue, image, figure, likeness) upon which words were inscribed. It may be that divine words prompted and combined both auditory and visual modes of hallucinations in ways we do not yet understand.

INTERCESSIONARY BEINGS

As the god-ordered and ordained cosmopolity gradually lost its predictability and assuredness over the centuries, evil-doing entities began to inhabit the psychoscape of individuals. Natural calamities, disease, personal misfortune, nightmares, and what we might call mental disorders became personified as demons, as bicameral authorization went into decline; individuals searched for explanations in a progressively complex world. The realm of haunting and harassing numina expanded. On the other hand guardian spirits acted as intermediary beings, who granted mortals favors. This was a pattern visible all over the ancient world, including Mesopotamia, which saw an increase in witchcraft, various forms of protective magic, demonology, recourse to omens, and appeals to oracles. These practices lasted into the Late Period and beyond.[141]

Ghosts, Welcome and Unwelcome

Evidence that the ancient Egyptians believed in the living dead is textually and architecturally corroborated. Ritner notes that because a "pervasive system of necromancy" permeated ancient Egyptian life, it "has typically gone unnoticed."[142] Indeed, communication with the dead, "whether for blessing, advice, information, healing or protection, is a central feature of state-sponsored literature, public veneration and oracles, funereal spells, private correspondence, and domestic cult." It could be that not all communication with ancestors (or any supernatural entity, for that matter), being relatively routine and casual, left a trace.[143] Communication was neither rigidly formulaic nor prayer-like. It was characterized by a matter-of-fact chattiness and focused on family matters, personal guilt, family property, inheritance, the fertility of spouses, or affliction by ghosts. Petitioners could be anxious, cajoling, or indignant.

The deceased were categorized as either the blessed, justified dead (Akh) or as the unjustified dead (*mt / mwt*).[144] The former might appear as benevolent ghosts, while the latter were associated with nightmares and other vexations. Those who died violently or prematurely or did not receive the proper funerary offerings could cause nightmares, illnesses, and what we describe as mental or emotional disorders. One might feel they were being watched by a ghost. Those unjustified dead or ghosts seem to have been part of a general category of assorted troublemakers — demons and evil spirits — from the beyond. Lettuce, garlic, and honey (poison to ghosts) were used to keep the returning dead away.

Evidence of the belief in ghosts is abundant, as seen in execration, or the ritualized destruction of depictions or objects related to individuals. Execration texts could be inscribed on pottery or figurines and listed cities and even individuals in Palestine and southern Syria as enemies. By damaging such portrayals, the numinosity of the deceased depicted was diminished or even destroyed. Such rituals could also be used against the living. "Breaking the reds pots" (*sḏ dšrt*) was an execration ceremony in which pottery was inscribed with the names of one's enemies and smashed. The execration of tombs became prevalent in the New Kingdom Period. Images of the Pharaoh-queen Hateshepsut (1473–1458 BCE) were vandalized. The entire city of Akhetaten was razed, after its founder Akhenaten passed away, taking with him his unorthodox henotheistic belief in the Aten.

The Egyptians did not fear ghosts because they were uncanny intrusions from the beyond. Rather, they were apprehensive about the trouble they might visit upon the living. Their "ghost stories" lack the eeriness we moderns associate with such tales. Consider a "ghost story" dated to the Ramesside Period, which recounts an encounter with the ghost Nebusemekh and Khomsehab, a high priest of Amun at Thebes. Nebusemekh worked in the service of Rahotep II (ca. 1640 BCE), in Dynasty 17. Rahotep arranged Nebusemekh's burial, but the tomb of the latter was destroyed. The tale is incomplete, but Khomsehab seems to have found a new tomb for the ghost on the western shore of Thebes.

Probably related to ghosts and demons are what we call spirit possession/personation (an instance of eroding or vestigial bicamerality). This is evidenced by terms such as *šnw*[145] (conjurer, magician, exorcist) and *rḫt*[146] (wise woman, female healer, skilled woman); these may have been shamanistic mediums who relied on Heka.

Demons and Spiritual Guardians

Demons are difficult to define or distinguish from other beings. They were rarely depicted visually and they came in different types. Some were blamed for possession or sicknesses. An instance of the latter is *wḫdw*,[147] which meant not only "disease demon" but also illness, pain, and inflammation (Table 6.5). Demons, the unjustified dead, and other enemies of Maat were forced to live a reversed life in the Duat. These beings, who were not immediately relegated to a permanent death, were condemned to suffer tortures. These might include "upside down, inside out, with even their digestion reversed: in Egyptian terms eating their own feces and drinking their own urine."[148] These were known as "the bound ones," or "those who are under the punishing knife." A number of what seem to be demonic beings appear in funerary literature such as the *Coffin Texts*, *Book of the Dead*, and other texts.[149] These beings are often represented as knife-wielding animals or hybrids of animals. Typically they are unnamed but are known by epithets, such as Big and Fiery; Bellower; the Rapacious One; He Whose Face Is Hot (*nby m ḥr f*);[150] God Who Lives on Meat-sacrifice; Dog-faced; Human-skinned; Keeper of the Bend of the Waterway of Fire; Who Swallows Shadows; Who Snatches Hearts; Throws the Lasso and Yet Is Not Seen."[151] Though categorized as gods (*nṯr*), they were clearly not grouped with the major gods who had their own names and cults.[152] They were depicted as fierce and violent, but they were not necessarily hostile to people. Some were tasked with protecting the gods and ensuring the safe passage of the justified dead. They guarded the sacred routes and doorways of the afterlife. In this sense they are best understood as genii or guardian spirits.[153]

Table 6.5. Types of Demons.

No.	Term	Possible Translation
1.	*nbd*[154]	Demon, evil one
2.	*'ḥꜣ*[155]	Demon
3.	*gmtyw*[156]	
4.	*ḥꜣytyw*[157]	
5.	*ḫndw*[158]	
6.	*nḏr*[159]	
7.	*sỉtỉw*[160]	
8.	*'ḏn*[161]	Disease demon (a demon that causes illness)
9.	*ỉbsn*[162]	
10.	*ỉnyt*[163]	
11.	*wrt*[164]	The Great One
12.	*ḫꜣyty*[165]	Knife demon, disease demon, demon that causes illness
13.	*nỉk*[166]	Serpent Demon
14.	*ỉtmw*[167]	Demon that causes disease of the nose
15.	*nbd*[168]	Evil One, demon
16.	*nsyt / nsyy*[169]	Demon that causes illness, epilepsy
17.	*nḫt*[170]	Demon, water spirit
18.	*hyt*[171]	Demon monster, female beast, disease demon
19.	*kꜣp*[172]	Hidden One, a disease demon
20.	*sbỉ*[173]	Rebel Serpent, a demon
21.	*smḥ*[174]	Demons with the evil eye
22.	*sḳr*[175]	Stroke, a demon causing illness
23.	*spspw*[176]	Disease demon
24.	*wꜣy*[177]	
25.	*ṯmḳn*[178]	
26.	*mḥy*[179]	Serpent demon
27.	*swꜣ*[180]	The Passer By
28.	*ḫmyw*[181]	Evil entity, demon, destroyer

FESTIVALS AS THEOPHANIC ENCOUNTERS

Usually the deities hid away in dark temple shrines, but at festivals the masses had the opportunity to encounter the gods, if only indirectly. Processional festivals permitted the faithful to steal a glimpse of the awe-inspiring supernatural beings (or at least the portable shrine within which they were concealed) as they paraded through the streets. Sometimes they were floated down the Nile on boats to visit local shrines or necropolises.

It seems that "appear" (*ḫ'i*) and "festival" (*ḫ'*) are cognates,[182] and Morenz suggests[183] that "festival" and "appearance" were semantically linked in *ḫ'*[184] and *ḫ'w*.[185] Egyptians had a long list of words for types of festivals (Table 6.6 lists a brief sampling). It was at these gatherings that the gods made an appearance, together with the pharaoh and the priests, who staged and managed the events. Gods would leave their secluded temple sanctuaries and then be carried on a barque in a small shrine by the priests. Indeed, the appearance of the god was regarded as the key element of a festival. The link between theophanies and festivals is indicated in numerous expressions, such as a festival of appearance (*ḫ'*);[186] festival of the arrival of the gods (*pḥ nṯr*);[187] a festival relating to the unveiling of a god's image (*wn ḥr*);[188] a festival for the arrival of the gods (*pḥ nṯr*);[189] festival for entry of a god in a procession (*s'ḳ nṯr*).[190]

Table 6.6. Terms for Festival.

No.	Term	Translation
1.	*tp ȝbd*[191]	Festival of beginning of the month
2.	*tp nwy*[192]	Festival
3.	*tp*[193]	
4.	*hdn ḫtwt ḫr*[194]	
5.	*ḏt*[195]	
6.	*hȝkr*[196]	
7.	*wp*[197]	
8.	*msyt*[198]	
9.	*'ḫ pt*[199]	Festival, celebration
10.	*ȝbd*[200]	Monthly festival
11.	*'k r pt*[201]	Festival of accession into heaven

Answers from the Gods

Oracular practices can be traced to preconscious times, but as bicameral mentality broke down and the gods grew silent, individuals searched for new ways to commune with the divine. This is why most documents relating to oracles do not predate the New Kingdom; most come from the Ramesside and Third Intermediate Periods.[202] Four sources of oracles can be discerned: (1) oracular decrees engraved on temple walls or delivered on papyrus to private persons to use as amulets; (2) oracular deliverances appearing in administrative or private records; (3) a few original petitions on papyrus or ostraca laid before a god; and (4) statues and reliefs linked to oracles.[203] Terms that can be translated as oracle include *bi͗ꜣyt / bi͗ꜣty* (also means omen, wonder, marvel)[204] and *ḫrtw*.[205] The latter term can mean, in addition to oracle, dictum of god or king.[206] Here we should note the related term *sr*,[207] which means prophesy.

By the New Kingdom, festivals and celebrations occasioned an increase in oracular practices. Ceremonies in which a vessel carried by priests rocked back and forth among a sea of worshipers were key rituals. The god-statue, usually hidden away in a temple, boarded a sacred barque and took questions from the swarming crowd. Then the god-statue, in response to the queries, piloted his barque in such a way that its directionality answered questions, swaying it to one side or another, moving one way for yes, in the opposite direction for no. Special shrines or stations of the gods were set up as resting places for the bearers of the barque-riding gods. These were decorated and positioned on elevated small stages, on top of which the god-statues were displayed. At these stations, oracles were also given. Priests incensed and purified participants as they paraded through the streets. These traditions probably developed from processions during festivals in which portable statues verbalized oracular utterances.[208]

Certain cult centers enshrined statues that "spoke" to devotees. Undoubtedly as individuals became conscious, priests hid behind walls and provided answers to queries for the gullible. Also, the statues of kings were asked questions and responded, indicating yes or no, by slight movements. Sacred bulls were another source of oracles. Questions were posed to the bull in a temple. The animal then answered by entering one of two chambers, indicating negative or positive responses. A famous example of an oracle temple is that of Amun in the Siwa Oasis, which supposedly was visited by Alexander the Great, the Spartan general Lysander, the poet Pindar, and the Greek geographer Strabo.

DREAMS IN ARCHAIC EGYPT

As in other archaic civilizations, the significance of dreams was far greater than moderns can appreciate. For example, the Famine Stela, located on Sehel Island, south of Aswan, dates to the Ptolemaic Period (304–30 BCE) but it is an account of a food crisis that took place in the reign of Djoser (2650–2620 BCE). The Nile had not flooded for several years. Djoser dreamt that the god Khnum chastised him for not maintaining a sacred site on Elephantine Island. When Djoser renovated and expanded the shrine, the Nile resumed its normal inundation levels. Another famous account of a divinely inspired dream concerns Thutmose IV (1400–1390 BCE); his experience has parallels in the Mesopotamian tradition. While resting beside the Great Sphinx after a hunting trip, he heard the Sphinx complain about its deplorable state. It told Thutmose that if he restored the Great Sphinx he would become pharaoh. Thutmose decided to follow through on the request and erected a stela between the giant paws of the Sphinx to commemorate the dream and his restoration work.

A distinction needs to be drawn between two types of dreams. The first type are preconscious dreams and were experienced before about 1000 BCE. These were sometimes like divination or oracles and could be a means of obtaining guidance or revelations; in some instances they might be called dream–visions. Such experiences were taken very seriously and "divine visitations"[209] while asleep were more frequent in preconscious times.

The second type are consciously interiorized dreams, which modern people typically have. Conscious dreams do not possess all the features of conscious interiority (cf. "lucid dreaming"). However, they have two related characteristics distinguishing them from preconscious dreams: (1) vicarial, or doing something other than lying in one's bed while sleeping; one's "I" in one's psychoscape is able to move about; and (2) translocal, or one believes while dreaming that one is anywhere else except in bed.[210]

To muddy the waters even more, we must make note of "waking visions," whose dream-like characteristics were perhaps interpreted as full-fledged dreams. It was "often hard to distinguish divine visitations and visions sighted in dreams from actual divine epiphanies taking place in a waking state."[211] In any case, in Egypt it is difficult to know how common visitation dreams actually were. It may have been that, even if they were common, "religious decorum generally did not allow the possibility of recording them for people of non-royal status."[212]

In the archaic Egyptian language, one did not typically dream (verb); rather one would see (*mꜣ*[213] or *mꜣw*[214]) a dream (*rswt*; a noun) whose root, strangely enough, is "awaken" (Table 6.7).[215] Thus, a dream is expressed in hieroglyphics by the symbol of bed, combined with the symbol for an open eye.[216] Dreaming meant to "awaken within sleep," so that "dreams are similar to wakefulness, despite being asleep."[217] The dream content is the "object of inner sight, an internal spectacle."[218] Asaad wonders if what we call "lucid dreaming" is being indicated, but this form of cognition was absent among people lacking full-blown conscious interiority (while dreaming transpires when some features of conscious interiority are engaged, lucid dreaming occurs when more features of conscious interiority are activated).

A Change in Dreaming Patterns

Having left behind the super-religious era when the presence of the gods was more routinely experienced, Egyptians were now in search of reconnecting with the supernatural. Dreaming opened up a door to the otherworld. Evidence of this is apparent in the practice of incubation — a person slept within a sacred precinct in an attempt to evoke meaningful dreams by having a god provide instructions to the sleeping individual.[225] Though supposedly it can be traced back to the First Intermediate Behavior (2125–2125 BCE), incubation became very common in the Late Period. Indeed, note Szpakowska's claim that for the first two millennia of Egypt's history, the mantic use (for divination or prophecy) of dreams or rituals intended to solicit such dreams is not evident.[226] We can hypothesize that as the gods and ancestors ceased communicating directly during

Table 6.7. Terms for Dreams and Nightmares.

No.	Term	Possible Translation
1.	*rswt*[219]	Dream (noun), vision
2.	*rswt / rswt tp*[220]	
3.	*rswt*[221]	Awakening, dream a vision
4.	*snḏt*[222]	Fear, nightmare, bad dream
5.	*snḏw*[223]	Terrors, bad dream
6.	*ḳdt*[224]	Dream (noun)

waking hours, dream–visions increased during later bicameral times. The "letters to the dead" from the Old Kingdom onwards requested assistance and information that were probably visualized in dreams.[227]

Prada notes that during the Graeco-Roman Period, visions of gods in "one's dreams become more and more common, or, at least, the practice of recording them becomes more widespread."[228] It is not clear if here "visions of gods" meant dreaming about gods or experiencing some sort of theophany while dreaming, but in any case by the postbicameral era a "clear line is now drawn between two types of visions of gods." The first are conscious dreams, whose subject (charged with a symbolic value) might be gods or god-like beings such as the pharaoh; "many dream accounts talk about or alluded to visions of gods."[229] This "symbolic type of divine dream" became "extremely common."[230] Dreams about gods might require recourse to exegesis and oneiromancy as their messages were not readily understandable. It makes sense, then, that the earliest Egyptian oneirocriticon (a book to interpret dreams) is from Dynasty 19 (1292–1190 BCE).[231] The second type were visitation dreams or dream–visions in which the deities themselves directly conveyed information to the dreamer.[232] Interestingly, this type of dream, in which the deity communicates a clear message, was well-attested.[233]

Explaining the Fear of Nightmares

No one likes bad dreams, but we need to ask why the archaic Egyptians so feared them. Surely such a concern, reverberating through the centuries and well represented in material culture (e.g., amulets), cannot be explained away as mere superstition. I submit that the great consternation caused by nightmares is due to how such dreams possessed a realistic intensity that is different from what modern conscious people experience.

Having a bad dream was an instance of being contacted by an entity; the dream itself seems to have been initiated by a supernatural being, rather than by the dreamer who lacked control over the experience. "When that vision was spawned by a deity, it was welcomed as an awe-inspiring theophany. But when instigated by the dead, the feelings it evoked were not necessarily so pleasant."[234] Also unwelcomed was the unsettling sensation of being watched by the dead or a demon while dreaming.[235] Three basic experiences accompany bad dreams that can be recognized in a number of spells: (1) intense dread; (2) paralysis or the inability to move; and (3) a sensation of oppression on the chest.[236] All this suggests that, in the case of nightmares, uncontrollable phenomena perceived to be "external to the dreamer" were in play.[237]

Archaic Egyptians took the threat of nightmares very seriously, as these were powerful and frightening experiences that instilled overwhelming fear within the individual. Indeed, Szpakowska suggests that dreams "terrorized" the individual; this "more clearly expresses the idea of a force which seems to be directed toward the victim."[238] The concern with these experiences is apparent in how bad dreams were listed in execration texts and special amulets were intended to guard against them.[239] From the Old and Middle Kingdom onward, it was believed that one's enemies and demons, including the military foes of Egypt, could send nightmares.[240]

Notes to Chapter 6

1. Robbins, 2001, p. 149.
2. Lichtheim, 2006b, p. 35.
3. From sometime before 1365 BCE. Lichtheim, 2006b, p. 44.
4. Cited in Tyldesley, 2019, p. 111.
5. Morenz, 1992, p. 33.
6. Morenz, 1992, p. 33.
7. Jaynes, 1976, p. 134.
8. Morenz, 1992, p. 104.
9. Lichtheim, 2006c, p. 204.
10. Lichtheim, 2006c, p. 202.
11. L1-D21-G43-N33A; L1-D21-Z7-Z6-Z2.
12. L1-D21-Y1-Z7.
13. L1-D21-Z2; L1-G43-Y1-Z2; L1-L1-L1; L1-Z2.
14. L1-D21-Z2-G43; L1-D21-Z7; L1D21-Z7-A53-Z3.
15. L1-Y1-Z2.
16. D4-L1-D21-G43-A53-Y1-Z2.
17. L1-D21-A1-Z3.
18. Hoffmeier, 2015, pp. 143, 151.
19. N28-D36; N28-D36-D36-A40; N28-D36-Z7; N28-D36-Y1-M17-M17-G7.
20. N28-D36-Y1.
21. N28-D35.
22. N28-D36-N5.
23. Aa1-D36-N28; N28-D36-Y1A.
24. N28-D36-Y1-M17-M17-A40.
25. N28-D36-X1-Y1.
26. N28.
27. N28-D36-Z2.
28. N28-D36-M17-M17-Y1-Z2; N28-D36-Z5-Z5-Z5-G7.
29. N28-Z2.

30. D28-D52-G1.
31. O1-D21-D54.
32. O1-D21-M17-D54-M17.
33. O1-D54.
34. W11-Q3-D54.
35. O1-D21-D54-P8-G43.
36. N37-I9-M17-M17-X1-Z5-Y1; Z2.
37. S29-N28.
38. S29-N28-D36-Z5-M17-M17; S29-N28-D36-M17-M17.
39. G43-D58-G23-N35-W24; G43-D58-N35-H8.
40. G43-D58-N35-N5.
41. G43-D58-N35-N5-G7; G43-D58-S3-N5.
42. Z7-D58-Z1-N35-N5.
43. Pinch, 2006, p. 36.
44. Pinch, 2006, p. 36.
45. Pinch, 2006, pp. 36–37.
46. Pinch, 2006, p. 39.
47. G29-G29-G29.
48. G29-Z1-G7-Z3A.
49. G29-Z1-Z3; G29-Z1-Z7-Z4-A40-Z3; G30-Z1-G7-G7-Z3A; G30-Z2.
50. G30.
51. G30-G43-Y1-Z2.
52. G30-Y1-Z2; G30-Z1-G7-Z2.
53. G30-Z1; G30-Z4; G30-Z6.
54. G53-Z1-A40-Z3; G53-Z1-Y1-Z2.
55. Frankfort, 2000, p. 81.
56. Frankfort also wrote that "There were no specific divine commands which gave man directives for the shaping of his actions" and he described the gods as "aloof" and indirectly relating to humankind. Frankfort, 2000, p. 81.
57. Frankfort, 2000, p. 81.
58. Morenz, 1992, pp. 57–67.
59. M23-X1-N35-G7-V5-Z7-V12-Z1.
60. Morenz, 1992, pp. 64.
61. Note that, despite its increased degree of psychologicality, Morenz writes that in its practical impact divine inspiration can have a "function very close to that to a divine command." Morenz, 1992, p. 65.
62. Baines and Malek, 2000, p. 210.
63. Morenz, 1992, p. 40.
64. Baines and Malek, 2000, p. 210.
65. Thompson, 2001, p. 330.
66. Wilkinson, 2003, p. 59.
67. V28-G43-A40; V28-G43-G7.
68. Along with Sia, *ḥw* embodies the divine creative power.
69. U5-D36-P8-G43-A2; U5-D36-Aa1-D21-P8. See also H6-P8.
70. Jaynes, 1976, p. 189.
71. S29-U1-Aa11-D36-P8-A2; S29-Aa11-D36-Y1-P8; S29-U5-D36-P8-A1.
72. O1-D21-D54-X1-X2-X4-Z2-P8-Z7-A2; O1-D21-X1-D54-D21-P8-G43-Z8-Z2. A simpler hieroglyph for *prt ḫrw* is of a house, a pitcher, bread, and voice (O3).

73. O1-D21-D54-P8-G43.
74. F21; F21-Y1.
75. F21-G17.
76. O34-I10-G17-F21; S29-G17-F21.
77. A53; A53-Z1; X1-G43-X1-A22, etc.
78. X1-X1-A53-Y1.
79. G43-X1-A53-Y1-Z2; X1-X1-A53-Z4-Y1, etc.
80. X1-G43-X1-A53, etc.
81. X1-X1.
82. D33-A53; D33-N35-U33-A22; D33-N35-U33-A53; D33-N35-X1-Z4; D33N35-X1-Z4-A22, etc.
83. D33-N35-U33-A22-S34-N35-Aa1.
84. G41-G1-D21-Aa1.
85. 2-Q3-A53; O42-Q3-E154; O42-Q3-G7, etc.
86. S29-T31-G17-G43-A40; S29-T32-G17-Y1A; S29-T32-I12, etc.
87. O34-T32; O34-T32-A40; S29-T31-Aa15-A40, etc.
88. M17-X1-D17; V13-M17-X1-D15; V13-M17-X1-D17; X1-D17, etc.
89. U33-X1-Z1-V39.
90. Vernant, 1991.
91. Assmann, 2005, p. 109.
92. Likeness (O34-N35-X1-X5-D54); copy (O34-N35-X1-X5-D54-D21); image, likeness, in same condition (O34N35-X1-Z4-A53-Y1A).
93. Assmann, 2005, p. 109.
94. O1-Z1-X1-G43-X1.
95. Assmann, 2005, p. 106.
96. Kjølby, 2009, p. 31.
97. O42-Q3-A53; O42-Q3-E154; 42-Q3-G7.
98. O42-A24.
99. O42-Q3-D40.
100. O42-Q3-D40-O34-N35-Y1-Z2.
101. Wilkinson, 2003, p. 59.
102. Kjølby, 2009, p. 38.
103. I10-X1-Z1, etc. As I10-X1-Z1-F51B it means body, person; as I10-X1-Z4-A-F51-B-Z1 it means "own" (self).
104. D36-F32-G17-G7, W10-N37-Aa15-G11, D36-F32-G17-N33-Z2, etc.
105. D36-N37-G17-G43-I3-Z2.
106. Kjølby, 2009, p. 42.
107. Kjølby, 2009, p. 42. For a detailed explanation of the various aspects of the agent–patient dynamic see Kjølby, 2009, p. 42.
108. Kjølby, 2009, p. 37.
109. Assmann, 2001, p. 37.
110. F31-S29-B3.
111. S29-S34-N35-Aa1-A1.
112. O34-S34-N3-Aa1.
113. S29-S34; S29-S34-N35-Aa1, etc.
114. M17-G1-Aa1-G43-A40; N8-G43-A40.
115. G43-D58-N35-N33-M7-N7.

116. Wilkinson, 2003, p. 46.
117. Baines, 1991, p. 181.
118. It is possible, of course, that ear depictions may have had to do with ear-related illnesses or hearing difficulties.
119. Murdy and Pirsig, 2007, pp. 84–85.
120. Jaynes, 1976, p. 169. See his proposal of an "eye index" to measure the impact of ocular iconography.
121. Nyord, 2014, p. 32.
122. Nyord, 2014, p. 32.
123. G43-U28-D10, G43-U28-G1-X1-D10, etc.
124. D10.
125. M13-M17-M17-I12, M13-M17-M17-X1-H8-I12, etc.
126. D4-N6.
127. Pinch, 2002, pp. 128–129.
128. Price, 2018.
129. Price, 2018, p. 138.
130. G43-O26; M13-G43-O39-Z1; V2-G43-I10-O26; V24-G43-O39; V24-O26; V24-G43-O26, etc.
131. P6-Z1-M17-M17-O39-Z2; P6-Z1-O39, etc.
132. P6-D36-G43-O26; P6-D36-M17-M17-O26; P6-D36-Z7-O26-Z3A; P6-Z1-O39-Z2, etc.
133. Harrington, 2010, p. 59
134. Harrington, 2010, pp. 58–59.
135. Pinch, 2004, p. 21.
136. R8-S43; R8-S43D46-Y1-Z2, etc.
137. R8-S43-D46-G43-A2; R8-S43-S43-S43, etc. Mdw *nṯr* can also mean letters or literature, suggesting that this medium of communication, no matter the topic, was infused with some degree of spirituality.
138. David, 2001, p. 27.
139. Morenz, 1992, p. 6.
140. A53; A53-Z1; X1-G43-X1-A22 X1-G43-X1-A57, X1-G43-X1-Y1, etc.
141. Wilson, 1965, p. 305.
142. Ritner, 2012, p. 183.
143. Ritner, 2012, p. 183. See also Lesko, 2012.
144. G17-X1-A14. Also *mtt* (G17-X1-X1-A14) for evil spirit of a dead woman.
145. V7-N35-W24-Z7-A2-A1.
146. D21-Aa1-Y1-B1.
147. Z7-Aa1-D46-Z7-Aa2-Z2.
148. Szpakowska, 2009, p. 802.
149. Szpakowska, 2009, p. 802.
150. N35-D58-Q7-G17-D2-Z1-I9-G7.
151. Szpakowska, 2009, p. 802.
152. Szpakowska, 2009, p. 802.
153. Szpakowska, 2009, p. 802.
154. D3-Z6.
155. D34-G1.
156. G28-X1-G4-A40-Z3.
157. V28-G1-M17-M17-X1-G4-A40.

158. Aa1-N35-D46-Z7-A53-A40.
159. N35-G1-U28-G1-E23-Z1-F27.
160. O34-M17-X1-G4-F51-Z2.
161. D36-I10-N5-A1.
162. M17-D58-Z7-M23-Z7-N35-G1-Aa2.
163. M17-K1-N35-M17-M17-X1-A14.
164. G36-D21-Z5-X1-H8-I12.
165. M12-G1-M17-M17-X1-Z4-A24-G7; Aa1-M12-G1-G43-U33-M17; Aa1-M12-G1-X1-G43-D12; Aa1-M12-G1-X1-G43-T30.
166. M17-N35-M17-Z7-V31-I14-A13; N35-M17-V31-I14, etc.
167. M17-X1-U15-G17-G43-P5.
168. N35-D58-D46-D3-Z6.
169. N35-F20-O34-M17-M17-Z6.
170. N35-M3-Aa1-X1-A24-G7.
171. O4-M17-M17-X1-A14.
172. R5-Q3-Z7-A14.
173. S29-D58-M17-I15.
174. S29-G17-V28-D6.
175. S29-N29-D21-D36.
176. S29-Q3-S29-Q3-Z7-T31-Z2-G7.
177. V4-G1-M17-M17-A14.
178. V13-Z7-G17-D36-N29-G1-N35-G1-Aa2.
179. V22-V28-M17-M17-O14.
180. Z9-Z7-Z7-D54-A14.
181. Aa1-G17-M17-M17-Z7-A14.
182. Morenz, 1992, p. 89.
183. Morenz, 1992, p. 33.
184. N28-D36-Y1.
185. N28-D36-M17-M17-Y1-Z2; N28-D36-Z5-Z5-Z5-G7.
186. N28-D36-Y1.
187. R8-F22-D54.
188. E34-N35-O31-D2-Z1-W3.
189. R8-F22-D54.
190. R8-S29-G35-N29-W3.
191. D1-Z1-N11-N14-W3.
192. D1-Z1-N35-U19-W24-Z7-M17-M17-N35A-N36-N23.
193. D1-Z1-W3.
194. O4-D46-N35-M34-O6-D2-D21-C9; O4-G1-D46-N35-O6-D2-D21-C9; O4-D46-N35-M2-O6-D2-D21-C9, etc.
195. I10-X1-W3.
196. O4-G1-V31-D21; O4-G1-V31-D21-A2; O4-G1-V31-D21-W3; O4-G1-V31-W4, etc.
197. F13-Q3-A2-Z3; F1-Q3-G43-W3-N5; F13-Q3-M9;F1Q3-Z9-W3-N5, etc.
198. F31-G43-M17-M17-X1-W3; F31-S29-M17-M17-X1-W3.
199. D36-Aa1-Z7Q3-X1-N1.
200. N11-N14-D46-X4.
201. G35-N29-D54-D21-Q3-X1-N1.

202. Kruchten, 2001, p. 609.
203. Kruchten, 2001, p. 609.
204. D58-G40-G1-M17-M17-X1-Z5-V12-Z2.
205. Aa1-D21-X1-Z7-V12-Z1; Aa1-X1-Z5-V12-Z1; D58-M17-G1-X1-Z5-U16-Y1-Z2; Aa1-D21-A2-Z1-X1-Z7-G7; Aa1-D21-U33-Z5-G7; Aa1-D21-X1-M17-M17-A2; Aa1-D21-X1-Z7-G7.
206. Aa1-D21-A2-X1-Z7; Aa1-D21-X1-Z7.
207. S29-D21-X1-Z5-A2.
208. Kruchten, 2001, pp. 609–612.
209. Prada, 2014, p. 251.
210. Jaynes, 2012, p. 199.
211. Prada, 2014, p. 262.
212. Prada, 2014, p. 261.
213. Also meaning look upon; regard; see to; inspect; diagnose; examine; look on; dream (D12-D12).
214. Also meaning look on (at event); look (at); dream; and other meanings (U2-D4-G1-G1)
215. Other relevant terms include: *nhs* (awake, wake up; N35-O4-G1-M17-S29-D6); *snhs* (awaken; O34-N35-O4-S29-U40-D5); *srs* (awaken; S29-D21-O34-U40-D5); *rs* (wakeful; D21-O34-T13-D4).
216. Asaad, 2015, p. 13.
217. Asaad, 2015, p. 13.
218. MacDonald, 2005, p. 237.
219. D5-D21-Aa18-Z1-U40; D21-S29-G43-X1-T13-D4.
220. D21-O34-S29-U40-D5D1-Z1.
221. D21-O34-T13-Z7-X1-D4-Z2; U40-Z7-X1-D4-Z2.
222. G54-Xa-Z1; O34-N35-I10-X1-G54.
223. S29-N35-D46-Z7-G54-A2-Z2, etc.
224. J28-X1-D6.
225. Lichtheim, 2006c, p. 22; Ritner, 2001b, p. 410.
226. Szpakowska, 2001, p. 34.
227. Ritner, 2001b, p. 410.
228. Prada, 2014, p. 262.
229. Prada, 2014, p. 261.
230. Prada, 2014, p. 262.
231. *Papyrus Chester Beatty 3*. Prada, 2014, p. 257.
232. Prada, 2014, p. 262.
233. Prada, 2014, p. 262.
234. Szpakowska, 2007, p. 24.
235. Szpakowska, 2007, p. 31.
236. Szpakowska, 2007, pp. 22–23.
237. Szpakowska, 2007, p. 23.
238. Szpakowska, 2007, p. 29.
239. Szpakowska, 2007, p. 26.
240. Ritner, 2001b, pp. 410–411.

Chapter 7

The Theocentric Social Order and Divine Kingship

"The king sits with those who row the barque of Re,
the king commands what is good and he does it,
for the king is the great god."
— *Pyramid Texts*

HUMANS DERIVE AUTHORIZATION for their behavior from different types of loyalty. These include personal (conscience, which might be called a fidelity to one's principles), kinship (familial), or extra-kinship (clan, tribal, chiefdoms). Over history, loyalties on the larger, political scale developed — city–states, kingdoms, national states, empires. For the most part, modern people are uncomfortable with surrendering their loyalties to monocratic rule, and except for a small number of outliers (North Korea), dynastic monarchies are kept in check by constitutions, parliaments, prime ministers, and public opinion. But something remains inherently attractive about one-person rule. Kingship is rooted in a very old notion, probably dating back to Neolithic times, when clans were ruled by chieftains, some who continued to govern from their graves. Over time, the status of these local rulers rose as they became either god-chosen or part-god. The divine right of kings is but a pale imitation of an elemental and primeval idea.

Modern societies lack the structural isomorphism that characterized archaic societies. In other words, before modern times the political, religious, military, and legal realms were indissoluble. And like other archaic civilizations, Egypt's society was strictly hierarchical, a description concretely reflected in visible structural form by its pyramids. At the top sat the pharaoh, his "great royal wife," and other royal family members.

Beneath them were the officials and a small aristocratic stratum of society. At this level, and together with high military officials, the vizier (a sort of prime minister) assisted the pharaoh. Other wives, high priests, and middle-ranking priests rounded out this second level. Below this level were the soldiers, scribes, junior priests, craftsmen, and artists. The lowest level was occupied by the vast majority of the population — peasant farmers, fishermen, servants, serfs, prisoners of war, and convicts. A "vertical solidarity"[1] among the different groups held the body social together. The goal of life was not autonomy, self-sufficiency, or independence. Rather it was tightening ties, fulfilling functions, and roles that bind the constituent parts together. The objective was to find one's place in the hierarchy, so that one lives as "if one is led by another."[2]

Archaic Egypt was certainly not a nation in the modern sense, as notions of rights-bearing citizens or nationalism as a unifying ideology were absent. An expansive, imperialist "kingdom" comes close. However, its imperialism was not religio-political but super-religious in nature (at least until the Late Period). Everything and everyone pivoted around a pharaonic monocracy (a system of government by only one person). Similar institutions, of course, were not unheard of in other parts of the world, but for millennia, ancient Egypt succeeded impressively as a theocentric monarchy. The Egyptians, like no other people, turbocharged a very primitive idea, i.e., that people are attuned to godly authorization, and in spite of serious challenges and modifications through the centuries, kept it alive.

ORDERING THE COSMOS AND STABILIZING THE SYSTEM

The Egyptian "sentient world" included the gods, the blessed dead, the king, and the rest of humanity.[3] The deities and transfigured deceased were not decorative details of an apologue or mythological flourishes. Nor can such a worldview be reduced to prettified propaganda that justified exploiter–exploited relations. The pharaoh was awe-inspiring, the gods integral to one's daily routines, and ancestors involved in one's life in ways we moderns would find incomprehensible.

The archaic Egyptians relied on several methods to stabilize their pyramid-shaped social order and ensure authorization.[4] The first was the pharaonic monocracy. At the center of this theocentric system was the king, whose primary role was to mediate between gods and mortals. Through daily rituals, he was expected to sustain the cosmopolitical order. He was the supreme political, religious, military, and legal authority, uniting in one individual the realms of power that modern societies segregate.[5]

Central state structures that supported and promoted the pharaoh as the only legitimate source of beneficence was the second stabilizing element. Modern historians and social scientists have a tendency to divide human behavior into the practical versus the symbolic. Motivations are either rooted in measurable material needs or difficult-to-discern ideas and beliefs. What cannot be understood in real-world economic terms or as utilitarian is promptly thrown into the basket of religious concepts, cultural preferences, myths, or irrational superstitions. Such an analytical approach does a grave injustice to understanding a society, past or present. So it is crucial to appreciate that in the case of archaic Egypt, no contradiction existed between practical power and its system of governance, which was a unity, not a union, of religious and political authority. Even "when an Egyptian monument appears to be simply commemorating a specific event in history, it is often interpreting that event as an act that is simultaneously mythological, ritualistic, and economic."[6] In archaic Egypt, what peeked through the theopolitical structures as seemingly "secular" was always subordinate to the all-embracing realm of the cosmopolitical order. Moreover, there was no conflict between the demands of the gods and the deceased (symbolic) and the needs of the living (economic): "One could visualize a system where most of the national product would, in theory, be earmarked for the needs of the deceased kings, their sun-temples, and shrines of the local gods, but would, in fact, be used to support most of the Egyptian population."[7]

The third stabilizing element was how the king entered into a close relationship with community powers, whether mortal or divine (local deities). The latter were the protectors of villagers and townspeople, but though in principle they belonged to a different realm than the king, in a sense they were subordinate to him. Egypt was divided into provinces called nomes (*spꜣt* or *ḏꜣtt*). These administrative regions probably started as an amalgamation of separate Predynastic chiefdoms. Each had a capital city with its own cult center, a small temple, and a priesthood, overseen by a local deity (*nṯr niwt*) and totems. Their number changed through the centuries, but forty-two is a good approximate number. This political unit was first mentioned in Dynasty 3 during the reign of Djoser (2650–2620 BCE).

Nomes were governed by a nomarch or "great overlord" (*ḥry tp*), an aristocratic hereditary title. Originally nomarchs were rotated, but by Dynasty 5 they became hereditary and began to spend most of their time in one nome where they would be buried. They were responsible for taxation, tribute, and military levies demanded by the central authorities. Besides representing the pharaoh, nomarchs raised their own armies and defended their borders. When the monarchy was weak, the nomarchs loosened their ties with the king and became independent. Over time, nomarchs developed their own traditions, as evident in the cliff tombs of Assiut and Beni Hasan, as well as other monuments. The bureaucratic structures of the nomes proved resilient and useful for rulers. Later, the Ptolemies utilized the legal traditions of the nomes to stabilize their power, an endeavor that was continued through the Roman Period.

The fourth stabilizing element was the sheer aesthetic appeal of monumental architecture (ARCC), the inscribed mysterious "words of the gods," and other splendid artifacts. The sky-scraping steps to the heavens (pyramids), statues hidden away in the temples that whispered messages, and grand processions of barque-riding enshrined images all communicated an overwhelming super-religiosity. The average person did not have to witness the mysterious rituals held deep in temple chambers or be able to read hieroglyphics (the vast majority could only appreciate their pictorial impact) to experience a potent sense of the numinous about which most modern humans can only wonder. It is easy for us to cynically dismiss all this powerful, awe-inspiring imagery as ideologically-crafted and propagandistic. But surely something else must have been at work, century after century, besides political machinations.

Maat was the fifth stabilizing element. Rather than scientific principles, natural laws, legalistic systems, political theories, theological dogmas, or general abstract philosophizing, the justification and authorization for one's behavior was ultimately grounded in Maat (*m3't*).[8] Meaning cosmic order, balance, and truth, in concrete terms it meant speaking honestly, dealing fairly in the marketplace, obeying one's parents, following the instructions of one's superiors, and expressing loyalty to the king. Sometimes Maat was described as something the gods consumed. The cosmic order was personified by the goddess Maat, daughter of the sun god Re. Maat was inextricably entwined with kingship, the routines of moral behavior at the everyday level, the constellation of gods, and the cosmos itself. From the reign of Sneferu (Dynasty 4) onward, Maat became a common part of the royal titular, seen in expressions such as "Possessor of Maat" or "He Who Arises with Maat."[9] And beginning in Dynasty 5, viziers and judicial officials might bear the title "priests of Maat" (*ḥm nṯr mꜣ't*).[10] The counterpart of Maat was *isft*[11] or chaos, evil, injustice, falsehood, and the related concepts of wrong, crime, and sin (*btꜣ*).[12] The earliest confession of sin is in the *Instructions for Merikare*, probably composed during the Middle Kingdom.[13]

For most of their history, the ancient Egyptians never developed a codified legal system, and the closest term to "law," *hp* (or *hpw*),[14] might mean rule, regulation, habit, rite, ceremony, and the cycle of a planet (it could also mean a measure on a sun dial).[15] *Hp* can be defined as "every kind of rule, either natural or juridical, general or specific, public or private, written or unwritten."[16] A semantically similar term is *nt'*,[17] often glossed as "custom" (it might also mean duty, regulation, ordinance, prescription, arrangement, treaty). The underlying idea common to both terms is "recurrence," the implication being that law had more to do with cosmic forces rather than social justice. After all, law was a manifestation of Maat.[18]

A MONARCHY OF ABSOLUTE MONOCRACY

To the modern mind, insistent on clear-cut categorizations, the ancient Egyptian monarch can be mystifying. No persistent theologisms were worked out as to the nature of divine kingship, and not being a static notion, definitions of kingship changed over the millennia. But one continuous idea was that kings were at the center of a royal ancestor cult, i.e., a lineage connected the living king, his forebearers, and the gods.[19] Most likely this evolved from a very ancient belief in how deceased chieftains or petty kings became the deified ancestor of the community. Over time, this was elaborated into the complex edifice of pharaonic monocracy. The royal Ka, the life-force or Double of the king, transmitted the divine energy of kingship from one holder to the next, thereby ensuring the mythical line of descent. The focus was on the perpetual recreation and continuation of kingship. This is why kings were known as the "repeater-of-births," i.e., a ruler who inaugurated a new era.

Resonating with the idea that all of society was conceived in kinship terms, with the state as the central domestic unit, was the very notion of "pharaoh" (*pr 'ꜣ*),[20] which originally meant "great house." This referred to the royal court or the king's palace and had a corporate connotation; it was used in the same way as Americans might say "White House."[21] But the word "pharaoh" was not used until the New Kingdom. Other terms include monarch or sovereign (*ity*),[22] ruler (*ḥḳꜣ*),[23] and lord, as in Lord of the Two Lands (*nsw bity nb tꜣwy*).[24]

The Gods and the Monarchy

Kings were associated with a range of gods, depending on the historical period and context. But no matter the era, it is safe to say that kingship was a manifestation of the creative powers of the cosmos; the pharaoh "reveals the deity by being a visible incarnation of it."[25] The *Instructions of Sehtepibre*, from around the time of Amenemhet III (1860 to 1814 BCE), equates the king with a list of deities and cosmic principles, indicating his role as demiurge and nurturer of humankind.[26] After death, multiple facets of the king's existence (Ka, Ba, an embodiment of a particular deity) would sail through the sky and underworld on a sacred barque and visit his earthly tomb, thereby infusing kingly numinosity throughout the different realms of the cosmos.

The Monarchy as High Priest–king

The pharaoh was the supreme priest–king, the master of rituals of every temple in the land. Though in theory he performed rituals every day, in practice high priests performed the necessary ceremonies in his place. The pharaoh was an interlocutor between the divine and human realms, whose offerings to the gods maintained reciprocal relations between the gods and their kingly representative on earth. The most common inscriptions in temples were theophanic encounters of the king, standing next to or directly facing the gods, often making offerings to ensure the continuation of prosperity and health of the spiritual community. Without a king on the throne, the gods would not be able to receive the offerings that they expected. Besides the daily rituals, the king participated in activities related to the dual kingship of Lower and Upper Egypt, and revivification rites to ensure the land's fertility. The pharoah was the center of attention in grand ceremonies of kingship, such as the Sed Festival (thirtieth regnal year and then every three years after that) and the Opet Festival (to renew the king's divine stewardship).

As the divine pivot around which the earth and heavens rotated, the king was responsible for upholding Maat and fighting off chaos, which was manifested as criminality, injustice, social disorder, wild beasts, and invading foreign enemies from the deserts. His role was to embody sacrosanct authorization. His speech carried a potency that moderns would find hard to comprehend. First there was his creative speech (*ḥw*) that he shared with the gods. He could utter efficacious formulas and spells (*ṯsw*) that were deadly to enemies and rebels. His sayings (*ḏdt*) and discourse (*mdt*) were inspired by and modeled on archaic writings. He composed laws (*hpw*) and issued orders (*wḏ snw*) whose authorization was rarely questioned. Besides his super-religious role, the king's economic role was immense. In principle he owned all the land and endowed temples with resources, workers, and livestock. He planned, built, and renovated monumental edifices, as well as commissioning statues and other OHFs. The architectural expression of the monarchy was "crushing and sumptuous," and the monumental cult overseen by the king ensured that the security of the universe was addressed, as was the creator god in his local form.[27]

THE PARALOGIC OF THE DUAL NATURE OF DIVINE RULERSHIP

If viewed through the lens of a Judeo-Christianity infused with a large dose of Greek categorical logic, the division between the Godhead and humans is absolute. If we drop the categorical "either/or" viewpoint and adopt a more paralogic "and/or" perspective, debates about pharaonic divinity becomes less confounding. Indeed, discussions about a king's true nature may be more of a modern concern; the archaic Egyptians, working with a paralogic mindset, were not as interested in theological hair-splitting. Any treatment of divine rulership must use expressions such as "identified with," "embodiment of," and "attributes of," not in any strict technical sense but rather as descriptive approximations.

In any case, it is safe to state that the king possessed a dual nature that depended on from which perspective one viewed the king: from the perspective of the gods, he was a human who acted on behalf of other mortals, while from the perspective of his subjects, he was a divine being. A statue of Amenhotep III illustrates this: it displays the king as a god, while on its obverse is an image of the human king prostrate before the god Amun.

The dual nature of divine kingship is apparent in terminology. On the one hand, a king possessed majesty that was incarnated in a particular individual (*ḥm*);[28] this mortal and bodily nature put a limit on the notion of an all-powerful divinity. Meaning the King of Lower Egypt, *bity*[29] pointed to the current human holder of the office in the line of kingly succession. Another related term is *nsw*,[30] which meant King of Upper Egypt; this was also used in many expressions concerning royalty. At the same time, the king was somehow linked to forces beyond this world and various terms were used to indicate this above-and-beyond the ordinary sense. Though called "god" (*nṯr*) or "great god" (*nṯr ꜥ3*)[31] and officially entitled "good god" (*nfr nṯr*),[32] such designations may have meant that, though semi-divine, the king was still a lesser god of some sort. Sometimes kings were described being "like" (*mi*) a god. This description seemed to modify the god-like qualities of kings and granted them a status not far below the deities.

THE NATURE OF THE MONARCHY

Several approaches can help us come to terms with the role of archaic Egyptian kingship: (1) attributes of a human while alive; (2) identified with/embodiment of a god while on earth; and (3) identified with a god after death (Chart 7.1).

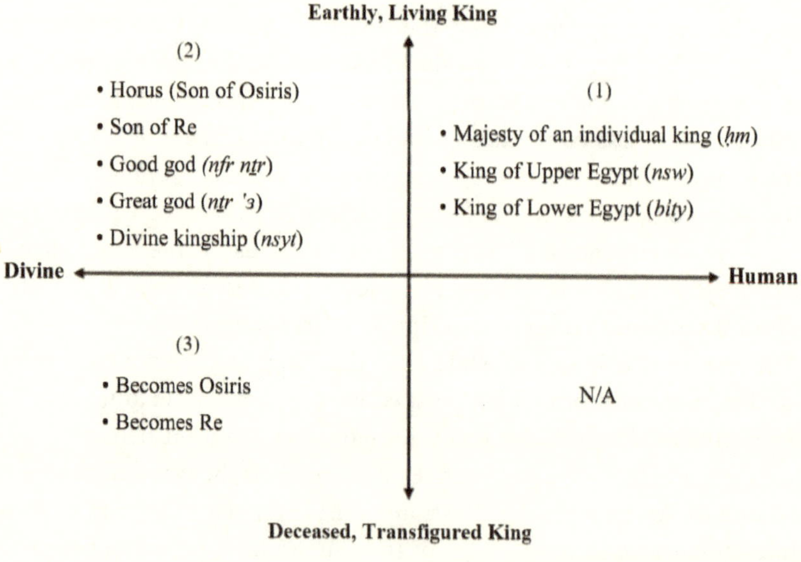

Chart 7.1. The Nature of the King.

(1) Attributes of a Human while Living

The Egyptian king, whether dead or alive, was never regarded as completely divine. In writings, kings could be portrayed with human frailties and weaknesses. Arguably, it was "not the king who was honored as a god but the incarnate power of the gods that was honored in the king."[33] While he was "numbered among the gods," he was still forced to kneel before them.[34] Any kingly traits he possessed were gifts from the gods. The gods were inherently immortal, but kings had to earn their immortality. As a representative of mortals and mediator between worlds, his nature was never on par with the gods. Despite his incarnation as a deity and concomitant divine attributes, then, the king-on-earth was not regarded as a complete deity in his own right. Whether conceived as identifying with a god, incarnating a god, or manifesting as a god, the king possessed a mortal aspect that was intertwined with the divine.[35] The divine office itself was designated by *nsyt*,[36] meaning kingship or the divine power given to the king and expressed in his monarchial roles. Sometimes *ḥm n nsyt* was used to designate the king; this meant the "incarnation of (divine) kingship."[37]

By the Middle Kingdom, the facial expressions of kings became even more human. But it was not until the New Kingdom that enough archaeological and textual evidence emerges to see the pharaohs "as something resembling well-rounded individuals."[38] This lack of individuation, however, has more to do with a weak sense of subjective consciousness among archaic Egyptians than with the depiction of special royal personages. Portraits as we think of them did not exist, and representations were idealized images. Though preconscious examples of what appear to be "portraiture" exist (suggesting self-individuation), it might be that each detail indicates an element of strictly codified super-religious symbolism. Such details are secondary to idealized portrayals. These are not examples of naturalism as we might understand it but rather a type of realism in the service of overarching theopolitical principles.

(2) Identified with/Embodiment of a God while on Earth

The paramount divine ruler was identified with several deities depending on the period. From predynastic times, the king embodied the god Horus, the falcon-headed god of the sky. This deity was also regarded as the guardian of the pharaoh as well as the embodiment of divine kingship. This was visually made apparent in the kingly "Horus name," the oldest part of royal titulary. In the Old Kingdom, a deceased king became one of the "imperishable stars." But this star cult was eclipsed by the solar cult of Re, and by Dynasty 4, monarchs had adopted the title "Son of Re." The solar cult continued to symbolize royal divinization (while in later periods Osiris came to mean the immortality of common people). "Just as the living monarch was held to be the son of Osiris but fused with the deity upon death, so the living king known as the 'Son of Re' could fuse with his father Re" upon his entry into the Afterworld.[39]

By the Old Kingdom the special sacredness of kings was marked by how only he could achieve eternal life. Kings simply dwelled in a different dimension and shared in the divinity of supernatural beings. This was symbolized in early periods by how a nonroyal individual could not be shown together with a god; only a king could be depicted this way.[40] The king was portrayed in "timeless and untiring majesty."[41] Moreover, they were believed to possess the three key powers of the gods: (1) Hu (divine utterance); (2) Sia (divine wisdom); and (3) Heka (divine energy/magic and knowledge of efficacious techniques). From Dynasty 5, he was also the Son of Re and the father's earthly representative.

By the Middle Kingdom, the common formulation was the living king as Horus (the Younger) and the dead king, Osiris.[42] For their part, deified queens were frequently associated with the goddess Hathor (and later Isis-Hathor), the daughter of Re. By the New Kingdom, it was thought that the king's birth was of divine origin.[43] The divine births of Hatshepsut (1473–1458 BCE) and Amenhotep III are seen on the walls of the mortuary temple at Deir el-Bahri and the Temple of Luxor, respectively. By Dynasty 18 (1539–1292 BCE), the monarch was identified with Amun-Re. Horus took two forms, both linked to the king. The first was Horus the Elder, a great falcon whose eyes were the sun and the moon. The second was Horus the Younger, or the son of Isis and Osiris, who inherited kingship from his murdered father (Horus avenged his father Osiris, and succeeded Seth as Egypt's ruler in the mythical past).

(3) Identified with a God after Death

During the Old Kingdom, the king was considered the progeny of the sun god Re (*s3r'*). After his death, he ascended to the heavens to join Re. But the spread of the Osiris cult signaled a massive shift in beliefs. The deceased pharaoh now became identified with Osiris. While alive on the throne, the pharaoh became Horus, Osiris's son. Osiris, symbolized as a shepherd with a crook and flail, may have been a real ruler from Predynastic Period (5000–3100 BCE) in the Nile Delta who was deified. According to myth, Osiris had ruled the Afterworld. His violent death at the hands of his brother Seth led to a power struggle between him and Horus, another son of Osiris. To resolve this, Osiris threatened that the Afterworld would rise in revolt if no just solution was reached. Re and his court therefore declared Horus the rightful ruler. Consequently, the person of the king was paralogically equated with Horus during his life and with Osiris, ruler of the Afterworld, after his death.

The *Contendings of Horus and Seth* may in fact be more than just a mytho-literary text; it may have its origins in actual events. This colorful and complicated tale describes the struggles over who will succeed Osiris as ruler. In its present form it dates from Dynasty 20, though its ultimate origins go back much further. "There has been some astonishment that mythology and reality should be so mixed that the heavenly contention of Horus and Seth is over real land, and that the figure of Osiris in the last section has a real grave in Memphis, and also that each king at death becomes Osiris, just as each king in life is Horus."[44] Jaynes proposes that these gods were VVVs "heard by kings and their next in rank, and that the voice of a king could continue after his death" and become the "guiding voice of the next, and that the myths about various contentions and relationships with other gods are attempted rationalizations of conflicting admonitory authoritative voices mingled with the authoritative structure in the actuality of the society."[45]

Osiris was "not a 'dying god,' not 'life caught in the spell of death, or 'a dead god,' as modern interpreters have said."[46] Rather, Osiris was the hallucinated voice of the deceased king, "whose admonitions could still carry weight. And since he could still be heard, there is no paradox in the fact that the body from which the voice once came should be mummified, with all the equipment of the tomb providing life's necessities: food, drink, slaves, women, the lot."[47] The "mysterious power" emanating from Osiris was the latter's "remembered voice which appeared in hallucinations to those who had known him and which could admonish or suggest even as it had before he stopped moving and breathing."[48] The relationship between Horus and Osiris, then, represented in "each new king and his dead father forever." This "can only be understood as the assimilation of a hallucinated advising voice into the king's own voice, which then would be repeated with the next generation."[49]

Even after death, some kings were so popular that they were worshiped separately and operated as intermediaries between commoners and other gods. A good example of this phenomenon was Amenhotep I (1514–1493 BCE), who continued to be the object of worship for centuries after his death.[50] During the New Kingdom Period, votive stelae were inscribed with prayers to him, and in the Ramesside Period his oracle was often consulted for legal rulings.

Cult of the Living King

Full deification of a monarch typically occurred upon death. However, examples of living deified kings existed. The "cult of the living king" became salient after the chaos of the first two Intermediate Periods, when monarchs struggled to re-assert pharaonic dominance.[51] During the New Kingdom, the "practice of worshipping the still-living ruler, both in person and through his cult," became well accepted.[52] The supplication for aid was part of this deification of living kings. Kings honored by a cult during their lifetime included Sneferu; Senusret III; Amenemhet III; Amenhotep III; Tutankhamun; Sety I; Ramesses II; and Ramesses III.

ROYAL TITULARY

The king's royal titulary spelled out the close relationship to several gods. The first was the Horus name, written within a serekh (*srḫ*),[53] or a rectangle containing the royal appellation. This indicated that the monarch was the embodiment of Horus on earth, i.e., he was the king of the living, while the father of Horus, Osiris, was the king of the dead. The second was the Two Ladies name (He Who Belongs to the Two Ladies). This title placed the monarch under the protection of the goddesses Nekhbet and Wadjet. They symbolized the king's rulership over Upper and Lower Egypt, respectively. The meaning of the third or "gold name" is somewhat unclear but it may have signified the rising sun as well as the king's divinity. "King of Upper and Lower Egypt" was the fourth or throne name (prenomen); literally, He Who Belongs to the Sedge and Bee (*nsw bity*).[54] The final appellation is the birth name (nomen), sometimes referred to as the "Son of Re" (modern scholars use the birth name when referring to a particular king). The last two names were written within a cartouche, representing a rope folded and tied at one end, symbolizing everything that the sun encircled; this in turn symbolized the monarch's "overlordship of the cosmos."[55]

PRIESTS, PRIESTESSES, AND PROPHETS

Though local variations existed, priests were organized in a strict hierarchy and arranged "watches" that took turns working as "servants of the gods"[56] or "prophets" (*ḥm nṯr*).[57] Most did not hold permanent positions but were part of a rota system. The priesthood was generally hereditary, so that they belonged to a family that was connected to a particular cult or temple. Though allowed to marry, they were required to adhere to strict regulations that involved fasting before and after rituals. Not surprisingly, archaic Egyptian was replete with terms for priest (Table 7.1). Some terms were titles, specific to a temple or deity. A high ("head") priest was called *ḥm nṯr tpy*.[58] Epithets were also used. The high priest of Ptah in Memphis was the "Greatest of the Master Craftsmen" (*wr ḫrp ḥmwt*),[59] while the high priest of Re was called the "Greatest of Seers" (*wr m3w or m33 wr*).[60]

Priestesses, or wives of the god (*ḥmt nṯr*),[81] were often married to priests. Some danced and sang at ceremonies and were recruited from the ranks of the elite. Musician priestesses were called *ḫnwt*[82] or *iḥyt*.[83] Others had epithets or titles, e.g., the Hand of God (*ḏrt nṯr*)[84] or Female Watcher (*wršt*).[85] The appellations of priestess indicated they also specialized and fulfilled crucial roles, e.g., Ka-priestess or priestess of the dead (*ḥmt k3*)[86] and Wab priestess (*w'bt*[87] or *w'b ḥmt*).[88]

Though men for the most part dominated the priesthood, women and priestly power were not complete strangers. In Dynasty 18, a form of temple service was established that was referred to as God's Wife of Amun. It was initiated by the consort of Ahmose (1539–1514 BCE), Queen Ahmose-Nefertari, who served as a priestess in the cult of Amun. Though this office had a precursor in the Middle Kingdom, when royal consorts officiated certain temple ceremonies, Hatshepsut (1473–1458 BCE) prepared her daughter, Neferure, to take over what by then was a powerful title (also known as the Chieftainess of the Harem). It would also become known as the Divine Adoratress of Amun (*dw3t nṯr n imn*).[89] Subordinated to this office were the large number of women officiating as votaresses or adoratresses (*dw3 nṯr*),[90] singers, dancers, and ritual priestesses. In Karnak, the God's Wife was referred to as the Mother of God or the Prophetess.

Table 7.1. Terms for Priests.

No.	Term	Possible Translation
1.	*ẖry ḥbt*[61]	Lector-priest
2.	*sm*[62]	Sem-priest
3.	*ḥm kꜣ*[63]	Ka-priest
4.	*w'bi*[64]	Wab-priest
5.	*ḥry wr*[65]	
6.	*'ḳꜣv*[66]	
7.	*ꜣnḳ*[67]	
8.	*ỉgrtỉ*[68]	Priest
9.	*hỉh*[69]	
10.	*ḥm tꜣ*[70]	
11.	*ḳd w*[71]	
12.	*ỉt nṯr*[72]	God's father, priest
13.	*wr nṯr / nṯr wr*[73]	Priest, officiant in ritual
14.	*mn bỉt*[74]	High priest title
15.	*šmꜣyt*[75]	
16.	*sꜣdt*[76]	
17.	*mꜣdtx*[77]	Priestess
18.	*ỉns*[78]	
19.	*wprt*[79]	
20.	*ẖtys*[80]	

After the collapse of the New Kingdom, the Theban high priests of Amun elevated the God's Wives of Amun, granting them even more power and prestige. By Dynasty 21 (1069–945 BCE), the God's Wife of Amun ruled all priestesses, some of whom acquired titles and great wealth, controlling the estates of Amun. Dynasty 25 (728–657 BCE) even saw women "married" to the god and deified upon death. Well known God's Wives included Amenirdis I and II, Nitocris, Shepenwepet I and II, and Ankhesneferibre.

Some priests were charged with specific functions. Sem-priests, Ka-priests, mortuary priests (*wt ỉnpw*),[91] and funerary priests (*ḏꜣy*)[92] performed as mortuary ritualists. There were also libation priests (*ỉbḥw*)[93] and music priests (*ỉḥwy*).[94] The priest who walked behind the procession carrying an image of the god was called *w'b n pḥwy*.[95] The Wab priests purified temples, monuments, or sacred barques during rituals and cultic rites. They might be associated with smaller temples. Lector-priests were called *ẖrjw-ḥb*. Some priests were dedicated to washing and feeding god-statues. Stolist priests who dressed the gods were known as *ḏbꜣty*,[96] *smꜣ*,[97] or *smꜣwty*.[98] Some priests functioned as scribes, writing legal documents, composing religious writings, and copying texts in the Houses of Life attached to temples. A type of priest or scholar was a *ẖ sꜣ*.[99] Some priests were associated with medical knowledge. Others were the master of the secrets (*ḥry sštꜣ*)[100] and officiated at funeral ceremonies for royal families. These were also the guardian of the mysteries of the god's seal (*iry sštꜣ n ḫtmti nṯr*).[101] Some worked as astrologers and determined lucky and unlucky times or auspicious days for festivals.

Over time, especially beginning after the Old Kingdom, different types of communication lines developed around administrative and military areas of expertise, indicating the growing segregation of domains of power. However, as a testament to the potency of a theocentric mentality, the priesthood continued to exercise considerable influence. The intersection of religious and political authority is apparent in (*ḥꜣt ʿ / ḥꜣty ʿ*),[102] which meant ceremonial priest, local prince, nomarch, mayor, or high official.

During certain periods, priests would more or less take over the theocentric system. At the end of Dynasty 20, though he never claimed complete royal power, Herihor, a high priest of Amun at Thebes and a general, claimed royal prerogatives while the throne was occupied by Ramesses XI (1099–1069 BCE).

THE EXCELLENT SPIRITS OF THE DEPARTED ONES

Underpinning the theocentric structures was ancestor worship. Indeed, one can argue that the entire theocentric edifice evolved from CAW in which the ancestors of divinized rulers became gods issuing VVVs. "That the 'gods' really are the ancestral spirits is shown by the puns which are meant to effect the union."[103] Domestic units were the building blocks of the theocentric order, parts of an overarching architecture of royal ancestor worship. Reverence towards one's predecessors was officially sanctioned and encouraged (as seen in the *Instructions of Ani*).[104]

Writing about Dier el-Medina, one researcher notes that "One rather gets the impression that dead ancestors count among the 'actual' inhabitants of the village at any particular time, as their presence was made visible through stelae, busts, inscriptions, etc. in people's homes, nearby shrines and tombs."[105] The ancestors were petitioned to deal with illness, childbirth, and infertility, as well as protection against nightmares, snakes, scorpions, and the spirits of the malevolent dead. Though in principle ancestors acted as intercessors between the living and the gods, the sense is that they could be more effective and supportive than remote deities.[106]

The dead were multi-locational, distributed, and could manifest themselves in various forms. They might contact one in dreams. Ancestor worship was not confined to domestic dwellings and could take place in chapels, shrines, temples, and pilgrimage sites.[107] Offerings and prayers were provided for ancestors at their tombs. Ancestor worship was at the heart of the dynamics of intergenerational dependence and reciprocity, though probably devotion to a group of the predeceased was abandoned after several generations.

Ancestors were called the Excellent Spirit (Departed Ones) of Re: Akh-ikr-en-Re (*ꜣḫ ỉḳr n r*'). These were the deceased of the nonroyal family. It was believed that the Akh-ikr-en-Re traveled on Re's sacred barque. They were sometimes portrayed as the rays of the sun in commemoratives. By the New Kingdom, worship ceremonies employed representations (busts and stelae) to commemorate Akh-ikr-en-Re. About 150 red stone effigies of ancestors were found in Deir el-Medina, the artisan district near the Valley of the Kings at Thebes.

A strong link between the dead and domestic dwellings is clear in the archaeological record.[108] Household shrines from the New Kingdom Period have been found. It needs to be stressed that the house was where "most of the regular cultic activity in relation to the dead took place."[109] Houses were central to making offerings to the dead, with their lustration slabs and offerings tables, though these could have been used to make offerings to the gods as well. Some houses apparently had a false door that allowed egress and ingress for spirits. Clay figurines of the deceased were used in later eras and manufactured on an industrial scale. A cache of 17,000 such figurines was found in Karnak. Ephemeral materials that were presumably used — vulture feathers, pieces of weed, flowers, figures made of bread, hair, bodily fluids, blood — have obviously been lost.[110]

So-called "letters to the dead" might be written on stelae, clay vessels, or strips of linen, and deposited in or not far from tombs. Perhaps due to the fragility of materials, only sixteen definite examples have survived.[111] Some messages inquired about life "in the West" or, fearful of being haunted, tried to placate the deceased. Other letters pleaded for intercessions, hoping that the spirits would intervene in legal proceedings on earth or even in the judgment courts of the dead.

THE STABILIZING EFFECT OF RITUALS

Every morning in temples across the land, priests greeted, dressed, incensed, anointed, and fed the god-statue in their temples' hidden sanctuary. Priests poured water that "soaked into the offerings and the fabric of the temple, energizing and bringing life; the provision of food, with its smells and taste, activated the senses and power of the gods."[112] In the evening more offerings were made. On special days, perhaps several times a month, the god-statue was carried on barques into the streets to make their appearance among the masses to receive petitions and to provide oracles. Sometimes the gods boarded a boat and were taken down the Nile. Daily services, festivals, and special rituals were described as "mysteries" (*sštꜣ*).[113] Knowledge among the priesthood of these mysteries maintained their sacred prerogatives, thereby bolstering their position in the theopolitical order as well as the authorization of the theocentric system itself.

Ancient Egyptian was rich in terms describing ritual objects and occasions. It had a number of generic terms for ceremonies, rituals, rites, and ritual acts (*iʿ ḥr ḥb,*[114] *ỉrwt,*[115] *ntʿ,*[116] *sḫʿʿw*[117]) in addition to more specific terms, such as ceremony for the dead (*hry*)[118] and "procession around the walls" (ceremonial for accession of the king) (*pẖr ḥꜣ inb*).[119]

For the archaic Egyptians such rituals were real encounters with the divine. In other words, behaviorally acting out an action was tantamount to actually doing it.[120] The boundaries between act/behavior and image/representation were, by modern standards, fluid.[121] It was not until after about 1000 BCE that paralogic thinking was eroded and the inseparability of symbolic activity and event was presumably questioned. Though still believed in for the most part, the gods had grown silent and retreated to the heavens. Dealing with them became probably even more ritualistic as officiants and commoners alike became desperate for engagement with the divine.

Sacrificing for the Gods and Ancestors

Many rituals were about making offerings to the numinous beings, driving a complicated cosmic circuitry of gift exchanges, favors, and return favors. A common subject for tomb paintings and carvings were the living dead seated at offering tables laden with food.[122] Provisions were laid out on tables in between the sealed burial chamber and the funerary chapel or in front of the false door. Making offerings was a means of communication between the earthly and otherworldly realms; it knitted together the various regions of the cosmos. The word for offering, *ḥtp*,[123] also meant to satisfy, make content, or pacify. Originally real food was presented to the gods and one's ancestors, but as time passed it became more common to utilize inscribed offering lists, offering formula, and pictorial representations in place of actual consumables.[124] But for the archaic paralogic Egyptians, any representation was in effect just as "real" as actual food. The invocation offering formula (*prt ḫrw*[125] or *prt r ḫrw*[126]) describes making offerings to the deities. Its literal meaning, "going forth of the voice," indicates the significance of the verbalized component of offerings.[127]

At the center of the circuitry of divine exchange was the king. He was the "lord of the ritual" (*nb irt ḫt*)[128] and was typically shown officiating before a statue of a god and making offerings (though in practice such activities were delegated to the head priest of each temple).[129] Through the "reversion of offerings" the beneficence of the gods was spread throughout the local community. The proffered gifts to the deities were actually consumed by priests, temple staff,[130] their families, dependents of the temple estate, and perhaps the poor at the temple gate. No doubt enjoying consumables brought everyone, from the high born to commoner, into the embrace of the gods. In some cases what was offered went from the temple out to lesser gods or to the necropolises.

A Pyramid of Ceremonies

Rituals could be ranked in a hierarchy (household → local temple → state temple) capped off with those performed at the theocentric apex of the pharaonic monocracy. Their execution afforded a reassuring routine that undoubtedly stabilized the psychosocial system. In principle, the pharaoh was the high priest of every temple in the land and only he was shown officiating before the gods. An example of what a daily temple ritual may have looked like can be seen in the New Kingdom temple of Seti I (ca.

1294–1279 BCE) at Abydos. It provides the most complete record ever found.[131] The king was purified by two priests, who acted out the parts of the gods Horus and Thoth (this "acting out" may have been personation, an archaic form of spirit possession). The king, who dressed simply to demonstrate his humility before his divine superiors, approached the sanctuary carrying a censer. Within the sanctuary was a sacred barque and a shrine housing the god-statue. The king sprinkled incense and lit a lamp, breaking the seal and removing the bolt called the Finger of Seth. He then informed the god-statue that he had brought him the Eye of Horus to resurrect him.[132] The king next opened the Doors of Heaven (shrine doors), bowed twice before the god-statue, sang hymns of praise, and then anointed the god-statue and burnt incense. He embraced the statue and offered the Eye, just as Horus did to Osiris in the mythic account. He repeated this ritual twice in his capacity as king of the Two Lands. The king then removed the god-statue from its niche and placed it on the primeval mound of sand. The king presented a basket of linen, precious ointments, and incense. He walked four times around the statue (presumably to symbolize completeness) and purified it with water and incense. Then he dressed the statue, adorned it with jewelry, anointed it with perfumed oil and ointments, and offered it bread. Next the king returned the sacred image to its niche, retreated while sweeping traces of his footprints with a broom, and then bolted and sealed the doors.

Another important ritual was the "raising the Djed-pillar." This object perhaps originally symbolized a pole with grain tied around it, but by the New Kingdom it stood for the backbone of Osiris and was linked to his resurrection. Besides being apparently practiced in temples, the Djed-pillar was also a part of the king's jubilee festival.

Major Ceremonies of the Pharaohs

The Beautiful Feast of Opet (*ḥb nfr n ỉpt*)[133] was held each year to honor Amun and to renew the king's divine stewardship. By Dynasty 20 it lasted 27 days. Statues of Amun, Mut, and Khons would be taken from the Temple of Karnak and brought to the Temple of Luxor. Led by the pharaoh, they were carried by priests on richly ornamented barques (named Mighty of Prow). Dancers, singers, wrestlers, and other performers mixed with onlookers. Gifts to the gods were placed on offering tables along the processional way. Originally, the shrines holding cult images were carried overland on divine barques and then a return journey was made on the Nile. Later the entire journey took place on the Nile in ceremonial boats.

The Sed Festival, or *ḥbsd* (Royal Jubilee),[134] was celebrated on the thirtieth year of a king's reign. Thereafter it would be held every two or three years. It was meant to regenerate the king's strength. This celebration can be traced to Den of Dynasty 1 and in the funeral complex at Saqqara. Djoser (2650–2620 BCE) built a courtyard and chapels just for this festival. Not all monarchs celebrated the Sed Festival, and there was variation in expense devoted to its preparations. Besides Djoser, other kings constructed monumental halls and courtyards to celebrate their royal jubilees.

Dramatizing Super-religiosity

In regards to "secular drama," no "archaeological or textual evidence for theaters" has ever been found from archaic Egypt. Neither are there words for drama, play, or actor in Middle Egyptian.[135] This is a controversial conclusion. However, religious texts categorized as "dramatic texts"[136] do exist, but these compositions were certainly not drama in the modern sense, and have been variously translated as "dramatic ritual," "liturgical drama," or "sacred drama."[137] Stage directions and notes about roles are evident, but these were firmly rooted in cultic practices.[138] What we have is material for the commemorative reenactments of myth. The point of these "performances" was to have gods appear speaking and acting.[139] In acts of personation, priests donned masks of gods to "become" the gods, i.e., the identity of the "actors" and deities were paralogically blurred. The relevant rituals were undoubtedly dramatic re-enactments of super-religious themes, but such practices were not theater as we understand it. They were acts of worship, not art for the sake of entertainment. The age-old principle of "as above, so below" finds expression in how the reenactment of an activity in the earthly realm could cause the intended effect in the divine realm. Thoughts, deeds, words, images/representations, and divine energy were deeply interconnected and shared the same essential reality.

The purpose of these dramatizations, then, was not to instruct or to reflect upon. An analysis of human behavior and motivation is simply absent. There was no "I" that could direct or stage-manage one's "me" (part, role), the hallmark of conscious interiority. Art in the modern sense, which demands a hypothetical as-if-ness, did not exist, though certainly aesthetic elements were employed for super-religious purposes (legitimizing theopolitical rulership, instilling awe and wonder in subjects, inspiring spiritual feelings, etc.). A distinction, then, should be made between "theatrical elements," apparent in super-religious re-enactments, and full-blown drama in the post-bicameral, conscious sense.

THEOPHORIC NAMING PRACTICES AND THEOCENTRICITY

In archaic civilizations, descriptions of the world functioned like a giant hall of mirrors, every person or natural phenomena isomorphically reflecting some key aspect or principle of the way the cosmos cohered. A vital facet of theocentricity was theophorous names (bearing the name of a god). Egypt was no exception. In fact, such names were extremely common in all periods of ancient Egyptian history. These appellations expressed a "relationship between the name-bearer, or his parents, and a deity (or deities)."[140] They might be one-word names, compound names not constituting a complete structure, or names constituting a complete sentence (Tables 7.2 and 7.3). Besides theophoricity, basilophorous names (incorporating a king's name) and throne names "were widely used as personal names during and after the reigns of those kings."[141] "Pure, unextended divinity names" were not used as personal names in the Old Kingdom. But by the Middle and New Kingdoms, names such are Bastet, Ptah, Isis, Horus, Seth, and Khons were used.[142] One might be associated with a sacred emblem, e.g., a common Late Period name was "S/He Belongs to the (Holy) Staff."[143] Sometimes, the theophorous element is embedded in a suffix, as in "They (the Gods) Are Content" or "May They be Content!"[144] In the Old and Middle Kingdoms, Ka (Double) appears in names, e.g., "Who Repeats My Ka" and "Whom My Ka Loves." Some names were inspired by oracles, e.g., "Ptah Said, He Will Live." Anything that was part of the Egyptian cosmos (plants, animals, and anything associated with divine rulers), was drawn into the symbolic web of nomenclature.

Table 7.2. Theophoric Name Patterns.

Theophoric Name Pattern	Examples
Belonging to god N	• Who Belongs to Bastet • Who Belongs to Ptah • S/He of N • He of Amun • She of Amun • S/He Belongs to N • S/He Belongs to Khons
As servant of god N	• (male/female) Servant of Re • Servant of Khons • The (female) Servant of Mut • The Dog of Horus
Beloved or praised by god N	• Loved by Sakhmet • Praised by Re
Protected or saved by god N	• Isis Has Saved Him • May Isis Save Him! • He Whom Horus Has Protected • Heka Is His Protection • Nefertem Rescued Him • May Nefertem Rescue Him!
As a gift of god N	• (She Who Has Been) Given by Mut • S/He Whom N Has Given • He Whom Isis Has Given • It Is N Who Has Given Him/Her • It Is Amun Who Has Given Him/Her • Gift of N • Gift of Min • The Gift of (the Goddess) Iusaas
Son/daughter of god N	• Son of Sobek • Daughter of Hathor • The Son of Khons • The Son of the Gods • Scion of the (Sacred) Ibises
Made by god N	• Made by Re • He Who Is Made by the Moon (God)
Kept alive by god N	• Ptah Keeps Me Alive
Sentences expressing action (e.g., seizing enemies), quality, or state of deity	• Khons Has Come • May the Apis Bull Live! • Horus Is Hale • May Horus Be Hale! • The Apis Bull Is Enduring • Thoth Has Been Born • Sobek Is Strong • Montu Is Strong • Khons Is in Festival • Ptah Is Content • May Khons Kill the Evil Eye • May Apis Take Hold of Them!

Source: Günther, 2013.

Table 7.3. Basilophorous Name Patterns.

Basilophorous Name Patterns	**Examples**
Unextended royal names: Birth name	Amenemhat Senusret Thutmose Shoshenq Psammetichus Amasis
Unextended royal names: Throne name	Amenemhat I: Sehetepibre Amenemhat I: Kheperkara Thutmose III: Menkheperra Psammetichus I: Wahibre Psammetichus II: Neferibre Amasis: Khenem-ibre
Royal name (sometimes in a complete sentence)	Beloved by Teti Merira (Pepy I) Is Alive Ramesses Is Strong or Victorious May Shoshenq Live Khenemibre (i.e., Amasis) Is Enduring Seneferu Is Content Khufu Is Strong or Victorious Khufu Is Beloved by the Gods Khufu Is in the Horizon My Life Is in the Hand of Radjedef

Source: Günther, 2013.

In addition to theophorous and basilophorous names, other appellative practices signaled the super-religious and theopolitical nature of archaic Egypt. Very frequently, a divine epithet is used instead of a god's proper name, e.g., Lord of Sumenu (= Sobek); Great Sycamore (= Hathor); and less obviously, The Ox-herd (an epithet of Anubis and other gods). Some names were based on administrative, military, or priestly titles (as well as other professions). These were not appellative but true personal names. Their various functions were regarded as crucial for maintaining the theocentric order: The Overseer of the Granary; The General; The Overseer of the Archers; The Troop-commander; The God's Father; The Prophet; The Water-carrier; and The Prophet of Maat. During the Ramesside Period, the names of the royal butlers (especially those of presumably foreign origin) were frequently based on the names of the reigning pharaoh, e.g., Merenptah Is in the House of Ptah; Neferkara (= Ramesses IX) Is in the House of Amun; Neferibra (= Psammetichus II) is Beloved by Ptah; Wahibre (= Psammetichus I) Is in the Horizon; Amasis Is Enduring in the Great Mansion (of Heliopolis).[145] Besides deities, some were named after divinized individuals, such as Imhotep (Djoser's vizier, probable architect of Djoser's step pyramid, high priest of Re, and other legendary roles, such as being a physician) and Amenhotep, son of Hapu (architect, priest, scribe).

By the Late Period, if not earlier, animal names with religious associations had become popular. Examples include: The Falcon; The Lion; The Cat; The Crocodile; The Snake; The Sacred Snake; (The) Lizard; The Frog (linked to regeneration). Plant names were also common in the Old and Middle Kingdom: Tamarisk; Lotus Bundle; Asphodel; The Rose; The Rose of Min; Great Sycamore; and Lotus Flower (the ultimate origin of Susan — *Sššn*). In the latter half of the Ptolemaic Period, The Son/Daughter of (the parent) N became frequent. However, it is often impossible to tell whether such naming practices indicated either "the son/daughter of (the parent named after the divinity) N; or The Son/Daughter of God N."[146]

Notes to Chapter 7

1. Assmann, 1990, p. 35.
2. Assmann, 1998, p. 386
3. Hays, 2009, p. 16.
4. Cf. Pinch, 2004, p. 70.
5. Robins, 2001, p. 286.
6. Shaw, 2000, p. 16.
7. Malek, 2000, p. 111.
8. Maat is perhaps cognate with to steer, guide, direct; it resonates with the "embodiment of the order given to the organized world by the demiurge at the origin of the cosmos." Kruchten, 2001, p. 277. Morenz contended that the concept's origins are from a geometrical and physical term denoting straightness, evenness; it "probably represented the straightness of the scale of the pharaoh's throne, which in turn may be regarded as a stylized form of the primeval mound." Morenz, 1992, p. 113.
9. Teeter, 2001b, p. 319.
10. Morenz, 1992, p. 13.
11. M17-M40-S29-I9-X1-G37-Z3, etc.
12. D58-X1-U30-G1-Z4-G37; D58-X1-U30-G1-F18-A2, etc.
13. Morenz, 1992, p. 132.
14. O4-G1-Q3-V12-Z2.
15. Kruchten, 2001, p. 277.
16. Kruchten, 2001, p. 279.
17. N35-X1-D36-V12.
18. Kruchten, 2001, p. 277.
19. Wilkinson, 2003, p. 61.
20. O1-O29; O1-O29-G7; O29-O1, etc.

21. Silverman, 1991, p. 59.
22. A23, etc.
23. N29-S38.
24. S2-S4.
25. Morenz, 1992, p. 41 (italics in original).
26. Bonhême, 2001a, pp. 161–163.
27. Bonhême, 2001b, p. 244.
28. U36-Z1; U36-A40. Note that U36-Z1-G7 is glossed as "majesty, incarnation."
29. D58-M17-X1-S4; L2; L2-X1, etc.
30. A41; A43B0; M23; M23-A45; M23-G7, etc.
31. R8-O29A.
32. R8-F35.
33. Wilkinson, 2003, p. 55.
34. Morenz, 1992, p. 41.
35. Silverman, 1991, p. 66.
36. M23-X1-M17-M17-X1-Y1; M23-M17-X1-M17, M23-M17-M17-X1-Z2, etc.
37. Wilkinson, 2003, p. 56.
38. Tyldesley, 2019, p. 8.
39. Wilkinson, 2003. p. 63.
40. Baines and Malek, 2000, p. 201.
41. Wilson, 1965, p. 54.
42. Pinch, 2004, p. 71.
43. Robins, 2001, p. 287.
44. Jaynes, 1976, p. 187.
45. Jaynes, 1976, p. 187.
46. Jaynes, 1976, p. 187.
47. Jaynes, 1976, p. 187.
48. Jaynes, 1976, p. 187.
49. Jaynes, 1976, p. 187.
50. Silverman, 1991, p. 57.
51. Silverman, 1997, p. 113.
52. Silverman, 1991, p. 55.
53. O34-D21-Aa1-O33.
54. M23-L2, etc.
55. Leprohon, 2001, p. 409.
56. R8-U36-A1.
57. R8-U36; R8-U36-G7; R8-U36-Z1-A1; R8-U36-Z1-G7; R8-Z5-Z5-Z5. A prophet of Maat was *ḥm nṯr mꜣ't* (R8-U36-H6).
58. R8-U36-A1-D1-Q3-Z5.
59. G36-D21-S42-U24.
60. G36-D21-U1-M17-A40B.
61. T28-D21-V28-D58-W3-N5-A1; T28-D21-W3-A1; T28-D21-Z4-Y1-V28-D58-W3-N35-Z3; T28-V28-D58, etc.
62. M21; S29-G17-A1; S29-G17-A51; S29-G17-X1; S29-X1-G17-A1; S29-Xa-G17-A2, etc.
63. D31.

64. A6; A60; D60-A1; D60-N35A; D60-N35A-A1.
65. D2-G36.
66. D36-N29-D50-D50-A1; D36-N29-T14-T14-A1; G35-N29-A1-Z2; G35-N29-D50-D50-A1; G35-N29-T14-T14-A1; W10-N29-D50-D50-A1; W10-N29-M17-M17-A1-Z3; W10-N29-T14-T14-A1.
67. G1-N35-N29-A1.
68. M17-W11-D21-U33.
69. O4-M17-O4-M17-D60.
70. U36-N16.
71. Aa28-G36-D4.
72. R7-R8-M17; X1-R8; X1&R8-M17; X1&R8-M17-X1-D21-A1.
73. R8-G36; R8-M17-X1; R8-M17-X1-I9-A1; R8-X1.
74. Y5-N35-U32-L2-X1-Z5-A40.
75. N37-U1-J15-M17-M17-X1-B1.
76. S29-G1-D46-X1.
77. U1-D46-X1.
78. M17-K1-N35-O34-B1.
79. F13-D21-X1-Z2.
80. F32-X1-M17-M17-S29.
81. R8-N41-X1; R8-U36-X1.
82. J1-N35-W24-X1-G43-B1-Z3.
83. B47.
84. R8-D46-X-Z1.
85. G6-D21-N37-X1.
86. D31-X1; D31.
87. D60-X1.
88. A6-N42-X1.
89. R8-N1-X1-Z1-N35-M17-Y5-N35, etc.
90. R8-N14-G1-Z5-Z5-A30-G7.
91. E15-G43-X1; E15-G43-X1-Aa2-A1; E15-X1-G43; M17-N35-Q3-X1-G43.
92. U28-G1; U28-G1-A1.
93. M17-D58-E8-V28-G43-N35A.
94. M17-V28-G43-Z4; M17-V28-M17-S42.
95. D60-N35-F22-Z7-Z4.
96. T25-D58-X1-Z4-A40.
97. F36-G1; Aa25-A1; S29-Aa25.
98. F26-G43-X1-Z4.
99. F26-N35-V16-Z2; F26-V17.
100. D2-D21-S29-N37-X1-U30-G1; D2-D21-S29-N37-X1-U30-Y1A; D2-D21-S29-N37-X1-U30-Y1A-Z2.
101. M17-D21-A47-O34-N37-X1-U30-G1-Y1A-N35-S19-X1-Z1-R8.
102. F4-D36.
103. Frankfort, 1978, p. 114.
104. Harrington, 2010, p. 29.
105. Toivari-Viitala, 2001, p. 225.
106. Harrington, 2010, p. 102.

107. Harrington, 2010, p. 148.
108. Harrington, 2010, p. 72.
109. Harrington, 2010, p. 102.
110. Harrington, 2010, p. 83.
111. Harrington, 2010.
112. Wilson, 2003, p. 452.
113. Wilkinson, 2003, p. 45.
114. M17-D36-N35A-D2-Z1-W3.
115. M17-D4-G43-X1-Y2-Y2-Y2.
116. N35-X1-D36-Y1-Z2.
117. S29-N28-D36-D36-G43-Y1-Z2.
118. O4-D21-M17-M17-I12.
119. F46A-M16-O36.
120. Shaw, 2000, p. 16.
121. Wiebach-Koepke, 2001, pp. 498–500.
122. Englund, 2001, pp. 564–569.
123. R4.
124. Englund, 2001, pp. 564–569.
125. O3; O1-D21-D54-X1-X2-X4-Z2-P8-Z7-A2; O1-D21-D54-X1-X2-X4-Z2-P8-Z7-A2.
126. O1-D21-X1-D54-D21-P8-G43-Z8-Z2.
127. Leprohon, 2001, pp. 569–572.
128. V30-D4-X1-Aa1-X1; V30-D4-Aa1-X1; O3.
129. Englund, 2001, pp. 564–569.
130. Englund, 2001, pp. 564–569.
131. Summarized from Oakes and Gahlin, 2006, pp. 164–165.
132. This refers to the story of Osiris.
133. M17-X1-Q3-X1. This was originally the name of the ancient goddess who was patroness of the southern district of Thebes.
134. O23-W4.
135. O'Rourke, 2001, p. 408.
136. Frankfort, 2000, p. 136.
137. O'Rourke, 2001, p. 407.
138. Morenz, 1992, p. 7.
139. Frankfort, 2000, p. 135.
140. Günther, 2013, p. 3.
141. Günther, 2013, p. 5.
142. Günther, 2013, p. 4.
143. Günther, 2013, p. 3.
144. Günther, 2013, p. 5.
145. Günther, 2013, p. 6.
146. Günther, 2013, p. 3.

Chapter 8

Inspiring Awe and Radiating Authority: Monumental Architecture

"The house of death is for life."
— *Instructions of Prince Hardjedef*

FROM THE PERSPECTIVE OF THE MODERN MIND, it is not easy to understand the reasons for "such huge and seemingly wasteful projects as the building of pyramids,"[1] as well as other impressive architectural feats. We have a tendency to impute "practical" motivations. For example, shafts in pyramids, once believed to be for air circulation, are now believed to have had religious meaning, perhaps to allow the king's Ba to come and go from the burial chamber. The accounts offered in this chapter on the reasons behind devoting so much physical and intellectual effort to building monumental architecture makes sense if contextualized within a paralogic super-religious mentality.

RADIATING DIVINE POWER

From temples, tombs, and other edifices, divine beings emitted influence (ARCC). Of course, the most prominent example were the pyramids, some of which were personified as divinities and given a name. Awesome splendor, pharaonic monocracy, and cosmic symbolism all converged in monuments of unassailable authorization. The word for monument, *mnw*,[2] was used for sanctuary (*ntr mnw* / *ntr mnw*),[3] image of god (*mnw*), and idol.[4] Urban dwellings, farms, ranches, and settlements in the environs were dominated by ARCCs, which by their very visual presence broadcast a type of implicit control over local inhabitants and reminded everyone of the TSO. ARCCs can be understood as multilayered accretions built around OHFs, such as a cult god-statue or gloriously entombed king.

Urban centers functioned as ARCCs. The first capital was Memphis (White Walls), on the east side of the Nile in Lower Egypt, established around 3000 BCE. Other capitals included, depending on period, Alexandria, Sasi, Tanis, Akhetaten (el-Amarna), Thebes, Hierakonpolis (Nekhen), Avaris, Piramesse, and Itj-Tawy. Important centers were Saqqara (west side of the Nile, Lower Egypt); Abydos (west side of the Nile, Upper Egypt); Aswan (east side of the Nile at the Frist Cataract near Elephantine); and Giza (Lower Egypt on the west side of the Nile Delta).

Each population center had its own unique history and features. Consider Thebes (Waset). Once a small town during the Old Kingdom, Thebes was promoted to the capital in Dynasty 11 (2080–1938 BCE). It sits on the east side of the Nile, Upper Egypt. It was described by Homer as the "city of 100 gates," due to the many pylons fronting its palaces and temples, such as the Temple of Karnak, dedicated to Amun, Mut, Khons, and Montu (the local warrior god and protector of the city). During the New Kingdom, beginning with Thutmose I (1493–1481 BCE), pharaohs began to be entombed in the Valley of the Kings on the West Bank, opposite Thebes.

In general, accessibility for the average person to the numinous became more restricted as one moved from private to larger, more communal edifices: (1) one's domestic dwelling or personal spirituality; direct contact with and immediate access to ancestors and household deities; (2) tomb or personal/familial spirituality or communication with the dead and state/local gods; (3) chapel/shrine or local spirituality; exchange with or via local priesthood; (4) temple or state-sanctioned spirituality; contact with gods of officialdom via (intermediary) priesthood.[5]

TOMBS:
HOUSES FOR THE LIVING DEAD

Tombs evolved from simple Badarian-culture grave pits dug out on the edge of the desert. Some pits were lined with reed matting. Similar burial patterns continued into the Naqada Period. By then graves were covered with reed mattings, branches, and wood planks. A few even had painted walls and multiple chambers. By Dynasty Zero, multichambered substructures appeared. By Dynasties 1 and 2, "palace façade" (a pattern of niching) decorated tombs.[6] It was at this time that tombs for royalty and nobility became standardized. Significantly, tombs were inspired by domestic architectural design, indicating the blurring of this-world dwellings and other-world mortuary sites (i.e., houses for the deceased). Nonroyal tombs might have a substructure, a reception hall, guest rooms, a master bedroom (the burial chamber), a living room, women's quarters, a bathroom, and a lavatory.[7] Tombs constructed completely from stone appeared in the early phases of the Old Kingdom. Funerary goods of pottery, jewelry, tools, cosmetic palettes, and ivory or wooden figurines of women and animals were placed in tombs, evidencing early concepts of a Doubleworld (Table 8.1).

For the elite, *mastaba* were used. Their main level had a room for ceremonies, plus a *serdab* (Arabic for cellar), where a statue of the deceased was placed. This image permitted the living dead to observe offerings being made to them. The first phase of royal pyramids began with the "step pyramid" at Saqqara. These led to more conventionally-shaped pyramids, which were components of town-scale complexes, some the size of small cities. Cenotaphs were also constructed. Meanwhile, nonroyalty were buried near the desert. Some were buried in cliff tombs.

A Microcosmos of the Cosmos

A grave is a liminal, transitional space. It is an "ambiguous and unstable position between two spheres of existence ... located simultaneously in the realm of the living and the underworld."[17] Simply put, the dual function of tombs evolved into its two basic parts. The first was an area where the living dead could communicate with those in this world. This was the part for cultic practices, where offerings were presented (on an offering stone) — a

Table 8.1. Terms for Tombs.

<table>
<tr><th>No.</th><th>Term</th><th>Translation</th></tr>
<tr><td>1.</td><td>ꜣḫt[8]</td><td>Horizon, tomb of king, palace</td></tr>
<tr><td>2.</td><td>mr[9]</td><td>Pyramid, tomb</td></tr>
<tr><td>3.</td><td>st[10]</td><td rowspan="5">Tomb</td></tr>
<tr><td>4.</td><td>ỉs[11]</td></tr>
<tr><td>5.</td><td>''ỉ[12]</td></tr>
<tr><td>6.</td><td>r st ꜣ[13]</td></tr>
<tr><td>7.</td><td>m'ḥ't[14]</td></tr>
<tr><td>8.</td><td>ḥrt[15]</td><td>Tomb, necropolis, realm of the dead</td></tr>
<tr><td>9.</td><td>ỉ' / ''[16]</td><td>Tomb, mastaba</td></tr>
</table>

"dwelling for the dead" accessible to the living, priests, relatives of the deceased, and passers-by. As a permeable site, it allowed the "living to interact directly with the dead."[18] The second part was the actual burial chamber. It was decorated with portrayals of the earthly environment — scenes of hunting, fighting, farming, and banquets. These were not mere representations; they would paralogically "acquire vitality by the performance of certain rituals."[19]

The spatiality of tombs originally symbolized the distinction between the chthonic and solar domains. This dates back to the *Pyramid Texts*. By the New Kingdom, the layout of tombs corresponded to the three cosmic realms inhabited by the deceased. The first is the solar or heavenly domain (superstructure, pyramidion, stelephorous statues in recess). The second is the earthy realm (courtyard, tomb chapel, stelae, false door, statues, shaft entrance),[20] and the final realm is the Afterworld (substructures, shaft, burial chamber).[21] The symbolic associations of the tomb chamber, netherworld, or abyss come together in the term *dwꜣt*.[22] The body and tomb of the deceased were believed to be a personal Osiris (this is why they were sometimes addressed as Osiris) as well as a personal Duat.

Portals between This World and the Doubleworld

The living and the deceased communicated with each other through stylized faux portals (false doors) in temples. These thresholds, which for the archaic Egyptians were not representatively symbolic but functionally symbolic, also allowed the deceased and deities to enter and exit this world. False doors, which symbolized liminality, had two purposes. First, they allowed a passage for the Ka of the deceased — who was able to transition between the realms of the living and the dead — between the chapel or shrine room and the great beyond. This is why they are known as Ka-doors. Tombs were regarded as "houses of the Ka," or as houses for the dead (*pr ḏt*)[23] (this also meant estate, foundation). Second, false doors provided a focus for the Ka-priest who made offerings.[24] Here we should note Ka chapels have been found in tombs as well as temples (*ḥwt kꜣ*[25] or *ḥwt kꜣ ptḥ*).[26]

False doors were found in so-called "mortuary temples"[27] and date from the Old Kingdom. Inscriptions detailed the deceased's name, titles, offering lists, offering formula, and wishes for a long blessed existence in the necropolis. It was an architectural element that condensed and concentrated the personality of the deceased for all eternity.[28] Some tombs had multiple false doors. Statues of the deceased might be incorporated into some false door niches. In some cases a false door was represented by stela encased in a wall. Sometimes the dead were depicted as returning from the Duat in resurrected form.

By about 1200 BCE, a "drastic change" transpired: Within two or three generations, the "tomb had discarded its devotion to this world and dedicated all its wall space to death and the next world."[29] Given that this was around the period of the final breakdown of bicameral mentality, this alteration in tomb aesthetics indicates, arguably, that definitions of the Afterworld had become more interiorized, i.e., they changed from a literal view to a more psychospiritual understanding.

The Purpose of "Empty Tombs"

Cenotaphs present an intriguing architectural item of archaic Egypt, as their purpose is unclear. Labeled spiritual tombs, dummy tombs, or secondary royal tombs, they are similar to the so-called false doors in that they have been described as "fictive architecture" (DWMP).[30] However, for the archaic Egyptians they had a very real function, which makes sense once we apply a paralogical analysis.

Egyptian seems to have lacked a single, specialized word for cenotaph, though *'ḥ't* or *m'ḥ't*,[31] which might also mean tomb, were used. Despite originating from the Greek appellation "empty tombs," centotaphs were in fact not always empty and sometimes contained a sarcophagus or grave goods. Centotaphs were utilized for both royal and private tombs and for funerary and cultic structures.[32] They come in two types: (1) tombs that did not contain the actual interment of a body, but clearly had a function related to the Afterworld; and (2) mortuary buildings where a funerary or offering cult was maintained; the actual burial of the deceased was elsewhere.[33]

Now for the paralogical explanation. Cenotaphs may have functioned as a god's tomb or were simply abandoned burial projects,[34] but they have also been called Ka-tombs and Ka-pyramids.[35] The idea is that they were a type of "housing and support" for the king's Ka[36] and intended for his "otherworldly aspects." Some kings had multiple secondary tombs, presumably for their various Kas. Note that statues were understood as a substitute for the king's actual body and might be buried elsewhere.[37] The idea here is that the archaic Egyptians did not merely believe that a personage could manifest themselves in more than one place; they actually experienced such multiple appearances.

STAIRWAYS TO THE SUN

Especially during the Old Kingdom, pyramid complexes operated like an "economic engine." They were massive labor projects that employed farmers, herdsmen, bakers, brewers, and craftsmen of all kinds, who delivered goods and services to hundreds, if not thousands, of consumers. They functioned like Mesopotamian city-states in how they generated a massive circuitry of socioeconomic exchange with the environs. The pyramid was the largest of what have been called "pious foundations," or "enormous endowments of people, lands and produce," for the sustenance and upkeep of tombs, temples, as well as pyramids.[38] Politically, pyramids were a "major catalyst for internal colonization" of what would become the provinces, triggering the development of Egypt as one of the world's first true states.[39]

The tomb-temple complexes were the "temple and ritual center at the core of the Egyptian state; reliquary of a king; embodiment of light and shadow; and the union of heaven and earth, encapsulating the mystery of death and rebirth."[40] They were a site of transformation and transfiguration, a womb from which the king would be reborn, a radiant shrine of glorification. They were a means of access for the king to reach heaven and also to return to his place of interment where he could receive offerings. These nexuses of cosmopolitical energies concentrated and emanated power and were utilized by an elite to awe and govern the masses and nearby settlements (ARCC). A newly constructed pyramid, freshly covered with smoothed white limestone and capped by a glistening pyramidion (associated with the sun god Re), must have been "so brilliant as to be almost blinding."[41]

The allure of the pyramid complex was appreciated well beyond Egypt. Nubia (in modern Sudan) was greatly influenced by Egyptian civilization. There the rulers of the Kingdom Napata (from ca. 720 BCE) and the Kingdom of Meroe (ending about 350 CE) built pyramids on a smaller scale. However, they ended up constructing 180, about twice as many as were built by the Egyptians.

The Evolution of Places of Ascension

The pyramid, or as it was known to the Egyptians, a "place of ascendance" (*mr*),[42] evolved from two elemental structures: a substructure (for burial) and a superstructure marking the burial site, where offerings to the deceased could be made.[43] The place of ascension is "simply the mound transformed to sublime geometry and expanded into a man-made mountain."[44] The architectural antecedents of places of ascension were mound graves, designed like imitation palaces in the form of open rectangular courts with mudbrick walls. By around 2900 BCE, the graves of rulers and the elite were neat mud-brick boxes, sunk in the earth and divided up like a domestic dwelling into several rooms. They were covered by a mound and marked by two stelae. These structures became the *mastabas.*

The tombs of Dynasty 1 kings (ca. 2950–2750 BCE) reflect the relatively simple structure of what would become mountain-sized monumental mortuary architecture. Aha's tomb had two stelae that recorded the king's name, and underground burial chambers lined with cedar and covered with planks. It was capped with a superstructure of a brick-covered mound. Not far from the tomb was an offering chapel, open spaces, and buildings made from mud-brick and wattle of reed.[45] Den was the first king to utilize stone in his mostly mud-brick tomb. The royal tomb–temple complexes of Dynasty 1 included subsidiary graves of those who supported the king, indicating that a proto-state was forming. Djer's mortuary complex included 338 graves for the king's personal retinue, his servants, minor officials, and young women (it cannot be determined definitively whether they were ritualistically killed or committed suicide).[46]

Employing his architect Imhotep, Djoser (or Netjerikhet; 2650–2575 BCE) materialized his great ambitions by laying the foundations for subsequent pyramid-shaped achievements by building the first "step pyramid" at Saqqara. He heralded the classic age of tomb–temple complex construction (he also established a necropolis at Memphis). During the Old Kingdom, step pyramids evolved into what we now recognize as pyramids. Sneferu (2575–2545 BCE), the first king of Dynasty 4, commissioned three places of ascension and is considered the builder of the first "true" pyramid. Sneferu's son and successor, Khufu (Cheops; 2545–2525 BCE), built the first and largest of the three pyramids of Giza. His son, Khafre, built the second (as well as the Great Sphinx), and the third was built by Menkaure. These are the most impressive places of ascension ever built and indicate an "accelerated cultural development, comparable to our modern space programme or computer revolution."[47] Within three generations, the majority of Egypt's pyramids were built. "All the other pyramids of Egyptian kings combined (excluding queens' and other satellite pyramids) contain only 41 per cent of the total mass of the pyramids of Sneferu, his son Khufu, and grandson Khafre."[48]

After Khafre, the aspiration and size of pyramids are considerably smaller. The break came around the time of Menkaure (2532–2510 BCE). Though the pyramids were less impressive, their pyramid temples grew in scale, complexity, and craftsmanship. Social changes of some sort may be reflected in the diminishing scale of pyramid building, but we can only speculate on what they were. Scaled-down tomb construction may have indicated changes in the theocentric status of the king. Though this sacred personage was still pivotal in Egypt's cosmopolitical worldview, perhaps other centers of power increased, thereby robbing the god-king of his original divine charisma and thus resources.

At the beginning of Dynasty 5, Userkaf reinstated the construction of places of ascension, but the age of ambitious, sky-scraping monumental tomb building had ended. Massive tomb-temple complex construction came to end during the First Intermediate Period. Just Sneferu's (2575–2545 BCE) pyramid at Meidum is 638,733 cubic meters, far larger than anything built after Khafre's reign.[49] An analysis demonstrates the startling changes in monumental construction.[50] Table 8.2 shows the average volume (cubic meters) of the first eight pyramids (1,096,899) and Table 8.3 shows the average of 22 later pyramids (137,425). By Dynasty 5, the pyramids were smaller but more standardized. This reflects a less centralized theopolitical order, or at least one that could not mobilize the requisite resources for such massive monumental mortuary projects. It was also during Dynasty 5 that the first examples of the *Pyramid Texts* appear in Unas's (2350–2325 BCE) pyramid.

Beginning in the Old Kingdom, for almost one millennium, places of ascension were used to inter kings. At first the construction of tomb-temple complexes was concentrated near Memphis and then from about the Middle Kingdom around Itjtawy (near modern el-Lisht). During the Old Kingdom, actual funerary objects were replaced by representations on walls and inscriptions with offering lists, prayers, and biographies. Temple reliefs were essentially illustrated text. Depictions of interactions of kings and gods were "accompanied by dialogues, as if the reliefs were snapshots of Egyptian drama which could be reenacted eternally through their presence on the walls and columns."[51] The phrase used to introduce the illustrated speeches was the same as that used for speeches in the *Book of the Dead*: *ḏd mdw*[52] or "recitation."

Table 8.2. The Average Volume (cubic meters) of the First 8 Eight Pyramids.

King	Dynasty	Volume (cu. meters)	Notes
Djoser	3	330,400	
Sekhemkhet	3	33,600	Unfinished
Khaba (?)	3	47,040	Unfinished
Sneferu (?)	4	638,733	
Sneferu	4	1,237,040	
Sneferu	4	1,694,000	
Khufu (Cheops)	4	2,583,283	
Khafre	4	2,211,096	
Total = 8,775,192; Total Divided by 8 = 1,096,899			

Source: Lehner, 1997, p. 17.

Table 8.3. The Average Volume (cubic m.) of Later Pyramids.

King	Dynasty	Volume (cu. meters)	Notes
Menkaure	4	235,183	
Shepseskaf	4	148,271	
Khentkawes	4	6,372	
Userkaf	5	87,906	
Sahure	5	96,542	
Neferirkare	5	257,250	
Niuserre	5	112,632	
Djedkare-Isesi	5	107,835	Approximate
Unas	5	47,390	
Teti	6	107,835	Approximate
Pepi I	6	107,835	Approximate
Merenre	6	107,835	Approximate
Pepi II	6	107,835	Approximate
Ibi	8	6,994	
Amenemhet I	12	129,360	
Senusret I	12	225,093	
Senusret II	12	185,665	
Senusret III	12	288,488	
Amenemhet III	12	274,625	
Amenemhet III	12	200,158	
Amenemhet IV or Soberkneferu	13	30,316	Unfinished
Khendjer	13	44,096	
Total = 3,023,351; Total Divided by 22 = 137,425			

Source: Lehner, 1997, p. 17.

The Purpose of Pyramids

There is an "almost complete reticence on the subject by Egyptian texts" about the reason for building pyramids.[53] But enough archaeological and textual evidence exists to confidently piece together an explanation. The place of ascension is both a mammoth symbol for a grave mound and resurrection, as well as a chapel to commune with the departed and to leave offerings.[54] Its prime function is to sustain the royal ancestor cult complex and transform the mortal king into an immortal being. Though for convenience's sake we use "tomb" when discussing an Egyptian pyramid, it was not in fact a tomb as we understand it. Rather it was a "station for transitional or spiritual events";[55] it was "regarded not so much as an eternal resting place for the king's mummy but as a location where the king could be reborn, transformed and gain access to heaven."[56] After all, death "was not regarded as the end of individual existence, but merely a means of access to the next world."[57]

A place of ascension, like other super-religious edifices and artifacts, dripped with symbolism. Besides a tomb for the king, a place of ascension was also a temple to Horus (who the king identified with while alive) and a temple to Osiris (who the king became after death). With its close connection to the solar cult, the true pyramid, with its smooth, sloping sides encased in white limestone, may have been an attempt to recreate the sun's rays descending from the heavens to the earth. The king scaled places of ascendance to join Re; the *Pyramid Texts* speak of the sun's rays as a ramp by which the king climbs to reach the sun. The place of ascension was also conceptualized as the phoenix (*bin / bnw*),[58] an incarnation of Re, who perched on the primeval mound at the dawn of creation (the primeval mound was also isomorphically represented in temples).[59] It symbolized both the "mound of primeval earth [chthonic aspect] and the weightless rays of sunlight, a union of heaven and earth."[60] Places of ascension were topped with gilded-capstones (*bnbnt*),[61] as were obelisks. These pyramidions, which represented the sun's sacred rays made solid as they shimmered in the sky, also symbolized the primeval mound. The latter was depicted as the Benben stone (*bnbn*).[62] It was upon this holy stone, which emerged from the primordial watery abyss (Nun), upon which the creator deity Atum settled in the Heliopolitan creation myth.

At the beginning of Dynasty 4, places of ascension started to be given names (Table 8.4). Some pyramid names contain a reference to the king's Ba. Note the use of "appear," hinting perhaps at theophanic hallucinatory experiences. "Six of the 26 known pyramid names refer to the rising of the king, while five refer to his perfection. Five others affirm that the king is 'established' and 'endures,' while eight pyramids are named for the king's 'places' or 'thrones' which 'rise,' 'flourish, and are 'established,' 'pure,' 'divine' and 'perfect.'"[63]

The Standard Pyramid

We can describe, in its most basic form, the standard pyramid complex that had taken shape by Dynasty 4 or 5. It had about a dozen distinct components. The tomb superstructure, i.e., the pyramid itself, was the most conspicuous component.[64] Other key elements included the satellite pyramid (a cenotaph; presumably for the king's Ka);[65] a "mortuary temple"; an enclosure wall; causeway; pits for sacred barques; a valley temple; smaller pyramids for the queen or principal wives; cemeteries for officials and noblemen; numerous domestic buildings for priests, servants, and craftsmen; and other structures needed to sustain the funerary cult.[66]

Table 8.4. Examples of Pyramid Names.

Name of Place of Ascension	Dynasty
Sneferu Endures	4
The Southern Shining Place of Ascension	4
The Shining Place of Ascension	4
Great is Khafre	4
Menkaure is Divine	4
The Purified Place of Ascension	4
Pure are the Places of Userkaf	5
The Rising of the Ba Spirit	5
Place of Ascension of the Ba of Neferirkare	5
The Place of Ascension which Is Divine of the Ba Spirits	5
The Places of Niuserre Endure	5
The Perfection of Pepi Is Established	6
The Perfection of Merenre Appears	6
The Places of the Appearances of Amenemhet	12
Senusret Appears	12
Amenemhet Lives	12

Source: Lehner, 1997, p. 17.

The Last Age of the Pyramids

Amenhotep I (1514–1493 BCE), probably looking for a place less vulnerable to robbers, began a trend of selecting the cliffs on the western shores of Thebes for burial. Also established was the Valley of the Queens. Common during the First Intermediate and Middle Kingdom Period were free-standing structures, called staff tombs; these were arranged in rows and cut into the rock. By the New Kingdom, at least 62 pharaohs were interred in a communal royal burial ground — the Valley of the Kings — on the Nile's west bank at Thebes. Unlike the older mortuary complexes, the "mortuary temple" components were built on the edge of the desert, separately away from the rock-cut tombs.[67] The latter contained stairways, halls, passages, shafts, and burial chambers. The so-called "mortuary temples" were now conspicuous and more accessible. The peaked mountains perhaps served as the symbolic place of ascension sitting atop the tomb.[68] Canals linked the tombs to the Nile and each tomb had at least one artificial harbor.

TEMPLES: HOUSES OF GODS

In the Predynastic Period, portable shrines were probably used to house deities (OHFs). As time passed, larger, more permanent structures enveloped the god's image, becoming shrines that were slightly larger than the typical house to signal their special status. They were made of wood, wickerwood, reed, and mud. It was in these structures, primitive ARCCs, that the gods dwelled. These may have been placed within "fortresses of the gods," where assemblies of gods met for ceremonies, perhaps in the form of standards, emblems, or banners.[69] A court was enclosed by mud brick, paneled walls (*tennos*) meant to symbolically keep chaos on the outside and preserve the sanctity of the inner area. In the center was a sacred mound where the king would stand with the gods (Followers of Horus). These structures evolved into proto-temples that contained the cult image. They had a hooped roof and were foregrounded by a courtyard surrounded by a fence or wall. Two poles with banners of the gods' emblem stood guard at the enclosure's entrance. In the courtyard's center, in front of the shrine, a flagpole flew a banner; this probably became the hieroglyph *nṯr* for "god" or "divine." Later stone temples replicated and scaled-up the basic architectural layout and features apparent in these early structures.[70]

Before Dynasty 12 (1938–1755 BCE), temples had been "small, often irregular constructions of mud brick, with only a sparing use of stone for doorways, thresholds, and the like."[71] The most impressive buildings were not the temples that housed deities, but rather the pyramids of pharaohs. The tradition of monumental edifices dedicated to the major gods and goddesses has its origins in the early part of the Middle Kingdom, perhaps reflecting how the kings shifted from the center of theopolitical focus, making more room for the deities.[72] This change may have had to do with a reaction to a growing social complexity that outstripped pharaonic monocracy.

Unlike churches, mosques, or synagogues, temples were not places for organized public worship. Ordinary individuals were excluded from the inner areas, though they could petition the gods in the outer precincts. By the later periods, however, commoners were permitted into the peristyle court; this became a place to pray to and supplicate the gods and kings, who were manifested as statues. Some temples had "healing statues" that were inscribed with spells for curing or protecting one from snake bites, scorpion stings, etc.

A temple was known as a "mansion of god" (*ḥwt nṯr*),[73] indicating the assumption that the deities, though different from mortals in certain ways, could co-exist in the same earthly realms with ordinary beings. The temple was a stone microcosmos of the cosmos, condensing within itself the energies of the heavens, earth, and other worlds. It was also considered a great sarcophagus in which the miracle of the sun god's rebirth occurred each day.[74] The pylon symbolized the land through which the Nile flows to Egypt, as well as the mountains in between which the sun rises. As the Island of Creation, the temple emerged from the roiling primeval ocean. This is why its walls were constructed to symbolize waves, with alternating concave and convex sections that formed a wave-line pattern. Each temple also had a sacred lake that symbolized the watery chaos from which creation arose.

Temples, as well as the tombs of early dynasties, contained a mound of earth that evoked the primeval mound. This symbolized a divine force that promised new creation and eternal rebirth. It was personified by the god Tatenen (Rising Land), who was associated with Re or Nefertum, the lotus deity. Incidentally, the lotus was widely used in decorations, symbolizing the sun, creation, and the primeval waters.

The first mound, Benben, and the pyramids, given their common shape, all isomorphically resonated as symbols of cosmic points of renascence and regeneration. The aim of this feature, as well as monumental architecture in general, was to "make the inhabitant of the temple (or tomb) partake symbolically in the process of creation itself or in the cosmic cycles," especially that of the sun.[75]

Key rituals linked to the construction of a temple were the foundation (*bȝ*)[76] and consecration ceremonies. The former saw the delineations of a new temple measured out, while the latter saw the bestowal of a new temple to its deity. Daily rituals were performed perhaps three times a day: dawn, noon, and evening.

Temples as Theopolitical Points of Focus

In the ancient Egyptian worldview, divine kingly rule, monumental architecture, and mortuary practices (here "mortuary" is qualified as "not completely deceased") all converged in a theopolitical perspective. This intersection of meanings is clear in terms that meant both palace or temple: *'ḥ*,[77] *'ḥt*,[78] and *pr nsw*.[79] A similar sense is apparent in the "horizon of eternity" that was a name of a temple/palace/tomb (*ȝḫtt nt nḥḥ*).[80] In later periods, the innermost parts of temples may have been regarded as the tombs of the gods.

In earlier scholarly literature, a distinction was made between "mortuary temples" and "cult temples." The idea was that the former were dedicated to a god, while the cult temples, called "House of Millions of Years," were the sites for rituals connected to deceased kings (usually built at the east side of a pyramid, but in the New Kingdom placed separately away from the tombs). But this classification is problematic, as the roles of temples and tombs varied and were not always clearly separated. Temples were not designated either for a (deceased or living) king or a god, and in any case the archaic Egyptians themselves never made this distinction. Another more tenable categorization is "royal cult complexes" and "divine cult complexes." In the former, the cult of a king (usually deceased) was maintained, while the worship of another god was sometimes practiced. In divine cult complexes, the worship of gods and sometimes of a king (usually living) was performed. By the New Kingdom, divine cult complexes were housed in elaborate edifices, as evident in the Temples of Karnak and Luxor. Note also that the real purpose of royal cult complexes was not funerary; rather they provided a place where the deceased king could continue to be sustained in the Afterworld and where the god would grant the king eternal life in exchange for ritual offerings.[81]

Temples as Centers of Socioeconomic Activity

From the beginning, sacred structures were at the heart of economic functions. At these centers, not only were ceremonies conducted, animals sacrificed, and prisoners of war ritually slaughtered, but taxes were also collected. Such early examples may have existed at Abydos, Heliopolis, and Hieraconpolis.[82] Temples were more like medieval monasteries, since they were powerful landowning institutions that served as the hubs of the local economy (indeed, from a purely objective perspective, one could argue that they were primarily places of employment). And thanks to Ramesses III (1186–1155 BCE), who donated huge stretches of land to the state and local cults, the temples controlled almost one third of Egypt's agricultural land.[83]

Temples might even serve as a refuge against foreign attackers. Significantly, working in a temple as a priest was "virtually the only form of advancement available to talented Egyptians."[84] They were also places of learning and stored records. Temples might have a scriptorium or House of Life (*pr 'nḥ*),[85] in which, depending on the period, treatises on medicine, magic, ritual, or dream interpretation were written.

Though atypical given its size, the Temple of Karnak provides an idea of how central a sacred site could be economically. At least according to the *Papyrus Harris*, by Dynasty 20 it employed 81,322 people and controlled over 924 square miles of arable land, 433 orchards, 421,362 head of livestock, 65 villages, 83 ships, and 46 workshops.[86]

A Typical Temple: Wrapping an Object of Hallucinatory Focus with Architectural Layers

Typically a mudbrick wall surrounded the temple precinct. Behind the enclosure were residences for priests, shrines, a "sacred lake" for lustrations, work places, storage areas, slaughter yards for the preparation of meats offered to the god-statue, and other areas for preparing offerings. Temples were typically divided into front courts open to sky and a roofed area that housed the more sacred chambers.

By the New Kingdom, temple complexes had evolved into their most elaborate form. Despite changes over time and local variation, an idealized "typical" temple from the New Kingdom, in its basic features, can be described. A temple's components architecturally "wrapped" around — thereby protecting — the cosmic power-emitting god-statue kept in the inner recesses. Different degrees of divine energy filled the areas surrounding the inner shrine that housed the god. A paved processional way (dromos) led to the entrance of the temple, lined by an alley of statues or sphinxes. The temple's façade was of a grand gateway composed of two tapering towers (pylons). Flagpoles with divine emblems graced the façade. Next came the inner court (peristyle); this was an open area framed with colonnaded corridors. Then came a colonnaded hall (hypostyle), a closed, sparingly illuminated hall with a ceiling supported by columns. The latter were decorated with capitals that reflected Egypt's flora: lotiform (lotus), papyriform (papyrus), palmiform (palm), or composite (mixed plants).

At the very back and darkest part of the temple, perhaps surrounded by side chapels, storage rooms, and the anteroom with the god's barque, was the inner sanctuary — *db3r*[87] — which concealed the god-statue. This part of the temple, the most holy area that contained the OHF, was set apart from the rest of the edifice.

Royal Palaces as Temples

Though buildings that we base our analysis on mostly survive from the New Kingdom or later, we can get an idea of what the typical royal palace was like. In effect it was an administrative center, but not surprisingly seems to have resembled a temple, radiating both sacred and political power. A number of words were used to denote palace, but note that *ʿḥ*[88] meant both palace and temple. Like a temple with its naos, the king's residence had a throne room and a columned hall (again an architectural feature seen in temples), and a "window of appearances" at the front. This was an opening in the wall where the king stood to observe ceremonies or bestow largesse on his courtiers.

Notes to Chapter 8

1. Malek, 2000, p. 92.
2. Y5-N35-W24-G43-Y1-Z2; Y5-N35-W24-W24-W24; Y5-N35-Y5-W24-Z7-A53; Y5-N35-W24-Z7-A53-G7-Z3A, etc.
3. R8-X1-D21-Y5-W24-W24-W24.
4. Y5-N35-W24-W24-W24-A53-A40.
5. From Harrington, 2010, p. 102, with my modifications.
6. Weeks, 2001, pp. 418–425.
7. David, 2003, pp. 71–72.

8. G25-X1-N27-O1; G25-Aa1-X1-N18; N27; N27-X1-O1.
9. O24; U23-D21-O24; U23-G17-D21-O24; U23-G17-D21-O24-O1; U3-G17-D21-O24-O1-X1-Z3A, etc.
10. Q1-G43-X1-O1-O1-Z3A; Q1-O1; Q1-Z5-Z5; Q1-Z7-X1-O1-O1-Z3.
11. M2-X1-O1; M40-O34-O1.
12. O29-D36-O24.
13. D21-Z1-V2-X1-Z1.
14. G17-P6-D36-O26; N36-N21-P6-D36-X1-O1; N36-N23-P6-Z1-O1; N36-N23-P7-M17-M17-X1-O1-Z3A; P6-D36-D54-O1, etc.
15. D2-D21-N18; D2D21-X1-N1-N25; D2-D21-X1-N25, etc.
16. D36-D36-O24.
17. Harrington, 2010, p. 86.
18. Harrington, 2010, p. 86.
19. Morenz, 1992, pp. 202–203.
20. The courtyard and tomb chapel were accessible to the living.
21. Harrington, 2010, pp. 86–87.
22. D46-G1-X1-N15; D46-G1-X1-O49; D46-V4-X1-N15; D46-V4-X1-O1.
23. O1-Z1-I10-X1-N16; O1-Z1-N35-I10-X1-N16.
24. Wiebach-Koepke, 2001, pp. 498–500.
25. O6-X1-D28; O6-X1-D29; O6-X1-D29-O49; O7-D28O7-X1-D28-O1.
26. Q3-X1-V28-O7-D28.
27. "Mortuary temple" has been used to describe temples attached to pyramids in the Old and Middle Kingdoms. However, "royal cult complex" is probably a more appropriate term. David, 2003, pp. 104–105, 186–187.
28. Wiebach-Koepke, 2001, pp. 498–500.
29. Wilson, 1965, p. 297.
30. Dieter, 2001, pp. 429–430.
31. N36-Z1-P6-D36-X1-O1; G7-P6-D36-X1-O1; P6-X1-Z1-O1, etc.
32. Wegner, 2010, pp. 244–245. But see Dieter who denies their private use. Dieter, 2001, pp. 429–430.
33. Wegner, 2010, pp. 244–245.
34. Dieter, 2001, pp. 429–430.
35. Wegner, 2010, p. 245.
36. Wegner, 2010, p. 245.
37. Wegner, 2010, p. 245.
38. Lehner, 1997, p. 9.
39. Lehner, 1997, p. 9.
40. Lehner, 1997, pp. 14, 9.
41. Lehner, 1997, p. 35.
42. O24.
43. Lehner, 1997, p. 16.
44. Lehner, 1997, p. 18.
45. Tyldesley, 2019, p. 24.
46. Tyldesley, 2019, p. 27.
47. Lehner, 1997, p. 16.
48. Lehner, 1997, p. 14.

49. Lehner, 1997, p. 17.
50. This analysis does not include unfinished pyramids of Nebka (Dynasty 4) and Raneferef (Dynasty 5) and excludes satellite pyramids and those of queens.
51. Goelet et al., 2015, p. 158.
52. I10-D46-S43-Z1-Z2; I10-S43; I10-S43-Z1-Z3A.
53. Malek, 2000, p. 92.
54. Lehner, 1997, p. 16.
55. Dieter, 2001, p. 425.
56. David, 2003, p. 105.
57. David, 2003, p. 105.
58. D58-M17-M17-N35-G1-G31, etc.
59. Silverman, 1997, pp. 172–173.
60. Lehner, 1997, p. 35.
61. D58-N35-D58-N35-X1-O24.
62. D58-D21-D58-D21-O21-O24-O39; D58-N35-D58-N35-M44; D58-N35-D58-N3-O24, etc.
63. Lehner, 1997, p. 24.
64. Lehner, 1997, p. 16.
65. Lehner, 1997, p. 16.
66. Dieter, 2001, p. 423.
67. Though rock-cut tombs existed in Dynasties 3 and 4, they became more common by the Middle and New Kingdoms.
68. Tyldesley, 2019, p. 98.
69. David, 2003, p. 69.
70. David, 2003, p. 70.
71. Wilkinson, 2010, p. 143.
72. Wilkinson, 2010, p. 143.
73. R8-O6; R8-O20; R8-O6-X1-O1.
74. David, 2003, 189.
75. Baines and Malek, 2000, p. 61.
76. D58-G29-G1-U7-D40; D58-G41-G1-M17-G1-Z9-D40.
77. O11-D36-X1-O1; O11; O11-D36-O1; O11-O1; O11-Z1-D36-O1-G7; O12-O1.
78. O12-X1-O1; O12-X1-O1-A40.
79. O1-Z1-M23-X1-N35.
80. N27-X1-O1-N35-X1-V28-N5-V28.
81. David, 2003, p. 187.
82. David, 2003, pp. 69–70.
83. Tyldesley, 2019, p. 168.
84. Pinch, 2002, p. 37.
85. O1-S34; O1-S34-O1.
86. Oakes and Gahlin, 2006, pp. 358–359.
87. Also shrine or naos (D46-D58-G29-G1-Z4-D21-Z1-M3-O1).
88. O11-O1; O11-Z1-D36-O1-G7; O12-01; O12-X1-O1, etc.

Chapter 9

The Realms of the Afterworld, Transfiguration, and Multiple Existences

"He knows the gateways of the Netherworld and the gateways of the Fields of Reeds, his heart joyful with the calendrical offerings of the processions of every god on the Wag-festival, the Thoth-festival and an eternity of years therein."
— *The Neferhotep Stela*

WHAT WAS THE SO-CALLED "MORTUARY CULTURE" of ancient Egypt really about? Were funerary customs (e.g., mummification) meant to prevent the corpse from rotting or were they practices intended to transform the deceased into ancestral messengers?[1] What was the nature of postmortem existence for the ancient Egyptians? It seems to have been a parallel realm — a Doubleworld[2] — populated by the not-quite-dead, who communicated with the living via divine voices and visitations. We need to abandon the notion of "preserving the body for eternity and focus instead on mummification and grave goods as the material aspects of the transformation of the deceased into an ancestor."[3] Moreover, we must appreciate the archaic view that the deceased was involved in the "creation and maintenance of the world's order." We need to question our assumption that the ultimate goal of the individual was to survive as a highly self-individuated entity in the Afterworld. "Rather, the deceased is dissolved into a myriad of roles all serving, not the deceased 'himself,' but the world itself, which is maintained through the activities of the ancestors-as-gods."[4]

TRANSFORMING THE DECEASED TO ENSURE THE CONTINUATION OF THE VOICES

ḫpri Transform (L1-M17-Z5-Y1-Z2)

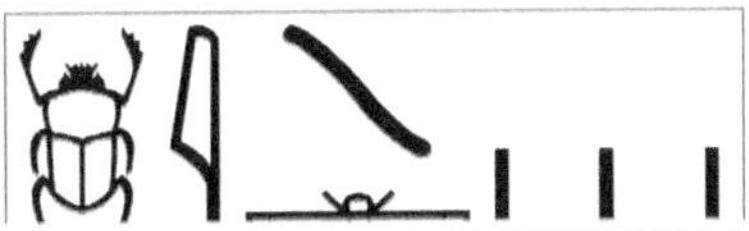

Nyord suggests that much of Egyptology is weighed down by "Victorian baggage" and the traditional notion that a "quest for immortality" explains the spirituality of archaic Egypt.[5] He contends that the "afterlife" hypothesis and its concomitant ideas about "eternal life" and an emphasis on "not perishing" may mean something else.[6] Significantly, he points out that the ancestor's presence in the tomb does not exactly square with a "transcendent personal afterlife in the beyond." The pursuit of transformation is a well-attested Egyptian notion, while the "quest for immortality" is mainly a Victorian conception.[7] Mortuary practices were deeply implicated in the social context of the ancestor cult.[8] With this said, the point of the elaborate mortuary practices may have been less about preserving the corpse (though certainly preservation was a factor) and more about transforming (*ḫpri*) the deceased into an ancestor.[9] I would go one step further and apply a Jaynesian interpretation: after individuals died, turning them into an ancestor was a method of ensuring that their authoritative voices continued to be heard (Table 9.1).

Table 9.1. Some Hieroglyphic Variants of "Transforming."

No.	Term	Possible Translation
1.	*ḫprỉ*[10]	Shape, transformation
2.	*ḫprỉ*[11]	Form, shape, transformation
3.	*ḫprỉ*[12]	Form, transformation
4.	*ḫprỉ*[13]	Form, shape, transformation
5.	*ḫr*[14]	To happen, to become
6.	*ḫr*[15]	Occur, happen, come to pass, to develop, arise, originate, befall, exist
7.	*ḫr*[16]	(1) occur, happen, come to pass, exist, be, come into being, become, change into; (2) take place, be effective, go by, be past, continue
8.	*sḫpr*[17]	Bring into being, create, make, make grow (a garden)

THE AFTERWORLD

For the archaic Egyptians, the Afterworld (my term that subsumes the various postmortem modes of existence) was not ethereal but corporeal. Originally, the spatiality of the Afterworld was conceived to be actual, locatable, and physical. However, by the time people became consciously interiorized, such otherworldly places became more psychospiritual in nature. In other words, an individual's introcosmos was somehow conceived as possessing elements of the other-worldly macrocosmos.

In archaic Egypt, two views co-existed about what happened to the deceased. The first was a transfiguration into a new type of being (Akh). The second viewed life in the Afterworld as a continuation of life in the earthly realm. One went into the Afterworld in various ways: riding on the back of a falcon, goose, or some other bird; being wafted upwards with burning incense; climbing up a ladder formed by the outstretched arms of the gods; or traveling on a reed boat or towed along in a barque. Whether the aim of the deceased was to journey on the solar circuit, reach the circumpolar stars, or to be joined in life with Osiris, the "essential wish is the same: to be absorbed in the great rhythm of the universe."[18] The individual finds peace and immortality by "becoming part of one of the perennial cyclic rhythms of nature";[19] hence the phrase "repeating life" (*wḥm 'nḫ*).[20]

The Watery Paradise of the Duat

Celestial bodies were conceived as sailing across the heavens in a sort of sky-ocean; this was the surface where the waters of the primordial ocean met the atmosphere of the world. Nut, or the Watery One, stretched above the recumbent Geb (land) with Shu (dry, empty) in between. The sky was where the transfigured king would "go forth." It was also in this sun-soaked realm that birds, Kas, Bas, Akhs, gods, and goddesses dwelled, as well as the circumpolar stars known as the Imperishable Ones. But eventually most archaic Egyptians associated their otherworldly existence with the Duat, which was associated with the realm of the dead and necropolises, as evident in the terms *igrt*,[21] *iwgrt*,[22] and *iḳrt*.[23] The Duat was where the deceased and gods dwelled (*dwꜣtyw*).[24] It was the realm of the distinguished (*wꜣšyw*),[25] as well as oppressors or demons (*ꜣ'bw*).[26] It was also the kingdom of Osiris, as seen by one of his epithets, Foremost of the Duat (*ḫnty dwꜣt*).[27] Duat could be written with a star in a circle,[28] a reference to Orion, the stellar expression of Osiris (the Duat may originally been connected to the stars, but overtime it became associated with chthonic regions). Though often rendered as "Underworld" or "Netherworld," these words can be misleading as the deceased "ascended" to the Duat. In the darker parts of the Duat, demons lived upside-down, eating their own feces and drinking their own urine (Table 9.2).

The entrance to the Duat was somewhere below the horizon at the intersection of the sky and earth. The horizon (*ꜣḫt*[44] or *ꜣḫty*[45]) is an example of spatial liminality, a mysterious place where the sky and land embraced each other. It is written with the same root for Akh (effective spirit). It was where the deceased were transfigured into horizon dwellers ("effective inhabitants"; *ꜣḫtyw*[46] or *ꜣḫty*[47]) of the world beyond death.[48] This "light land" or "bright place" was where gods and spirits came into being. The term for horizon could also mean the tomb of a king or palace.[49]

The Duat contained, like the earthly realm, rivers, islands, lakes, hills, and caverns, as well as fantastic features, such as turquoise trees, iron walls, fiery lakes, etc. These would have to be traversed and overcome by the deceased. Descriptions of the Duat are found in the *Book of Gates*, *Book of*

Table 9.2. Terms for the Afterworld.

No.	Term	Possible Translation
1.	*dwꜣt*[29]	Duat, Netherworld
2.	*dwꜣt*[30]	Netherworld, Duat, tomb chamber, abyss
3.	*dwꜣt*[31]	Duat, Netherworld, underground burial chamber
4.	*snṯt*[32]	Hereafter
5.	*ẖrt*[33]	Hereafter, Netherworld
6.	*ḥmt*[34]	Hereafter, Netherworld
7.	*nfrt*[35]	Netherworld
8.	*ỉmḥt*[36]	Netherworld
9.	*ḳrtyw*[37]	Netherworld
10.	*štiw*[38]	Netherworld
11.	*šn'w*[39]	Netherworld
12.	*ỉmḥt*[40]	Right side, west side, Netherworld, the West, Realm of the dead, necropolis
13.	*sḫt ỉꜣrw*[41]	Fields of Reeds (a location in the Netherworld)
14.	*'nḫt*[42]	West, Netherworld
15.	*šn'*[43]	Netherworld, tomb

Caverns, *Coffin Texts*, *Amduat*, and *Book of the Dead*.[50] Rather than merging with the sun god Re as the king did, the ordinary deceased person would be judged by having their hearts weighed by Osiris against the feather of Maat. If found worthy, they would pass into the Fields of Reeds (*sḫt iꜣrw*), the Ka of the Nile Delta.[51] This was a place somewhere on the eastern horizon where the deceased would continue to eternally labor as they had done in this world. But this was a paradise of reward and a superabundance of produce, full of fruit trees laden with dates and figs, emmer wheat, barley, and flax.

It was through the Duat that the solar god Re journeyed, echoing the rhythms of life, death, and rebirth. The journey of the sun underpinned creation myths and the death and rebirth of the manifest cosmos in all its overflowing beauty. At sunset, Re, along with the deceased king riding in the solar barque, entered the sky's mouth and sank below the shimmering horizon into the Duat, where he encountered the mummified Osiris. Feeding off each other's cosmic energies, they gave each other sustenance needed for another cycle of regeneration. While in the Duat, the sun god would battle against Apophis, the giant serpent who stood for chaos, the opposite of order and daylight. At dawn, the sun would re-emerge between Nut's legs. Later in Egyptian history, nonroyals were believed to merge with the solar god along with the king.

Here we should note that during the Amarna period, the dead were restricted to their tombs and did not enter the Afterworld. By day, they "visited the temples of Amarna in an invisible or altered form, and by night, they returned to their tomb."[52] Such a belief reflected the idiosyncratic views of Akhenaten and his Atenism.

THE PARALOGIC OF TRANSFIGURATION AND MULTIPLE EXISTENCES

By the Middle Kingdom, three general concepts of the Afterworld had emerged that reflected sociopolitical divisions.[53] The first, which applied to the vast majority of the people, saw commoners idyllically cultivating their plots of land in the kingdom of Osiris in the Duat. The second was for wealthier commoners who could afford to furnish lavish tombs where they could enjoy at least part of the Afterworld. Finally, the king would join the gods to sail around the heavens in the sacred barque.

Mortuary rituals were intended for purposes of transfiguration or to make a dead person into a living being (*s3ḫ* is translated as glorify, glorification[54] or to bless, to beautify, glorify, make effective, glorification spell).[55] Scenes from the tomb of Rekhmire, vizier of Thutmose III and Amenhotep II, during Dynasty 18, provide us with a general idea of the component rituals constituting a funeral: (1) procession to the necropolis (involving crossing over to the west bank by boat); (2) procession to the embalming place; (3) embalming and mummification; (4) post-embalming rituals; (5) procession to the tomb/funeral; (6) opening of the mouth ritual (*wpt r3*); (7) mortuary service.[56]

After death, a person's earthly deeds were judged by the fertility-vegetation god Osiris as well as other deities. Assuming one was not condemned to a second, more permanent death, the deceased could then live out multiple existences, simultaneously dwelling in different spiritual dimensions. While the body rested in the tomb, it waited to be brought to life by one's Ka (life force). Scenes of mortuary banquets in tombs are paralogically timeless in the sense that they are "situated simultaneously in the worlds of the living and the dead."[57] In the evening, one's Ba (manifestation of one's personality) would ride in Re's solar barque through the Duat. For the deceased, their body and their tomb in a sense became their personal Osiris and a personal Duat. For this reason they are often addressed as "Osiris." Though individuals retained their individuality, they simultaneously and paralogically shared the nature of Osiris.

RITUALS FOR THE LIVING DEAD

Two sets of funerary rituals can be discerned by the time of the New Kingdom.[58] The first set, using glorification or transformation spells (*s3ḫt*),[59] was intended to cause the deceased to become a glorified spirit and join the gods.[60] This set of activities was performed once. Within the initial set, the first rituals revolved around embalming, in which a number of different types of priests and officiants fulfilled their duties: lector-priests (*ḫry ḥbt*), Ka-priests, sem-priests (*sm*), and embalmers ("bandagers" or "binders") (*wt*)[61] who assisted in their own way with mummification and the incantations. The god Anubis oversaw the mummification. A processional journey transported the mummy (or perhaps an anthropoid coffin; the mummy could be regarded as the deceased's statue) to the tomb. Also part of the procession was the mysterious human-headed sack-like object or

Tekenu (*tknw*),[62] which was dragged by cattle on a sled. Animal sacrifices were carried out in the necropolis. Sacrifices were also made to the Tekenu. It is unclear what the Tekenu was for; it may have contained body parts. After arriving at the part of the tomb that would eventually be sealed, the mummy was stood upright to receive censing, libations, and blessings. The mummy, sarcophagus, Tekenu, and canopic chest (containing the canopic jars with the removed viscera) were presented with offerings and protective ritual recitations. Finally, the mummy was placed in the sarcophagus.[63]

The second set of rituals were performed after the funeral. Cult functionaries, family members, or others visiting the deceased at the tomb-chapel maintained the tomb (supported by a perpetual mortuary endowment). Ideally the relevant ceremonies were performed daily.[64]

REANIMATION BY OPENING THE MOUTH

At least by Dynasty 4, the Opening of the Mouth Ceremony (*wpt r3*)[65] was a key part of the preparations for burial. It was originally performed on cult statues and then on mummies (of royalty and nonroyalty) later in the Old Kingdom. However, in later centuries, it was performed on scarabs, crowns, figurines, and even structures, such as tombs. Though it changed through the centuries, this ritual,[66] given its ubiquity, was probably the most important ceremony of ancient Egypt.[67] It involved other auxiliary activities such as purification, censing, anointing, and incantations.

The point of this ceremony was to transform the deceased into a new type of being (reanimate its recipient). A secondary rite for "opening the eyes" might accompany the Opening of the Mouth ritual.[68] The Opening of the Mouth ritual was associated with what we might term the "birth of an image." The term *msi͗*[69] means giving birth, as well to form or fashion. Originally this ritual took place in the goldsmith workshop (*ḥwt nbw*)[70] that was affiliated with a temple or royal residence. The point was to animate and invest the image with *mnḫt* (effectiveness, efficiency, ability; these terms might mean the ability to emit voices).[71] The metaphor of a sculptor or *s ʿnḫ*[72] described someone who reanimates images. This is evident in (*s ʿnḫw*),[73] around which revolves a web of semantically-related terms: maker of statues, life giver;[74] bestower of life, perpetuate;[75] make live; preserve; revive (dead); nourish; feed; perpetuate (name);[76] create; bring into being.[77]

The Opening of the Mouth Ceremony required special instruments to reanimate the deceased. These included a wood-carving adze, whose significance, and by implication the significance of the Opening of the Mouth Ceremony itself, is shown by the different terms used that referred to this long finger-shaped instrument[78] applied to the mouth of the mummy (*dwȝ wr*,[79] *msḫtyw*,[80] *nṯrty*[81]) and the Adze of Wepwawet (*nwȝ wpwt*[82] or *nwȝ wpwt*[83]). Wepwawet was the jackal-headed god whose name means Opener of the Ways. Other instruments included an obsidian *pesesh kȝf* knife (also applied to the mouth)[84] and other items, such as a staff in the form of a ram-headed cobra. The heart of an ox (due to its links with strength, masculinity, and fertility) was also used to touch the mouth of the mummy.

The common view is that the Opening of the Mouth Ceremony was done so that the spiritual body would be able to move about in the Afterworld. However, this may be a modern assumption. This ritual was more likely intended to transform the deceased into a type of living dead that could interact with the living. After all, the purpose of this ritual was to allow the recipient to eat, breathe, see, hear, and enjoy offerings. It is important to note that this ritual had its counterpart in Mesopotamian practices, demonstrating a parallel bicameral development focusing on reanimation, thereby allowing communication with the deceased.

THE MUMMY AS GLORIFIED BODY

For the archaic Egyptians, the problem was not the immortality of the soul, but rather the "establishment of a connection and cooperation between the surviving components of the person, such as body, heart, and soul."[85] Thus the body had to be effectively preserved, and it was here that the Egyptians, with their arts of mummification, excelled. Moreover, the burial chamber was individuated and made as personal as possible, using paintings and objects to exhibit events, scenes, and achievements from the deceased's time on earth. Bodily preservation permitted the Ba to return to the tomb at the night, and to rise to a new life as the morning dawned. However, complete Akhs were also thought to appear as stars. Initially, nonroyal Egyptians did not expect to unite with the sun god, as this was the privilege of royals.

The mummy was "treated like a statue, and the statue was treated like a mummy; both served the deceased as bodies."[86] The *ḏt*, or body (also image, bodily form of god, statues, one's own self, person), erased the distinction between representation and body, so that corpse (mummy, body) and representation (statue, picture, form, etc.) were referred to by the same term.[87] A representation was paralogically not a "depiction of a body; it was itself a body."[88]

By the First Intermediate Period, the mummy form was intended to resemble Osiris, and it was at this time that tomb statues and mummification became separated. The former, which had portrayed the dead wearing the clothes of the living, "left the hidden spaces of the tomb and were increasingly set up in the accessible cult rooms, until, during the Old Kingdom, the *serdab* disappeared altogether."[89] The corpse, which in some sense was divine and assumed the form of Osiris, remained hidden. Not only was the deceased identified with Osiris, but each part of the body was associated with a specific deity. A number of terms denote corpse: *ḫꜣt*;[90] *ẖꜣt*;[91] *mẖꜣ*;[92] *ỉfd*;[93] *ẖꜣt*.[94] Other terms seem to relate to dealing with a dead body that requires some type of preparation or putting it back together: pull together, rejoin (corpse), collect (parts of corpse) (*sꜣḳ*);[95] restore the limbs of a corpse (*spdḏ*);[96] leaping of corpse (*nhp ẖꜣt*);[97] be revived (condition of corpse's flesh) (*nkꜣkꜣ*).[98]

A component of the mummy was the "mummy mask." But this mask was not intended to hide or conceal anything. Instead, it was considered the "head of a god" that allowed the deceased to become god-like; it was referred to as the Lord of Vision.[99] The mummy mask may have had the same function as the so-called "reserve heads," "heads of mystery," or "mysterious heads" (*tp štꜣ* or *tp n sštꜣ*).

A long list of terms (not all shown here) related to mummies, mummification, mummy masks, associated objects, wrappings, bandages, etc., indicating the central role of this complexive idea. The most relevant term was *sꜥḥ*. This term could also mean, appropriately, eternal image.[100] It also appears related to an array of words having to do with dignity;[101] ennoble;[102] be noble;[103] noble/privileged person/aristocrat;[104] rank/dignity (of royalty);[105] and noble/dignitary.[106] Clearly the idea here is that being a mummy was primarily a designation of status,[107] indicating the intertwining of theopolitical power and individual transfiguration (Table 9.3).

THE THREE SPHERES OF COSMOGEOGRAPHY

For the archaic Egyptians, existence can be divided into three spaces. The first was the ordinary, commonplace, and mundane sphere in which one carried out the expected routines of daily life. The ultimate goal was to reach and enter the second place, the sacred sphere as depicted in funerary

Table 9.3. Terms for Mummification and Related Concepts.

No.	Possible Translation	Term
1.	Body[108]	*ḏt*
2.	Body, image, bodily form (of gods), statues, self, person[109]	
3.	Body, person[110]	
4.	Own (self)[111]	
5.	Mummy, mummified person[112]	*sʿḥ*
6.	(1) be noble, dignitary, rank, dignity, honor; (2) bind (with bandages), mummify, reward honor, endow[113]	
7.	Mummy, mummified person, deceased[114]	
8.	Mummy, insignia, dignity, reward (?)[115]	
9.	(1) dignitary, rank, dignity, dignities, honors; (2) bind (with bandages), mummify, reward honor, endow[116]	
10.	Dignitary, rank, dignity, dignities (plural), honors (plural)[117]	

texts where one was either transfigured into an Akh spirit or continued to live a sort of spiritualized earthly existence. Positioned between the first and second spheres was the "betwixt-and-between" cosmogeography. This was a place where the mundane and sacred overlapped and afforded portals, in the form of tombs and temples, to other planes of existence. Here one might be visited by a numinous being, glimpse a ghost in a dream, commune with ancestors, gain sacred knowledge, or begin one's journey into the Afterworld. Though often a place of opportunities and new beginnings, this transitional location could be dangerous, with its wrathful gods, goddesses, and vengeful revenants (Table 9.4).

DEPICTIONS THAT COME TO LIFE

Within the tomb, numerous objects were used to ensure the sustenance of the deceased in their transfigured state: the tomb itself, statues, figurines, stelae, offering tables, anthropoid busts, and mummiform figurines called shabtis or ushabtis (*wšbty*).[118] These were instruments of a life

Table 9.4. Types of Space.

Everyday Space	Liminal Space	Extraordinary Space
Alive, living, awake, places of daily life	Sleep, dream, visions (SV), death, transformation, journey, horizon, tomb, temple	Afterworld, transfiguration, blessed existence, rebirth, new knowledge

uninterrupted. During the Middle Kingdom, tombs would become well equipped with pottery models of houses,[119] graniers, breweries, slaughter-houses, boats, groups of servant statuettes, animal figurines, troops of soldiers, and toys. These grave goods were not representations or reminders, but objects that were believed to paralogically possess the innate properties of the originals, "including the ability to become full-sized" so as to function as the real thing in the Afterworld.[120]

Shabtis[121] originally may have represented the deceased themselves, but over time became regarded as workers in the fields. There were also so-called "concubine figures," that presumably provided sexual pleasure for the owner in the next world. Made from clay, faience, word, or stone, shabtis first appeared in Dynasties 9 and 10 and were used until end of ancient Egyptian history. But were they intended to labor on behalf of the deceased? Arguably since one's social status was continued in the Afterworld, these images were not created as substitutes to take one's place to avoid labor.[122] It was only later that these figurines evolved into servants for the deceased. Nyord pushes this line of argumentation. He writes that though the funerary use of shabtis from the New Kingdom onwards is well understood and generally supports the conventional "substitute labor" interpretation, the evidence calls this idea into question. The original shabtis (i.e., inscribed with the certain spells) are not funerary per se, but rather were used as a type of substitute burial.[123] This conflicts with the idea that they were intended to take the place of the deceased in their role as laborers.

The evidence points to the idea that the "person depicted wanted to be able to carry out work in a place where he was not actually buried."[124] The practice of depositing so-called "stick shabtis" in the Theban region also challenges the conventional interpretation.[125] Shabtis were positioned in the accessible parts of a tomb by dedicants; "they were doing so on behalf of the dedicator as much as the tomb owner."[126] The evidence, though hard for the modern mind to accept, is that working in the fields was not an unpleasant task, but "rather something desirable which the figurine enabled its dedicant or depositor to do. The fact that the figurines were deposited in sacred places could be taken to mean that the work in question was not the unpleasant corvée labour usually assumed."[127]

Another example of tomb goods suggests the paralogic use of life-sized stone likenesses of heads of the deceased. These were placed near tombs, in burial chambers, or at the bottom of grave shafts. These "true portraits of the deceased" (whose purpose is unclear) displayed a high degree of individuation and apparently the "impulse to preserve the corporeal form."[128] Only about 37 have so far been discovered. They date to Dynasty 4, and have been found mainly in Giza, Abusier, Saqqara, and Dashur. One theory is that they were "reserve" or spare heads, i.e., if an individual's actual head was for some reason unavailable, the wandering Bas or Kas of the deceased could still recognize their own graves and be able to return safely. These heads have been found with damaged ears and distinct scoring marks. Such damage could have been the consequence of the accidental breaking of molds (made out of linen and thin plaster). But oddly, the heads were not repaired or restored. Another explanation is that the ears were intentionally damaged for some reason involving the belief that the departed should be prevented from hearing the living.

FUNERARY TEXTS

Changes in funerary texts illustrate the expansion of conscious interiority; the *Pyramid Texts* (from ca. 24th century BCE), the *Coffin Texts* (from ca. 22nd century BCE), and the *Book of the Dead* (from ca. 16th century BCE) follow a trajectory of increasing personalization and self-individuation.

The Pyramid Texts

The *Pyramid Texts* are probably the "world's oldest extant substantial body of religious" writings.[129] They obtained their name from inscriptions on the walls of antechambers, passageways, vestibules, ramps, and burial chambers of pyramids. They may have been chanted by priests or perhaps, it was believed, read by kings as they rested in their tombs. They were composed by the priests of Heliopolis and reached their fullest form for the tomb of Unas (2350–2325 BCE). Due to economic pressures, the pyramids of Dynasty 5 were being reduced in size, and eventually the *Pyramid Texts* provided an alternative method of attempting to ensure that the king ascended the "sun-ladder" toward the heavens, where he would merge with the solar disc. The *Pyramid Texts* came to serve as the standard for later inscriptions, funerary formulas, spells, and incantations. They were discontinued as the tombs became smaller at the end of the Old Kingdom.

The *Pyramid Texts* illustrate how for the archaic Egyptians word and effect were paralogically the same. Their overarching theme is the eternal existence of the king in the Afterworld. They can be categorized into a number of types. The first, dating from Dynasties 2 and 3, concern recited speech, prescribed action, and spells related to lamentations, offering rituals, the provision of the king's crowns, and other grave equipment. Spells for the Opening of the Mouth and other statue-related rituals were included, as were instructions for officiators who took on the ("dramatized") persona of the gods. The second type are hymns and name formulae which set the cult symbols, actions, rituals, and objects of the dramatic texts in the context of the mythical stories or allusions. The third category are litanies, structured verses that consist of enumerations and sequences of names pertaining to divine beings (from Dynasty 4). The fourth type are the "glorification spells" (*s3ḫ*),[130] which transfigure one into an Akh. These were composed mainly during Dynasties 5 and 6. Finally, the oldest texts dealt with brief protection spells for contending with snakes and other dangerous beings.

The Coffin Texts

As part of a general democratization of spirituality during the First Intermediate Period and Middle Kingdom, the *Pyramid Texts* were subsumed into the *Coffin Texts* (developed in Herakleopolis Magna). The latter were inscribed in the tombs of high-ranking officials, wealthy commoners, and nomarchs.[131] They were for those who could attain individual eternity distinct from that of the king's immortality. These writings, more than a thousand spells, ritual texts, hymns, and prayers, were intended to help the deceased on their journey to the Afterworld. They were more psychologically interiorized in how they addressed the individual's fear of death. The *Coffin Texts* used pictorial vignettes not found in the *Pyramid Texts* and were written inside coffins. They also appeared on walls of the burial chambers, papyrus rolls, and mummy masks. Texts had to be transferred to the coffins as tombs became smaller and wall space for inscriptions shrunk. Some spells in these texts are monologues spoken by a deity, beginning with "I am the N god." Dialogues among deities are also recorded.

The Book of the Dead

By the end of the Middle Kingdom, the *Coffin Texts* were no longer commonly used and a new spiritual guide had become popular. Called the *Book of the Dead* (or in Egyptian *prt m hrw*,[132] which means *Coming Forth by*

Day), this was a collection of 190 independent "chapters." It was intended to assist a person in avoiding the dangers of the Afterworld, so they would not die a second, permanent death. Spells and passwords were placed in tombs from about 1600 BCE onward, although there are indications that they were included in the sections called "chapters" as early as Dynasty 12.

The *Book of the Dead* took its final form by (Saite) Dynasty 26 (664–525 BCE). Chapters 1–16 concern the deceased entering the tomb and descending to the underworld as the body regains its powers of movement and speech. Chapters 17–63 explain the origins of the gods. The deceased is re-animated and reborn with the rising sun. Chapters 64–129 depict the deceased traveling across the sky in the solar barque as one of the blessed dead while in the evening the deceased visit the underworld to appear before Osiris. Chapters 130–189 describe how having been justified and vindicated, the deceased becomes gods. The final chapters also deal with protective amulets, provision of food, and sacred places.

A key paralogic feature of the *Book of the Dead* involves the theme of transfiguration and allowing the deceased to become a part of the divine cosmic order. It not only affords passwords necessary for admittance into certain stages of the underworld, but through spells it enables individuals to assume the identity of gods and otherworldly creatures. A commercialized self-individuation is indicated by how the individual decided which chapters and illustrations to have produced and the quality of the papyrus to use. In the *Book of the Dead*, the visual impact of the illustrations seemed to be given primacy over the writings (presumably many Egyptians of the time probably could not read anyway). It was "apparently sufficient to supply just a few lines of the relevant text, so that often a chapter will break off in the middle of a phrase or even a word."[133]

Other Funerary Texts

A number of other funerary works, adopted for non-royal purposes, were copied onto the walls of tombs. The *Book of Two Ways*, a precursor to the *Book of the Dead*, mapped out the roads and canals through the Duat. *The Amduat* (also known as *That Which Is in the Afterworld*, *Text of the Hidden Chamber Which is in the Underworld*, or *Book of What Is in the Underworld*) is from the fifteenth century BCE or earlier. *The Litany of Re*, from the fifteenth century BCE, offers praise to the deity and lists the 75 forms assumed by Re as the supreme solar deity. The *Book of Gates*, from the fourteenth century BCE or earlier, contains formulas for making the sun rise and traces the road of the gods and the deceased, showing various openings through which the barque of Re would have to pass in order to be free from peril. This work describes fierce guardians, a lake of fire, and the secret caverns of the deity Sokar. The *Book of Caverns*, from the thirteenth century BCE, is a variation on the traditional *Book of the Dead* that depicts the vast caverns that formed the Duat. Other texts include the *Book of the Earth* (thirteenth century BCE); the *Books of Night and Day* (fourteenth century BCE or earlier); the *Book of the Opening of the Mouth* (from Dynasty 18); the *Book of the Pylons* (another version of the *Book of the Dead*); and the *Book of the Heavens* (from Dynasty 19). Much later the *Book of Breathing* (from the Ptolemaic period) and the *Book of Traversing in Eternity* (Roman period) appeared.

Notes to Chapter 9

1. In many cultures after the VVVs of the ancestors fade away, their remains are permanently interred (secondary burials). In Egypt the hope was that passers-by would remember them and make an offering so as to maintain their existence.
2. Bolshakov, 1997, pp. 261–81.
3. Nyord, 2018, p. 78.
4. Nyord, 2018, p. 81.
5. Moreover, the "antiquarian tradition means that the act of collecting details, be they archaeological or philological, often comes to be seen as an end in itself, without necessarily engaging with the wider consequences of what they imply about Egyptian experiences and conceptions of the world." Nyord, 2018, p. 73.
6. Nyord, 2018, p. 78.
7. Nyord, 2018, p. 78.
8. Nyord, 2018, p. 78.
9. Nyord, 2018, p. 79.
10. L1-D21-Z5-Y1-Z2.
11. L1-M17-Z5-Y1-Z2.
12. L1-D21-Z2-G43.
13. L1-D21-Z7-A53-Z3.
14. L1-D21-Z7-Y1.
15. L1-D21.
16. Aa1-Q3-L1-D21; Aa1-Q3-D2.
17. S29-L1; S29-L1-D21.
18. Frankfort, 2000, p. 106.
19. Frankfort, 2000, p. 107.
20. F25-S34.
21. M17-W11-D21-X1-N35; M17-W11-D21-X1-X1-N25.
22. M17-G43-W11-D21-X1-N25.

23. M17-N29-D21-X1-N25.
24. N14-N14-N14-A40; D46-V4-X1-O1-A40-Z2A; N14-G4-X1-O1-A40-Z3. Other related terms are "dweller in the Netherworld" (*dwꜣti*) (D46-G1-X1-O49-U33-M17; N14-X1-O1-A40-Z3) and "those in the Netherworld" (*imyw dwꜣt*) (Z11-G43-N33A-N14-X1-O1).
25. V4-N37-M17-M117-G43-Y1-Z2-A40.
26. G1-D36-D58-G43-A2-A40-Z3.
27. W17-N35-X1-Z4-N14-X1-O1.
28. N15.
29. D46-V4-V13-O1; N14-V13-O1; N14-Z1-X1-O1; N15; N15-O1; N15-X1; N14-G1-Z7-X1-O1.
30. D46-V4-X1-O1; N14-X1-O1.
31. N14-X1-O1.
32. O34-N35-V13-X1-N25.
33. T28-D21-X1.
34. V28-X1-Q1-U15-X1-G17-G39-O1; M17-Aa15-VV28-X1-O1.
35. F3-I9-D21-X1-O1.
36. M17-M1-G17-V28-X1-O1; M17-Y5-N35-A5-X1-X1-N25; M17-Y5-N35-X1-A4-N25; Aa15-V28-X1-O1.
37. N29-D21-G4-Z3A.
38. N37-X1-Z4.
39. U13-D36-G43-O1.
40. M17-Y5-N35-X1N25.
41. M20-X1-N21-M17-G1-D21-G42-M2-O49.
42. S34-N35-Aa1-X1-N25.
43. U13-D36-O1-Z3A.
44. G25-X1-O1; G25-Aa1-Y1-N18; G25-Aa1-Y1-N27, etc.
45. N27-X1-O1-O1-G7-G7.
46. N27-X1-O1-G4-A40-Z3; N27-X1-G4.
47. X1-G25-Aa1-N19-A40; N27-X1-Z4-O1-O1-A40-A40; N27-X1-Z4; G25-Aa1-X1-N18-U33-M17; G25-V13-Z2-N16, N27-N27-A40; also "Who Is from the Horizon" (N27-N27)..
48. Lehner, 1997, p. 29.
49. G25-Aa1-X1-N18; G25-X1-N27-O1; N27, etc.
50. The *Pyramid Texts* emphasized the celestial world of the sky more than the earthly and watery Netherworld.
51. M20-X1-N21-M17-G1-D21-G43-M2-O49. Also known as the Field of Offerings.
52. Assmann, 2005, p. 15.
53. David, 2002, p. 161.
54. S29-G25-Aa1, S29-G25-Aa1-Z7-A2-Z3, etc.
55. S29-G25-Aa1-Y1. A related term is *sꜣḫw* (S29-G25-Aa1-G43-Y1-Z2) meaning recitations (ritual), or hymns.
56. Hays, 2010, pp. 2, 5–6; cited in Harrington, 2010, pp. 102–103.
57. Harrington, 2010, p. 16.
58. Roth, 2001a, p. 580.
59. S29-G25-Aa1-X1-A2.

60. That deities were a crucial component of the ceremonies, at least in the background, was seen in the expression "here comes the god performing the *s3t3* ritual (funerary procession)" (*ỉ nṯr s3t3*).
61. Z7-X1-Aa2-D36-A1; Z7-X1-Aa2-D40-A1; G43-X1-Aa2-A1; Z7-X1-Aa2-D40-A2; Aa2-D36-A1; Aa2-X1-A1, etc.
62. U33-V31-W24; X1-V31-N35-W4-G43.
63. Roth, 2001a, p. 580.
64. Roth, 2001a, p. 580.
65. F13-X1-D21-Z1.
66. Roth, 2001b, pp. 605–609.
67. Roth, 2001b, pp. 605–609.
68. Roth, 2001b, pp. 605–609.
69. F31-S29; F31-S29-Z5; F31-S29-Z5-Y1.
70. F31-S29-X1; F31-S29-X1-Y1.
71. O6E.
72. Y5-N35-Aa1-U22; Y5-N35-Aa1-X1-U22; Y5-N35-Aa1-X1-U22-Y1.
73. S29-S34-N35-Aa1-A1.
74. S29-S34-N35-Aa1-Z7-A1-Z2.
75. S29-S34-N35-Aa1-D51-D40.
76. S29-S34.
77. F31-S29-Z7-Z5.
78. The association with the finger may have come from cleaning the mouth of a newborn infant.
79. D46-V4-N14-G36-U19; N14-G36-U19.
80. F31-Aa1-G4-F23; F31-Aa1-G4-U19; F31-Aa1-G4-U21.
81. R8-R8-X1-D21-X1-Z4-U19.
82. N35-U21-E15.
83. N35-V4-E19.
84. Q3-O34-N37-V31-19.
85. Assmann, 1998, p. 384.
86. Assmann, 2005, p. 108.
87. Assmann, 2005, p. 106.
88. Assmann, 2005, p. 106.
89. Assmann, 2005, pp. 105–106.
90. M12-G1-X1; M12-X1, etc.
91. F32-G1-X1; K4-G1-Z7-Aa2; K4-X1-G1-A14, etc.
92. G17-D36-K4-G1-Z7-Z2.
93. A55.
94. F32-G1-X1.
95. S29-Aa17-G1-N29-N29-I5-Y1; I5.
96. S29-Q3-D46-I10.
97. S3-O4-D153-N37-G39-V13-D12.
98. N35-D28-D28.
99. Assmann, 2005, pp. 106–107
100. O34-D36-V28-A40B.
101. S29-V28-D36-S20.

102. E31-Y1A; E31-Y1-Z2.
103. E31-Z1.
104. E31-Z1-A50.
105. S29-D36-V28-S6.
106. O34-D36-V28-E31-A40; O34-D36-V28-E31-A52; S29-D36-V28-E31-A1; S29-M17-V28-E31; S29-V28-A53; E31-A1; O34-D36-V28-A40.
107. Assmann, 2005, p. 89.
108. I10; I10-X1-N17.
109. I10-X1-Z1.
110. I10-X1-Z1-F51B.
111. I10-X1-Z4A-F51B-Z1.
112. O34-D36-V28-A53; O34-D36-V28-A51-A1-Z6; O34-D36-V28-G43-A51-Z3; O34-D36-V28-S20; O34-D36-V28-S20-A50; S20-A50.
113. O34-D36-V28-S20-Y1.
114. O34-D36-V28-Z7-A51-G7.
115. O34-D36-V28-Z7-S20.
116. S29-D36-V28-E31.
117. S29-D36-V28-S20.
118. Harrington, 2010, p. 2.
119. Whose open courtyards were used as an offering tray.
120. David, 2001, p. 21.
121. G43-N37-D58-X1-Z4-A53. Also *šwbty / sɜwɜbti* (M8-D58-X1-Z4-A53); šwbty (M8-G1-D58-X1-Z4-A40); *šwbty* (M8-G1-V4-D58-X1-Z4-A40); *šwbty* (M8-G1-V4-D58-X1-Z4-A53).
122. Assmann, 2005, p. 110.
123. Nyord, 2018, p. 75.
124. Nyord, 2018, p. 75.
125. Nyord, 2018, p. 75.
126. Nyord, 2018, p. 75.
127. Nyord, 2018, p. 75.
128. Assmann, 2005, p. 107.
129. David, 2002, 91.
130. S29-G25-Aa1-Y1.
131. David, 2001, pp. 90–91; Lehner, 1997, p. 31.
132. O1-D21-X1-D54-G17-O4-D21-Z7-N5-Z1-V12-Z1.
133. Goelet et al., 2015, p. 151.

Chapter 10

Spiritual Doubles, Divine Manifestations, and Communicative Life-forces

"Your Ba shall not forsake your corpse. Your Ba is divine among the spirits, the worthy Bas converse with you."
— *Prayers of Paheri*

A CONSTELLATION OF PHYSICOSPIRITUAL SELVES

DOPPELGÄNGERS ARE AN UNSETTLING but understudied phenomenon. Appearing in art and literature and haunting religious accounts and folklore, these are a species of auto-visions, i.e., hallucinations of "seeing oneself." A *vardøger*, from Norse mythology, is a spectral double seen performing a person's actions in advance. Finnish mythology has the *etiäinen* or "first comer." The Irish have their *fetch* or "apparition of a person living." Variously called "mirror hallucinations," "syndrome of floating experience," or "pseudo-doubled auto-vision,"[1] these out-of-body experiences are associated with stressful episodes, often occurring after a severe accident or during surgery.[2] Such experiences can be truly odd. Consider heautoscopy — observing not just a reduplication of one's body but also seeing one's observing self.[3] I contend that such "second" or autoscopic bodies[4] are hallucinated when vestigial neurostructures are activated, i.e., they are descendants of the apparitional entities from preconscious civilizations. As evidence for this contention, I argue that the Ka (spiritual Double), Ba (human-headed bird body-soul), and possibly other entities (e.g., Shadow, *šwt*) from the spiritual landscape of archaic Egypt were extraceptive phantom images.[5]

To the modern mind, the archaic Egyptian view of the individual may seem disjointed and fragmented beyond repair. But one key element of archaic Egyptian super-religiosity that strongly resonates with other traditions is the notion of multiple souls and how one part of one's spiritual self stays behind in this world to communicate with mortals (DWMP). Persons were regarded as complex beings that could exist both before and after death in a myriad of manifestations (*ḫprw*).[6] They expressed themselves via a multiplicity of constituents in a constellative manner.[7]

In this chapter I delineate the main elements that, for the Egyptians, composed the individual (the Ba, Ka, Akh, and Shadow are the most frequently mentioned). Table 10.1 lists key concepts that will be addressed.

Table 10.1. Summary of Key Facets of a Person.

Expression Used	Historical Meaning	Term
Akh	Powerful, transfigured state of entire being	*3ḫ*
Ba	Manifestation of being/soul	*b3*
Corpse, body	Corpse, body	*ḫ3t*
Heart	Emotion/intellect/morality	*ỉb*
Heart	Physical heart	*ḥ3ty*
Heka	Cosmic energy/magic	*ḥk3w*
Ka	Double	*k3*
Life-force	Life-force	*sḫm*
Mummy	Mummy, spiritualized body, glorified body	*s'ḥ*
Name	Name, reputation	*rn*
Shadow	Spirit-shadow	*šwt*
Statue, image	Statue, image	*twt*

THE KA: A VITAL FORCE THAT CONNECTS AND COMMUNICATES

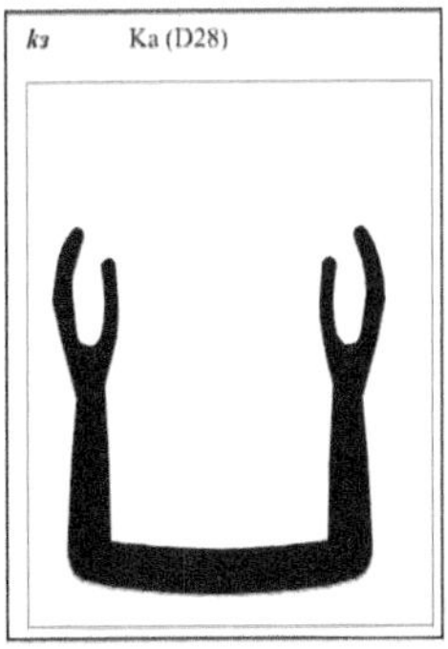

Let us begin with Ka, certainly one of the most important notions of the archaic Egyptians.[8] The very name of Egypt itself suggests the significance of Ka: our word for Egypt comes from *Aiguptos*, the Greek rendering of *ḥw k3 ptḥ*.[9] This means "palace of the Ka of Ptah," the name of the god's temple at Memphis. The concept of the Ka dominated Egyptian spiritual thought for millennia, though it lost its importance by the New Kingdom. However, even during the Late Period, it still received offerings and respect, e.g., an inscription from the Victory Stela of King Piye (715–657 BCE) reads "By his Ka, I act not without him; it is he who commands me to act!"[10]

An uncomfortable weirdness surrounds Ka. Jaynes describes it as a "particularly disturbing concept,"[11] a description that echoes Frankfort's view.[12] Some note it is impossible to translate, though many have tried: soul, spirit, ghost, vital force, will power, life-spirit, nature, luck, genius, destiny.[13] None of these glosses are satisfactory. This "slippery diversity of meanings"[14] indicates that we are missing a crucial aspect of this remarkably alien concept. The problem of the Ka is

> so enormous that one cannot hope to work it out within the framework of a single book ... Properly speaking, it cannot be solved by a single scholar, for its utterly complex and versatile nature requires ... vast knowledge in all fields of Egyptology unattainable in our epoch of specialization. In short, the Ka problem can be successfully treated as an integral whole only by a team of scholars having various views but working in a well-coordinated joint project. The present writer can hardly imagine such a team, and thus, any study of the Ka will inevitably remain fragmentary and incomplete.[15]

Often translated as a person's Double, the Ka could detach from a sleeping person. It could move about freely and required food and drink. Animals, plants, and rocks might have their own Kas; the god Osiris was called the Ka of the pyramids. Like a doppelgänger, the Ka could appear to others while its owner was still alive.

The Ka is born twice. In its first birth it appears with the "original." Its second birth (after the death of its owner) requires ritually bringing representations in the tomb to life, thereby inviting the Ka's owner into eternal life. But Bolshakov points out that we should not assume that the "mere potentiality to be realized" was "only at the second stage." As long as a person is alive, the Ka maintains an individual's vital and mental activities.[16] When one dies "one goes to one's Ka" and the dead are called "masters of their Kas." Before interment one was "neither dead nor alive," and this was a crucial liminal period during which embalming was intended to prepare the corpse for the arrival of the Ka. It was known to linger in the deceased's tomb, inhabiting the mummified corpse or statue representing the deceased. But strangely for us, Kas were also described as entities that belong in this life and move among the living.

The root meaning of Ka concerns ideas of plurality, augmentation, and growth; more concretely, it involves a fertility and reproductive energy that animates the vegetable, animal, human, and divine worlds. But this energy is not just about sustenance; it also denotes a power that connects individuals to their ancestors, the king, and the gods with whom communication becomes possible. And for the archaic Egyptians, communicating with divine beings was cognition. Moreover, *kꜣ* seems to tie together thinking (intention), speaking (formulation), and working (execution of what is planned); this is the ontological basis of the notion that the world is created by a god's thought and word.[17] A variant of Ka written with the symbol of the *kꜣ* — two upraised arms — rests on a standard supporting the emblem of a divinity.[18]

Below I rely on Bolshakov's detailed linguistic analysis (with my own additions and insertions) in order to delineate the crucial role Ka played in Egyptian spirituality.[19] I suggest nine interrelated semantic domains that account for the significance of this key complex: (1) alive while dead—the Ka and its Doubleworld; (2) offerings to the Ka; (3) communicative life-force; (4) cosmic and creative energies; (5) reproduction, fecundity, and creation; (6) agriculture and sustenance; (7) magic and sorcery; (8) the authorization of thought and behavior; and (9) Ka as one's guide.

Alive While Dead: The Ka and Its Doubleworld

As previously mentioned, the hieroglyph for Ka is of two upraised arms, interpreted to mean embracing and offering protection.[20] Another interpretation is "doubling." Since this concept appears to be the core meaning of *kꜣ*, it will initiate a discussion of what Ka denoted.

A Ka[21] was not an incarnation of a certain component of a person; rather it was an individual's complete copy, encompassing what we would understand as both physical and psychological attributes.[22] Morenz describes the Ka as a "hyper-physical vital force."[23] As if indicating the very earthly nature of the Ka, a euphemism for human feces is "peace of the Ka" (*ḥtp kꜣ*).[24] At the same time, Ka possesses what to our modern minds is a supernatural aspect, as in *ẖry kꜣ*, meaning "protection of a good spirit."[25] In myths, the king's Ka, considered his twin, performed the role of a doppelgänger, such as announcing the king's arrival to the gods in heaven. And like a doppelgänger, it repeated the actions of the monarch.[26] Table 10.2 lists words closely related to the idea of a person's or a god's Double.[27]

Table 10.2. Some Hieroglyphic Variants of "Double" and Its Ka-related Meanings.

No.	Term	Possible Translation	Explanation
1.	*kꜣ*[28]	Name	One's name, in the sense of an individual's essence, is an idea close to Ka as Double
2.	*kꜣr*[29]	Chapel, shrine	Place where the Double of the person represented dwells
3.	*ḥwt kꜣ*[30]	Ka chapel	Place where the Double of the person represented dwells
4.	*tkꜣw*[31]	Ritual of torch lighting	Light is of vital importance for the Double in the tomb's darkness
5.	*tkꜣ*[32]	Burn, be burnt, illumine	Light is of vital importance for the Double in the tomb's darkness
6.	*kꜣp*[33]	Cense, censer	Censing is a significant component of the rituals performed in front of representations in order to sustain the Double's existence
7.	sb*ỉ n kꜣ .f*[34]	The dead	"One who goes to his or her Ka"
8.	*kꜣ*[35]	Appear	Perhaps indicating a visual extraception of a Double
9.	*ḥm kꜣ*[36]	Ka priest	"Servant of the Ka" (the arms are lowered rather than raised)

As Double, the Ka's very existence implicated what may be called a Doubleworld, which was depicted in tomb murals. They might show a king sitting down to enjoy a meal while his Ka sat and ate with him. Part of this duplex existence was a false door, through which the Ka of the deceased god-king would enter this world and be heard. False doors were sometimes elaborate structures or they were simply painted on limestone walls.

Offerings to the Ka

Mortals were expected to make offerings to the Kas of kings and their ancestors, forming a ritualized dynamic of cosmic powers, sustenance, connection, and communication. Superiors and subordinates were interdependently linked in reciprocal relations. Beginning in the Old Kingdom, a special room called the *pr twt* (statue chamber)[37] housed the king's Ka statue, to which offerings were presented. Typically a small slit or hole allowed the aroma of offerings to waft through to the statue and for the

Ka to move about freely. In the *Instructions of Ptahhotep*, a son is advised to teach "the great" what is useful: if you let your knowledge impress your lord, "your sustenance" will come from your lord's Ka (ca. 2374–2191 BCE).[38] Offerings, using the formula *n k3 n* (for the Ka of so-and-so), were made to a statue or representation of the deceased, in which presumably the Ka dwelled. And like ancestral spirits in so many other cultures, a Ka might haunt those who neglected making offerings to it. The linkage between tomb representations and the Ka is apparent in scenes of households and the delivery of offerings, e.g., "milking a cow for the Ka of so-and-so"; "choice meat for the Ka every day"; "bringing goods for the Ka of so-and-so"; "bringing choice meat and fowl for the Ka of so-and-so"; "bringing … the best of the offering table and every good thing, every day, for the Ka"; "this is for the Ka of so-and-so."[39] Attention to such offerings would last beyond the bicameral period. An inscription from *Two Speeches of Sishu Father of Petosiris* describes the king making an offering to Osiris-Khentamenti: "Having filled my heart with gods' way, / From my youth until this day! / I lay down with his might in my heart, / I rose up doing his Ka's wish … I was pure as his Ka desires" (from the last decades of the fourth century BCE).[40]

Communicative Life-force

However one translates Ka, it is clear that it possessed a complex mediating function among the gods, kings, and their subjects, transmitting divine authority and the exchange of influence and cosmic forces via offerings. All beings have Kas, including gods, who become the Kas of the kings.[41] The divine aspect of *k3* is evident, according to Bolshakov, in how the word "god" (*nṯr*) belongs to the same root as "Double."[42] Bolshakov speculates that this may be due to the idea of the plurality of god's manifestations, a central characteristic of ancient Egyptian thought.[43]

Below the gods in the cosmopolitical hierarchy were the kings, who were referred to as the "Ka of all the gods." Except for royalty, the Ka is never depicted, perhaps symbolizing a privileged position of divine authorization of the monarch. Only the monarchical Ka was portrayed on monuments, "sometimes as a standard bearer holding the staff of the king's head and the feather, or as a bird perched behind the king's head."[44] In one significant scene, the god Khnum is shown creating identical small figures of the king and his Ka on a potter's wheel. The Ka has his left hand pointing to his mouth, perhaps indicating that it will eventually issue commands to the king.

King Mernere, in the *Autobiography of Weni*, is described as someone "who lives forever, is august, exalted, and mighty more than any god" and "everything came about in accordance with the ordinance commanded by his Ka" (around 2300–2150 BCE).[45] In inscriptions we read of courtiers stating that "I did what his Ka loved" or "I did that which his Ka approved." The king's subjects experienced the monarchical Ka as personified power and authoritative potency;[46] they were expected to execute the demands of the king's Ka: "He made me carry out a mission in whatever his Ka desired" (Stela of the Treasurer Tjetji, ca. 2000 BCE).[47] Individuals were dependent on the pharaoh and his potency affected each and every subject.[48] An inscription on the Stele of Sehetepibre from ca. 1860–1840 BCE reads: The "king gives his servants Kas and feeds those who are faithful."[49] The ritualized, cosmos-enhancing actions of the king supported the vitality of his subjects; they were able to experience his life's energy.[50] Meanwhile, individuals tried to please the king's Ka in order to enhance his vital power.[51] Some texts report that the king made the Kas of individuals. Certain scholars[52] have translated Ka in this context as "fortune," but this is a misleading modern imposition if this word is interpreted as luck, since the notion of random happenings was unthinkable in preconscious civilizations.[53] Perhaps a better interpretation is found in the expression *kꜣ nsw*, meaning the "king's grace."[54]

An individual's Ka was his admonitory extraceptive voice, which he or she "heard inwardly, perhaps in parental or authoritative accents, but which when heard by his friends or relatives even after his own death, was, of course, hallucinated as his own voice."[55] The attitude of the Egyptians toward their Kas seems passive. Hearing it is "tantamount to obeying it. It empowers what it commands."[56] The Ka of the god-king was probably heard by the "king in the accents of his own father." However, it was "heard in the hallucinations of his courtiers as the king's own voice."[57] The dead king is the Ka of the living successor.[58]

> Each king then is Horus, his father dead becoming Osiris, and has his ka, or in later ages, his several ka's, which could best be translated now as voice-persona. The king's ka is, of course, the ka of a god, operates as his messenger, to himself is the voice of his ancestors, and to his underlings is the voice they hear telling them what to do. And when a subject in some of the texts says, "my ka derives from the king" or "the

> king makes my ka" or "the king is my ka," this should be interpreted as an assimilation of the person's inner directing voice, derived perhaps from his parents, with the voice or supposed voice of the king.[59]

Jaynes attempts to describe what it was like to dwell in a world with Kas. He asks us to relax his insistence upon the nonconsciousness of the archaic Egyptians and "for a moment, believe that they were something like ourselves." Imagine

> a worker out in the fields suddenly hearing the ka or hallucinated voice of the vizier over him admonishing him in some way. If, after he returned to his city, he told the vizier that he had heard the vizier's ka (which in actuality there would be no reason for his doing), the vizier, were he conscious as are we, would assume that it was the same voice that he himself heard and which directed his life. Whereas in actuality, to the worker in the fields, the vizier's ka sounded like the vizier's own voice. While to the vizier himself, his ka would speak in the voices of authorities over him, or some amalgamation of them. And, of course, the discrepancy could never be discovered."[60]

As political structures became more elaborate, the king's extraceptive persona had to be in more than one place simultaneously performing different roles. This explains why eventually kings could have more than one Ka, as evident from the mid-second millennium BCE.[61] Ramesses II (1290–1224 BCE) had 20 Kas.

Cosmic and Creative Energies

The Ka "not only organizes the mental processes"; it is "also the center of human vital activity as a whole."[62] This is why some have translated it as a life energy, a force animating the individual. The Ka is a type of cosmic force that can be present to varying degrees in a person.[63] Though one's Ka requires food to survive after one dies, and seems in certain respects to possess a personality of sorts, it is impersonal. As a life-force, the Ka appears to be passed down through the generations. The addressee in the *Instructions of Ptahhotep* is reminded that his son was begot by his own Ka (from Middle Kingdom, 2040–1650 BCE).[64]

Reproduction, Fecundity, and Creation

As a cosmic power, *kꜣ* is related to the world of nature — reproduction, fertility, and the act of creation itself. Bulls, as manifestations of power and vitality par excellence, were closely associated with *kꜣ*. Indeed, a word for bull was *kꜣ*, and numerous words for bull contain the hieroglyphic components of *kꜣ*, a bull, and a penis.[65] "Bull of bulls" (*kꜣ kꜣw*) is represented as a bull followed by three ejaculating penises.[66] Work and labor mean creating something new or augmenting what already exists, so perhaps it should not be surprising that a number of terms related to *kꜣ* have to do with labor, building, and making objects. For example, *kꜣt*[67] meant work, construction, craft, or profession, while *kꜣwty*[68] meant workman, worker, or porter (Table 10.3).

Agriculture and Sustenance

Ka, as a cosmic power, is related to that which grows and provides sustenance (Table 10.4). This linkage to plants, crops, and natural augmentation can even be extended to human-made containers of produce (Table 10.5).

Table 10.3. Some Hieroglyphic Variants:
Fertility and Creative Power and Ka-related Meanings.

No.	Term	Possible Translation
1.	*bk / bꜣkꜣ*[69]	Breeding cow
2.	*bkꜣ*[70]	Be pregnant
3.	*bkꜣt*[71]	Mother cow
4.	*kꜣ*[72]	Cow
5.	*kꜣ*[73]	Bull
6.	*kꜣ ḥḏ*[74]	White bull (sacred animal)
7.	*kꜣi*[75]	Prostitute, harlot
8.	*kꜣt*[76]	Vagina, private parts
9.	*kꜣt*[77]	Cow
10.	*ms kꜣ*[78]	Male calf
11.	*nk*[79]	Copulate, have sex with
12.	*nk*[80]	To debauch
13.	*nkꜣkꜣ*[81]	Be revived (condition of corpse's flesh)
14.	*nkiki*[82]	Impregnate
15.	*nkw*[83]	Lover, adulterer, dirty ox (derogatory)
16.	*sbkꜣ*[84]	To fill, impregnate
17.	*ṯꜣy / kꜣ*[85]	Bull calf

Table 10.4. Some Hieroglyphic Variants:
Agriculture and Sustenance and Ka-related Meanings.

No.	Term	Possible Translation
1.	*kꜣm*[86]	Grape-harvest, vintage
2.	*kꜣmw*[87]	Vinter, vine grower
3.	*kꜣmw / kꜣnw*[88]	Vineyard, orchard
4.	*kꜣmw*[89]	
5.	*kꜣny*[90]	Vintner
6.	*kꜣry*[91]	Gardener
7.	*kꜣw*[92]	Food
8.	*kꜣw*[93]	Food, sustenance
9.	*kꜣw / kꜣy*[94]	Sycamore figs
10.	*skꜣ*[95]	Plough lands, plough fields
11.	*skꜣ*[96]	Plough, cultivate, till
12.	*skꜣ*[97]	Plough-ox
13.	*skꜣw*[98]	Harvests, crops

Table 10.5. Some Hieroglyphic Variants:
Vessels and Ka-related Meanings.

No.	Term	Possible Translation
1.	*kꜣkmn*[99]	Container, pot, vessel
2.	*kꜣt mrẖt*[100]	Container, pot
3.	*ṯꜣb n kꜣ*[101]	
4.	*tkꜣ*[102]	

Magic and Sorcery

As a type of power, *kꜣ* can be manipulated and put to magical uses. In this sense, it resonates with the Polynesian notion of mana and can be described as an efficacious cosmic energy (Table 10.6).

Table 10.6. Cosmic Energy and Ka-related Meanings.

No.	Term	Possible Translation
1.	*ḥkꜣ*[103]	Magic
2.	*ḥkꜣ*[104]	Bewitch, be bewitched
3.	*ḥkꜣ*[105]	Charms
4.	*ḥkꜣw*[106]	God Heka, personification of magic
5.	*ḥkꜣw*[107]	Magic, magic spells
6.	*ḥkꜣw*[108]	Magic, magic spells, incantations, charms
7.	*ḥkꜣwt*[109]	Sorcery, magic
8.	*ḥkꜣy / ḥkꜣw*[110]	Magician
9.	*ḥry ḥkꜣ*[111]	
10.	*rkꜣ / rk*[112]	Enchant, to spellbind, bewitch
11.	*wr ḥkꜣw*[113]	Great of magic, epithet of gods

Authorization of Thought and Behavior

Thinking, especially during times of stress or novel experiences, is really a type of talking to one's self, a reflective cognition, a dialogue between self-as-subject and self-as-object. In bicameral times, such self-communication occurred between a person and a divine entity, while in post-bicameral times it transpires between an "I" and a "me." Bolshakov writes that among the Egyptians, thinking was regarded as a "dialogue with some internal interlocutor." This is why the verb *kꜣi* (speak) shares the same root as *kꜣ* (Table 10.7).[114] Intriguingly, Bolshakov suggests that the word *ḫmt* (three or to treble), which can also mean foretell, expect, think, intend, plan, anticipate, or desire,[115] describes cognition as a "trilateral process" occurring among the Ka, Ba, and the person.[116] And *kꜣ* as thinking possesses a temporal dimension that is worth mentioning: any event-to-come is something thought about at present. The same future sense is embodied in the word *bkꜣ*,[117] meaning tomorrow or morning.[118]

Table 10.7. Hieroglyphic Variants: Thinking and Speaking and Ka-related Meanings.

No.	Term	Possible Translation
1.	*kꜣ*[119]	Speak
2.	*kꜣ*[120]	Cry out, scream
3.	*kꜣ*[121]	Think about, plan
4.	*kꜣt*[122]	Thought, plan, device, plot
5.	*nkꜣ*[123]	Meditate on, think about, take counsel
6.	*nkꜣy*[124]	One must think about

Ka as One's Guide

A Ka sometimes functioned like a guardian angel, at other times like a being that acquired earthly knowledge. Like the personal god (*ili*) of the Mesopotamians, Kas seem to have co-existed alongside an individual as his or her guide or genius. Indeed, one translation of *kꜣ* is "genius."[125] A formula to "appease the Ka" states "Hail to you, my Ka, my helper! / Behold, I have come before you, / Risen, animated, mighty, healthy!"[126] And like the *ili* of Mesopotamian officials, Ka appears in names of Egyptian superiors: Kaininesut, "my Ka belongs to the king" or Kainesut, "the king is my Ka."[127] Kas also functioned as something like a conscience (though this is a post-bicameral notion), a guiding force that urged kindness, compassion, and quietude. One's Ka disapproves of outbursts, whether great or small.[128] In the *Instructions of Ptahhotep,* we are told that it is the Ka that makes one's "hands reach out."[129] We are also told that the "nobleman, when he is behind [before] food / Behaves as his Ka commands him."[130] We are advised not to offend the Ka of a dinner host[131] or not to upset those who are worried: "If he gets angry at him who foils him, / The Ka will part from him who loves him."[132] Peace will come from the Ka of a "great man" after he rages at a person.[133] "In the belly" of superiors "who love you" is a Ka "who loves to listen."[134]

To conclude this section, I cautiously offer a tentative definition of the Ka: an animating force that provides beings with the ability to be connected to, communicate with, and to guide and be guided by other beings.

THE BA: MANIFESTING A PERSON'S ESSENCE

Another crucial concept from Egyptian archaeopsychology is the Ba. This was often depicted as a human-headed bird, sometimes with arms (or the same hieroglyph of the Jabiru stork; later changed to a human-headed hawk). It was believed to fly between the entombed, immobilized physical body, the Ka, and the otherworld. Other interpretations saw the Ba spending time in the tomb during the day but accompanying Re on his solar barque

bꜣ Ba (GLC = G53)

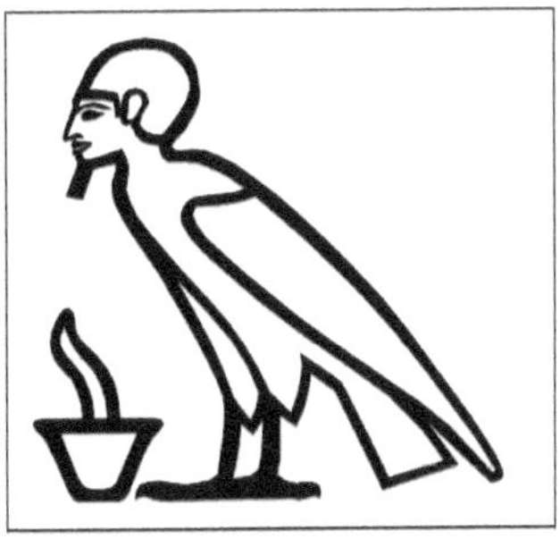

during evenings. Bas destined for damnation were *mt*; those rewarded with a peaceful eternity were *mnḫ*,[135] meaning the beautified or perfected souls.[136] A Ba that had reached paradise was *'nḫ*.[137] Bas were believed to be armed with spells and amulets (*'pr*).[138] One writer mentions that in some cases, the Ba was described as the soul of the Ka.[139] Unlike the Ka, which has attributes that make it impersonal, the Ba is personal and embodied an individual's personality and in some ways acted like a ghost.[140] The Ba had wide-ranging freedom of movement through the different realms of the cosmos.[141] Gee sees Ba as a "general category" of which a person (*rmṯ*), god (*nṯr*), transfigured being (Akh), and demon or damned (*mwt*) are "specific entities"; he suggests "angel."[142] Funerary rituals, such as the Opening of the Mouth, not only reanimated a deceased individual's physical abilities, but also liberated a Ba's attachment from the body.[143] This allowed the Ba to merge with the Ka in the Afterworld, forming the Akh.

Arguably, like the Ka, the Ba was experienced as an authoritative extraception. At least during the Old Kingdom, the Ba was conceived as the visual counterpart of what (perhaps) aurally was the Ka. The Ba could not speak, but did make bird-like chirping noises and was often "depicted as a small humanoid bird, probably because visual hallucinations often have flitting and birdlike movements. It is usually drawn attendant to or in relationship to the actual corpse or to statues of the person."[144] While the Ka is power, the Ba possesses power.[145] The Ba was both a being and a quality of a being.[146] More specifically, it can be understood as either the "manifestation of the power of a being" or a "being whose power is manifest."[147] The Ba and Ka could appear together: "May your Ba swoop from heaven to your house every day, / At the welcoming voice of your priestly singer! / May you hear the chantings of your steward, / As he sets things before your Ka!" (*Hymn to Imhotep* in the Temple of Ptah at Karnak).[148]

Like the Ka, the notion of the Ba implicates a wide semantic field that covers monarchical authority, godly manifestations, transformations of the deceased, and cosmic power (Table 10.8).[149]

Divine and Kingly Bas

Kings, one step below the gods on the ladder of divine emanations, had their monarchic powers embodied as Bas (as evident in the *Pyramid Texts*), and they frequently possessed more than one Ba. This plural aspect can be understood as an "intensification of the meaning of the Bas as the

Table 10.8. Some Hieroglyphic Variants: Ba-related Concepts.

No.	Term	Possible Translation
1.	*bꜣ*[150]	Soul
2.	*bꜣ*[151]	Holy ram, ram, Ba
3.	*bꜣ*[152]	Might, power
4.	*bꜣ*[153]	Be a Ba, possess a Ba
5.	*bꜣ rpwt ity*[154]	Ba of the sedan chair of the monarch
6.	*bꜣbꜣti*[155]	Testicles
7.	*bꜣgywv*[156]	The Languid Ones (dead)
8.	*bꜣw*[157]	Souls (of dead), manifestations
9.	*bꜣw*[158]	Power, might, strength, will, glory, prowess, frame, wrath
10.	*bꜣw*[159]	Glory, respect, authority, power, strength, fate
11.	*bꜣw*[160]	Plural of Ba
12.	*bꜣy*[161]	He of the Ba
13.	*bꜣyw*[162]	Ba-like creatures
14.	*sbi n bꜣ-f*[163]	One Who Goes to His Ba

emanation of power."[164] Ba is sometimes translated as "might," "power," "fame,"or "glory," though these terms do not fully capture the full significance of what the Egyptians meant.[165] Other glosses might be "impressiveness, "effect," or "reputation."

More so than kings and ordinary people, gods were beings whose power was pre-eminently manifest, and it was the function of Bas to make visible divine presence (e.g., as evident in the *Pyramid Texts*). The Bas of the gods took various forms, e.g., the Bennu Bird was called the Ba of Re and the Apis Bull (Orion) was the Ba of Osiris. Gods might also be the Bas of other gods. Inanimate objects could be the Ba of a god (though in the world view of the Egyptians, everything was essentially animate).[166] Indeed, anything could paralogically be a manifestation of a deity's power. A lion-shaped amulet may be referred to as the Ba of Shu.[167] The Bas of cities were the "divinized dead kings of those cities."[168] Sacred writings might be referred to as the Bas of Re. When the Ba of Re is in the underworld, it would be represented as Khnum, the ram god, who was associated with the annual inundation of the Nile and was also the "potter god" who fashioned unborn infants. Re would then be known as Khnum–Re.

Evolution of a Concept

Different periods of Egyptian history reflected changing understandings of the Ba. During the Old Kingdom, only gods and deceased kings — those sitting on the top of the theopolitical pyramid — possessed Bas. Evidence does not exist that living kings had Bas in the Old Kingdom. Bas had the prerogative of manifesting their authorization through visions and voices. After the decline of the more monarch-dominated Old Kingdom, the Ba adopted some of the bicameral functions of the Ka. This was "indicated by a change in its hieroglyph from a small bird to one beside a lamp," i.e., to lead the way like a guardian spirit.[169] By the First Intermediate Period (from around 2190 BCE) and into the Middle Kingdom (as reflected in the *Coffin Texts*), the gods and living kings were in possession of Bas, as were the deceased.

Beginning in the Middle Kingdom, a type of pottery called "Ba houses" were placed in tombs of commoners who could not afford the more expensive offertory chapels. These acted as resting places for the Bas and contained clay images of food and gifts. In the New Kingdom (after around 1550 BCE), it was primarily living kings and the deceased who had Bas, as seen in the *Book of the Dead*. Among the common people, the Ba was understood as an alter ego of those who had passed, as well as the "personification of the vital forces, physical as well as psychic."[170]

To conclude this section: the Ba was one mode of being through which a person continued to live after death. It was not so much an immanent part of a person, but a state of existence attained after death; it was not a component of the deceased but the deceased themselves.[171] The Ba, then, was the totality of an individual's physical and psychological capacities.[172] Like the Ka, the Ba is something whose traits characterize it as corporeal, not incorporeal. Rather than something other-worldly, the Ba was more of a this-worldly being. Because it performed physical activities such as eating, drinking, and copulating, it required a corpse (or statue) to anchor its existence in the earthly realm.[173]

A Proto-conscience?

In *A Dispute between a Man and His Ba*, from around 1900–1785 BCE, a man gripes about the hardships of this world and praises death. Jaynes contends that we should take the meaning of this composition at face-value — the man is engaged in a dialogue with an "auditory hallucination, much like that of a contemporary schizophrenic."[174] Upset by his complaining, his Ba threatens to desert him. This greatly disturbs the man, because being abandoned by one's Ba would not only prevent him from moving on to the next phase of existence but would mean complete annihilation and the loss of eternal life. The man debates with his Ba, asking it not to leave him and to accept his longing for death. The Ba advises the man that death is not anything to be welcomed and he should enjoy the blessings of this life. The Ba seems to function as the man's moral sense or a type of proto-conscience. The Ba finally agrees to remain with him. Interestingly, the man does not appear to consider suicide, but rather contemplates a "natural, though greatly welcomed, death."[175] The point of the story seems to be that this life is worth living. It does not in any fundamental way question Egypt's super-religiosity.

AKH: THE INDIVIDUAL TRANSFIGURED

3ḫ Akh (G25-Aa1)

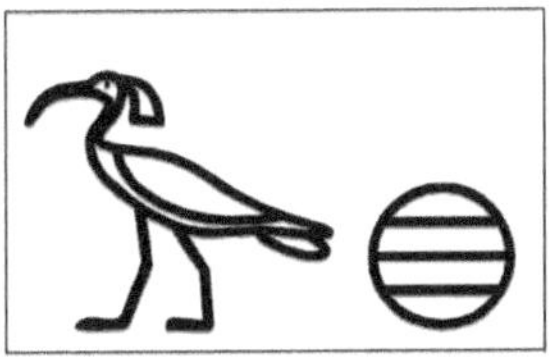

While the Ka was associated with the tomb and the Ba was believed to move between earthly existence, heaven, and the Afterworld, the Akh (*3ḫ*), whose hieroglyph represented the crested ibis, was a "transfigured spirt" that dwelled among the stars. The Akh was associated with a cosmic, primordial, and luminous potency. "Akh" appears to have two roots. The first means what is "beneficial" or "effective." The other relates to what shines and various forms of light.[176] This symbolically linked it to the twinkling stars as well as solar imagery; indeed, "effective light" was exemplified by sunlight.

The Akh can be conceived as implicating two spheres. In the living sphere Akh referred to the effectiveness of kings, officials, or anyone else who acted on behalf of their gods, kings, lords, or one another."[177] The Akh therefore had a relationship with the living.[178] To be an Akh for someone means doing helpful deeds for others who were still alive.[179] Akh-effective deeds could be mundane (performed by ordinary individuals) or of major proportions (e.g., a king's accomplishments). Unlike the Ka, Ba, or Shadow, the Akh would more readily communicate with the living. The Akh, who could speak (VVV), was "not so much an element of the deceased as the transfigured deceased in his entirety who had attained the status of an ancestor … [it] was able to communicate with the living, and appeared before them in corporeal form."[180]

In the mortuary sphere, the transfiguration of the Akh only occurred once the proper funeral rites had been performed. Moreover, regular offerings were required to keep the Akh animated. The Akh may be the closest archaic Egyptian idea to our notion of an individuality that survives death. A transfigured spirit with mighty "effective powers," it lacked material or earthly ties and was the "most spiritualized" of the various concepts of the deceased.[181] It indicated that a person had attained a shining, glorious state in the great beyond.

A mortuary ritual used to transfigure the deceased into an Akh is evident in the Early Dynastic Period. This Akh-transformation was performed by a priest called an "Akh seeker" (*sḫn ꜣḫ*).[182] To facilitate this transfiguration, a "god must speak and act," so "one may perceive the priest as god reciting the efficacious, Akh-making words to the deceased king."[183] By around the eleventh century BCE, it was believed that if a tomb was not cared for, the Akh would haunt the living; such stalkings might manifest themselves as bad dreams or illnesses. But an Akh could also be petitioned to aid the living. To be effective in the Afterworld, the Akh required offerings and needed proper tomb goods, food, and knowledge of magical spells.[184] As the Akh might be angered, it needed to be pacified and appeased, requiring "voice offerings" (*prt ḫw*). The anthropoid busts of New Kingdom ancestor worship may be representations of Akhs (Table 10.9).[185]

Akhs were notably powerful. As Gee points out, they had power over the damned, the living, and could cause health; illness; childbirth; financial

Table 10.9. Some Hieroglyphic and Conceptual Variants of Akh.

No.	Term	Possible Translation
1.	*ꜣḫ / ꜣḫw*[186]	Become a spirit, beneficial, useful, profitable, successful, right, glorious, glorified, splendid, excellent
2.	*ꜣḫ*[187]	Spiritual power, intellectual ability, be glorified, be blessed, be holy
3.	*ꜣḫ*[188]	Spirit, good spirit
4.	*ꜣḫ*[189]	Spirit
5.	*ꜣḫt*[190]	Transfigured, glory, glorious, splendid, splendor
6.	*ꜣḫt*[191]	Spirit state, transfiguration, spiritual power
7.	*ꜣḫt*[192]	Spirit, the deceased
8.	*ꜣḫ ʿpr*[193]	The Perfectly Blessed

distress; send dreams; guide individuals; do work; fight off demons; light lamps; kill; and even move ships. They could transform themselves into lotuses; barley; falcons; phoenixes; herons; geese; swallows; ibises; vultures; various birds; bulls; crocodiles; snakes; spirits; gods; fire; air; or whatever they desired. They could open doors and travel through fire. They could drive away dangerous and annoying animals and pests (crocodiles; snakes; vultures; pigs; cockroaches). They had power over water; winds; fire; and one's enemies. They could provide bread; water; beer; and other foods.[194] They could also act as a judicial personage in the Afterworld tribunals.

The relation between the Akh and Ka was complicated. They could both be present in order to receive offerings, and while the Akh could observe the living from another spiritual dimension, the Ka was the invisible force within an image.[195]

The Body as Earthly Anchor

In death, the body became not just a corpse, but also an "image" of the deceased.[196] The physical form itself was part of the spirit/soul. Thus mummification was vital, required to preserve an aspect of individual existence so that other manifestations — Ba and Ka — had something to which to return. It was also necessary so one could be judged by the guardians of the Afterworld (Table 10.10).

Table 10.10. Some Hieroglyphics Variants:
Concepts Related to the Body.

No.	Term	Possible Translation
1.	*ḥ'*[197]	Body, flesh
2.	*ḥ'w / ḥ't*[198]	Body, flesh, frame, sum of bodily parts
3.	*ḥ'*[199]	Body
4.	*ẖt*[200]	
5.	*ẖ3t*[201]	Corpse, body
6.	*ḫ3t*[202]	Body, corpse
7.	*ẖ3wt*[203]	Corpse
8.	*ẖ3t*[204]	
9.	*ẖ3k*[205]	Corpse, body

THE SHADOW AS POWER

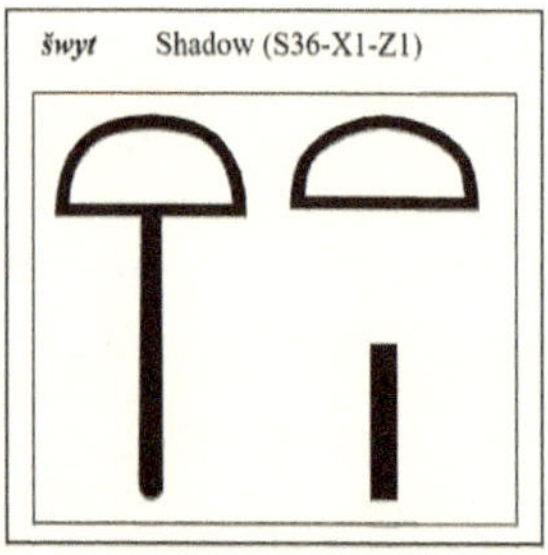

The Shadow (*šwt*) was paralogically considered to contain something physical of its owner, as well as be a separate mode of existence. Some individuals, though usually kings, had a special box in which a part of their Shadow was kept. Its earliest references are found the First Intermediate Period (the *Coffin Texts*) and the Middle Kingdom. It was often mentioned together with the Ba, and seems to have been related to the entombed body. The Shadow might obtain food for the deceased, and like other manifestations of a person, was "understood as corporeal rather than ethereal."[206] Shadows lacked a voice, "producing only a whispering or buzzing sound, or screaming ... when in pain"[207] — like the banshee of Irish folklore. The Shadow was not often depicted, but it might be portrayed as a human silhouette or a small human figure painted completely black. Statues of individuals and deities might be referred to as Shadows. The image of a deity carved on a temple wall could be regarded as the god's Shadow; indeed, a temple might be called the Shadow of a god. The Shadow could accompany the Ba on the solar barque, feast on offerings, or perhaps rest in its owner's tomb (Table 10.11).

Table 10.11. Some Hieroglyphic Variants and Concepts Related to Shadow.

No.	Term	Possible Translation
1.	*šwt*[208]	Shadow, shade, Shadow (as part of an individual)
2.	*šwt / šwyt*[209]	Shadow, shade (as part of a person)
3.	*šwbyt*[210]	Shadow, shade
4.	*ḫ3byt / šwbyt*[211]	
5.	*ḫ3b / ḫ3byt*[212]	
6.	*šwyt*[213]	
7.	*šwt / ḫ3byt*[214]	Shadow
8.	*ḫ3ybt*[215]	
9.	*šwyt nṯr*[216]	Sacred figure, image (of god), god's Shadow
10.	*šwyt*[217]	Spirit (of god)
11.	*šwyt*[218]	Shadow (as part of a person's individuality), spirit of god

The Power of Names

rn	Name (D21-N35-G7)

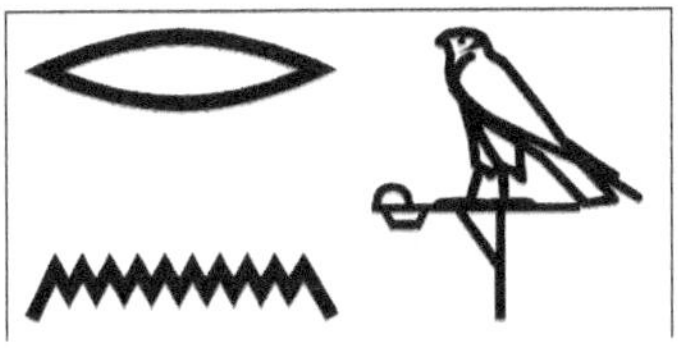

Another essential aspect of a person's identity was his or her name (*rn*).[219] Naming and the uses of names indicates paralogic identification. Names "emanated from the objects they represented."[220] Because all things came into existence by appellation, it was believed that controlling names through magical means afforded power over others. In the Old Kingdom, the hieroglyphs for animals might be rubbed out to prevent them from coming to life and harming the deceased or consuming offerings intended for them.

It was believed that one would survive in the beyond as long as one's name was evoked. This explains why efforts were made to protect it and the practice of placing it in numerous writings. Inscribing it on mortuary stelae ensured that one's spiritual existence continued after death. The idea was that the more places it appeared, the greater the chance it would survive to be spoken and read, thereby guaranteeing one's existence. One's name needed to be mentioned after death so one could live on in the Afterworld, and recognition of one's social status was equated with eternal existence. In other words, having others remember one lacked a psychologically-interiorized value; it was "not a matter of an inner, autonomous life force but of constellative integration and acknowledgment."[221]

Names, then, had to be guarded; royal names were inscribed or written in a cartouche (an oval with a horizontal line at one end) (note when written differently, *rn* meant "name of a king"[222]). The cartouche was the hieroglyphic form of the Shen ring, a circle with a line tangent to it. Meaning to encircle, Shen granted eternal protection. Here it should be noted that Ka is often glossed as "name."[223]

DIVINE ENERGIES AND POWER

The deceased, both during funerary rituals and while in the Afterworld, were animated and energized by Heka.[224] Less clear in the record is *sḫm* (Table 10.12). It appears to have been a living force or life-force that existed in the Afterworld or the ethereal personification of the life force of the person. It is also defined in the *Book of the Dead* as "power" and as a location in the Afterworld where Horus and Osiris dwelt.

Table 10.12. Terms Related to *sḫm*.

No.	Term	Possible Translation
1.	*sḫm*[225]	Have power over an enemy, gain control
2.	*sḫm iry*[226]	Ruler, potentate
3.	*sḫm*[227]	Powerful
4.	*sḫm*[228]	Mighty, to be
5.	*sḫm*[229]	Power, personified as a deity
6.	*sḫm*[230]	Cult figure, likeness (of god on earth)
7.	*sḫm*[231]	Mighty one, cult figure, likeness (of god on earth)
8.	*sḫm*[232]	Powerful (of Horus)
9.	*sḫm*[233]	Power
10.	*sḫm*[234]	Powerful, to be
11.	*sḫm spd*[235]	Powerful and effective one
12.	*sḫm*[236]	Mighty one
13.	*sḫm*[237]	Have power
14.	*sḫm*[238]	Book of spells, magical book

Notes to Chapter 10

1. Also called "excursion of the ego," "visuo-vestibular splitting of the somatosensory body image," or "ecstasy while looking back at oneself."
2. They have three phenomenological elements: (1) feeling outside one's body (disembodied); (2) a distanced and elevated visuospatial viewpoint (perspective); and (3) seeing one's body (autoscopy).
3. Also called deuteroscopy or dissimilar doubled auto-vision.
4. Sometimes called parasomas.
5. I provide a more detailed exploration of autoscopic phenomena, as well as a literature review, and how they relate to religious experience. McVeigh 2016a, esp. pp. 165–69, 234–38.
6. L1-D21-G43-N33A; L1-D21-Z7-Z6-Z2.
7. Assmann, 1998, p. 384; Assmann, 2005, pp. 88–89.
8. Bolshakov, 1997, p. 132.
9. O6-X1-O1-D28-Z1-Q3-X1-V28-A40.
10. Cited in Lichtheim, 2006c, p. 73.
11. Jaynes, 1976, p. 190.
12. Frankfort, 1978, p. 61.
13. Bolshakov usefully reviews 150 years of scholarly attempts to decipher the meaning of Ka. Bolshakov, 1997, pp. 123–131.
14. Jaynes, 1976, p. 190.
15. Bolshakov, 1997, p. 291.
16. Bolshakov, 1997, pp. 209–210.
17. Bolshakov, 1997, p. 164.

18. D29.
19. Bolshakov analyzed the uses of Ka into five semantic groups; my approach is somewhat different. Bolshakov, 1997, pp. 159–165. Though he admits some of the connections he makes are hypothetical, most of them are supported by strong evidence.
20. For the word *ḥm kꜣ*, meaning Ka priest or "servant of the Ka" (D31; D31-X1), the arms are lowered.
21. D28; D29.
22. Bolshakov, 1997, p. 153.
23. Morenz, 1992, p. 170.
24. R4-X1-Q3-D28-Z1-J2.
25. T28-D21.
26. Frankfort, 1978, p. 69.
27. From Bolshakov, 1997, p. 160. Other semantic elaborations related to *kꜣ* as Double include a sense of otherness: *ky* (other), *ky* (another); *kwy* (others); and *kw y* (enemies). These interpretations are based on the assumption of the very early transition *ꜣ* > *y*. Bolshakov 1997, p. 164.
28. D28-Z1; D28-Z1-A40.
29. D28-D21-O18.
30. O6-X1-D28.
31. X1-D28-G43-Q7.
32. V13-D28-G1-Z7-Q7-Z2, X1-D28-G1-Q7.
33. D28-Q3-R5.
34. O35-N35-D29-I9-A55.
35. D28-D52-G1.
36. D31.
37. O1-Z1-X1-G43-X1. Often described using the Arabic *serdab*.
38. Cited in Lichtheim, 2006a, p. 71.
39. Cited in Bolshakov, 1997, pp. 148–49.
40. Cited in Lichtheim, 2006c, p. 50.
41. Frankfort, 1978, p. 78.
42. The "transitions *ṯ* > *k* and *r* > *ꜣ* are quite natural, and so 'god' obviously belongs to the same root as Double." Bolshakov 1997, p. 164.
43. Bolshakov, 1997, p. 164.
44. Jaynes, 1976, p. 192.
45. Cited in Lichtheim, 2006a, p. 22.
46. Frankfort, 1978, p. 72.
47. Cited in Lichtheim, 2006a, p. 92.
48. Frankfort, 1978, p. 69.
49. No. 20538, Cairo Museum.
50. Frankfort, 1978, p. 69.
51. Frankfort, 1978, p. 69.
52. Cf. Frankfort: The king could have an effect on a person's "innermost vitality," thereby improving their "fortune." An intensification of vitality would accompany one's success. Frankfort, 1978, p. 68.
53. Jaynes, 1976, p. 191.
54. M23-X1-N35-D28-Z1-G7.
55. Jaynes, 1976, p. 190.

56. Jaynes, 1976, p. 191.
57. Jaynes, 1976, p. 192.
58. Frankfort, 1978, p. 114.
59. Jaynes, 1976, p. 193.
60. Jaynes, 1976, pp. 190–191.
61. Jaynes, 1976, p. 193.
62. Bolshakov, 1997, p. 163.
63. Frankfort, 1978, p. 61.
64. Cited in Lichtheim, 2006a, p. 66.
65. E.g., D28-D52-E1.
66. D28-D53-D53-D53.
67. A9-Xa-Y1-Z2; D28-X1-A9; D28-X1-A9-Y1-Z2.
68. V31-G1-G43-X1-Z4-A9.
69. D58-G41-G1-D28-Z1-B2-E1-Z2.
70. D58-D28-B2.
71. D58-G29-G1-D28-Z1-B2-E1.
72. F1.
73. D28-Z4-Z5; D28-D52-E1-A40; D28-E1; D28-X1-D52-F27; D28-Z5-Z5.
74. D28-D52-E1-T3.
75. D28-G1-M17-D3.
76. D28-G1-X1-F51B.
77. D28-Z1-X1.
78. F31-S29-Z5-E1.
79. N35-V31-D53.
80. N35-V31-D53-Y1.
81. N35-D28-D28.
82. N35-V31-M17-V31-M17.
83. N35-V31-G43-D280.
84. S29-D58-D28-B1.
85. D52-E3.
86. D28-Z-J5-M43A-Z3.
87. D28-G1-G17-G43-M17-M17-D40-Z2.
88. D28-G1-N35-M43.
89. D28-G1-G17-O1-Z3A.
90. D28-Z1-N35-59-M17M17-M43-A1.
91. D28-D21-M17-M17-A24.
92. D28-G1-Z7-Z8-Z2.
93. D28-Z1-N37-Z2.
94. D28-Z1-M17-M17.
95. S29-D28-G1-Z7-U13-U7-D40-X1-N23-Z1.
96. S29-D28G1-U13.
97. S29-D28-G1-U13-E1.
98. S29-D28-U13-N33-78-Z2-78.
99. D28-Z1-V31-63-Y5-N35-U28-O39-Z7-W23-Z1.
100. D28-X1-Z1-D3-U7-D21-Aa1-X1-W22.
101. V13-D58-Z7W22-N35-D28-Z1-Y1-Z2.
102. X1-D28-Z5-Z5-Z5-W23-Z1.

103. V28-D28-Z5-Z5-A2.
104. V28-D28-G1-A2.
105. F18-D28-A2-Z2.
106. V28-D28-Y1-A40-Z3.
107. V28-D28-Z2.
108. V28-D28-G1-A2-Z3.
109. V28-D28-G1-G43-X1-A1-Z2.
110. V28-D28-M17-M17-Y1-40-A40.
111. D2-D21-Z3-V28-D28-Z3.
112. D21-Z1-V31-G1-Z29-A24.
113. G36-D21-V28-D28-Z2.
114. Bolshakov, 1997, p. 163.
115. Aa1-D52-X1-Z3-A2.
116. Bolshakov, 2001, pp. 215–217.
117. D58-G29-D28-N14.
118. Bolshakov, 1997, pp. 163–164.
119. V31-G1-A2.
120. V31-G1-M17-M17-A2.
121. D28-Z1-M17-M17-A2.
122. V31-G1-X1-A2.
123. N35-V31-G1-A2.
124. N35-V31-G1-Z4-M17-M17-A2-A1.
125. D28-Z1-Z2.
126. Chapter 105, An Address to the Ka, the Book of the Dead (Coming Forth by Day). Cited in Lichtheim, 2006b, p. 123.
127. Jaynes, 1976, p. 191.
128. *Instructions of Ptahhotep*. Cited in Lichtheim, 2006a, p. 65.
129. *Instructions of Ptahhotep*. Cited in Lichtheim, 2006a, p. 65.
130. Cited in Lichtheim, 2006a, p. 65.
131. Cited in Lichtheim, 2006a, p. 65.
132. Cited in Lichtheim, 2006a, p. 70.
133. Cited in Lichtheim, 2006a, p. 70.
134. Cited in Lichtheim, 2006a, p. 71.
135. G17-X1-D12.
136. U22.
137. S34-N35-Aa1-A1.
138. Aa20.
139. Though it is not stated what the Egyptian term for "soul" was in this context. Bunson, 2002, p. 62.
140. Frankfort, 1978, p. 61.
141. Žabkar, 1968, p. 162.
142. Gee, 2009, p. 14.
143. In a sense the Ba was a complement to the body. Frankfort, 1978, p. 61.
144. Jaynes, 1976, p. 193.
145. Frankfort, 1978, p. 64.
146. Žabkar, 1968, p. 160.
147. Žabkar, 1968, pp. 161–62.

148. Imhotep, vizier and architect for King Djoser (ca. 2686–ca. 2649 BCE). He became a god of healing. Cited in Lichtheim, 2006c, p. 105.
149. When the Egyptians became Christianized they adopted the Greek word (psyche) for soul rather than Ba. Žabkar, 1968, p. 162.
150. E10-Z1.
151. E10.
152. G29-Z1.
153. G53-Z1.
154. G29-M17-X1-D21-Q3-X1.
155. G29-X1-G29-X1-D283.
156. D58-G29-G1-W11-A7-A40-Z3.
157. G30-Z2.
158. G30-Z4.
159. G30-Z6.
160. G29-Z1-G7-Z3A.
161. D58-G29-G1-M17-M17.
162. G29-Z1-M17-M17-G7-Z3A.
163. O35-D54-N35-G29-Z1-I9.
164. Žabkar, 1968, p. 161.
165. Žabkar, 1968, p. 161.
166. Žabkar, 1968, p. 161.
167. Frankfort, 1978, p. 61.
168. Žabkar, 1968, p. 161.
169. Jaynes, 1976, p. 193.
170. Žabkar, 1968, p. 2.
171. Žabkar, 1968, p. 162.
172. Žabkar, 1968, p. 3.
173. Žabkar, 1968, p. 162.
174. Jaynes, 1976, pp. 193–94.
175. Lichtheim, 2006a, p. 163.
176. Harrington, 2010, p. 7.
177. Friedman, 2001, pp. 47–48.
178. Friedman, 2001, pp. 47–48.
179. Assmann, 2005, p. 309.
180. Harrington, 2010, p. 7.
181. Frankfort, 1978, p. 64.
182. Friedman, 2001, pp. 47–48.
183. Hays, 2009, p. 28.
184. Friedman, 2001, pp. 47–48.
185. Friedman, 2001, pp. 47–48.
186. G25.
187. G25-Aa1.
188. G25-Aa1-A1.
189. G25-Aa1-A51.
190. G25-Aa1-X1.
191. G25-Z1.
192. G25-Z1-A51.

193. G25-Aa20-D21-Y1.
194. Gee, 2009, pp. 10–11.
195. Harrington, 2010, p. 8.
196. Assmann, 2005, p. 105.
197. V28-D36-F51B.
198. D36-F51B-F51B-F51B.
199. V28-D36-F51B.
200. F32-X1-Z1-F51B-G7.
201. M12-G1-X1; M12-G1-X1-A14; M12-G1-X1-A55; F32-G1-X1.
202. M12-X1.
203. K4-X1-A14; K4-X1-Aa2.
204. K4-X1-G1-A14; K4-G1-Z7-Aa2.
205. N37-F32-G1-X1; N37-G1-V31; N37-G1-X1.
206. Harrington, 2010, p. 11.
207. Harrington, 2010, p. 7.
208. N37-G43-X1-S36; S36-X1-Z1-A14; X1-S36-Z1.
209. H6-G43-M17-M17-X1-N5.
210. H6-M17-M17-D58-X1-S36; H6-D58-M17-M17-N8; H6-Z7-D58-Z7-N8-Z3A.
211. H6-D58-X1-N8.
212. M12-G1-D58-Z7-N8; M12-G1-M17-M17-D58-X1-S36.
213. H6-X1-N5; H6-G43-X1-N5; H6-Z7-M17-M17-X1-N5.
214. H6-X1-S36-X1-N8.
215. M12-G1-M17-M17-D58-X-S35.
216. R8-S86-X1-Z1; R8-X1-H6.
217. S36.
218. S36-X1-Z1.
219. D21-N35-A2; D21-N35-G7; V10; D21-S3-A2; D21-N35-V10-A1.
220. MacDonald, 2005, p. 234.
221. Assmann, 2005, p. 52.
222. D21-N35-V10.
223. Bolshakov, 1997, pp. 154–155.
224. Harrington, 2010.
225. S29-S42-Aa1-G17; S42-G17-A24.
226. S29-S42-Aa1-G17-D4.
227. S42-G17-D40.
228. Y8-G17-Z7-Y1-A24.
229. S29-Aa1-G17-S42-A40.
230. S42.
231. S42-A40.
232. S42-G7.
233. S42-G17; S42-Aa1-G17-Y1.
234. S42-G17-Z1.
235. S42-M44.
236. S42-Z1-G7.
237. S42-Z5-Z5-Z5-A24.
238. S42-Z7-V12-Z1.

Chapter 11

"Heart" in the Psycholexicon of Ancient Egypt

"O my heart which I had from my mother! O my heart of my different ages! Do not stand up as a witness against me, do not be opposed to me in the tribunal, do not be hostile to me in the presence of the Keeper of the Balance, for you are my Ka which was in my body, the protector who made my members hale."

— *Papyrus of Ani*

THE EMBRYONIC PSYCHOLEXICON HYPOTHESIS

If Jaynes's argument is correct that conscious interiority was undeveloped before about 1000 BCE, then Bronze Age languages should be relatively weak in psychological terminology. Archaic sociopolitical systems, though certainly complex, did not require linguo-concepts of interiorized psychologicality. Such idioms did not emerge in any robust fashion until after ca. 1000 BCE. The Embryonic Psycholexicon (EmPL) hypothesis is intended to test such an argument.[1] Three points should be made about embryonic psycholexicons. First, their vocabulary of mental words is limited, i.e., psychological idioms were incipient. Second, archaic psycholexemes are characterized by a concrete, literal, action-oriented, and behavioristic quality. The third point is admittedly more difficult to illustrate: in super-religious times a well-developed language revolving around religiosity — gods, ancestors, spirits, sacred edifices, ceremonial paraphernalia, etc. — took the place of a self-reflective, self-conscious psychologicality.[2] In other words, since supernatural entities functioned as our inner selves, a well-developed psycholexicon was unnecessary. Super-religiosity accounts for the primordial state of a psychological vocabulary, so that the need for an inventory of mind-words was minimal before the emergence of conscious interiority.

PRECONSCIOUS HYPOSTASES: TRAJECTORIES OF EVOLVING MIND-WORDS

The first mind-words were substratal building blocks upon which metaphorical forms were constructed to reflect ever increasing sociopsychological complexity. As psycholexicons developed, they followed a basic linguo-conceptual scaffolding grounded in physiological and perceptual sensations. This line of reasoning resonates with basic "pre-conceptual structures"[3] and "embodied schemata." The latter are patterns that emerge as meaningful structures primarily at the level of our bodily movements through space, the manipulation of objects, and perceptual interactions with the environment.[4]

Jaynes offers an analysis of the embodied and metaphoric roots of psychological language. He refers to words that later came to mean something like modern conscious interiority as "preconscious hypostases" (from the Greek: "what is caused to stand under something"). Hypostases are the "assumed causes of action when other causes are no longer apparent."[5] They "are thus seats of reaction and responsibility which occur in the transition from the bicameral mind to subjective consciousness."[6] When the gods and ancestors became absent, individuals assumed that preconscious hypostases caused their actions. As the bicameral organization of mind began to weaken, the "decision-stress in novel situations would be much greater than previously, and both the degree and duration of that stress would have to become progressively more intense before the hallucination of a god would occur." This "increased stress would be accompanied by a variety of physiological concomitants, vascular changes resulting in burning sensations, abrupt changes in breathing, a pounding or fluttering heart, etc."[7]

To illustrate how bodily sensations resulting from physiological processes shaped mind-words, Jaynes examined the trajectory of ancient Greek terms that are variously and misleadingly translated as heart, mind, spirit, or soul: *thumos* (the most important term, probably originally referring to something external to the person but eventually taking on the meaning of a bodily container); *phrenes* (probably associated with the lungs); *noos* (from "seeing," originally external perception); *psyche* (associated with breathing or possibly bleeding); *kradie* (from quivering but evolving to mean the beating of the heart); *ker* (apparently related to kradie, it was usually referred to as the organ of grief); and *etor* (perhaps from *etron* for "belly").[8]

Jaynes hypothesized a four-stage trajectory.[9] His framework for the historical evolution of linguistic terms describing psychological processes resonates with a similar schema developed by MacDonald (Table 11.1).[10]

THE MEANING OF "HEART" IN ARCHAIC EGYPT

At first glance, Middle Egyptian appears to have a fairly developed vocabulary of mind-words. However, to what degree these terms actually describe an interiorized mental world subjectively experienced or pre- or semi-conscious behavioral actions is the key question. For my present purposes I restrict my analysis to two terms typically translated as "heart." But first I introduce the theoretical framework for dissecting these two terms. Cross-culturally "heart" is one of the most common tropes to describe psychological events (though this writer wonders if, as in archaic Egyptian, "body interior" [or "bodily core"] is a more appropriate definition; see below).[13]

Table 11.1. The Historical Evolution of Psychological Terms.

Jaynes's Theory	MacDonald's Theory
(1) Objective: terms used for mental events originally referred to simple external things and observations outside the person	(1) Concrete + Outward
(2) Internal: terms became associated with processes occurring within the body, such as internal physiological sensations. Bodily organs also began to represent places where cognitive, emotional, and volitional events transpire	(2) Concrete + Inward
(3) Subjective: linguo-concepts "have moved from internal stimuli supposedly causing actions to internal spaces where metaphored actions may occur"[11]	(3) Abstract + Inward
(4) Synthetic: terms "unite into one conscious self capable of introspection"[12]	(4) Self-referring or Reflexive

Being of Two Sensations

Jaynes, discussing how modern translators misinterpret expressions in the *Iliad* as ponder, think, be of divided mind, be troubled about, try to decide, etc., makes the point that these terms concerned being in conflict about two actions, *not* two thoughts. In other words, the *Iliad*'s language is behavioristic, not psychological.[14] Similarly, Lichtheim points out that the belly is sometimes contrasted with the heart;[15] the latter is the "center of reason" and the former is the seat of unreasoning feelings, desires, and appetites. Examples of physically experiencing being pulled in different directions are found in the *Instructions of Prince Hardjedef*: "He whose heart obeys his belly / Puts contempt of himself in place of love, / His heart is bald, his body unanointed; / The great-hearted is god-given, / He who obeys his belly belongs to the enemy" (2450–2300 BCE).[16] In the *Instructions of Amenemope*[17] we are told that "He who makes gain by lying oaths, / His heart is misled by his belly" (from the Ramesside period).[18]

The Metaphor of the Heart

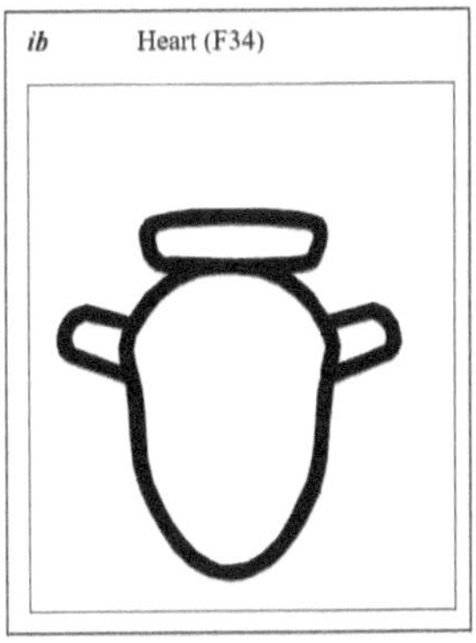

Two terms are central to any discussion of archaic Egyptian pre- or proto-psychology: *ỉb* and *ḥꜣty*. These are conventionally translated as "heart" and apparently both had metaphoric and literal uses, though Nyord notes that *ỉb* tended to be employed more metaphorically than *ḥꜣty*.[19] The former appears in a long list of compound expressions, but singularly it is translated as understanding, intelligence, will, desire, mood, wish, take care, and most problematically for this writer, the very abstract "mind." Believed to be the seat of emotion, thought, will, and intention, it may have been the closest notion the Egyptians had to what we would label as psychological (the distinction between emotion and thought may not have been as clear among archaic Egyptians). At the same time, note that there was nothing "mental" in the modern sense about the physical heart, as this organ was preserved and stored with other mummified remains. The term for heart as a physical entity (or central chest or breast)[20] was *ḥꜣty*; note, though, that *ḥꜣty* might be metaphorically employed to mean thought, courage, or will.[21]

ḥ3ty Heart (F4-X1-Z4A-F34)

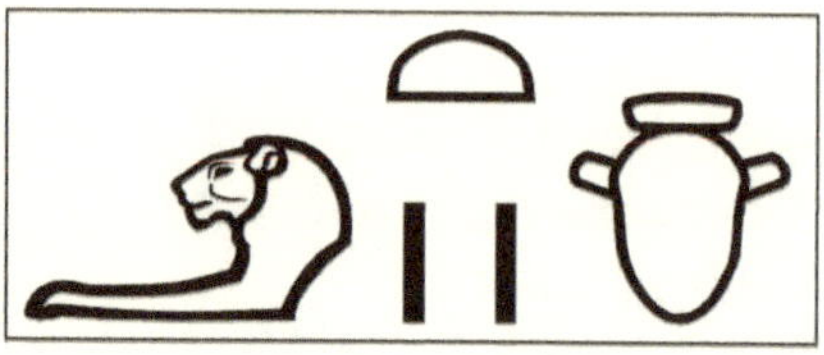

Believed to be formed from one drop of blood from the mother, the heart was a crucial concept in Egyptian understandings of the person. One must care for one's heart since it is a "gift of god." Beware of "neglecting it."[22] Not just mortals, but gods also have hearts. Significantly, like the Ka and the Ba, the heart is often portrayed as something imbued with its own agency. The heart can be followed and it can command or guide an individual. One's heart can have plans or even intentions that may not be known by its possessor.[23] Like a person, it could be happy, greedy, arrogant, inflamed (angry), or tired. The heart can be soothed or it might languish. The heart can be "washed" to relieve it of feelings; depending on the context, this may mean to satisfy (someone), please, slake, vent (one's feelings), be pleased, or rejoice.

An Archaic "Unconscious"?

Before proceeding, a slight detour: no textual records indicate that the "unconscious" (as understood in the modern sense, since the nineteenth century CE) existed among the archaic Egyptians. This is not surprising, since to be unconscious first requires consciousness (here consciousness/unconscious does not denote being awake/asleep or being in a coma). The term *db3ḫ*,[24] for unconscious or to lose consciousness, seems related to falling asleep. This is also the case for (*dgmt*),[25] which can be glossed as unconsciousness. To be "unconscious of" is one of the definitions of *ḫm*,[26] but given that it also means to not know, be ignorant, and to forget, it is very doubtful that it meant unconscious in the modern sense.

The Centrality of the Heart

Listening to one's heart determined whether one was favored by the gods: "He who hears is beloved of god, / He whom god hates does not hear. / The heart makes to its owner a hearer or non-hearer, / Man's heart is his life-prosperity-health!"[27] Having an "open heart" (*wb3 ỉb*)[28] can mean being clever, but it can also denote being ready to listen to the gods.[29] A heart hears the words of another or answers one's own questions. In the *Complaints of Khakheperre-Sonb* (ca. 1900 BCE), a heart is interrogated: "Come, my heart, I speak to you, / Answer my sayings!" and "I spoke to you, my heart, answer you me, / A heart addressed must not be silent."[30] A basic feature of love poems is a monologue in which the writer addresses his or her own heart.[31]

The heart possesses a metaphoric spatiality, i.e., it is something in which things can be placed and then pondered upon; its contents can be poured out (when in distress); it can be wide and long (i.e., patient); and it might be filled with the thoughts of another. In archaic Egyptian, numerous linguistic terms that incorporate this word attest to its crucial role. I have compiled a basic list of *ỉb* and *ḥꜣty*-related expressions (Appendix A). If we compare the number of heart-related psycholexemes from Appendix A with terms from Appendix B (Basic List of Ancient Egyptian Psycholexmes), the former occupy 80.9% of the total number of psycholexemes.[32] We can see how in Middle Egyptian psychological terminology the heart played a salient role.

Here I would caution that we must not assume that the metaphoric-versus-literal distinction — i.e., heart pressed into service to describe psychological processes *or* conceived as an organ — was familiar to the Egyptians.[33] Indeed, I submit that metaphors have historically come in two varieties: (1) *figurative*; these describe how an individual interprets an analogical experience as a mere figure of speech; and (2) *literal*; these depict how an individual interprets an analogical experience as being literally true.[34]

The Body Interior

sḫꜣ Classifer: speak, think, eat, drink, love, hate (A2)

Above this writer followed convention and deferred to other translators of archaic Egyptian, glossing *ỉb* as "heart" for the sake of convenience. Intuitively, "heart" may seem like an appropriate translation for *ỉb*. However, if we take Jaynes's theorizing on hypostases into account, perhaps *ỉb* referred to the thoracic-abdominal region — or for the sake of convenience, the "body interior." Indeed, *ỉb* appears to lack a precise anatomical location and may have meant internal organs. In any case, *ib* may be thought of as a container, i.e., a locus of spatialization. It was in the thoracic-abdominal area that various sensations were registered and used to comment on sociopsychological interactions and behaviors. Note that *r ib*[35] and *r3 ib*[36] mean abdomen or stomach. Not surprisingly, then, given how we do not experience psychophysiological reactions (except for headaches) in the head, expressions that utilize heart far outweigh those that contain "head."

Written Egyptian utilized classifiers,[37] or "extra metalinguistic and semantic information,"[38] that aid the reader in determining the meaning of a word.[39] Terms that appear to describe the mouth's activities (eating, drinking, speaking, keeping silent, etc.) and mental activity (thinking, feeling, senses and emotions) often have the classifier that depicts a man with his hand touching his mouth.[40] This hieroglyph is predicated on the idea that the body is a container and ideas are food,[41] i.e., things are put in/come out from the body/container through the mouth.[42]

The Heart Remembers: A Shift in Mentality

During the Middle Kingdom (2010–1630 BCE), one had to undergo a judgment-of-the-dead-like trial only if guilty of some misdeed. However, by the beginning the New Kingdom (1539–1069 BCE), all the deceased were required to stand before a divine tribunal, including the king. A major shift in mentality had occurred. This is evident in how the heart had become even more interiorized as the seat of psychologicality. This organ contained not only an individual's emotions, intellect, and moral worth; it was now also a record of one's deeds. More than this, the heart was assumed to have a will and existence of its own. Egyptians believed that after death individuals had to navigate a treacherous path in the Duat, the underworld. If they survived, they had to undergo the Weighing of the Heart, a final judgment in a court of divine justice presided over by Osiris. He was aided by 42 deities called the Assessors of Maat. The deceased would declare their innocence before each god, and each god judged a particular crime, ranging from serious misdeeds (stealing, adultery, murder) to those expected to attract censure in a super-religious society, such as damaging a god's image or blasphemy. Other sins included sullenness, babbling, quarreling, being unduly active, wading in water, or being of loud voice.[43]

Proceedings began when the deceased made offerings of a lotus flower, which symbolized birth and resurrection. The jackal-headed Anubis led the deceased to the Hall of Judgment where the Weighing of the Heart against the feather of an ostrich (symbolized by the goddess Maat) would be conducted.[44] Then the deceased made their "negative confessions," denying any wrongdoings. Thoth recorded the results of the Weighing the Heart (he was shown in the form of a baboon perched on top of the scales) while Horus checked the accuracy of the scales. If declared innocent, the deceased entered the Fields of Reeds and Offering as a transfigured spirit (Akh).

The heart performed a pivotal role after one died, since it provided evidence for or against its possessor; this organ was after all the seat of intellect, wellspring of emotion, and the storehouse of memories. While a heart could be one's companion, it was also feared since it might blurt "out untruths (or hidden truths) that might seal its owner's fate"[45] during the Weighing of the Heart. In order to prevent the heart from speaking against the individual and confessing transgressions, a scarab amulet engraved with a protective spell was placed in the mummy.[46]

What is interesting is how the heart was granted agency, as if it were a person in its own right. In a section called the "heart as witness" from the *Book of the Dead*,[47] a magical formula is recorded for not letting one's heart oppose one when being judged by the gods. Interestingly, here the individual's heart is described as the Ka within his or her body.[48] If the heart — measured against the standards of how a person should have behaved as dictated by Maat — was weighed down by sins, the terrible "devourer of the dead," or Ammit, went to work. This part crocodile, part lion, and part hippopotamus monstrosity summarily gobbled up the unworthy organ on the spot, thereby condemning the individual to permanent death.

ANGRY GODS

We instinctively associate emotions with internal experiences. But in the animal world emotions signal to their conspecifics behavioral consequences. This was true for preconscious individuals (and though of course conscious individuals posit intentional states within conspecifics, they too monitor the affective states of others to predict observable behavior). Though Tait's analysis of the representation of expressions of anger (*ḫ'r*)[49] is from demotic sources (and thus originating in the conscious period), the relevant examples are arguably formulaic holdovers from an earlier period. Expressions of anger possess a "largely fixed phraseology" that "occur in restricted types of context"; they function as "structural signposts." What is notable is that mentions of anger are set alongside certain phrases which are "all actions, not expressions of a state of mind."[50] These "refer to public outburst or displays of anger" and were "intended to make an impression: quite the opposite of smouldering, concealed resentment."[51]

The point is that, in preconscious times, emotions were not mentally registered as interiorized experiences. They were for display and possessed a behavioral import. This is why a "display of anger is followed by decisions, by command, by action."[52] I submit that besides anger, an analysis of the use of emotion words in texts, especially from the preconscious period, will reveal that what we moderns confidently assume *must* be internally experienced (i.e., emotions and feelings) were in fact nonconsciously processed. Appendix B intends to demonstrate how Middle Egyptian psychological terms are related to behavioral or perceptual cognates (this list is preliminary and speculative).

Any god or goddess could vent their anger, though more than any other deity, Seth was associated with wrath. Deities might become wrathful because a festival was neglected, a tomb robbed, or someone caused harm or injury to others. Divine wrath can be directed toward a god's own town and devotees and punishment can take the form of disease or plagues. A deity might take on a certain manifestation, such as a fierce animal, to drive home the point of their rage. But deities could be pacified. Attestations of divine wrath date from the Old Kingdom up through and including the Graceo-Roman period in texts dealing with the Afterworld.[53] Significantly, however, they became quite common in Ramesside texts. This was an era when the deities, now closer to the average individual because of a rise in personal piety, replaced the king as the dispensers of justice.[54]

THE IMPORTANCE OF "FACE"

In Egyptian, "face" (*ḥr*[55]) denoted head, front, mask, sight, vision, and attention. The latter two terms strongly suggest the visage of a deity appearing in the hallucinations of devotees (SV). Face could also mean what we might call "mind." Other terms for face were *ḥ3wty*[56] and *ḥ3wt*.[57] The former could also specifically mean face or countenance of god.[58] Perhaps related to visitations by deities were how "face" was used in the epithets of some gods (i.e., coming face-to-face with a deity), as in With the Beautiful

Face, i.e., Hathor (*'nt ḥr*)[59] and The One Fair of Face, i.e., Ptah (*nfr ḥr*).[60] Face was also used metaphorically to designate some aspect of a deity.

Notes to Chapter 11

1. McVeigh, 2018.
2. Of course we need to use "religious" in quotations since during the first millennium BCE "religion" as a clear-cut category of intellectual inquiry did not exist, i.e., this notion is a modern invention.
3. On embodied experiences and language see Gibbs, 2004. See also Gibbs and Colston, 2005.
4. Johnson, 1987, p. 29.
5. Jaynes, 1976, p. 258.
6. Jaynes, 1976, p. 259.
7. Jaynes, 1976, p. 258.
8. Jaynes, 1976, pp. 257–272.
9. Jaynes, 1976.
10. MacDonald, 2003.
11. Jaynes, 1976, p. 260.
12. Jaynes, 1976, p. 260.
13. Cf. Nyord, 2009a.
14. Jaynes, 1976, p. 70.
15. Lichtheim, 2006a, p. 78.
16. Cited in Lichtheim, 2006a, p. 67.
17. Chapter 11.
18. Cited in Lichtheim, 2006b, p. 155.
19. Nyord, 2009b, p. 174.
20. Nyord, 2009a. The term *ḥry ib* meant innermost parts of or contents of the torso.
21. It possess both verbal and nominal forms.
22. Chapter 24, the *Instructions of Amenemope*. Cited in Lichtheim, 2006b, p. 160.
23. In the *Coffin Texts* a god stated that "I did not command that they [humans] do evil, [but] it was their hearts which violated what I had said."
24. D36-D58-G1-D12-A15.
25. D46-W11-G1-G17-X1-D6.
26. Aa1-Aa15-G43-D35-Z2; Aa1-D35; Aa1-D52-Aa15-D35-Z2; Aa1-D52-Aa15-X1-G43-D35-D54, etc.
27. From the *Instructions of Ptahhotep*. Cited in Lichtheim, 2006a, p. 74.
28. U26-D58-Y1V-F34-Z1.
29. Morenz, 1992, pp. 64–65.
30. Cited in Lichtheim, 2006a, p. 148.
31. See examples from Lichtheim, 2006b, pp. 182–93.
32. If we include "head" (from Table 11.2), the percentage of body-related terms becomes, at 82.3%, slightly higher.
33. This does not mean that archaic Egyptians could not always distinguish between metaphors and literal definitions.
34. McVeigh, 1996.

35. S29-Aa1-D21-Y1A-F32-57-X1-Z1.
36. S29-V31-V29-F32-57-X1-Z1.
37. Sometimes still referred to as determinatives.
38. Goldwasser, 2005, p. 96.
39. The Egyptian language is "not a classifier language but a nonclassifier language recorded in a classifier script." Goldwasser, 2005, p. 99.
40. A2.
41. Goldwasser, 2005, p. 111.
42. Goldwasser, 2005, p. 99; italics in original.
43. Wilkinson, 2003, p. 84.
44. The Weighing of the Heart is recorded in chapter 125 of the *Book of the Dead.*
45. Wilkinson, 2010, p. 139.
46. For a detailed examination of how the body is pressed into service to express meanings, see Nyord, 2007; 2009b; 2014.
47. Chapter 30B.
48. Cited in Lichtheim, 2006b, p. 121.
49. N28-D36-D21-D40; N28-D36-D21-G43-E32.
50. Tait, 2009, p. 79.
51. Tait, 2009, p. 81.
52. Tait, 2009, p. 82.
53. Joseph, 2019, p. 52.
54. Joseph, 2019, p. 58.
55. D2-D21-Z1; D2-Z1-A40; D2-Z1-G7; D2-Z1-D21; D2; D2-Z1.
56. F4-Z7-X1-X1-Z4-A40-B1, etc.
57. F4-X1-Z2.
58. F4-G43-X1-Z4-A40-A40.
59. D36-N35-D6-D2-Z1-X1-H8.
60. F35-D2-Z1-A40.

Epilogue

Lessons from Archaeopsychology

"For even a single day can contribute toward eternity, an hour can embellish the future, and God recognizes him who works for him."
— *Instructions for Merikare*

WHAT CAN WE LEARN: LESSONS FROM THE RECONSTRUCTION OF OLDER MENTALITIES

In this book I have selected a number of topics from archaic Egypt and interpreted them through the lens of Jaynesian psychology. Archaic Egypt is a storehouse laden with riches that evoke a different mental universe. An honest archaeopsychology is not about making past lives more familiar; it is about reconstructing mentalities foreign and different. This does not restrict our understanding of humanity; it expands it.

The Interaction between Demographic and Cognitive Scale

A number of general lessons can be gleaned from the reconstruction of archaic mentalities. The first is that as societies increase in demographic scale and complexity, communication systems (whether psycholinguistic or technological) must adapt to ensure some measure of sociopolitical stability and efficient economic exchange. This is not a terribly original perspective, but it illuminates how human mentality has changed through history.

The Role of Superceptive Experiences

The second lesson concerns evidence from earlier mentalities in which hallucinations were adaptive. The reactivations of vestigial neurostructures cause audiovisual hallucinations in modern times, e.g., "hearing voices" (both in clinical pathological and nonclinical benign populations), autoscopy, out-of-body experiences, and heautoscopy. Such phenomena, similar to the ubiquitous theophanies recorded in archaic texts (e.g., Bible), are remnants of an older neuroculture. Understanding present-day anomalous behaviors aids us in appreciating the hallucinatory nature of subjective inner visualizations as adaptations.

The affinities between introceptual images and hallucinations can be taken one step further. I suggest links exist between divine visitations and visions in archaic times and modern-day therapeutic endeavors. In other words, learning about a vestigial mentality can help us enhance therapeutics (e.g., mental imagery and visualization), cultivate self-transcendent practices, and understand atypical cognition and semi-hallucinatory experiences among present-day "voice-hearers."

The Logic and Paralogic of Political Authorization

Vestigial bicameral mentality is still manifest at the individual level (spirit possession, hypnosis, etc.). Less obviously vestigial bicamerality, like a faded and waned ghost, also roams our current halls of congress, parliaments, political assemblies, court houses, and city squares. Historically, polities have had to balance mundane practicalities with spiritual aspirations, while modern political arrangements are infused with reassuring traditionalisms that hark back to the ancient past.

The search for authorization, once a super-religious, then religious, and now for many of us a political endeavor, can be understood as vacillating between explicitly verbalized rules open to question that are modifiable, and a venerable mystique with its attention to continuity and the customary. It is too simplistic and misleading to postulate a neuropolitics directly configured by bicameral mentality, but we can at least argue that the affairs of state and government equivocate between logic and paralogic. Some of these distinctions are expressed in the differentiation between heads of government (prime ministers, presidents, chancellors) and heads of state (e.g., monarchs, whose role is largely ceremonial).[1]

In his *The City of God,* St. Augustine distinguished between the realm of heaven and the earthly city. The latter was the temporary, passing world of pleasures associated with evil and the Devil who struggles against God's design for humankind, which are to be realized in the City of God. Even if the worldly realm of the empire was in peril, threatened by mundane politics and the crises of the day, St. Augustine reassured his readers that ultimate authorization and triumphal salvation were to be found in the heavenly city of the New Jerusalem.

The complex relationship between the secular and sacred resonates with the "two bodies" argument of the medieval king as put forth by Ernst Kantorowicz.[2] The "body natural" was the monarch's mortal and corporeal being, while the perfect, immutable "body politic" of the entire realm implicated the mystique of the state. By the time of the European Reformation, increasing religious toleration began to force a separation of religion from politics, though in some ways the divine right of kings still had considerable sway as a justification for monarchical rule.

As a testament to the centuries-long influence of the theocractic mindset, note that as of this writing, 44 national states have a head of state who is a monarch. Though absolute monarchies still exist (e.g., Saudi Arabia), the more common trajectory for societies that successfully modernized with a robust kingship was to become a constitutional monarchy (e.g., Belgium, Denmark, Japan, Kuwait, Luxembourg, the Netherlands, Norway, Spain, Sweden, Thailand, the United Kingdom). Great Britain's polity was analyzed by Walter Bagehot who noted its "double set" of institutions or its two part composition. One part was the "efficient" government. This describes the cabinet, civil service, and day-to-day rational operations.[3] The other part was the "dignified" monarchy, with its displays of splendor, pageantry, pomp, and ceremony. My own book on rationality and rituality in the modern Japanese polity was an attempt to reconcile nominally conflicting impressions of Japan: a high-tech economic powerhouse versus a sociopolity suffused with rigid civility and ceremonial traditionalism as personified by the emperor.[4] Japan's Emperor Shōwa renounced his divinity as recently as 1946 in the "Humanity Declaration."[5]

Some places combine strong religious sentiments with modern political arrangements, such as the Islamic Republic of Iran, in which a "supreme leader," the highest religious and political authority, is the head of state and oversees a system imbued with theocractic clericalism. The State of Israel is another ambiguous case, since it is secular but rabbinic law plays a special role. In Italy, Roman Catholicism ceased being the official state religion in 1985. Officially, the United States is a secular system and the separation of church and state is explicitly constitutionalized. Nevertheless, strong religious impulses subtly configure the national sociopolitical landscape. The United Kingdom and certain Scandinavian countries have an established church, and in some of these places ministers are close to being civil servants.

A number of modern polities justify authorization with liberalism, human rights, and capitalist consumerism. On the darker side, others have also attempted to ground authorization in racial purity, class warfare, ideological purity, and monocratic loyalty — the "personality cults" of Stalin and Mao or Hitler as *Führer* (leader) and Mussolini as *el duce* (both meaning leader). The competition between logic and paralogic governance was visible in the People's Republic of China, with its tension between "expertise" (practical skills needed to administer a modern state) and "redness" (ideological purity and loyalty to the party; the successor to the centuries-old authorization of the Mandate of Heaven). These tensions exploded into the Cultural Revolution (1966–1976), a horrific state of internecine strife that shredded the fabric of Chinese society. Indeed, one-party states, whether on the right or left, attempt to construct utopian polities of dogmatic perfection that attack the slightest deviation with a religious fanaticism that would make the most committed medieval inquisitor blush. North Korea — whose official name, the Democratic People's Republic of Korea, is tarted up with several tragically ironic appellations — is run by a blood-splattered family dynasty whose mythologized politics, absurd fantasies, and paranoid insistence on obsessive devotion make it the most zealously religious society in history.

FUTURE RESEARCH DIRECTIONS AND THE BCI HYPOTHESIS

A long list of subjects deserves exploration that, at least for this writer, confirm Jaynes's contentions. Additional issues await a detailed treatment in a more comprehensive project, such as analyses of archaic languages that, when doable, should demonstrate that what would become abstract mind-words were shaped by bodily experiences and concrete metaphors. In the case of Egypt, a comprehensive review of its literary tradition from a Jaynesian perspective is also in order.

Archaic Egypt must be contextualized with what we know about other civilizations. Moreover, if the BCI hypothesis possesses any validity, it must be found to apply to other civilizations. Though their secrets are still being unearthed, a sampling of archaeological discoveries, some relatively recent, require attention in order to fill in the gaps.

Gobekli Tepe (ca. 10,000 BCE). This may be the world's oldest temple. Located in modern-day Turkey, it consists of sixteen-feet tall, seven-to-ten ton megalithic carved stones. These were constructed before the known invention of metal tools and are arranged in sixteen circles, with the largest measuring sixty-five feet in diameter. Carvings of foxes, lions, scorpions, and vultures climb over the stones. Gobekli Tepe seems to up-end the conventional view that settled agriculture precedes urbanization (or at least monumental architecture) with its elaborated theopolitical ideologies. Not far from this site is Sanliurfa (originally named Urfa), a major center of Syrian culture. It is speculated that people travelled from Sanliurfa to Gobekli Tepe for ceremonies of some sort.

Mehrgarh (ca. 7000 BCE). Located in what is now Pakistan, with a population of around 25,000, this may have been one of the oldest civilizations in the world. It appears to have been a highly developed society with trade links to other regions. A complex of mud-brick buildings as well as a cemetery has been discovered.

Vinča Civilization (ca. 5000–3500 BCE). Apparently predating Mesopotamian and Egyptian achievements, evidence for this civilization has been found along the banks of the Danube River. It may have possessed the earliest writing systems in the world, with around 700 characters (carved on pottery). The population also used advanced agricultural techniques and by Neolithic standards were quite sophisticated. A settlement housed several thousand people in dwellings made from wattle and daub clay. Evidence has also been found of gold artifacts and copper utensils, predating their use in the Middle East by one millennium.

Konar Sandal (ca. 4500–3000 BCE). In 2002, a large ziggurat-like structure (probably dating to around 2200 BCE) was discovered in Jiroft, a city in southern Iran. Two mounds and dwellings have also been excavated, as well as a thickly-walled two-story building. The edifices may have been built by the Aratta, a Bronze Age kingdom depicted in Sumerian texts. Konar Sandal may provide evidence of the world's oldest written language.

Indus Valley Civilization (ca. 3300–1300 BCE). Located in what is now Pakistan, Afghanistan, and India, Mohenjo-Daro and Harappa are its two main urban centers. It is unclear whether it formed part of a larger kingdom or was a civilization in itself. The cities had an impressive underground drainage system and dwellings had their own wells and bathrooms.

Attempts to decipher the writing system have to date been unsuccessful. Why this enigmatic civilization declined is unclear. Evidence of this civilization appears in Sumerian records.

Norte Chico Civilization (ca. 3500–1800 BCE). Located in what is now Peru (situated north of modern-day Lima), this may be the oldest known civilization in the Americas. There is evidence of six large pyramids and complex irrigation systems. Interestingly, these people did not appear to know how to make pottery. For unknown reasons the settlements were abandoned ca. 1800 BCE.

Caral-Supe Civilization (ca. 2600 BCE). Located in the Supe Valley of Peru, Caral is one site in a constellation of eighteen sites. With their massive pyramids they represent one of the earliest known civilizations in the Americas.

Dilmun (ca. 2000 BCE). A site located in what is now Bahrain in the Persian Gulf, Dilmun was the center of extensive trade networks connecting parts of Asia, Africa, and the Indian subcontinent.

Aryans (ca. 1500 BCE). The birth of Indian civilization can be traced to the Aryans. It is unclear whether they came to the subcontinent as invaders or as refugees from a natural disaster. They may have been from the Indus Valley civilization. Evidence of the Aryan civilization is apparent in references in the collection of religious texts known as the *Vedas*, but archaeological remains are few.

Olmec Civilization (ca. 1200–400 BCE). This Central American civilization was very influential for the development of later monumental architecture in other regions (including North America).

Moche Civilization (ca. 100–800 CE). This civilization, located on the coast of what is now Peru, produced gold artifacts and ceramic sculptures including lifelike portrait heads.

Notes to the Epilogue

1. Depending on the polity, a head of state may be either executive or ceremonial. In some polities the head of government and head of state are the same, e.g., in presidential systems.
2. Kantorowicz, 1957.
3. Bagehot, 1867.
4. See McVeigh, *The Nature of the Japanese State: Rationality and Rituality*, 1998.
5. McVeigh, 1998.

Appendix A: Expressions with "Heart"

No.	Faulkner's Translit-eration	Faulkner's Translation	Linguistic Element + Body Interior (BI)	Gardiner's List Code
1.	*ṯ3 ib*	able	? + BI	G47-Y1A-F34-Z1
2.	*r mḏdw n ib n*	according to the will of	press hard on + BI + to	D21-J23-D46-G43-N35-F34-Z1-N35
3.	*fnḫ ib*	acute (?)	wise + BI	I9-N35-Aa1-U20-F34-Z1; I9-N35-Aa1-V1-F34-Z1
4.	*mtt(nt)ib*	affection (?)	midst of, belonging + BI	D52-X1-X1-T14-T14-Y1V-N35-X1-F34-Z1
5.	*špt-ib*	anger	discontent, angry + BI	N37-Q3-X1-K7-F34-Z1
6.	*rdi ib m-s3*	anxious about	place + BI at the back of	D21-D37-F34-Z1-G17-Aa17-Z1
7.	*ḥw' ib*	apprehensive	short + BI	V28-G43-D36-G37-F34-Z1
8.	*ḥw' ib*	arrogant	great of size + BI	O29-D36-G1-Y1A-F34-Z1
9.	*šnṯ ib*	be angry	revile, oppose + BI	V7-N35-V13-A24-F34-Z1
10.	*ḳb ib*	be calm, be refreshed	cool + BI	N29-D58-D58-W15-F34-Z1
11.	*'m ib*	be discreet, dissem-ble, regret, forget, be unconscious, become faint, neglect	swallow, breathe in, absorb + BI	D36-G17-F10-A2-F34-Z1
12.	*mr ḥr ib n*	be displeasing to	painful + BI	U23-G17-D21-G37-D2-Z1-F34-Z1-N35
13.	*wnf ib*	be frivolous, content	joyful, content, amused + BI	E34-N35-I9-V12-F34-Z1
14.	*pḏ ib*	be glad	stretch cord + BI	Q3-I10-T9-F34-Z1
15.	*wḏ3 ib*	be glad	hale, uninjured, prosper-ous + BI	G43-U28-G1-Y1A-F34-Z1

16.	*ḫnti ib*	be glad of heart, outstanding of mind	sail (?) + BI	W18-N35-U33-M17-F34
17.	*ḫnti ib*	be helpless (?)	fall out, destroyed + BI	G43-N37-G37-F34-Z1
18.	*ḫ3ḫ ib*	be impatient	be speedy, swift + BI	M12-G1-Aa1-D54-F34-Z1
19.	*ḏnd ib*	be infuriated	angry + BI	I10-N35-D46-F5-F34-Z1
20.	*w3ḥ-ib*	be kindly, patient	lay aside, discard, reprieve, pardon + BI	V29-V28-Y1-F34-Z1
21.	*3d ib r*	be oppressive to	be savage, aggressive, angry + BI	G1-D46-F34-Z1-D21
22.	*grg ib r*	be ready	found, establish + BI + to	W11-D21-U17-Y1-F34-Z1
23.	*im3-ib*	be well-disposed	kind, gentle, well-disposed + BI	M1-G17-F34-Z1
24.	*hnn ib r*	be well-disposed to	attend to, consider + BI	O4-N35-N35-D1-F34-Z1-D21
25.	*ḥtp ib ḥr*	be well-disposed toward	be pleased, be happy + BI toward	R4-X1-Q3-F34-Z1-D2-Z1
26.	*'ḳ ib*	become intimate	enter + BI	G35-N29-D54-F34-Z1
27.	*wḥ'-ib*	capable, skilled	understand + BI	P4-D36-A2-F34-Z1
28.	*pḫ3 ib*	clean of heart	purge + BI	Q3-Aa1-Y1-F34-Z1
29.	*'rḳ ib*	clever	know, perceive, gain full knowledge of, be wise, skilled + BI	V12-N29-Y1V-F34-Z1
30.	*nḫt ib*	confident	strong, stiff, hard, victorious + BI	N35-M3-Aa1-X1-A24-F34-Z1
31.	*hr ib*	contented	pleasing + BI	O4-D21-M17-M17-F34-Z1
32.	*srf ib*	deliberate	warm, inflammation, fever + BI	S29-D21-I9-Q7-F34-Z1
33.	*ḫntš ib m*	delight in, over	have enjoyment, be glad, make glad + BI	Aa1-N35-X1-N37-D19-Y1-F34-Z1-G17
34.	*r(di) m ib*	determine	place in + BI	D21-D37-G17-F34-Z1
35.	*rḳ-ib*	disaffected man	turn aside (from), oppose + BI	D21-N29-D41-F34-Z1-A14
36.	*ḫ3kw ib*	disaffected persons	shifty + BI	K4-G1-V31-G43-F34-Z1-A13-Z3
37.	*mṯ3 ib r*	disagree with someone	flout, vex + BI to	G17-G47-G1-A2-F34-Z1-D21
38.	*sḫmḫ ib*	distract the heart, take recreation, enjoyment	forget, ignore + BI	S29-Aa1-G17-Aa1-F34-Z1
39.	*ir ib*	do the will of	do + BI	D4-F34

40.	*hb ỉb*	far ranging of desire (?)	tread out + BI	O4-D58-U13-D54-F34-Z1
41.	*imy ỉb*	favorite	tread out + BI	M17-Z11-F34-Z1
42.	*st-ỉb*	favorite, f. place, wish, affection	seat, throne + BI	Q1-X1-O1-F34-Z1
43.	*šms ỉb*	follow one's desire	follow for the love of + BI	T18-S29-D54-F34-Z1
44.	*n ỉb n*	for the sake of	to + BI + to	N35-F34-Z1-N35
45.	*smn ỉb*	fortify the heart	make firm + BI	S29-Y5-N35-U32-Y1-F34-Z1
46.	*dšr ỉb*	furious	red + BI	D46-N37-D21-G27-F34-Z1
47.	*wsḫ ỉb*	generous	broad, wide, extensive + BI	G43-S29-Aa1-W10-Y1-F34-Z1
48.	*rdỉ ỉb ḫnt*	give attention to	place + BI in front	D21-D37-F34-Z1-W17-N35-X1
49.	*snfr ỉb*	gladden	make beautiful, embellish + BI	S29-F35-I9-D21-Y1V-F34-Z1
50.	*snk-ỉb*	haughtiness	pretense + BI	O34-N35-V31-F34-Z1
51.	*ḳꜣ ỉb*	haughty	tall, high + BI	N29-G1-A28-F34-Z1
52.	*mr ỉb n*	have compassion for, be sorry for	painful + BI to	U23-G17-D21-G37-F34-Z1-N35
53.	*ḫrp ỉb*	having authority (?)	govern, control, administer + BI	Aa1-D21-Q3-D44-F34-Z1-A24; Aa1-D21-Q3-D44-F34-Z1
54.	*ḥꜣty*	heart	heart	F4-X1-Z4-F34; M16-X1-F34; V28-G1-X1-Z4-F34
55.	*ỉb*	heart (physical), mind, understanding, intelligence, will, desire, mood, wish	BI	M17-D58-F34; M17-Z4-D58-F34
56.	*wrḏ ỉb*	heart is weary	grow weary, tire + BI	G36-D21-I10-D81-F34-Z1
57.	*ṯꜣ ỉb*	hot tempered	hot, hot-tempered + BI	X1-U30-G1-A24-F34-Z1
58.	*ꜣḫ .n < i > m ỉb f*	"I found favor in his heart"	it will be well within + BI him	G25-Aa1-Y1-N35-A1-G17-F34-Z1-I9
59.	*rḳt-ỉb*	ill-will	bend + BI	D21-N29-X1-F34-Z1
60.	*ꜣs ỉb*	impatient	hurry, flow fast + BI	G1-S29-V2-D54-F34-Z1
61.	*ḥr ỉb n*	in the opinion of	front, face + BI + to	D2-F34-Z1-N35
62.	*pẖr ỉb n*	incline the heart to	turn, turn about + BI + to	F46-D21-D54-F34-Z1-N35
63.	*ẖs ḥr ỉb*	incompetent	weak, feeble + BI	F32-O34-G37-D2-Z1-F34-Z1

64.	*rdi wḏꜣ ib*	inform	place well-being in + BI	D21-D37-G43-U28-G1-Y1A-F34-Z1
65.	*swḏꜣ ib ḥr*	inform about	make healthy, keep safe, calm (fear), make prosperous + BI + face, front	S29-G43-U28-G1-Y1A-F34-Z1-D2-Z1
66.	*swḏꜣ tw ib*	inform yourself	make healthy, keep safe, calm (fear), make prosperous + you + BI	S29-G43-U28-G1-Y1A-V13-G43-F34-Z1
67.	*ḥmw ib*	ingenious	be skilled, skillful + BI	U2-G43-Y1V-F34-Z1
68.	*wr-ib*	insolent	great, many + BI	G36-D21-F34-Z1
69.	*btn ib*	insolent man	disobey, defy + BI	D58-X1-N35-D19-A24-F34-Z1
70.	*'ḳ ib*	intimate friend	enter + BI	G35-N29-D54-F34-Z1-A1; G35-N29-Y1-F34-Z1
71.	*ꜣwt ib*	joy	length of time + BI	F40-X1-F34-Y1
72.	*nḏm ib*	joyful, joy	sweet, pleasant, pleasing + BI	M29-Aa15-Y1-F34-Z1; N35-M29-G17-Y1-F34-Z1
73.	*ims ib*	kindly disposed, pleasant	cow (?) + BI	M17-F31-S29-A2-F34-Z1; E9-F34-Z1
74.	*siꜣ ib*	know, be aware of	recognize, perceive + BI	S32-G1-A2
75.	*is ib*	ight-minded	be light of weight + BI	M17-M40-O34-M2-F34-Z1
76.	*sḥḏ ib n*	make glad	illumine + BI	S29-T3-I10-N5-F34-Z1
77.	*sꜣw ib (n)*	make glad	lengthen + BI	S29-F40-G43-F34-Z1
78.	*snḏm ib*	make glad, please	give pleasure + BI	S29-M29-G17-Y1A-F34-Z1
79.	*šptw-ib*	malcontents	discontent, angry + BI	N37-Q3-X1-G43-K18B-F34-Z1-A14-Z3
80.	*ḫns ib*	meanness	narrow, constricted + BI	N35-V28-S29-Z1; V28-M2-N35-S29-G37-F34-Z1; V28-M2-N35-S29-N31-F34-Z1
81.	*th ib*	misguided	go astray + BI	X1-O4-D54-F34-Z1
82.	*mht ib*	misguided	be forgetful, neglectful + BI	G17-D36-O4-X1-G37-F34-Z1
83.	*mḥ ib*	one who is trusted, confidant	faithful + BI	V22-D40-F34-Z1-G7; V22-F34-Z1; V22-Y1-F34-Z1
84.	*wbꜣ ib n*	open heart to, confide in	drill stone, open + BI + to	U26-D58-Y1V-F34-Z1-N35
85.	*swbꜣ ib*	open the heart (to wisdom)	open + BI	S29-U26-Y1V-F34-Z1

86.	*pgꜣ ib*	open-hearted	open, reveal + BI	Q3-W11-G1-D32-D40-F34-Z1; Q3-W11-G1-Z9-F34-Z1
87.	*wbꜣ ib*	open-hearted	drill stone, open + BI	U26-D58-Y1V-F34-Z1
88.	*'ḥ'*	persistent	stand, stand still, stand erect + BI	P6-D36-D54
89.	*sḥtp ib (n)*	please	propitiate, please + BI	S29-R4-X1-Q3-Y1-F34-Z1
90.	*nfr ḥr ib*	pleasing	good, fine, goodly + BI	F35-I9-D21-Z1-F34-Z1
91.	*mnḫ ib*	pleasing to the heart	well-disposed, devoted + BI	Y5-N35-Aa1-Y1-F34-Z1
92.	*mnḫ ḥr ib*	pleasing to the heart	well-disposed, devoted to + BI	Y5-N35-Aa1-Y1-D2-Z1-F34-Z1
93.	*ḥwrw ib*	poor of understanding	poor, in need, miserable + BI	V28-G36-D21-G43-G37-F34-Z1
94.	*'wn-ib*	rapacious	rapacious + BI	D36-E34-N35-A24-F34-Z1
95.	*nḫꜣt ib*	sadness, sad matter	contrary, perverse, terrible, abnormal + BI	N35-M16-Aa2-X1-F34-Z1; N35-M16-G1-X1-Aa2-F34-Z1-G37-Z2
96.	*i' ib*	satisfy someone, please, slake one's ardor, vent, one's feelings	wash + BI	M17-D36-N35A-F34-Z1
97.	*dꜣr ib*	self-denial, self-control	control + BI	D46-G1-D21-T12-Y2V-F34-Z1; T12-A24-F34-Z1
98.	*sꜣḳ ib*	self-possessed	pull together + BI	S29-Aa17-G1-N29-I5-Y1V-F34-Z1
99.	*ꜣḫ ib n*	serviceably minded towards	glorious, splendid, beneficial, useful, profitable + BI to	G25-Aa1-Y1-F34-Z1-N35
100.	*d ib r*	set one's heart on	give, place, put + BI	D46-F34-Z1-D21
101.	*sꜣḳ ib r*	set one's heart on	pull together + BI + towards	S29-Aa17-G1-N29-I5-Y1-F34-Z1-D21
102.	*sn'' ib*	soothe, calm	make smooth, polish + BI	S29-N35-D36-D36-Y3-Y1-F34-Z1
103.	*mds ib*	spiteful	sharp, acute + BI	G17-D46-S29-T30-F34-Z1
104.	*dfꜣ-ib*	stolid (?)	wipe + BI	D46-I9-G1-G37-Y1-F34-Z1
105.	*wsr ib*	stout of heart	strong, powerful, wealthy + BI	F12-F34-Z1; F12-S29-D21-F34-Z1; F12-S29-F34-Z1; F12-S29-D21-D40-F34-Z1

106.	*rwḏ ib*	stout-heart, assiduous	shard, firm, strong + BI	D21-G43-D46-T12-F34-Z1
107.	*sḫm ib*	stout-hearted	powerful + BI	S29-S42-Aa1-G17-F34-Z1
108.	*wmt-ib*	stout-hearted	thick + BI	G43-D52-X1-Y1-F34-Z1
109.	*'ḳ3 ib*	straightforward	precise, accurate + BI	D36-N29-G1-D50-D50-Y1V-F34-Z1
110.	*ḥry(t) ib*	terror	terror, dread + BI	D2-D21-M17-M17-X1-Aa19-D40-Z2-F34-Z1
111.	*ib th*	the heart is astray	BI + astray	F34-Z1-X1-O4-D54
112.	*mh ib*	the heart is forgetful	be forgetful, neglectful + BI	G17-O4-Z4-G37-F34-Z1
113.	*ib*	think, suppose	hide from, seek shelter, be thirsty, wish for, want + BI	M17-D58-E8; M17-D58-E8-A2; M17-D58-A2
114.	*ḥ3tyw*	thoughts	heart	F4-X1-Z1-F34-Z2
115.	*kf3 ib ḥr*	trust in	be discreet + BI	V31-I9-G1-F22-Y1-F34-Z1-D2
116.	*kf3 ib*	trustworthy	be discreet + BI	F22-Y1-F34-Z1; F22-Y1-F34-Z1-A1
117.	*ḥḏ ib*	upset, annoyed	injure, destroy + BI	T3-I10-Z9-F34-Z1
118.	*k3k3 ib*	vainglorious (?)	look (up), to tower + BI	N29-G1-N29-G1-F34-Z1
119.	*ḫnn ib*	violent man	disturb, interfere with + BI	D33-N35-N35-A24-F34-Z1
120.	*ib f mḥ*	weak in action	drown, be drowned + BI	F34-Z1-I9-V22-V28-N35A
121.	*iḳr ḥr ib n*	well-pleasing to the heart of	pleasing + BI + to	M17-N29-D21-Y1A-D2-Z1-F34-Z1-N35
122.	*bint ḥr ib*	what is displeasing	evil + BI	D58-M17-N35-X1-G37-D2-Z1-F34-Z1
123.	*pty irf p3 ib*	what is this mood?	who?/what? then/now, this + BI	Q3-X1-Z4-M6-A2-M17-D21-I9-G40-F34-Z1
124.	*šsp n ib n*	who are dear to	take, accept + BI	O42-Q3-D40-F34-Z1
125.	*ḫrt-ib*	wish, desire, favor	state, condition + BI	Aa1-D21-X1-F34-Z1; Aa1-D21-X1-Y1-Z2-F34-Z1
126.	*m ḥḥy n ib*	with ingenious mind	seek, search for + BI	G17-V28-V28-Z4-D54-N35-F34-Z1

Appendix B: Basic List of Ancient Egyptian Psycholexemes*

No.	Term	Transliter-ation	Possible Behavioral or Perceptual Cognates	Gardiner's List Code
1.	adoration	*i͗3w*	praise	A30
2.	adore	*i͗3i͗*	praise	M17-G1-A30
3.	adore	*dw3*	worship, praise	D46-V4-G1
4.	agreeable, pleasing	*nḏm*	sweet, charming	M29-G17-Y1A
5.	amazed	*ggwy*	stare, dazzled	W11-W11-G43-Z4-D6
6.	anger	*nsr*	inflammation (wound), flame	N35-F20-S29-D21-A2
7.	anger, discontent, discontented	*špt*	Nile puffer fish (?)	N37-Q3-X1-Aa2; K7-X1; N37-Q3-X1-D5; N37-Q3-X1-K7; N37-Q3-X1-K1-A2; N37-Q3-X1-K18; N37-Q3-X2-K7
8.	angry	*ḏnḏn*	arduous task	I10-N35-I10-N35-F5-A24; I10-N35-I10-N35-F5-A24
9.	angry	*i͗w*	stranded (?)	E9-G42-P1; E9-G43
10.	angry (with), bear a grudge (against), rebuke	*ṯsi͗*	put on, lift up	V13-O34-A2; V13-O34-U39-A2; V13-O34-U39-Y1V; V13-O34-A2; V13-34-U39-Y1A; V13-O34-U39-Y1A
11.	angry with , rage against	*fnḏ r*	snort	I9-N35-D46-D19-D21
12.	angry, annoyed	*šnty*	quarrelsome	V7-N35-X1-Z4-A14
13.	angry, become	*ḥs3*	fierce	V28-S29-Aa18-G1

14.	angry, become	*ꜣty*	have a care, to bother (with)	G1-X1-Z4-I3
15.	angry, rage	*ꜣd*	aggressive	I10-N35-D46-F5; G1-D46-I3-A14A
16.	anxious, be	*mḥi*	overflow	V22-D36-A2
17.	assent to	*hnn*	bow down	O4-N35-N35-D41-D40
18.	awe	*šfšft*	look upon	N37-I9-N37-I9X1-F7
19.	boast, brag	*ʿbʿb*	shine	D36-D58-D36-D58-F16-F16; D36-D58-D36-D58
20.	brave	*ḳni*	conquer, be strong	N29-N35-A24
21.	calculate, count, examine, reckon	*ip*	allot, allocate, distribute	M17-Q3-Y1
22.	care for	*nhp*	shield	N35-O4-82-Q3-82-A2
23.	care for, take care	*snr*	tame, train	O34-N35-D21-H4
24.	careless, be	*mhy*	neglectful	G20-O4-G1-G37-Z4
25.	character, good	*ḳd*	reputation	Aa28-D46-D12-Y1
26.	concern, a	*sšr*	thing	V6-Z1
27.	confuse	*šbi*	mix, mingle	N37-D8-Z9
28.	consider	*hnn*	bend (back), bow (head), listen	O4-N35-N35-D41D40
29.	content, make	*shri*	make peace	S29-O4-D21-M17-Ma7-X1-Y1
30.	contentment	*ḥpt*	setting sun	R4-X1-Q3-G43-Z3
31.	contentment	*hrt*	peace, pleasantness	O4-D21-X-Y1
32.	contentment	*ḥtpw*	peace, offering	R4-X1-Q3-G43-Y1-Z2
33.	contentment	*hrt*	peace, pleasantness, offering	O4-D21-X1-Y1
34.	count, reckon	*ḥsb*	counting	V28-S29-D58-Aa2-Y1; Z9-D48
35.	covetous, rapacious, greedy	*ʿwn*	plunder	D36-E34-N35-A24
36.	coward	*ḥm*	unmanly	N41-G17-D52-Z2
37.	coward	*ḫsy*	weak	F32-O34-G37-Z4-A1
38.	cowardly	*ḫs(y)*	weak	F32-O3-G37
39.	cowardly, be	*ḫst / ḫsyt*	weak	F32-O34-X1-G37
40.	deliberate	*wꜣwꜣ*	take counsel	V4-G1-V4-G1-A2
41.	desire	*mrwt*	love	U7-D21-X1-A2
42.	devoted	*mnḫ*	invent, see about	Y5-N35-Aa1-U22-Y1

43.	differ (argue), dispute	*ḏ3is*	oppose, hostility	U28-M17-S29-A24
44.	difficult (become), oppressive	*wdn*	weighty	G43-D46--N35-U35-U32-O39
45.	disapprove of, angry, wound up, furious, unwilling	*ḥḏnw*	separate, cut	V28-I10-N35-W24-Z7-D19-A2
46.	discern, judge	*wḏ'*	separate, divide	G43-I10-D36-T14-D54; G43-I10-D36-Aa2
47.	discern, judge	*wpỉ*	separate, divide	F13-Q3; G43-F13-Q3
48.	disgust	*ft*	tired, weary	I9-X1-G37
49.	dislike, hate, condemn	*msḏỉ / msd*	condemn, scold, tell off	F31-S29-D46-A2
50.	dispute	*sḫwn*	quarrel	S29-Aa1-E34-N35-A2
51.	dispute with	*mdw ḥn'*	words with	S43-D46-G43-A2-V28-N35-D36
52.	disregard	*wnỉ*	hostile	E4-N35-D54
53.	distress	*sny mnt*	calamity	O34-N35-Z4-X5-D54Y5-N35-X1-G37-Z2
54.	dread	*ḥr*	respect	D2-D21-Aa19-A24
55.	dread, fear	*nrw*	disturbance	N35-D21-G43-G14-Z3; N35-D21-G3-G14-Z3
56.	dumb	*ỉnb3*	speechless	M17-K1-N35-D58-G29-G1-A2
57.	ease	*snḏm*	sit down, rest	S29-M29-G17-Y1A
58.	enjoyment	*ṯnf*	drinking spree	V13-N35-I9-A2
59.	exalt	*rnn*	bring up, nurse	D21-N35-N35-A2
60.	exalted	*ḳ3ỉ*	uplifted, raise	N29-G1-A28
61.	exalted	*w3š*	honor, respect	V4-G1-N37-A28
62.	examine	*smtr*	give testimony, interrogate, witness	S29-D52-X1-D21-T14-T14-A2
63.	experience	*dp*	bite, taste	D46-Q3-F20-A2
64.	exultation (to king, god)	*ḥknw*	cheer, praise	V28-V31-W2-Y1A
65.	farsighted	*3w ḥr*	length + sight	F40-Y1-D2-Z1
66.	fear (someone), overawe	*nrỉ*	shudder	N35-D21-M17-M17-H4-D40
67.	foolishness	*nf*	wrong, evil, injustice, nonsense	N3-I9-G37
68.	forget, ignore	*smḫ*	be fallen	S29-G17-Aa1-D35; S29-17-Aa1-A2

69.	forgetful, ne-glectful	*mhy*	careless	G17-D36-O4-Z4-G37
70.	full of oneself	*špt (r)*	inflated, full of wind	N37-Q3-X1-M17-M17-D54; N37-Q3-X1-M17-M17-K1-D54
71.	generous	*ꜣw ḏrt*	extend the hand	F40-G43-D46\58-X1-Z1
72.	gentle, merciful	*sfn*	show mercy	S29-I9-N35-D19-A2
73.	glad	*ẖnm*	comfort	Aa1-N35-T34-G17-F63-Y1
74.	glad	*wnf*	cheerful	E34-N35-I9-S28
75.	gladden	*sbḥ / sḥb*	shout, cry out	S29-D58-V28-W3-N5
76.	gladden	*sḥḏ*	illumine, make clear, brighten	S29-T5-N5; S29-T3-N8; S29-T3-I10-N5; S29-T4
77.	gracious	*imꜣ*	charming	M1-G17-Y1A
78.	gracious	*imꜣt*	charming	M1-G17-X1-Y1
79.	gracious, kind, pleasant	*iꜣm*	offer	U4-G17-M1
80.	gracious, peace, mercy	*ḥtpt*	offering	R4-X1-3-X1-Y1; R4-X1-Q3-X1-Y1
81.	gracious, peace, satisfied	*ḥtp*	offering	R4-X1-Q3
82.	grasp, meaning of	*hꜣi*	descend, befall, discharge, accede (to office), charge at, beat, saw	O4-G1-D54
83.	grief	*imw*	wail	M17-Aa15-G17-A2-Z2
84.	grief, groans, woe to, attention	*iʿnw*	plaintive cry, groan	M17-D36LN35-W24-Z7-A2-Z3A
85.	grieving	*imt*	groan, wail	M17-Aa15-G17-X1-A2
86.	happily	*nfr*	appropriate, good things	F35-I9-D21
87.	hateful	*ẖbd*	rebuke, reprehend	Aa1-D58-D46-G37
88.	hesitate	*sin*	delay, wait for	S29-M17-K1-N35-D54
89.	honest	*mty*	exact, correct	D52-X1-D50-D50-Y1A
90.	hostile	*bḳ*	unruly, rebel	D58-N29-Y1
91.	humble, modest	*dḥi*	hang down, be low	D46-V28-M17-G37
92.	idle, become, procrastinate, laziness	*wsf*	take leave from work, hesitate, sluggish, lack	G43-S29-I9-G39-D54; G41-G37
93.	ignorant	*ẖm*	neglect	Aa1-G17-D35
94.	ignorant	*wẖꜣ*	incompetent, foolish	G43-Aa1-M12-G1-G37-A1

95.	impetuous	*sḫm*	hasty	O34-F32-G17-A24
96.	indifferent, be	*ḥbs ḥr*	cover one's head	V28-D58-S29-S28-D2
97.	indulgence, show, lenience	*ṯ3m ḥr m*	veil the face	G47-G1-G17-D40-D2-Z1
98.	insolent	*štm*	quarrelsome	N37-U15-G17-A2
99.	joy	*ḥ''wt*	glee	V28-D36-D36-G43-X1-A28
100.	joyful, exult	*ḥkn*	acclaim, praise	V28-V31-N35-Y1; V28-V31-W24
101.	kind	*'n*	beautiful, bright of face	D36-N35-D8
102.	kind	*im3*	gentle, gracious	M17-U1-M1
103.	kindliness	*sim3*	make well, disposed to	S29-M1-Y1A
104.	kindness	*nfrt*	good things	F35-I9-D21-X1-Y1-Z2
105.	know	*'m*	swallow	F10
106.	know	*šs3*	skill	N37-O34-Aa18-G43-F5-Y1
107.	know, learn	*'m*	find out, swallow, breathe in	D36-U2-G1-G17-D6
108.	know, learn	*rḫ*	find out	D21-Aa1-Y1
109.	know, perceive	*'rḳ*	skilled	D36-D21-N29-V12
110.	lamentation	*i'nw*	plaintive cry	D36-N35-W24-Z7-A2
111.	lazy	*wsfw*	sluggard, forgetter	G43-S29-I9-Z7-G41-D54-A1
112.	love, will, desire, bidding	*mrwt*	bidding	U7-D21-G43-X1-A2; U7-D21-G43-X1-A2
113.	mediate on, think about, counsel	*nk3*	because Ka	N35-V31-G1-A2
114.	memory	*sḫ3w*	recount, mention	S29-M12-G1-G43-A2
115.	mourn	*ḥ3i*	wail, screech, dance at funeral	V28-G1-A28
116.	mourn	*i3kb / 3gb*	wail, moan	G1-W11-R7-A2
117.	mourning	*irtyw*	misery, woe	M17-D4-G4-A2-Z3A
118.	mourning for	*tp ḥr m3st*	head on lap	D2-Z1-D1-Z1-U1-G1-Q1-X1-D56
119.	mourning, grief	*gmw*	weakness, daze, dizziness	G28-G17-Z7-G37-Z2
120.	neglect	*mkḥ3*	turn back on, ignore	G17-D38-V31-M16-D1
121.	obey	*sḏm*	hear, learn	F21-G17
122.	oppose	*šnt*	punish, argue, disparage, slander	V7-N35-X1-V1-A2; V7-N35-V13-A24
123.	passion, ardor	*šmm*	heat, hot, warm	N37-G17-G17-Q7-A14

124.	patient	*w3ḥ*	remain in good condition	V4-G1-V28-V29-Y1; V29
125.	perceive, know, aware of	*si3*	recognize	S32-G1-A2
126.	perception, knowledge	*si3*	recognize	S32-A2
127.	pity, have	*ḫ3tb*	treat with care	Aa1-M12-G1-X1-D58-D40
128.	plan, think about	*k3i*	Ka speaks	V31-G1-A2
129.	pleasant	*'3b*	desirable	O29-D36-G1-D58-M19-Y1A
130.	pleased	*ḫnm*	comfort, inhale, smell	Aa1-N35-T34-G17-D19
131.	pleasure, joy	*ḥ'wt*	jubilation	V28-D36-G43-X1-A28-Z3
132.	praise	*dw3t*	worship	N14-X; A30
133.	praise	*snsy*	worship	O34-N35-S29-A30
134.	propitiate, plea	*sḥtp*	pacify, satisfy	S29-R4-X1-Q3-Y1A
135.	rage, anger	*nhd*	tremble, weak (?)	N35-O4-D46-A24
136.	rage, angry	*fnd*	snort with rage	I9-N35-D46-D19-G37; I9-N35-D46-D19; I9-N35-D46-G37
137.	rejoice	*nḥn*	triumph	N35-G1-V28-N35-A2
138.	rejoicing (of suckling cow), glad, rejoice	*3ms*	friendly, pleasant	G1-F31-S29-E5
139.	relieved, comfortable	*nḏm*	sweet	N35-I10-M29-G17
140.	remember, call to mind, recollect	*sḫ3*	mention, recount	S29-M12-G1-A2
141.	respect	*šfšft*	look upon, consider	N37-I9-N37-I9-X1-F7
142.	reticent	*ḳmi spt*	glued lip	N29-W19-M17-S29-Q3-X1-D24
143.	sad	*snm*	mourn	O34-N35-T34-G17-G41-G37
144.	satisfy	*ss3i*	make wise	S29-S29-Aa17-G1-A2
145.	savage, anger	*3d*	aggressive, attack	G1-D46-Z7; G1-D46-I3
146.	skill	*šs3*	conversant	N37-O34-Aa18-G43-F5-Y1
147.	sorrow, mourning, sighing	*3hmt / ihm*	mourning, sighing	G1-O4-Aa15-X1-G37-Z2

148.	stop being angry, stop raging	*ḫsf ꜣd*	reply to anger	U35-A24-G1-D46-I3
149.	suffer	*nḳm*	afflicted, laid low (due to illness)	N35-N29-G7-C7
150.	sullen	*kni*	moan	V31-N35-M17-A2
151.	suppress (one's desires, thoughts)	*hrp*	sink	O4-D21-Q3-Y1; O4-D21-Q3-N35A
152.	take offence, angry	*šni*	argue, dispute	V49-N35-N35-G37
153.	terrifying, terrible	*nḥꜣ*	contrary, perverse, alarm-ing	N35-M16-G1-A24
154.	thought, plan, device, plot	*kꜣt*	device, plan	V31-G1-X1-A2
155.	vacillate	*nwd*	turn aside, deviate	N35-U19-W24-Z7-D4-G37-Z9
156.	wary of	*ʿḥꜣ ḥr*	weapon (?)	D34-A24-D2-Z1
157.	wise, prudent,	*sꜣi*	satisfied, become sated	S29-Aa17-G1-A2
158.	wonder, at	*biꜣi*	precious	D58-M17-G1-U16-Y1A
159.	wrath	*dšrw*	blood	D46-N35-D21-G43-G27-Z2

* Originally Appendix B contained 238 items. However, I could not confidently fill in the "Possible Behavioral or Perceptual Cognates" column for 79 items. A future project will hopefully complete the missing information and extend the list.

Glossary

Afterworld A term highlighting how bicameral individuals considered death not a finality but a transformation into another existence. From this other realm, the deceased could still communicate with those left behind, on a regular basis if necessary.

Authority-Radiating Ceremonial Complexes (ARCC) BCI item. Evolved from simpler focal points of deity–mortal interaction (often funerary sites). Examples include pyramids, ziggurats, temples, megaliths, and aggrandized tombs. Such monumental (frequently mortuary) architecture often housed divinized rulers and OHFs (ancestral tablets, idols, transfigured remains of rulers).

Bicameral Civilizational Inventory (BCI) Hypothesis A research proposition that postulates that from around 3500 to 1000 BCE certain traits characterized all civilizational cores. Our assumption that such features were somehow inevitable facets of early human history causes us to lose sight of how strangely remarkable such fact-patterning is. The BCI Hypothesis challenges conventional presumptions scientifically. In other words, if the null hypothesis is rejected (BCI list of items does not apply in any significant way to Bronze Age civilizations), then the alternative hypothesis is accepted (the BCI list of items does apply to Bronze Age civilizations).

Bicameral Hallucinations Usually auditory or visual (though haptic and olfactory are not unknown), these were a consequence of linguistic evolution in which volition occurs when an individual "hears" or "sees" gods or ancestors. See superceptions.

Bicameral Mentality From "two-chambered," an obsolete neurocultural arrangement in which a governing "god-side" (right hemisphere) would issue admonishing, advisory, and commanding hallucinatory voice–visions–volitions to an obedient human-side (left hemisphere).

Centrality of Ancestor Worship (CAW) BCI item. Arguably the germ of developed religion was some sort of ancestor cult (from which originated VVVs). As the edifice of sociopolitical systems became larger, household ancestor cults were nested within larger hierarchies of overarching royal ancestor-worship. Over time deceased rulers became divinized ancestors or gods whose authority persisted even after they were entombed with their favorite material accoutrements.

Coception Describes how typically perceptions and introceptions coincide; such overlapping deludes us into assuming that interior experiences are sensory reflections of reality.

Cognitive Relativism A perspective that, rather than assuming psychic unity and psychic structures, argues for psychic diversity, psychic (neuro-cultural) plasticity, and cognitive diversity.

Conciliation FOCI. Assimilating or making introcepted images conform to a previously learned schema. It fits together objects in our mental space the same way narratization strings together elements of a story for the sake of coherence.

Conscious Interiority (or consciousness or interiority) Due to cultural adaptation rather than a bio-evolutionary or genetic change, this mentality supplanted bicamerality in response to growing sociopolitical complexity. A package of mental abilities (FOCI), it includes the following features or functions: self-authorization; spatialization of psyche; self-individuation; self-autonomy; self-reflexivity; self-narratization; excerption; and conciliation.

Consciousness See conscious interiority.

Cosmopolity An inclusive term meaning the realm of nature and gods and everything in between as understood by archaic individuals.

Doubleworld Mortuary Practices (DWMP) BCI item. Belief that the deceased continue living in an Afterworld. An entire array of objects may be part of this Doubleworld, e.g., tombs, grave furnishings, retinues, slaves, figurines that assist in afterlife, mummification.

Excerption FOCI. Editing and picking out from the parade of mental content that bubbles up from the machinery of our psyche. It greatly enhances abstraction and reasoning. Excerption is not the same thing as memory, i.e., an excerpt of a thing is in consciousness the representative of the thing or event to which memories adhere, and by which we can retrieve memories.

Extraception A type of superception. Audiovisual hallucinations interpreted as divine voices and visitations in archaic times.

Features/Functions of Conscious Interiority (FOCI) See conscious interiority.

Indirect Divine Communication (IDC) BCI item. As the introcosmic psychologicality expanded and the gods retreated to the supernatural realms, VVV ceased. In order to keep the lines of communication open, divination, oracles, prophets, visions, and visitation dreams emerged (IB).

Induction Methods for Right-Hemisphere Activation (IMRHA) BCI item. The use of aesthetic and sensory experiences to trigger and evoke audiovisual, superceptive hallucinations. May involve ritual or complex induction procedures. Prompts may include OHFs (e.g., large, bejeweled eyes on statues), music, poetry, sacred writings (hieroglyphs), or monumental architecture (ARCCs).

Interiority See conscious interiority.

Intermediary Beings (IB) BCI item. As super-religiosity eroded over the centuries and VVVs became less common, intercessionary beings (angels, demons, ancestors, demi-gods, revenants, guardian deities, etc.) were needed to maintain a connection to the divine.

Introception FOCI and type of superception. The ability to experience inner quasi-perceptions within an individual's introcosmos, which is a mentally-constructed reflection of the real world.

Jaynes, Julian (1920–97) A psychologist trained at Harvard, McGill, and Yale Universities and a popular lecturer at Princeton University from 1966 to 1990. Known for his *The Origin of Consciousness in the Breakdown of the Bicameral Mind* (1976), he was also an accomplished researcher in ethology, animal behavior, and comparative psychology. He also was a playwright who composed plays and poetry and performed in England.

Metaphoric Mind-words (MMW) BCI item. Adapting to social complexity, underdeveloped psychological lexemes (UPLs) were replaced by more consciously-interiorized terms that utilize spatial and bodily metaphors to create novel psycholexemes.

Monumental (Mortuary) Architecture (MMA) BCI item. Pyramids, ziggurats, and other massive multi-leveled structures intended to be visible from great distances. These concretely symbolized the hierarchical relation between gods, their representatives on earth, and mortals. Often mortuary related, these functioned as gigantic aides mémoire of the theopolitical hierarchy.

Multiple Souls (MS) BCI item. Lacking a unified, individuated sense of selfhood, in archaic times a person's postmortem identity was distributed into multiple spiritual facets for different functions. Typically, one soul is divinized while another stays behind to communicate with and receive offerings from the living (DWMP).

Neuroculture The mind or psyche. The dynamic interaction of inborn and acquired psychological processes; the complex of information constructed by innate neurological structures as well as acquired via enculturation.

Objects of Hallucinatory Focus (OHF) Exopsychic aids that trigger superceptive experiences or a general attitude of deep veneration. They emitted holy power and authorized decision-making. They may be small (amulets), portable and taken into battle (the Israelites' Ark of the Covenant), larger (god-statues that are dressed, fed, paraded on barques, taken on journeys), or very large (temples or monumental mortuary architecture) (ARCCs).

Observing self ("I") FOCI. The self-as-subject. The active aspect of selfhood that "does things" in one's quasi-perceptual psychoscape.

Observed Self ("me") FOCI. The self-as-object or object of awareness. While the mind only generates one "I" (a sort of stage director for mental content) it produces multiple "me's" or roles in response to sociopolitical complexity and diversity, thereby increasing an individual's capability to adapt.

Origin of Consciousness in the Breakdown of the Bicameral Mind, The (1976). Nominated for the National Book Award in 1978, this controversial book by Julian Jaynes argued that until about three thousand years ago humankind lacked conscious interiority as we presently experience it and was governed by audiovisual hallucinatory voices attributed to supernatural beings.

Paralogic Cognition Putting aside an external standard of truth (the rules of logic) and overlooking contradictions, especially when assertions about reality are verbalized by powerful authority figures. Paralogic cognition was particularly pronounced during the preconscious bicameral period. A specific instance is paralogic identification or imbuing a representation and the thing it symbolizes with the same reality or essential nature (names, god-statues). Paralogic is still evident in hypnosis (VB) and hypnoidal mental states such as being in the "flow," dreaming, guided imagery, and autosuggestion.

Personation Conventionally called "spirit possession" in the modern world, the practice of incorporating an ancestor, god, or other divine entity into one's body and ritualistically acting out a role. Such practices became increasingly common as bicamerality declined and it was believed the gods had retreated to the heavens, far from this world. Personation was often linked to divinatory activities.

Postbicameral Civilization Inventory A list of holdovers of bicameral societies, e.g., hypnosis, shamanism, spirit possession, glossolalia, autoscopic phenomena (doppelgängers, heautoscopy), and neo-IDC. Remnants of an earlier mentality might also include folktales, myths, and legends about "little people."

Right-Hemisphere Dominance (RHD) BCI item. Audiovisual hallucinations originating in right hemisphere's linguistic regions (now vestigial).

Secondary Burials BCI item. When VVVs of supernatural beings cease (usually after two or three generations) the remains of the deceased are permanently interred (DWMP).

Self-authorization FOCI. Rather than supernatural entities or external divine powers, one attributes self-control to one's own person.

Self-autonomy FOCI. A strong sense of agency, intentionality, and responsibility for one's own actions; it bolsters the belief that each individual possesses an "inner person."

Self-individuation FOCI. In the same way that one's "I" is differentiated and comes to appear unique when set against the backdrop of interiorized excerptions, the individual's personal traits are highlighted and privileged within larger collectivities.

Self-narratization FOCI. Being able to "see" one's own personal trajectory on a well-defined storyline, affording one a sense of destiny and fate.

Self-reflexivity FOCI. The ability to excerpt, to "see" one's self in an interiorized place without any physical limitations, to imagine not-yet versions of our future selves, or produce an "I" that introspects upon a "me." Self-introspection causes a recursively regressive mirroring effect (i.e., self observing self), resulting in a highly individuated selfness that exists in opposition to others.

Spatialization of Psyche FOCI. The belief that, within the individual, an imaginary space or introcosmos exists upon which an "I" moves about and observes mental content which can be edited, arranged, and re-arranged. Linguistic metaphors cavitate the body, hollowing out a space or a psychoscape visible only to the individual.

Stratigraphic Psychology Premised on the belief that human mentality can radically change, the study of the strata that, accumulating through history, constitute human sociopsychological adaptation.

Superception A type of cognition that goes beyond what the immediate environment affords the individual. "Super" indicates the sense of something being layered over sensory perception and conceptions.

Supernatural Visitations (SV) BCI item. Messages from the divine world that authorized and legitimated the sociopolitical moral order (VVVs).

Theocentric Social Order (TSO) BCI item. Governance by divinely-deputized rulers or partly incarnate gods (e.g., pharaohs). Carvings, sculptures, texts, etc., typically depict the claim of rulers to "hear" and obey a deity's commands (RHD and VVVs).

Theophany The revelation from or manifestation of a god, ancestor, or other supernatural being.

Theopolity Among archaic individuals the modern concept of politics did not exist. Instead, government, state structures, and political organization were regarded as aspects of the realm of the gods and were governed by supernatural powers.

Transitional Mentalities Types of mentalities occurring between the periods of complex bicamerality and conscious interiority that exhibited characteristics of both these mentalities.

Undeveloped Psychological Lexicon (UPL) BCI item. Describes less than robust psycholexicons before approximately 1000 BCE. Sociopolitical systems did not configure sophisticated interiorized linguo-concepts until a new conscious mentality emerged.

Vestigial Bicamerality (VB) BCI item. Examples include spirit possession, automatic writing, channeling, mediumship, glossolalia, hypnosis, and audiovisual hallucinations in schizophrenics and the normal population.

Vestigial Extraceptions Hallucinations still experienced by schizophrenics as well as nonclinical populations ("voice hearers"). Also evident in spirit possession, channeling, and imaginary playmates.

Voice–Vision–Volition (VVV) BCI item. As demographic scale increases, social control-at-a-distance becomes more difficult. The adaptation is audiovisual hallucinations (RHD). These were originally attributed to absent clan leaders, chieftains, and ancestors, but eventually evolve into super-religious authoritative figures, and divinized kings, both living and deceased.

References

Andreski, Stanislav (1972). *Social Sciences as Sorcery*. London, UK: Andre Deutsch.

Asaad, Tarek (2015). Sleep in Ancient Egypt. In Sudhansu Chokroverty and Michael Billiard, eds., *Sleep Medicine: A Comprehensive Guide to its Development, Clinical Milestones and Advances in Treatment*. New York, NY: Springer Science, pp. 13–19.

Assmann, Jan (1990). *Ma'at. Gerechtigkeit und Unsterblichkeit im Alten Ágypten*. Beck, Germany: München.

Assmann, Jan (1997). *Moses and the Egyptians*. Cambridge, MA: Harvard University Press.

Assmann, Jan (1998). A Dialogue between Self and Soul: Papyrus Berlin 3024. In *Self, Soul and Body in Religious Experience* (Studies in the History of Religions, 78), Albert I. Baumgarten, and Jan Assmann, and Guy G. Stroumsa (eds.). Leiden, The Netherlands: Brill, pp. 384–403.

Assmann, Jan (2001). *The Search for God in Ancient Egypt* (trans. David Lorton). Ithaca, NY: Cornell University Press.

Assmann, Jan (2003). *The Mind of Egypt: History and Meaning in the Time of the Pharaohs*. New York, NY: Henry Holt.

Assmann, Jan (2005). *Death and Salvation in Ancient Egypt* (trans. David Lorton). Ithaca, NY: Cornell University Press.

Bagehot, Walter (1867). *The English Constitution*. London, UK: Chapman and Hall.

Baines, John (1991). Society, Morality, and Religious Practices. In Byron E. Shafer, ed., *Religion in Ancient Egypt: Gods, Myths, and Personal Practice*. Ithaca, NY: Cornell University Press, pp. 123–200.

Baines, John and Jaromir Malek (2000). *Cultural Atlas of Ancient Egypt*. New York, NY: Checkmark Books.

Bodel, John and Saul M. Olyan, eds. (2112). *Household and Family Religion Antiquity*. Oxford, UK: Wiley-Blackwell.

Bol, Cornelis (2005). *Frühgriechische Bilder und die Entstehung der Klassik. Perspektive, Kognition und Wirklichkeit*. Munich, Germany: Herbert Utz Verlag.

Bolshakov, Andrey O. (1997). *Man and his Double in Egyptian Ideology of the Old Kingdom*. Harrassowitz Verlag: Wiesbaden, Germany.

Bolshakov, Andrey O. (2001). Ka. In *The Oxford Encyclopedia of Ancient Egypt: 3 Volumes*. Donald B. Redford, ed. New York, NY: Oxford University Press, Vol. 2, pp. 215–217.

Bonhême, Marie-Ange (2001a). Kingship (trans. by Elizabeth Schwaiger). In *The Oxford Encyclopedia of Ancient Egypt: 3 Volumes*. Donald B. Redford, ed. New York, NY: Oxford University Press, Vol. 3, pp. 161–163.

Bonhême, Marie-Ange (2001b). Royal Roles (trans. by Elizabeth Schwaiger). In *The Oxford Encyclopedia of Ancient Egypt: 3 Volumes*. Donald B. Redford, ed. New York, NY: Oxford University Press, Vol. 2, pp. 238–245.

Breasted, J. H. (1912). *Development of Religion and Thought*. New York, NY: Scribner.

Breasted, J. H. (1933). *Dawn of Conscience*. New York, NY: Scribner.

Brunner-Traut, Emma (1990). *Frü hformen des Erkennens am Beispiel Altä gyptens*. First ed. Darmstadt: Wissenschaftliche Buchgesellschaft.

Bunson, Margaret R. (2002). *Encyclopedia of Ancient Egypt*. New York, NY: Facts on File.

Butzer, Karl W. (1999). Demography. In *Encyclopedia of the Archaeology of Ancient Egypt*. Kathryn A. Bard and Steven Blake Shubert, eds. New York, NY: Routledge, pp. 295–297.

Callender, Gae (2000). The Middle Kingdom Renaissance. In Ian Shaw, ed., *The Oxford History of Ancient Egypt*. New York, NY: Oxford University Press, pp. 148–183.

Cazeneuve, Jean (1972). *Lucien Lévy-Bruhl* (trans Peter Rivière). Oxford, UK: Basil Blackwell.

Cline, Eric H (2014). *1177 B.C.: The Year Civilization Collapsed*. Princeton, NJ: Princeton University Press.

Collier, Mark and Bill Manley (1998). *How to Read Egyptian Hieroglyphs*. Berkeley, CA: University of California Press.

Dark, K. R. (1998). *Waves of Time: Long Term Change and International Relations*. New York, NY: Continuum.

David, Rosalie (2003). *Religion and Magic in Ancient Egypt*. London, UK: Penguin Books.

Dieter, Arnold (2001). Royal Tombs. In *The Oxford Encyclopedia of Ancient Egypt: 3 Volumes*. Donald B. Redford, ed. New York, NY: Oxford University Press, Vol. 3, pp. 425–433.

Dodds, Eric R. (1951). *The Greeks and the Irrational*. Berkeley, CA: University of California Press.

Drews, Robert (1995). *The End of the Bronze Age: Changes in Warfare and the Catastrophe ca. 1200 B.C.* Princeton, NJ: Princeton University Press.

Englund, Gertie (2001). Offerings: An Overview. In *The Oxford Encyclopedia of Ancient Egypt: 3 Volumes*. Donald B. Redford, ed. New York, NY: Oxford University Press, Vol. 2, pp. 564–569.

Faulkner, Raymond O. (2017). *A Conscise Dictionary of Middle Egyptian* (modernized by Boris Jegorović). Oxford, UK: Griffith Institute.

Fernyhough, Charles (2016). *The Voices Within: The History & Science of How We to Talk Ourselves*. New York, NY: Basic Books.

Finnestad, Ragnhild Bjerre (1986). On Transposing Soul and Body into a Monistic Conception of Being: An Example from Ancient Egypt. *Religion* 16:359–373.

Foster, John L. (2001). Wisdom Literature. In *The Oxford Encyclopedia of Ancient Egypt: 3 Volumes*. Donald B. Redford, ed. New York, NY: Oxford University Press, Vol. 3, pp. 503–507.

Fóti, Véronique (2003). *Vision's Invisibles. Philosophical Explorations.* Albany, NY: State University of New York Press.

Fox, M. V. (1977). A Study of Intef. *Orientalia* 46, pp. 393–423.

Frankfort, Henri (1978). *Kingship and the Gods: A Study of Ancient Near Eastern Religion as the Integration of Society and Nature.* Chicago, IL. University of Chicago Press.

Frankfort, Henri (2000 [1948]). *Ancient Egyptian Religion: An Interpretation.* New York, NY: Dover Publications.

Frankfort, Henri, H. A. Frankfort, John A. Wilson, Thorkild Jacobsen, and William A. Irwin (1977). *The Intellectual Adventure of Ancient Man: An Essay on Speculative Thought in the Ancient Near East.* Chicago, IL: University of Chicago Press.

Friedman, Florence Dunn (2001). Akh. In *The Oxford Encyclopedia of Ancient Egypt: 3 Volumes.* Donald B. Redford, ed. New York, NY: Oxford University Press, Vol. 1, pp. 47–48.

Gee, John (2009). A New Look at the Conception of the Human Being in Ancient Egypt. In Rune Nyord and Annette Kjølby, eds., *"Being in Ancient Egypt": Thoughts on Agency, Materiality and Cognition.* Proceedings of the Seminar Held in Copenhagen, September 29–30, 2006. Oxford, UK: BAR Publishing, pp. 1–14.

Gibbs, R. W. (2004). Embodied Experience and Linguistic Meaning. *Brain and Language* 84:1–15.

Gibbs, Raymond W. and Herbert L. Colston (2005). *Interpreting Figurative Meaning.* New York, NY: Cambrodge University Press.

Goelet, Ogden, Raymond O. Faulkner, Carol R. R. Andrews, J. Daniel Gunther, James Wasserman (2015). *The Egyptian Book of the Dead: The Book of Going Forth by Day.* San Francisco, CA: Chronicle Books.

Goldwasser, Orly (2005). Where is Metaphor?: Conceptual Metaphor and Alternative Classification in the Hieroglyphic Script. *Metaphor and Symbol* 20/2, 95–113.

Günther, Vittman (2013). Personal names: Structures and Patterns. *UCLA Encyclopedia of Egyptology*, 1(1):1–15.

Harrell, James A. (2010). Cartography. In T*he Oxford Encyclopedia of Ancient Egypt: 3 Volumes.* Donald B. Redford, ed. New York, NY: Oxford University Press, Vol. 1, pp. 239–241.

Harrington, Nicola (2010). *Living with the Dead: Ancestor Worship and Mortuary Ritual in Ancient Egypt.* Oxford, UK: Oxbow Books.

Hays, Harold (2010). Funerary Rituals (Pharaonic Period). In W. Wendrich and J. Dielman, eds. *UCLA Encyclopedia of Egyptology.* Los Angeles, CA: http://www.escholarship.org/uc/item/1r32g9zn.

Hays, Harold M. (2009). Between Identity and Agency in Ancient Egyptian Ritual. In Rune Nyord and Annette Kjølby, eds., *"Being in Ancient Egypt": Thoughts on Agency, Materiality and Cognition.* Proceedings of the Seminar Held in Copenhagen, September 29–30, 2006. Oxford, UK: BAR Publishing, pp. 15–30.

Hoch, James (1997). *Middle Egyptian Grammar.* Mississauga, Ontario, Canada: Benben Publications.

Hoffmeier, James K. (2015). *Akhenaten & the Origins of Monotheism*. Oxford, UK: Oxford University Press.

Hornung, Erik (1996). *Conceptions of God in Ancient Egypt: The One and the Many*. Ithaca, NY: Cornell University Press.

Jaynes, Julian (1976). *The Origin of Consciousness in the Breakdown of the Bicameral Mind*. Boston, MA: Houghton Mifflin.

Jaynes, Julian (2012). The Dream of Agamemnon. In Marcel Kuijsten, ed. *The Julian Jaynes Collection*. Henderson, Nevada: Julian Jaynes Society, pp. 196–210.

Johnson, Mark (1987). *The Body in the Mind: The Bodily Basis of Meaning, Imagination and Reasoning*. Chicago, IL: The University of Chicago Press.

Joseph, Amgad (2019). Divine Wrath in Ancient Egypt. *Études et Travaux*, XXXI.

Junge, Friedrich (2003). Die Lehre Ptahhoteps und die Tugenden der ägyptischen Welt. Switzerland, Fribourg / Göttingen, Germany: Universitätsverlag / Vandenhoeck Ruprecht.

Kadish, Gerald (2001). Time. In *The Oxford Encyclopedia of Ancient Egypt: 3 Volumes*. Donald B. Redford, ed. New York, NY: Oxford University Press, Vol. 3, pp. 405–409.

Kantorowicz, Ernst (1957). *The King's Two Bodies: A Study in Medieval Political Theology*. Princeton, NJ: Princeton University Press.

Kirk, G. S. (1970). *Myth: Its Meaning and Function in Ancient and Other Cultures*. Berkeley, CA: University of California Press.

Kjølby, Annette (2009). Material Agency, Attribution and Experience of Agency in Ancient Egypt: The Case of New Kingdom Private Temple Statues. In Rune Nyord and Annette Kjølby, eds., *"Being in Ancient Egypt": Thoughts on Agency, Materiality and Cognition*. Proceedings of the Seminar Held in Copenhagen, September 29–30, 2006. Oxford, UK: BAR Publishing, pp. 31–46.

Kruchten, Jean-Marie (2001). Law. In *The Oxford Encyclopedia of Ancient Egypt: 3 Volumes*. Donald B. Redford, ed. New York, NY: Oxford University Press, Vol. 2, pp. 277–282.

Kruchten, Jean-Marie (2001). Oracles. In *The Oxford Encyclopedia of Ancient Egypt: 3 Volumes*. Donald B. Redford, ed. New York, NY: Oxford University Press, Vol. 2, pp. 609–612.

Krueger, Frederic (2017). The Stargate Simulacrum: Ancient Egypt, Ancient Aliens, and Postmodern Dynamics of Occulture. *Aegyptiaca: Journal of the History of Reception of Ancient Egypt*, 1, pp. 47–74.

Kuijsten, Marcel, ed. (2006). *Reflections on the Dawn of Consciousness: Julian Jaynes's Bicameral Mind Theory Revisited*. Henderson, NV: Julian Jaynes Society.

Kuijsten, Marcel, ed. (2012). *The Julian Jaynes Collection*. Henderson, NV: Julian Jaynes Society.

Kuijsten, Marcel, ed. (2016). *Gods, Voices, and the Bicameral Mind: The Theories of Julian Jaynes*. Henderson, NV: Julian Jaynes Society.

Kuijsten, Marcel, ed. (2022). *Conversations on Consciousness and the Bicameral Mind: Interviews with Leading Thinkers on Julian Jaynes's Theory*. Henderson, NV: Julian Jaynes Society.

Kulmar, Tarmo (2018). On a Possible Characteristic of the Governing System of Pharaoh Amenhotep (V (Akhenaten). *Folklore: Electronic Journal of Folklore* 74, pp. 115–128. http://www.folklore.ee/folkloe/vol74/kulmar.pdf

Lehner, Mark (1997). *The Complete Pyramids: Solving the Ancient Mysteries.* New York, NY: Thames and Hudson.

Leprohon, Ronald J. (2001). Titulary. In *The Oxford Encyclopedia of Ancient Egypt: 3 Volumes.* Donald B. Redford, ed. New York, NY: Oxford University Press, Vol. 3, pp. 409–411.

Leprohon, Ronald J. (2001). Offerings: Offering Formulas and Lists. In *The Oxford Encyclopedia of Ancient Egypt: 3 Volumes.* Donald B. Redford, ed. New York, NY: Oxford University Press, Vol. 2, pp. 570–572.

Lesko, Barbara S. (2010). Cults: Private Cults. In *The Oxford Encyclopedia of Ancient Egypt: 3 Volumes.* Donald B. Redford, ed. New York, NY: Oxford University Press, Vol. 1, pp. 336–339.

Lesko, Barbara S. (2012). Household and Domestic Religion in Ancient Egypt. In *Household and Family Religion Antiquity.* John Bodel and Saul M. Olyan, eds., Oxford, UK: Wiley-Blackwell, pp. 197–209.

Lesko, Leonard H. (1991). Ancient Egyptian Cosmogonies and Cosmology. In Byron E. Shafer, ed., *Religion in Ancient Egypt: Gods, Myths, and Personal Practice.* Ithaca, NY: Cornell University Press. pp. 88–122.

Lévy-Bruhl, Lucien (1910). *Les fonctions mentales dans les sociétés inférieures.*

Lévy-Bruhl, Lucien (1949). *Les carnets de Lucien Lévy-Bruhl* (published posthumously). Paris, France: Presses Universitaires de France.

Lévy-Bruhl, Lucien (1985). *How Natives Think* (trans. Lililian A. Clare). Princeton, NJ: Princeton University Press.

Lichtheim, Miriam (2006a). *Ancient Egyptian Literature: The Old and Middle Kingdoms, Volume I.* Berkeley, CA: University of California Press.

Lichtheim, Miriam (2006b). *Ancient Egyptian Literature: The New Kingdom, Volume II.* Berkeley, CA: University of California Press.

Lichtheim, Miriam (2006c). *Ancient Egyptian Literature: The Late Period, Volume III.* Berkeley, CA: University of California Press.

Liesegang, Diana (2014). The Phenomenon of "Personal Religion" in the Ramesside Period, from the "Poem" of Ramses II through to the Prayers of Ramses III. In *Cult and Belief in Ancient Egypt*, Teodor Lekov and Emil Buzov, eds. Proceedings of the Fourth International Congress for Young Egyptologists, 25–27 September 2012, Sofia, Bulgaria, pp. 97–101.

Littleton, C. Scott (1985). Introduction: Lucien Lévy-Bruhl and the Concept of Cognitive Relativity. In Lucien Lévy-Bruhl, *How Natives Think* (trans. Lililian A. Clare). Princeton, NJ: Princeton University Press, pp. v–lviii.

Lucarelli, Rita (2010). Demons (benevolent and malevolent). *UCLA Encyclopedia of Egyptology*, 1–9. http://escholarship.org/uc/item/1r72q9vv

MacDonald, Paul S. (2003). *History of the Concept of Mind: Speculations about Soul, Mind and Spirit from Homer to Hume.* Burlington, VT: Ashgate.

MacDonald, Paul S. (2005). Paleo-philosophy: Complex and Concept in Archaic Patterns of Thought. *Cosmos and History: The Journal of Natural and Social Philosophy*, 1(2):222-244.

Malefijt, Annmarie de Wall (1974). *Images of Man: A History of Anthropological Thought*. New York, NY: Alfred A. Knopf.

Malek, Jaromir, (2000). The Old Kingdom (c. 2686–2160 BC). In Ian Shaw, ed., *The Oxford History of Ancient Egypt*. New York, NY: Oxford University Press, pp. 89–117.

McVeigh, Brian J. (1996). Standing Stomachs, Clamoring Chests and Cooling Livers: Metaphors in the Psychological Lexicon of Japanese. *Journal of Pragmatics* 26:25–50.

McVeigh, Brian J. (1998). *The Nature of the Japanese State: Rationality and Rituality*. London, UK: Routledge.

McVeigh, Brian J. (2013). Mental Imagery and Hallucinations as Adaptive Behavior: Divine Voices and Visions as Neuropsychological Vestiges. *The International Journal of the Image* Vol 3(1):25–36.

McVeigh, Brian J. (2015). *The Propertied Self: A Psychology of Economic History*. Hauppauge, NY: Nova Publishers.

McVeigh, Brian J. (2016a). *Why Religion Evolved: The Living Dead, Talking Idols, and Mesmerizing Monuments*. Piscataway, NJ: Transaction Publishers.

McVeigh, Brian J. (2016b). *A Psychohistory of Metaphors: Envisioning Time, Space, and Self through the Centuries*. Boulder, Colorado: Lexington Books.

McVeigh, Brian J. (2016c). *Discussions with Julian Jaynes: The Nature of Consciousness and the Vagaries of Psychology*, editor. Hauppauge, NY: Nova Publishers.

McVeigh, Brian J. (2016d). *The History of Japanese Psychology: Global Perspectives, 1875–1950*. London, UK: Bloomsbury.

McVeigh, Brian J. (2018). *The "Other Psychology" of Julian Jaynes: Ancient Languages, Sacred Visions, and Forgotten Mentalities*. Exeter, UK: Imprint Academic.

McVeigh, Brian J. (2020). *The Psychology of the Bible: Explaining Divine Voices and Visions*. Exeter, UK: Imprint Academic.

McVeigh, Brian J. (2022). *The Self-Healing Mind: Harnessing the Active Ingredients of Psychotherapy*. New York, NY: Oxford University Press.

Millet, N. B. (1990). The Narmer Macehead and Related Objects. *Journal of the American Research Center in Egypt*, 27:53–59.

Morenz, Siegfried (1992). *Egyptian Religion* (trans. Ann E. Keep). Ithaca, NY: Cornell University Press.

Müller, Maya (2009). Self-perception and Self-assertion in the Portait of Senwosret III: New Methods for Reading a Face. In Rune Nyord and Annette Kjølby, eds., *"Being in Ancient Egypt": Thoughts on Agency, Materiality and Cognition*. Proceedings of the Seminar Held in Copenhagen, September 29–30, 2006. Oxford, UK: BAR Publishing, pp. 46–62.

Murdy, Albert and Wolfgang Pirsig (2007).The Ear in the Visual Arts of Ancient Egypt. *The Mediterranean Journal of Otology* 3:81–89.

Nørretranders, Tor (1998). *The User Illusion: Cutting Consciousness Down to Size* (trans. by Jonathan Sydenham). New York, NY: Viking.

Nyord, Rune (2007). The Body in the Hymns to the Coffin Sides. *Chronique d'Égypte* 82:5–34.

Nyord, Rune (2009a). Taking Phenomenology to Heart: Some Heuristic Remarks on Studying Ancient Egyptian Embodied Experience. In Rune Nyord and Annette Kjølby, eds., *"Being in Ancient Egypt": Thoughts on Agency, Materiality and Cognition*. Proceedings of the Seminar Held in Copenhagen, September 29–30, 2006. Oxford, UK: BAR Publishing, pp. 63–74.

Nyord, Rune (2009b). *Breathing Flesh: Conceptions of the Body in the Ancient Egyptian Coffin Texts*, Copenhagen, Denmark: CNI Publication 37.

Nyord, Rune (2013). Memory and Succession in the City of the Dead: Temporality in the Ancient Egyptian Mortuary Cult. Dorthe Refslund Christensen and Rane Willerslev, eds. In *Taming Time, Timing Death: Social Technologies and Ritual*. Farhham, UK: Ashgate, pp. 195–211.

Nyord, Rune (2014). Permeable Containers: Body and Cosmos in Middle Kingdom Coffins. In *Body, Cosmos and Eternity: New Research Trends in the Iconography and Symbolism of Ancient Egyptian Coffins*. Rogério, Souda, ed. Archaeopress Egyptology 3. Oxford, UK, pp. 29–44.

Nyord, Rune (2015). Vision and Conceptualization in Ancient Egyptian Art. *Sensuous Cognition. Explorations into Human Sentience: Imagination, (E) motion and Perception*, pp. 135–168.

Nyord, Rune (2017). An Image of the Owner as he was on Earth: Representation and Representation in Middle Kingdom Funerary Images. In *Company of Images. Modelling the imaginary world of Middle Kingdom Egypt: Proceedings of the International Conference of the EPOCHS Project held 18th–20th September 2014 at UCL, London*, eds. Gianluca Miniaci, Marilina Betrò, and Stephen Quirke. Leuven: Peeters, Orientalia Lovaniensia Analecta 262, pp. 337–360.

Nyord, Rune (2018). "Taking Ancient Egyptian Mortuary Religion Seriously": Why Would We, and How Could We? *Journal of Ancient Egyptian Interconnections* 17:73–87.

Oakes, Lorna and Lucia Gahlin (2006). *Ancient Egypt*. New York, NY: Barnes and Noble.

Ockinga, Boyo (2010). Piety. In *The Oxford Encyclopedia of Ancient Egypt: 3 Volumes*. Donald B. Redford, ed. New York, NY: Oxford University Press, Vol. 3, pp. 44-47.

O'Rourke, Paul F. (2001). Drama. In *The Oxford Encyclopedia of Ancient Egypt: 3 Volumes*. Donald B. Redford, ed. New York, NY: Oxford University Press, Vol. 1, pp. 407-410.

Ortner, Sherry. B. (1973). On Key Symbols. *American Anthropologist*, New Series 75(5), pp. 1338–46.

Petty, Bill (2012). *Egyptian Glyphary: A Sign List Based Hieroglyphic Dictionary of Middle Egyptian*. Littleton, CO: Museum Tours Press.

Petty, Bill (2013a). *Hieroglyphic List: Based on the Work of Alan Gardiner*. Littleton, CO: Museum Tours Press.

Petty, Bill (2013b). *Hieroglyphic Dictionary: A Middle Egyptian Vocabulary*. Littleton, CO: Museum Tours Press.

Petty, Bill (2016). *English to Middle Egyptian Dictionary: A Reverse Hieroglyphic Vocabulary*. Littleton, CO: Museum Tours Press.

Pinch, Geraldine (2002). *Egyptian Mythology: A Guide to the Gods, Goddesses, and Traditions of Ancient Egypt.* Oxford, UK: Oxford University Press.

Pinch, Geraldine (2004). *Egyptian Myth: A Very Short Introduction.* Oxford, UK: Oxford University Press.

Pinch, Geraldine (2006). *Magic in Ancient Egypt.* Austin, TX: University of Texas Press.

Prada, Luigi (2014). Visions of Gods. In A. M. Dodson, J. J. Johnston, and W. Monkhouse, eds. *A Good Scribe and an Exceedingly Wise Man: Studies in Honour of W. J. Tait.* London, UK: Golden House Publications, pp. 251–267.

Price, Robyn (2018). Sniffing Out the Gods: Archaeology with the Senses. *Journal of Ancient Egyptian Interconnections* 17:137–155.

Rankine, David (2006). *Heka: The Practices of Ancient Egyptian Ritual & Magic.* London, UK: Avalonia.

Ray, John D. (2010). Cults: Animal. In *The Oxford Encyclopedia of Ancient Egypt: 3 Volumes.* Donald B. Redford, ed. New York, NY: Oxford University Press, Vol. 1, pp. 345–348.

Redford, Donald B. (ed.) (2001). *The Oxford Encyclopedia of Ancient Egypt: 3 Volumes.* New York, NY: Oxford University Press.

Renfrew, Colin (1979). Systems Collapse as Social Transformation. In *Transformation, Mathematical Approaches to Culture Change.* C. Renfrew and K. L. Cooke, eds. New York, NY: Academic Press, pp.481–506.

Ritner, Robert K. (2001a). Magic. In *The Oxford Encyclopedia of Ancient Egypt: 3 Volumes.* Donald B. Redford, ed. New York, NY: Oxford University Press, Vol. 2, pp. 321–326.

Ritner, Robert K. (2001b). Dream Book. In *The Oxford Encyclopedia of Ancient Egypt: 3 Volumes.* Donald B. Redford, ed. New York, NY: Oxford University Press, Vol., 1, pp. 410–411.

Ritner, Robert K. (2008). *The Mechanics of Ancient Egyptian Magical Practices.* Chicago, IL: The Oriental Institute.

Ritner, Robert K. (2012). Household Religion in Ancient Egypt. In *Household and Family Religion Antiquity.* John Bodel and Saul M. Olyan, eds., Oxford, UK: Wiley-Blackwell, pp. 171–196.

Robbins, Manuel (2001). *Collapse of the Bronze Age: The Story of Greece, Troy, Israel, Egypt, and the Peoples of the Sea.* New York, NY: Authors Choice.

Robins, Gay (2001). Legitimation. In *The Oxford Encyclopedia of Ancient Egypt: 3 Volumes.* Donald B. Redford, ed. New York, NY: Oxford University Press, Vol. 2, pp. 286–289.

Rosalie, David (2002). *Religion and Magic in Ancient Egyp*t. London, UK: Penguin Books.

Roth, Ann Macy (2001a). Funerary Ritual. In *The Oxford Encyclopedia of Ancient Egypt: 3 Volumes.* Donald B. Redford, ed. New York, NY: Oxford University Press, Vol. 1, pp. 575–580.

Roth, Ann Macy (2001b). Opening of the Mouth. In *The Oxford Encyclopedia of Ancient Egypt: 3 Volumes.* Donald B. Redford, ed. in chief. New York, NY: Oxford University Press, Vol. 2, pp. 605–609.

Rowe, Bill (2016). The Ancient Dark Age. In *Gods, Voices, and the Bicameral Mind: The Theories of Julian Jaynes.* Marcel Kuijsten, ed. Henderson, Nevada: Julian Jaynes Society, pp. 78–94.

Sauneron, Serge (1960). *The Priests of Ancient Egypt* (trans. Ann Morrisett). New York, NY: Grove Press.

Shafer, Byron (1991a). Introduction. In Byron E. Shafer, ed., *Religion in Ancient Egypt: Gods, Myths, and Personal Practice.* Ithaca, NY: Cornell University Press, pp. 1–6.

Shafer, Byron E. (ed.) (1991b). *Religion in Ancient Egypt: Gods, Myths, and Personal Practice.* Ithaca, NY: Cornell University Press.

Shaw, Ian (2000). Introduction: Chronological and Cultural Change in Egypt. In Ian Shaw, ed., *The Oxford History of Ancient Egypt.* New York, NY: Oxford University Press, pp. 1–16.

Silverman, David P. (ed.) (1997). *Ancient Egypt.* New York, NY: Oxford University Press.

Silverman, David P. (1991). Divinity and Deities in Ancient Egypt. In Byron E. Shafer, ed., *Religion in Ancient Egypt: Gods, Myths, and Personal Practice.* Ithaca, NY: Cornell University Press. pp. 7–87.

Simpson, William Kelly (ed.) (2003). *The Literature of Ancient Egypt: An Anthology of Stories, Instructions, Stelae, Autobiographies, and Poetry.* New Haven, CT: Yale University Press.

Sörbom, Göran (1994). *Gombrich on the Greek Art Revolution.* Nordisk Estetisk Tidsskrift 12: 63–77.

St. Augustine (1972). *The City of God* (trans. by Henry Bettenson). Harmondsworth, UK: Penguin Books.

Strudwick, Helen (general ed.) (2008). *The Encyclopedia of Ancient Egypt.* London, UK: Amber Books.

Szpakowska, Kasia (2001). Through the Looking Glass: Dreams in Ancient Egypt. In *Dreams: A Reader on Religious, Cultural, and Psychological Dimensions of Dreaming*, Kelly Bulkeley, ed. NY & London: Palgrave, pp. 29–44.

Szpakowska, Kasia (2007). Nightmares in Ancient Egypt. In Jean-Marie Husser and Alice Mouton, eds., *Le cauchemar dans l'Antiquité: Actes des journées d'étude de l'UMR* 7044. Strasbourg, France: de Boccard, pp. 21–39.

Szpakowska, Kasia (2009). *Demons in Ancient Egypt.* Religion Compass 3/5:799–805.

Tait, John (2009). Anger and Agency: The Role of Emotions in Demotic and Earlier Narratives. In Rune Nyord and Annette Kjølby, eds., *"Being in Ancient Egypt": Thoughts on Agency, Materiality and Cognition.* Proceedings of the Seminar Held in Copenhagen, September 29–30, 2006. Oxford, UK: BAR Publishing, pp. 75–82.

Teeter, Emily (2001a). Cults: Divine Cults. In *The Oxford Encyclopedia of Ancient Egypt: 3 Volumes.* Donald B. Redford, ed. New York, NY: Oxford University Press, Vol. 1, pp. 340–345.

Teeter, Emily (2001b). Maat. In *The Oxford Encyclopedia of Ancient Egypt: 3 Volumes.* Donald B. Redford, ed. New York, NY: Oxford University Press, Vol. 2, pp. 319–321.

Thompson, Stephen E. (2001). Cults: An Overview. In *The Oxford Encyclopedia of Ancient Egypt: 3 Volumes.* Donald B. Redford, ed. New York, NY: Oxford University Press, Vol. 1, pp. 326–332.

Tobin, Vincent Arieh (2001). Amun and Amun-Re. In *The Oxford Encyclopedia of Ancient Egypt: 3 Volumes.* Donald B. Redford, ed. New York, NY: Oxford University Press, Vol. 1, pp. 82–85.

Toivari-Viitala, Jaana (2001). *Women at Deir el-Medina: A Study of the Status and Roles of the Female Inhabitants in the Workmen's Community during the Ramesside Period.* Egyptologische Uitgaven 15. Leiden, Nederlands Instituut voor het Nabije Oosten.

Turner, V. (1967). *The Forest of Symbols: Aspects of Ndembu Ritual.* Ithaca, NY: Cornell University Press.

Tyldesley, Joyce (2019). *The Pharaohs.* London, UK: Quercus.

Van de Mieroop, Marc (2016). *A History of the Ancient Near East, ca. 3000–332 BCE* (3rd edition). Oxford, UK: Wiley-Blackwell.

Van Der Toorn, Karel (2012). Family Religion in Second Millennium West Asia (Mesopotamia, Emar, Nuzi). In *Household and Family Religion Antiquity.* John Bodel and Saul M. Olyan, eds., Oxford, UK: Wiley-Blackwell, pp. 20–36.

Van der Veer, René (2003). Primitive Mentality Reconsidered. *Culture & Psychology* 9(2):179–184.

Vernant, Jean Pierre (1991). *Mortals and Immortals: Collected Essays.* Princeton, NJ: Princeton University Press.

Vygotsky, Lev (1962). *Thought and Speech.* Cambridge, MA: MIT Press.

Warburton, David A. (2009). Time and Space in Ancient Egypt: The Importance of the Creation of Abstraction. In Rune Nyord and Annette Kjølby, eds., *"Being in Ancient Egypt": Thoughts on Agency, Materiality and Cognition.* Proceedings of the Seminar Held in Copenhagen. September 29–30, 2006. Oxford, UK: BAR Publishing, pp. 83–96.

Weeks, Kent R. (2001). Tombs: An Overview. In *The Oxford Encyclopedia of Ancient Egypt: 3 Volumes.* Donald B. Redford, ed. New York, NY: Oxford University Press, Vol. 3, pp. 418–425.

Wegner, Josef E. (2010). Cults: Royal Cults. In *The Oxford Encyclopedia of Ancient Egypt: 3 Volumes.* Donald B. Redford, ed. New York, NY: Oxford University Press, Vol. 1, pp. 333–336.

Wegner, Josef F. (2010). Cenotaphs. In *The Oxford Encyclopedia of Ancient Egypt: 3 Volumes.* Donald B. Redford, ed. New York, NY: Oxford University Press, Vol. 1, pp. 244–248.

Wente, Edward F. (2001). Monotheism. In *The Oxford Encyclopedia of Ancient Egypt: 3 Volumes.* Donald B. Redford, ed. New York, NY: Oxford University Press, Vol. 2, pp. 432–435.

Wiebach-Koepke, Silvia (2001). False Door. In *The Oxford Encyclopedia of Ancient Egypt: 3 Volumes.* Donald B. Redford, ed. New York, NY: Oxford University Press, Vol 1, pp. 498–500.

Wilkinson, Richard H. (2003). *The Complete Gods and Goddesses of Ancient Egypt.* London, UK: Thames & Hudson.

Wilkinson, Toby (2010). *The Rise and Fall of Ancient Egypt.* New York, NY: Random House.

Wilson, John A. (1965). *The Culture of Ancient Egypt.* Chicago, IL: The University of Chicago Press.

Wilson, Penelope (2003). *Hieroglyphs: A Very Short Introduction.* Oxford, UK: Oxford University Press.

Žabkar, Louis V. (1968). *A Study of the Ba Concept in Ancient Egyptian Texts.* Chicago, IL: University of Chicago Press.

About the Author

Brian J. McVeigh received his BA in Asian studies and political science, MA in anthropology, and MS in counseling from the University at Albany, State University of New York, as well as a PhD in anthropology from Princeton University. He is interested in how humans adapt, both through history and therapeutically. Using the theories of Julian Jaynes as a theoretical framework, he has published extensively on the history of Japanese psychology, the origins of religions, the Bible, spirit possession, art and popular culture, linguistics, and changing definitions of self, time, and space. He has lived and worked in China and Japan for many years, taught at the University of Arizona for ten years, and now works in private practice as a licensed mental health counselor. His current projects include *Julian Jaynes for Beginners* and *Global Anthropology: Person, Politics, Property*.

Other books by Brian J. McVeigh:

The Self-healing Mind:
Harnessing the Active Ingredients of Psychotherapy

The Psychology of the Bible:
Explaining Divine Voices and Visions

The Psychology of Westworld:
When Machines Go Mad

The "Other Psychology" of Julian Jaynes:
Ancient Languages, Sacred Visions, and Forgotten Mentalities

The History of Japanese Psychology:
Global Perspectives, 1875–1950

How Religion Evolved:
Explaining the Living Dead, Talking Idols, and Mesmerizing Monuments

Discussions with Julian Jaynes:
The Nature of Consciousness and the Vagaries of Psychology

The Propertied Self:
The Psychology of Economic History

A Psychohistory of Metaphors:
Envisioning Time, Space, and Self through the Centuries

Interpreting Japan:
Approaches and Applications for the Classroom

The State Bearing Gifts:
Deception and Disaffection in Japanese Higher Education

Nationalisms of Japan:
Managing and Mystifying Identity

Japanese Higher Education as Myth

Wearing Ideology:
State, Schooling, and Self-Presentation in Japan

The Nature of the Japanese State:
Rationality and Rituality

Life in a Japanese Women's College:
Learning to Be Ladylike

Spirits, Selves, and Subjectivity in a Japanese New Religion:
The Cultural Psychology of Belief in Sūkyō Mahikari

Index

Afterworld 2, 21, 35–36, 40–41, 50, 58, 60, 62, 64, 68, 80–81, 84, 138–139, 159, 160, 169, 174, 176–178, 181, 183–184, 186–187, 204, 207, 208–209, 211, 227, 248–249
see also Doubleworld, Duat, Netherworld
agricultural revolution 1, 6, 102
Ahura Mazda 7
Akh 21, 177, 183, 186, 193, 204, 207, 208–209
Akhenaten 66–68, 115, 178
Akhetaten 67, 115, 157
Alexandria 157
Amduat, The 187
see also funerary texts
Amenhotep II 66–67, 179
Amenhotep III 66–67, 101, 107, 135, 138, 140
Amenhotep IV 66–67
amulets 35, 37, 56, 77, 81–82, 90, 110, 112–113, 119, 122–123, 187, 204–205, 225, 251
Amun-Re 85, 88, 101
ancestors 1, 5, 7, 9, 20–22, 25, 61, 77, 82, 103–104, 109, 114–115, 121, 130, 143–144, 146, 158, 175, 183, 188, 195, 197, 199, 218–219, 248–250, 254
see also Centrality of Ancestor Worship
Ankh 35, 68, 82, 86
appearances, divine 67, 76–78, 85, 97, 101, 104–106, 118, 145, 160, 166
archaism 43
Ardery, Philip x
Aryans 234
ascientific 2, 43–44
see also prescientific
aspective 2, 46–47, 68
see also perspective
Aten 4, 7, 30, 66–68, 75, 79, 84, 89, 91, 115
Authority-Radiating Ceremonial Complexes (ARCC) 20, 132, 156–157, 161, 167, 248, 250–251
authorization 5, 7, 9, 18–19, 23–24, 43, 103, 106, 114, 129–130, 133, 135, 145, 156, 195, 197, 202, 206, 230–232
see also self-authorization

autoscopy 2, 5, 21, 107, 192, 212, 230, 252
see also doppelgängers, heautoscopy, out-of-body experiences

Ba (human-headed bird body–soul) 2, 21, 28, 46, 65, 87, 89, 110–111, 156, 165–166, 179, 181, 192–193, 203–207, 209–210, 215–216
divine and kingly 204–205
as proto-conscience 206–207
BCI, *see* Bicameral Civilization Inventory
belly 48–49, 203, 220
Benben stone 165, 168
Bible 230
Bicameral Civilization Inventory (BCI) 19, 25, 29, 31, 233, 248–254
future research using, 232–234
bicameral mentality 6–7, 18–19, 23–25, 29, 45, 55, 71, 103, 119, 160, 230, 248
breakdown of 6–7, 23–24, 29, 55, 70–71, 103, 160
vestiges of 2, 5, 10, 19, 20–21, 25, 30–32, 116, 193, 230, 252, 254
see also extraceptions, hallucinations, superceptions, super-religiosity, Supernatural Visitations, Voice–Vision–Volitions
body interior 220, 223, 233, Appendix A
see also heart
Book of Caverns 188
see also funerary texts
Book of Gates 187
see also funerary texts
Book of Night and Day 188
see also funerary texts
Book of the Dead 26, 31, 41, 60, 82, 116, 163, 178, 185–188, 207, 211, 215, 225, 228
see also funerary texts
Book of the Earth 188
see also funerary texts
Book of the Heavens 188
see also funerary texts
Book of the Opening of the Mouth 188
see also funerary texts
Book of the Pylons 188
see also funerary texts
Book of Traversing in Eternity 188
see also funerary texts
Book of Two Ways 187
see also funerary texts
Bronze Age 3, 6, 103, 219, 234, 249

Caral-Supe Civilization 234

Centrality of Ancestor Worship (CAW) 20, 144, 249
  see also ancestors
ceremonies 49, 51, 119, 134, 141, 143–145, 147, 167, 169–170, 172, 180, 190, 233
  see also rituals
civilization, variables of 4
Cleopatra VII 6
coceptions 5, 249, *see also* introceptions
Coffin Texts 41, 60, 93, 95, 116, 178, 185, 186, 206, 227
  see also funerary texts
cognitive diversity 12, 249
  see also cognitive relativism, psychic unity
cognitive relativism 1, 12, 16–31, 249
  see also cognitive diversity, psychic unity
commands, divine 5, 18, 20, 22, 84, 95–96, 103–104, 106, 108–109, 124, 194, 198–199, 203, 222, 227, 248, 253
complexes 32, 37–39
  of spatiality 39–40
  of temporality 40–43
  see also concepts
concepts 37–39, *see also* complexes
conscious interiority 1, 7–8, 10–13, 15, 17, 21, 24–25, 29, 33, 45, 55, 72, 107, 120–121, 148, 185, 218–219, 249–251, 254
  defined 8
  see also consciousness, FOCI
consciousness ix, 12–14, 17–18, 22, 24, 48, 137, 219, 222, 249–251
  see also conscious interiority, FOCI
consilience (FOCI) 9
corpse 26, 174–175, 181–182, 193–194, 200, 204, 206, 209
cosmic fundament 86
creation myths 91–96
Cultural Revolution 232

Dedovic, Boban x
demons 82, 117, 122, 204
demotic 50, 60, 225
Dier el-Medina 143
Dilmun 234
Djed Pillar 35
doppelgängers 2, 21, 192, 194–195, 252
  see also autoscopy, heautoscopy, Ka
doubleworld 31, 158–159, 175, 195, 197, 249
  see also Afterworld, Duat, Netherworld
Doubleworld Mortuary Practices (DWMP) 20–21, 26, 160, 193, 249, 251–252
drama, lack of secular in ancient Egypt 148–149

dreams 5, 10, 18, 21, 39, 101, 120–123, 128, 144, 170, 183, 208–209, 250, 252
change in patterns of 121-122
lucid 121
preconscious 120
visitation 21
see also nightmares
Duat 39, 76, 117, 160–161, 176–179, 188, 225
see also Afterworld, Doubleworld, Netherworld

ears 112, 185
energies, 195, 198, 200
cosmic 40, 86, 90, 193, 201–202
divine 95, 133, 138, 148, 171, 194
see also life-force
excerption (FOCI) 9, 249, 250–251, 253
extraceptions 6, 196, 204, 250
vestigial 6, 254
see also bicameral mentality, hallucinations, superceptions, Supernatural Visitations, Voice–Vision–Volitions
Eye of Horus 60, 77, 112, 147
eyes 37, 111-113,
evil 38, 118, 150

face 226-227
Features of Conscious Interiority (FOCI) ix, 8, 10, 11, 44, 120–121, 249, 251–253
see also "I," "me," conscious interiority, consciousness, consilience, excerption, self-authorization, self-autonomy, self-narratization, self-reflexivity, spatialization
festivals 43, 76, 82, 105, 118–119, 134, 143, 145, 147–148, 150, 226
FOCI, *see* Features of Conscious Interiority
Frankfort, Henri 11–12, 16, 30, 48, 51–52, 73, 106, 124, 154–155, 188, 194, 213–216, 257
Frankfort, Henriette A. 16
funerary texts 184-188,
see also Book of Caverns, Book of Gates, Book of Night and Day, Book of the Dead, Book of the Earth, Book of the Heavens, Book of the Opening of the Mouth, Book of the Pylon, Book of Traversing in Eternity, Book of Two Ways, Coffin Texts

glossolalia 21
Gobekli Tepe 233
gods, angry 225-226,
monarchical 78–79
nature, types of 75-84
personal 82, 104, 203, passim

god-statues 76, 119, 145, 147, 157, 170–171, 251–252
Great Sphinx 120, 162
Greene, Barbara x
guidance, divine 2, 106–107, 120
guided imagery 18, 252

hallucinations v, 2, 5, 7, 15, 22–23, 28, 45, 102–104, 107–108, 111, 113–114, 139, 192, 198, 204, 206, 219, 226, 229–230, 248, 250, 252, 254
  population size and 102–103
  mirror 192
  see also bicameral mentality, extraceptions, superceptions, Supernatural Visitations, Voice–Vision–Volitions
head, in mental language 8, 224, 226, 234
heads of deceased, 184–185,
  depictions of 182
heart 28, 48–49, 52, 82, 96, 102, 107, 144, 170, 181, 193, 197
  centrality of 222–223
  in psycholexicon 218–228, Appendix A
  see also body interior
heautoscopy 5, 21, 192, 230, 252
  see also autoscopy, doppelgängers, out-of-body experiences
Heka 39, 80, 89–90, 95, 116, 138, 150, 193, 211
Heka, the god 202
hieratic 50
hieroglyphs xi, 2, 32, 37, 77, 85, 94–95, 105, 109, 121, 124, 132, 168, 175, 195–196, 200–203, 205–211, 224, 250
  as divine communication 114
  how [they] shape reality 49–50
high priest-king 134–135
high priests 48, 72, 80, 116, 130, 134, 141–143, 146, 152
history, of ancient Egypt, 54–74
  Egyptian conceptions of 41–43
  periodization of ancient Egypt's 55
  without time 42–43
  see also temporality, time
Hitler, Adolf 232
Horus 36, 57, 60, 76–77, 79, 81, 84, 86, 93, 107–108, 112–113, 137–140, 147, 149–150, 165, 167, 198, 211–212, 225
Hyksos 66, 83
hypnoidal mental states 18, 252
  see also hypnosis
hypnosis 21, 25, 230, 252, 254
  as paralogic thinking 18
  see also hypnoidal mental states

"I" (FOCI) 8–10, 45, 120, 148, 202, 251, 252–253
image 18, 34, 50–51, 76, 79, 85, 94, 103, 110–111, 118, 136, 143, 147, 156, 158, 180, 194, 210, 225
immortality 60, 137–138, 175–176, 181, 186
Indirect Divine Communication (IDC) 20, 250
Induction Methods for Right-Hemisphere Activation (IMRHA) 20, 31, 63, 250
Indus Valley Civilization 233–234
Intermediary Beings (IB) 20, 105, 250
introceptions (FOCI) 5, 8, 11, 47, 249–250
Isis 36, 76, 84, 94, 112, 120, 138, 149, 150

Jaynes, Julian *passim*
Jaynesian, approach 46
  archaeopsychology 6, 12, 19, 22
  interpretation 71, 175
  paradigm vi
  perspective 2, 232
  principles x
  psychology v, vi, ix, 3, 14, 19, 22, 108, 229
  therapeutics ix

Ka (spiritual double) 2, 21, 28, 150, 160, 178–179, 192–200, 203–204, 206–207, 209, 211, 213, 222, 225
  and authorization of behavior 202
  communicative life-force 197–198
  and cosmic and creative energies 199–200
  and Doubleworld 195–196
  monarchical 197–198
  offerings to 196–197
  as one's guide 203–203
king lists 43
kings 129–141
  cult of the living 140
  self-deification of 107
  two bodies of 231
  see also monarchs, pharaohs, *passim*
kingship 19, 58, 60, 77–78, 89, 107, 129–155, 231
  divine 2, 89, 133, 136, 138
Konar Sandal 233
Kuijsten, Marcel vi, viii, x

Late Bronze Age xi, 7, 21, 23, 55, 67, 70–72
Late Bronze Age collapse 7, 21, 55, 69–72
Lévy-Bruhl, Lucien 16, 30
Libyans 69

life-force 35, 95, 133, 192–193, 195, 199, 211
communicative 197–198
see also energies, Ka
Litany of Re 187, *see also* funerary texts
literature v, 21, 59, 61–65, 88, 115, 117, 126, 169, 192, 212
logic 16–18, 32, 34, 38, 44, 52, 135, 230, 232, 252
see also paralogic, truth

Maat 35, 44, 62, 116, 132–133, 135, 151–153, 178, 224–225
magic 19, 34, 36, 51, 89–90, 99, 138, 193, 195, 201–202
as complex idea 38–39
Mandate of Heaven 232
Mao Zedong 232
Marduk 7
masks 149, 226, mummy 182, 187
mastaba 56, 158–159, 162
"me" (FOCI) 9, 10, 148, 202, 251, 253
Mehrgarh 233
Memphis 6, 57–58, 66, 72, 80, 94, 139, 141, 157, 162–163, 193
mental space 8, 249
see also mind-space, spatialization of psyche
Merneptah 101
Mesopotamia 19, 49, 57, 114, 120, 161, 181, 203, 233
Metaphoric Mind-Words (MMW) 21, 259
see also metaphors
metaphors 8, 13–14, 21, 45, 180, 219, 220–221, 223, 227, 232, 250, 253
see also Metaphoric Mind-Words
mind-body dualism 2, 12, 45–48, 90
mind-space 8
see also mental space, spatialization of psyche
Moche Civilization 234
monarchs 22, 58–59, 67, 78–79, 96, 129–130, 132–135, 141, 148, 196, 198, 205–206, 230–231
nature of 136–140
see also kings, pharaohs
monocracy 58, 129–130, 133, 146, 156, 168, 232
monarch as absolute 133–135
see also kings, pharaohs
monotheism 7, 67, 87–89, 94
Multiple Souls (MS) 21, 193, 251
mummies 26, 80–81, 112, 165, 179–180, 183, 187, 193, 225
as glorified body 181–182
mummification 20, 26, 60, 72, 174, 179, 180–183, 209, 249
mythopoeic 16, 32, 42, 44

names, power of 211, 252
theophoric 61, 149–152
Neolithic period 5, 15, 29, 55, 102, 129, 233
Netherworld 159, 177, 189
see also Afterworld, Doubleworld, Duat
nightmares 114–115, 121, 144
fear of 122–123
see also dreams
Norte Chico Civilization 234
North Korea, 129, 232
Nubia 57, 59, 66, 72, 83, 107, 162
numina 24, 75, 104, 114
Nyord, Rune x, 39, 51–52, 126, 175, 184, 188, 191, 221, 227, 228

Objects of Hallucinatory Focus (OHF) 20, 109, 113–114, 135, 157, 167, 171, 248, 250–251
Olmec Civilization 234
Opening of the Mouth Ceremony 179, 180–181, 186, 204
Osiris 34–36, 42, 57, 62, 68, 75–76, 79–81, 88, 94, 108, 112, 138–139, 141, 147, 155, 159, 165, 176–179, 182, 187, 194, 197, 198, 206, 211, 224
out-of-body experiences 5, 192, 230
see also autoscopy, doppelgängers, heautoscopy

palaces 40, 133, 157, 158, 162, 169, 177, 193
temples as 171
pantheism 86, 94
paralogic 2, 10, 17, 18–19, 32, 34, 38, 42, 44, 49, 84, 87–88, 92, 95, 109, 135, 139, 145–146, 148, 156, 159, 160, 182, 184, 185, 187, 205, 210–211, 230, 232, 252
multiple existences, transfiguration and 178–179
see also logic
personal gods 82, 104, 203
personality cult 69, 232
personation 116, 147–148, 252
personhood, distributed 109–110
perspective 40, 44, 45, 46–47, 52, 68, 212
see also aspective
pharaohs 9, 20, 24, 37, 58, 60, 65–67, 72, 75, 88, 103–104, 115, 118, 120, 122, 129, 130–134, 137–139, 146–147, 151–152, 157, 167–168, 198, 253
see also kings, monarchs
piety, emergence of 54, 59, 88, 226
interiorization and 60–62
polytheism 86
Postbicameral Civilization Inventory (PBCI) 21, 252
preconscious 15–16, 24, 29, 44, 55, 137, 252
preconscious civilization 2, 34, 46, 192, 192

preconscious hypostases 219
preconscious individuals 10, 225
preconscious mentality 2, 3
preconscious people 18, 43
preconscious period/times 46, 103, 119–120, 226
prescientific 2, 32, 43–44
see also ascientific
priestesses 141–142
priests 36, 39, 47, 55, 58–59, 64, 72, 76, 89, 94, 110, 118–119, 130, 133–134, 141–148, 159, 166, 170, 180, 185
prophecy 62–65, 73, 121
prophets 8, 21, 63, 65, 76, 141, 151, 153, 250
psychic unity 13–14, 249
see also cognitive diversity, cognitive relativism
psycho-internalization 5, 59
see also socio-externalization
psycholexicon 218–219, 254
embryonic 218
Ptah 69, 94, 95, 100–101, 108, 111–112, 141, 149–150, 204, 227
Pyramid Texts 46, 58, 73, 89, 92, 94, 158, 163, 166, 185, 186, 190, 204–205
pyramids 18, 20, 22, 26, 33, 35, 58, 129, 132, 152, 156, 158–170, 172–173, 194, 206, 234, 249, 251
evolution of 161–163
purpose of 165–166
see also tombs

Ramesses II 43, 66, 70, 94, 107, 110, 140, 200
Ramesses III 69, 140, 170
Ramesses XI 143
Re 64, 82, 88–89, 94, 113, 138–139, 141, 150, 168, 178, 187–188, 203, 205
reason 17
see also logic, paralogic
Right-Hemispheric Activation (RHA) 19, 20, 102
rituals, stabilizing effect of 144–145
see also ceremonies
Roman Catholicism 231
Rowe, Bill x
royal cults 77

Sea Peoples 69
Secondary Burials (SB) 21, 188, 253
self-authorization (FOCI) 9, 59, 249, 252
see also authorization
self-autonomy (FOCI) 9, 59, 107, 249, 252
self-deification of kings 107

self-individuation (FOCI) 9, 60, 62, 64, 68, 88, 138, 185, 187, 249, 252
self-narratization (FOCI) 9, 250, 253
self-reflexivity (FOCI) 10, 69, 249, 252
Seligman, Martin ix, x
Shadow 2, 192–193, 207, 210
social Darwinism 14, 16, 30
socio-externalization 5, 59
  see also psycho-internalization
space 22, 33, 36, 39, 43, 46, 68, 84, 158, 160, 162, 182, 219, 221, 253
  types of 182–183
  see also spatiality
spatiality 2, 46, 159, 176, 223, complexes of 39–40, *see also* space
spatialization of psyche (FOCI) 8, 10, 47, 224, 249, 253, *see also* mental space, mind-space
sphinx 35, 51, 78, 120, 171
  Great 120, 163
St. Augustine 230, 231
Stalin, Josef 232
stelae 40, 55, 61, 77, 110, 112–113, 140, 144, 159, 162, 183, 211
superceptions 5, 248, 250, 253
  see also bicameral mentality, extraceptions, hallucinations, Supernatural Visitations, Voice–Vision–Volitions
Supernatural Visitations (SV) v, 2, 20, 106, 183, 226, 253
  see also bicameral mentality, extraceptions, hallucinations, superceptions, Voice–Vision–Volitions
super-religiosity 1, 2, 7, 24–27, 55, 57, 62, 68, 92, 109, 121, 130, 132, 135, 138, 148–149, 152, 156, 165, 193, 207, 218, 224, 230, 250, 254
  see also bicameral mentality
symbols 2, 32, 33–40
  identification type 18, 34–35, 37, 50, 109, 211, 252
  key 33–35, 38, 44
  reflective type 34, 64, 109, 202, 218, passim
syncretism 7, 84, 87–88

temples 6, 33, 34–35, 39, 41, 43, 50, 58, 64–65, 68–69, 72, 76–77, 79, 80, 92, 103, 107, 112, 118–119, 132, 134–135, 138, 141–145, 147, 156–157, 159, 161, 163, 164–166, 172, 178, 181, 183, 193, 204, 210, 233, 248, 251
  Authority-Radiating Ceremonial Complexes 20
  as centers of socioeconomic activity 170
  as houses of gods 167–169
  as Objects of Hallucinatory Focus 170–171
  royal palaces as 171
temporality 9
  complexes of 40–43
  see also history, time

Thebes 57, 59, 66, 72, 110, 113, 116, 143, 145, 155, 157, 167
Theocentric Social Order (TSO) 2, 20, 129–155, 253
theophoric naming 149–152
time 2, 32, 36, 40–42
  Egyptian conceptions of 41–43
  history without 42–43
  see also history, temporality
titulary, royal 140–141
tombs 20, 26, 35, 40, 42, 50, 57, 60–61, 65, 68, 76, 83, 113, 115–116, 132, 134, 140, 144, 146, 156, 161–163, 165–169, 172–173, 175, 177, 178–187, 194, 196–197, 204, 206–208, 210, 226, 248–249
  empty 160
  as houses for the living dead 157–160
  as microcosmos 158–159
  portals to Doubleworld 159–160
  see also pyramids
tomb-temple complexes 161–163
transformation of the dead 174–175
translation, problems of xi, 28
True of Voice 108
truth 17, 18, 252
  objective 17
  social 17

unconscious 222
Undeveloped Psychological Lexicon (UPL) 21, 250, 254

Vinca Civilization 233
Voice–Vision–Volitions (VVV) 5, 6, 19, 20–24, 26, 79, 88, 95, 101–102, 106, 139, 143, 188, 207, 249, 250, 252– 254
  apex 22, 24–25, 146,
  see also bicameral mentality, extraceptions, hallucinations, superceptions, Supernatural Visitations

Yahweh 66

www.ingramcontent.com/pod-product-compliance
Lightning Source LLC
Chambersburg PA
CBHW021055080526
44587CB00010B/254
* 9 7 8 1 7 3 7 3 0 5 5 4 5 *